NORTH CAROLINA
Small Claims
LAW

Joan G. Brannon

UNC
SCHOOL OF GOVERNMENT

THE UNIVERSITY
of NORTH CAROLINA
at CHAPEL HILL

The School of Government at the University of North Carolina at Chapel Hill works to improve the lives of North Carolinians by engaging in practical scholarship that helps public officials and citizens understand and improve state and local government. Established in 1931 as the Institute of Government, the School provides educational, advisory, and research services for state and local governments. The School of Government is also home to a nationally ranked graduate program in public administration and specialized centers focused on information technology, environmental finance, and civic education for youth.

As the largest university-based local government training, advisory, and research organization in the United States, the School of Government offers up to 200 courses, seminars, and specialized conferences for more than 12,000 public officials each year. In addition, faculty members annually publish approximately fifty books, book chapters, bulletins, and other reference works related to state and local government. Each day that the General Assembly is in session, the School produces the *Daily Bulletin*, which reports on the day's activities for members of the legislature and others who need to follow the course of legislation.

The Master of Public Administration Program is a full-time, two-year program that serves up to sixty students annually. It consistently ranks among the best public administration graduate programs in the country, particularly in city management. With courses ranging from public policy analysis to ethics and management, the program educates leaders for local, state, and federal governments and nonprofit organizations.

Operating support for the School of Government's programs and activities comes from many sources, including state appropriations, local government membership dues, private contributions, publication sales, course fees, and service contracts. Visit www.sog.unc.edu or call 919.966.5381 for more information on the School's courses, publications, programs, and services.

Michael R. Smith, Dean
Thomas H. Thornburg, Senior Associate Dean
Frayda S. Bluestein, Associate Dean for Programs
Todd A. Nicolet, Associate Dean for Operations
Ann Cary Simpson, Associate Dean for Development and Communications
Bradley G. Volk, Associate Dean for Administration

FACULTY

Gregory S. Allison
David N. Ammons
Ann M. Anderson
A. Fleming Bell, II
Maureen M. Berner
Mark F. Botts
Joan G. Brannon
Michael Crowell
Shea Riggsbee Denning
James C. Drennan
Richard D. Ducker
Robert L. Farb
Joseph S. Ferrell
Alyson A. Grine
Milton S. Heath Jr.
Norma Houston (on leave)
Cheryl Daniels Howell
Jeffrey A. Hughes

Joseph E. Hunt
Willow S. Jacobson
Robert P. Joyce
Kenneth L. Joyner
Diane M. Juffras
David M. Lawrence
Dona G. Lewandowski
James M. Markham
Janet Mason
Laurie L. Mesibov
Christopher B. McLaughlin
Kara A. Millonzi
Jill D. Moore
Jonathan Q. Morgan
Ricardo S. Morse
C. Tyler Mulligan
David W. Owens
William C. Rivenbark

Dale J. Roenigk
John Rubin
John L. Saxon
Jessica Smith
Karl W. Smith
Carl W. Stenberg III
John B. Stephens
Charles A. Szypszak
Shannon H. Tufts
Vaughn Upshaw
A. John Vogt
Aimee N. Wall
Jeffrey B. Welty
Richard B. Whisnant
Gordon P. Whitaker
Eileen R. Youens

21 20 19 18 17   6 7 8 9 10
ISBN 978-1-56011-607-3

Summary of Contents

Contents

III Contracts 51

VI Landlord–Tenant Law   147

VIII   Evidence   237

Preface

This book is a long time in coming. Several people deserve special thanks. Ingrid Johansen as a Research Assistant many years ago rewrote several chapters of the 1980 version of this book. I have used her versions as a starting point for several of the chapters in this book. Second, I would like to thank my colleague, Dona Lewandowski, for reviewing all of the chapters in this book and giving me constructive feedback. Third, Roberta Clark, as all good editors, improved this book. She caught me every time I was unclear about an issue and forced me to clarify my statements and be precise about my meaning. Finally, I would like to thank all of the magistrates who served in office during my tenure at the School of Government. Your questions shaped my knowledge and your support and friendship made my job exciting and rewarding.

Joan G. Brannon
February 2009

Chapter I

History of the
Office of Magistrate

The office of magistrate is rich in judicial traditions that, through the justice of the peace, go back to the twelfth century. In 1195 Richard I of England issued a proclamation for the preservation of public order requiring all men to observe the peace. Knights were assigned to see that the "King's Peace" was preserved.[1] These knights were the first keepers, or "conservators," of the peace, the direct ancestors of the justices of the peace. In 1327, during the reign of Edward III, the English Parliament, fearing an outbreak of lawlessness, enacted a law declaring, "For the better keeping and maintenance of the peace, the King wills, that in every county good men and lawful . . . shall be assigned to keep the peace."[2] In 1361 the original justice of the peace act[3] assigned one lord and several of the "most worthy" of each shire as justices to administer the king's law. Appointees to the office of justice of the peace came exclusively from the aristocracy and the landed gentry, and the office was deemed a high honor. After centuries of growth and development, the office reached a pinnacle of prestige and importance in England in the early eighteenth century.[4]

Considering this strong English ancestry, it is not surprising that the office of justice of the peace was brought to the English colonies in the New World. In the Charter of 1663, Charles II gave the Lords Proprietors of the Carolinas the right to appoint justices and other officials.[5] Restricted at first to the trial of nonfelonious criminal matters, the justices acquired "small claims" jurisdiction in 1715; this was limited to claims involving property valued at 40 shillings (about $512 today[6]) or less. The governor of North Carolina was given the power to appoint

1. Sir Thomas Skyrme, History of the Justices of the Peace (Chichester, Eng.: Barry Rose Law Publr. 1994), 45–47. See also Charles A. Beard, The Office of the Justice of the Peace in England: In Its Origin and Development (New York: Columbia University Press, 1904), 17–18.

2. Skyrme at 57.

3. Id. at 76–77. The Statute of Westminster transferred the keeper of the peace to the justice of the peace.

4. Id. at 409.

5. Albert Coates, "The Courts of Yesterday, Today and Tomorrow in North Carolina," Popular Government, March 1958 (Special Issue), 6.

6. This and all other conversions to 2007 dollars were computed on the website Measuring Worth, www.measuringworth.com. To convert British currency values to 2007 values, use the calculator at "Purchasing Power of British Pounds from 1264 to 2007" retail price index. To convert 2007 British currency to 2007

justices of the peace in 1773, and the North Carolina Constitution of 1776 authorized the General Assembly to nominate candidates for the office to the governor and vested the right of removal in the General Assembly.

In 1777 the Judicial Act established a North Carolina court system comprised of six judicial districts, each with a superior court and justices of the peace. The justices had jurisdiction over civil matters involving up to £5 (about $1,000 today) and over all nonfelony criminal offenses except those in which conviction would result in loss of "limb, or member." In 1785 the justices' civil jurisdiction was extended to controversies involving not more than £10 (about $2,040 today). As in England, the office was one of honor and was always filled by a leading citizen of the community.

In 1868 North Carolina statutes conferred on the justices' courts exclusive original jurisdiction in (1) all criminal cases in which the punishment did not exceed a fine of $50 or confinement for thirty days and (2) all contract actions in which $200 (about $3,009 today) or less was in controversy. These jurisdictional limits stood substantially unchanged for nearly a century while, with the gradual growth of mayor's courts and city and county courts after the Civil War, the justices' exclusive jurisdiction gave way in many localities to concurrent jurisdiction. The prestige of the office gradually declined. By the end of the nineteenth century the high-water mark of the justices of the peace had come and gone.

Since 1868, the parameters of the office have varied considerably. For example, the term of office in 1868 was two years. In 1876 it was changed to six years.[7] After 1895 it varied from two to four to six years, depending on the method by which justices were selected. In 1955 it became two years again, regardless of the method of selection.[8] The fees justices charged to hear a case also varied from time to time, place to place, and justice to justice; in the mid-1950s they ranged from $1.75 to $5.75, plus court costs amounting to another $4.50 to $15.[9] As justices received no salary, their compensation was the fees charged. And in criminal cases, they received no fee for their services unless there was a conviction. (Court costs were remitted to the county.)

The most revealing feature of the office of justice of the peace was the method by which the justice was selected. From 1868 to 1876 the voters of each township elected two justices. From 1877 to 1895 the General Assembly appointed the justices, sometimes in numbers bearing no relationship to the need.[10] From 1895 to 1917 the elective and the appointive methods flourished together.[11] In 1917 the General Assembly opened the post up to gubernatorial appointment.[12] The office continued as part of the patronage package until 1955, when the governor's power to appoint was rescinded and given to the resident superior court judges.[13] Apparently no accurate record of the total number of justices of the peace appointed in the first half of the

---

American dollars, use the relative values of British pounds to American dollars. To convert American dollars in the past to present-day value, use the relative value of American dollars converter.

7. S.L. 1876-77 Ch. 141 (codified as G.S. Ch. 22 § 819) 1 The Code of North Carolina (1883).

8. 1955 N.C. Sess. Laws ch. 910.

9. Coates, *supra* note 5, at 16–17.

10. *Id.* at 15.

11. 1895 N.C. Public Sess. Laws ch. 157.

12. 1917 N.C. Public Sess. Laws ch. 40.

13. 1955 N.C. Sess. Laws ch. 910 § 2.

twentieth century exists. Nonetheless, the average number in office at any one time—perhaps two thousand—was undeniably far greater than the need. The office had become a political football, and appointments proliferated with little or no regard for need or for the qualifications of the appointees. This "magistrate-making mania" was spotlighted by an eminent attorney, Kemp Battle of Rocky Mount, who publicly criticized the depravity, corruption, and disrepute into which the office had sunk through these political selections.[14]

A final important characteristic of the office of the justice was the informal nature of the justice's surroundings. A few full-time justices maintained an office and transacted business only in a clean, dignified, respectable setting. With the majority, however, it was different.

> Most of the . . . justices are "birds on the wing," and litigants find them on a "catch as catch can" basis. With no fixed time or place for tending to judicial business, the part-time justice of the peace can tend to judicial business anytime or anywhere, and the records show him trying cases in his back yard, on his front porch, in the rear end of a grocery store over chicken crates, over a meat counter in a butcher shop . . . in a garage, in an ice house, in a fairground ticket booth, and in a funeral parlor.[15]

North Carolina's system of justices of the peace served the needs of a horse-and-buggy society reasonably well. But the twentieth century brought conditions and problems with which the justices were not equipped to cope. The legislature, instead of restructuring the office to enable it to respond to the needs of the times, made the problem worse by flooding the counties with scores of justices. Not surprisingly, overproduction of justices compensated solely by fees led to a dishonest competition for fees (which were often too low). The record books overflow with instances of favoritism, bribery, and corruption.[16] The fee system itself, reasonable enough in a day when justices were well-to-do and served primarily from a sense of public duty, put impartiality and fair treatment at a disadvantage in an era when justices were largely dependent on fees for a livelihood. In addition, the typical justice was without legal training and operated free of supervision. It is little wonder that by the 1920s the office had sunk from one of dignity and honor to one of scorn and disrepute. Corrective action did not come, however, until Governor Luther Hodges's 1955 call for reform finally bore fruit in 1962 in a constitutional amendment that revised the state's judicial system.

The constitution's new judicial article[17] omitted any reference to the office of justice of the peace and provided for repeal of the statutes regulating the office. However, drafters of the new judicial article, recognizing a need for a judicial official at the level formerly served by the justice

---

14. Kemp D. Battle, *Open Court,* 6 N.C. L. Rev. 349, 354 (1928).

15. Coates, *supra* note 5, at 16.

16. *See* Battle, *supra* note 14, at 350–51.

17. Article IV of the North Carolina Constitution was rewritten in 1962 to adopt the uniform state court system under which the state now operates. *See* 1961 N.C. Sess. Laws ch. 313. In 1965 the implementing legislation, the Judicial Act of 1965, was enacted. 1965 N.C. Sess. Laws ch. 310.

of the peace, created the office of magistrate. The constitution made the following provisions for the new office:

1. Each county has at least one magistrate and as many more as the General Assembly may provide.
2. The magistrate is nominated by the clerk of superior court and appointed by the senior resident superior court judge.
3. Magistrates are compensated by a salary set without regard to their decisions in cases.
4. Magistrates are officers of the new statewide District Court Division and serve for a term of two years.[18]

On all other matters relating to the magistrate, the constitution is silent. Decisions about jurisdiction, powers, qualifications, and other details of the magistrate's office were left up to the General Assembly. In 2004 the constitution was amended to provide for an initial term of two years and subsequent terms for four years.[19]

The General Assembly continued the magistrate's jurisdiction in misdemeanor cases at the $50/30-day maximum sentence limit that had long been in effect for justices of the peace; but it withheld the power to try criminal cases in which the defendant pleaded not guilty, thus limiting greatly the magistrate's power to determine guilt or innocence. In 1969 the magistrate was given jurisdiction to try worthless-check cases of $50 or less.[20] The General Assembly has since increased that amount several times; the magistrate is now authorized, on approval by the chief district court judge, to try worthless-check cases of $2,000 or less.[21] In traffic, wildlife, boating, alcohol, and littering cases, the magistrate's discretion over the sentence is taken away by a schedule of offenses and punishments prescribed by the chief district judges, acting jointly.[22] In civil small claims cases, the magistrate's jurisdiction was originally limited to controversies involving $300 ($1,971 in today's dollars) or less. This jurisdiction has been expanded frequently and now includes controversies involving $5,000 or less.[23] Although the small claims jurisdiction is just an expansion of the justice's civil jurisdiction, the magistrate cannot try a small claim unless the plaintiff requests assignment of the case to a magistrate and the chief district judge concurs. In short, the magistrate's criminal jurisdiction is narrower than the former justice's; but his or her civil jurisdiction, though under rigid controls, is somewhat broader than the justice's. The magistrate is authorized to perform miscellaneous quasi-judicial functions like the marriage ceremony to substantially the same extent as the justices were.

In a number of other ways, however, the office of magistrate bears scant comparison to that of the justice of peace. Magistrates have offices provided by the county; in judicial duties, they are subject to assignment and supervision by the chief district judge; in record-keeping functions, they are subject to supervision by the clerk of superior court, acting under statewide regulations

18. N.C. Const. art. IV, § 10. See 1965 N.C. Sess. Laws ch. 310.
19. N.C. Const. art. IV, § 10. See S.L. 2004-128 §§ 16–19, approved by the voters in November 2004.
20. 1969 N.C. Sess. Laws ch. 876, sec. 2.
21. N.C. Gen. Stat. § 7A-273(6) (hereinafter G.S.).
22. G.S. 7A-148, -273(2).
23. G.S. 7A-210.

issued by the Administrative Office of the Courts (AOC). They cannot convene a jury; and their compensation, a straight salary (with the fringe benefits of state government employees) is paid by the state and fixed by statute according to their length of service as a magistrate.

A feature of the office of magistrate that has caused much concern is the means by which the office is filled. As noted above, the constitution provides that the clerk of superior court shall nominate and the senior resident superior court judge shall select the magistrate. This political compromise was apparently necessary to obtain approval from the 1961 General Assembly as part of the overall court reform package. The constitution also requires the state—through its responsibility for the operational support of the court system—to fix and pay the magistrate's compensation. Furnishing a facility in which the magistrate may transact business is left to the county. The General Assembly made the chief district judge responsible for assigning the times and places at which the magistrate would perform the basic duties of the office and for assigning or withholding small-claims cases. Thus, with five individuals or groups—representing the county, the judicial district, and the state—engaged in putting the magistrate in office and assigning his or her work, much cooperation and sharing of responsibility is required. It is hardly surprising that at times the cooperation has been less than ideal or that the process has not always produced the desired end product—a well-qualified magistrate functioning efficiently as a member of a smoothly operating district court judicial team. It is a tribute to those involved in this elaborate arrangement that the office of magistrate functions as well as it does.

Other important changes made since the 1963 creation of the office of the magistrate have increased the professionalism of the office. Beginning in 1977 new magistrates were required to attend and successfully complete a basic training course in order to be eligible for renomination for office;[24] since 1989 all magistrates have been required to attend twelve hours of continuing education every two years;[25] and in 1994 the educational qualification to be nominated as a magistrate was raised from a high school diploma to a four-year college degree or a two-year associate's degree plus four years of relevant work experience, as determined by the AOC.[26]

The creation and changes to the office of magistrate were designed to cure the evils that had contributed to the loss of respect for the office of justice of the peace: the fee system, the collection-agency practice, the competition for business, the undignified surroundings, the lack of uniformity. Some of the changes, especially the loss of power to try certain not-guilty misdemeanors, have detracted from the importance of the office; but in other respects the office's status has been enhanced. The magistrate is a judicial official, fully integrated into the General Court of Justice team. Magistrate's court is an arm of the district court. The office has been dignified by a state-paid salary and county-supplied office space. The magistrate's civil jurisdiction,

24. 1977 N.C. Sess. Laws ch. 945 (codified as G.S. 7A-171.2(c) through -177).

25. The director of the Administrative Office of the Courts (AOC) implemented the continuing education requirement after receiving a resolution requesting continuing education adopted by the North Carolina Magistrates Association on October 12, 1988, and after a vote of the Conference of Chief District Judges at their annual meeting on July 15, 1989. A copy of the N.C. Magistrate's Association resolution, a summary of the minutes of the meeting of the Conference of Chief District Judges, and a follow-up letter from Franklin Freeman, director of AOC, to Frank Plunkett, president of the N.C. Magistrate's Association, is on file in the author's office.

26. 1993 N.C. Sess. Laws ch. 769, sec. 7.13(a) (codified as G.S. 7A-171.2(b)).

in assigned small claims, has increased dramatically. Interestingly, in numbers of cases heard the magistracy disposes of a majority of the (nondomestic) civil litigation in North Carolina. In fiscal year 2005–6 magistrates disposed of 82.2 percent of the 336,395 civil cases disposed of in the state.[27] Furthermore, the General Assembly has increased their responsibilities by providing that that they hear cases enforcing liens arising out of the towing and repairing of vehicles,[28] by allowing magistrates to set aside their judgments in certain cases,[29] and by allowing magistrates to issue ex parte domestic violence orders.[30] If magistrates continue to demonstrate the skills and high ethical standards expected of a state judicial official, the General Assembly may increase their responsibilities further. In this sense, magistrates control their own fate. They must make their own contribution to the efficient administration of equal justice under law. If they do so, they may find that the prestige, honor, and respect that went with the office in the eighteenth and nineteenth centuries are not gone beyond recall.

27. Calculated from data provided in the North Carolina Courts FY 2005–6 Statistical and Operational Summary of the Judicial Branch of Government found at www.nccourts.org/Citizens/Publications/ Documents/stat_summary05-06.pdf.

28. 1977 N.C. Sess. Laws ch. 86 (codified as G.S. 7A-211.1).

29. 1981 N.C. Sess. Laws ch. 599 (codified as G.S. 7A-228(a)).

30. 1994 Sess. Laws ch. 4 (codified as G.S. 50B-2(c1)).

Chapter II

Small Claims Procedure

A special set of statutes governs the trial of small claims before a magistrate. The procedural rules set out in Article 19 of the North Carolina General Statutes, Chapter 7A (hereinafter G.S.) are for the most part simpler than those applied in district and superior court actions. However, when the small claim procedural rules are silent on an issue, the Rules of Civil Procedure applicable in district and superior court cases apply.[1] This chapter discusses the procedures magistrates follow in handling small claims cases as well as issues related to appeal to district court.

Definition of a Small Claim

The statute defines a *small claim* as a civil action in which (1) the amount in controversy does not exceed $5,000; (2) the principal relief sought is money, the recovery of specific personal property, summary ejectment, or any combination of the three; and (3) the plaintiff (the person suing) requests that the action be assigned to a magistrate.[2]

Amount in Controversy

The first requirement—that the amount in controversy cannot exceed $5,000—refers to the monetary value of the case and is determined at the time the complaint is filed. However, the statutory rules that apply to determining that amount often raise more questions than they answer.

---

1. N.C. GEN. STAT. § 1A-1, Rule 1 (hereinafter G.S.) provides that the Rules of Civil Procedure govern the procedure in the district courts in all actions and proceedings of a civil nature. *See* Provident Finance Co. v. Locklear, 89 N.C. App. 535, 366 S.E.2d 599 (1988) (Rule 58 applied to small claim case). Some rules of civil procedure, such as the discovery rules, may not apply because they do not seem applicable to small claims cases because trials are scheduled within thirty days of the complaint's filing date.

2. G.S. 7A-210.

When Plaintiff Seeks Monetary Damages

How is the amount in controversy determined in an action seeking monetary damages? One would think this would be easy to answer—the amount in controversy is the dollar amount requested in the complaint. Generally, that is the case. However, in an action for breach of contract the total amount prayed for includes a claim for a specific amount as principal and for prejudgment interest and then also asks for post-judgment interest and court costs, which are added by the clerk. The statute defining the *amount in controversy* provides (1) that the amount in controversy is computed without regard to interest and costs but then states (2) that when monetary relief is prayed, the amount prayed for is in controversy.[3]

> ***Example 1.*** Jordan borrows $5,000 from his friend, Sara Beth. He agrees to pay the money back in six months with interest at the rate of 10 percent per year. The loan repayment was due January 3, but Jordan doesn't pay. Sara Beth files the action at the end of July, one year after she made the loan. She sues for $5,000 principal, $500 interest, for a total amount prayed for of $5,500, plus interest from the date of judgment and costs.

If the first rule of determining the amount in controversy—computing it without regard to interest and costs—is read alone, it would seem that the amount in controversy in Example 1 is $5,000 and that the case can be assigned to a magistrate. But the second rule—in which the amount prayed for is in controversy—would indicate that the total amount prayed for ($5,500) is the amount in controversy, and therefore, that the case should not be assigned to a magistrate. Under the rules of statutory construction, a statute must be "considered as a whole and construed, if possible, so that none of its provisions shall be rendered useless or redundant."[4]

There is, however, a way to read the subsections of the statute to give meaning to both: this way interprets the total amount prayed for as the principal and prejudgment interest already accrued on the debt (in Example 1, the $5,000 principal plus the $500 interest) and excludes the language "interest and costs" from the amount in controversy, reading it instead as post-judgment interest and the court costs that the clerk will add to the judgment. The complaint would thus pray for $5,500, plus interest on the principal from the date of judgment and court costs; the "interest from the date of judgment and costs" are not computed in arriving at the amount in controversy, whereas the prejudgment interest is part of the total amount prayed for in the complaint. This interpretation rests on sounder policy grounds than determining that the amount in controversy is based solely on the principal amount of the debt, as the General Assembly clearly intended to limit the dollar amount of cases heard in small claims court. However, because no appellate decision has interpreted the interest subsection of the amount-in-controversy statute, there is no definitive answer to this question. Until there is, the interpretation of the statute rests with the chief district judge who determines which cases are assigned as small claims in his or her district. A chief district judge can resolve this issue for the district by specifying in an administrative order how the clerk assigning cases to magistrates should determine the amount in controversy.

---

3. G.S. 7A-243(1), (2).

4. Porsh Builders, Inc. v. City of Winston-Salem, 302 N.C. 550, 556, 276 S.E.2d 443, 447 (1981). *See also* State v. Bates, 348 N.C. 29, 35, 497 S.E.2d 276, 279 (1998).

A second question about determining the amount in controversy arises when the plaintiff prays for actual damages of a specified amount and then asks for that amount to be trebled because of an unfair and deceptive practice claim.

> ***Example 2.*** Tenant files a small claims action against landlord for constructive eviction and seeks damages of $2,500 for moving costs. In addition the complaint alleges a claim for unfair trade practice in which the tenant wants the $2,500 trebled.

The amount-in-controversy statute provides that when a single party asserts two or more properly joined claims, the claims are aggregated (added together) unless they are mutually exclusive and in the alternative (the test is whether the plaintiff can recover on only one of the claims), in which case the highest claim is the amount in controversy.[5] An unfair trade practice claim, like a claim for breach of contract, is a separate claim; but the plaintiff cannot collect damages for both breach of contract and unfair trade practices.[6] Thus the highest claim—the trebled amount of damages—would be the amount in controversy. In this example the amount in controversy would be $7,500 and the case should not be assigned to a magistrate.

When Plaintiff Seeks Return of Personal Property

How is the amount in controversy determined when the plaintiff is suing to recover possession of specific personal property that was either wrongfully taken or listed as collateral in a security agreement that is in default? "Where no monetary relief is sought but the relief sought would establish, enforce, or avoid an obligation, right or title, the value of the obligation, right, or title is in controversy."[7] In an action to recover property as a nonsecured party, the relief would establish the right to recover the property; therefore the amount in controversy is the fair market value of the property the plaintiff is seeking to recover plus any monetary damages sought for loss of use or damage to the property.

> ***Example 3.*** Acme Rent-All brings an action against James to recover a chain saw it rented to him. The fair market value of the chain saw is $250. Acme also seeks $50 damages for loss of use of the saw, since it was unable to rent the saw to another customer who sought to rent it during the period James wrongfully held the saw. In this case, the plaintiff is seeking to establish the right to recover the chain saw and is seeking monetary damages of $50. The establishment of the right is the value of the right, or $250. Therefore, the amount in controversy in this case is $300.

But what if the plaintiff is a secured party and is seeking to recover the specific personal property listed in the security agreement?

---

5. G.S. 7A-243(4).

6. *See. e.g.,* Britt v. Jones, 123 N.C. App. 108 (1996) (citing Marshall v. Miller, 47 N.C. App. 530, 542, 268 S.E.2d 97, 103 (1980) *modified on other grounds and aff'd,* 302 N.C. 539, 276 S.E.2d 397 (1981)) (Where the same course of conduct gives rise to a traditionally recognized action such as breach of contract as well as a cause of action for unfair trade practices, damages may be recovered for either breach of contract or unfair trade practices, but not both.).

7. G.S. 7A-243(3).

Example 4. Sears sells a refrigerator, stove, microwave, washing machine, and dryer to Virginia for $4,800. She pays $500 down and Sears finances the remainder. Virginia signs a security agreement listing all the items purchased as security for the extension of credit. One year later, she stops making her monthly payments and Sears brings an action to recover possession of the refrigerator, stove, microwave, washing machine, and dryer. At the time, the personal property Sears is seeking to recover has a fair market value of $4,100, but the total amount owed on the debt is $2,500.

It is not clear whether the plaintiff is establishing the right to possession of the property—in which case the value of the property is the amount in controversy—or whether the relief sought would enforce an underlying obligation—in which case the amount owed on the debt would be the amount in controversy. The standard small claims complaint form used by litigants assumes that the amount in controversy is the value of the property that plaintiff seeks to recover.[8] The better rule may be that the amount in controversy is the underlying obligation. Unlike the action by a nonsecured party, in which the plaintiff recovers property owned by the plaintiff, in an action by a secured party the plaintiff is recovering property owned by the defendant in order to apply it toward payment of the underlying debt owed by the defendant. Any surplus recovered is then returned to the defendant. As a practical matter, however, the determining factor is the value the plaintiff fills in on the complaint form. If the plaintiff indicates the value as $5,000 or less, the clerk will assign the case to the magistrate and the magistrate should hear it. On the other hand, if the plaintiff fills in an amount greater than $5,000, the case should not be assigned to a magistrate.

Actions to Enforce Motor Vehicle Lien

In motor vehicle lien cases in which the garage owner seeks a judgment allowing the lien to be enforced, the amount in controversy is the amount of the lien (the value of the obligation) and not the value of the motor vehicle.[9] The lawsuit authorizes enforcement of a lien on the motor vehicle, which means the garage owner must sell the motor vehicle and apply the proceeds to the amount owed, giving any surplus to the owner of the vehicle.

Principal Relief Sought

The second criterion defines a small claim according to the type of relief sought, not by the subject matter of the lawsuit. As long as no more than $5,000 is sought, a plaintiff can bring a suit in small claims court based on any subject: for example, an unfair trade practice, medical malpractice, fraud, or breach of contract. Nor is the plaintiff limited in the kinds of monetary damages allowed. As long as the amount in controversy does not exceed $5,000, the plaintiff is entitled to any kind of monetary damages authorized for the particular type of claim, such as damages for pain and suffering in tort cases, treble damages in unfair trade practice claims, and punitive damages in intentional tort cases.

8. *See* AOC-CVM-202, "Complaint to Recover Possession of Personal Property."

9. G.S. 7A-243(3), which governs the amount in controversy when the owner of the motor vehicle seeks to recover property on which a motor vehicle lien is asserted, specifies that the amount in controversy is that portion of the asserted lien that is under dispute.

What matters in determining whether an action may be brought as a small claim is the remedy sought by the plaintiff. Only three remedies are appropriate for small claims court: (1) requests for money, (2) recovery of specific personal property, and (3) summary ejectment. A magistrate cannot grant injunctive relief or specific performance (that is, requiring a party to perform some contractual obligation other than paying money). Nor can a magistrate hear domestic cases (divorce, custody, support, or equitable distribution).

> *Example 5.* Buster and Franklin enter into a contract under which Buster agrees to paint Franklin's car. Franklin pays Buster $500 when he picks up the car. One week later, spots appear on the car because it was not properly painted, and Franklin asks Buster to take the car back and get it right. Buster refuses. Franklin sues Buster and seeks to make him repaint the car.
>
> A magistrate cannot hear this lawsuit because the remedy sought—specific performance—is not within the definition of a small claim. If, however, Franklin had taken the car to another place to have it repainted for $500 and then sued Buster for $500, the case could be heard by a magistrate since the relief sought is money.

The only exception to the limitation of small claims cases to those seeking these three types of relief is an action to enforce a motor vehicle mechanic-and-storage lien arising under G.S. 44A-2(d) or G.S. 20-77(d). By specific statute, a magistrate may hear a motor vehicle lien claim seeking the right to enforce such a lien.[10]

Plaintiff Requests Assignment

North Carolina does not require that civil actions for $5,000 or less be heard in small claims court. Even a plaintiff who files a $5 lawsuit may choose to have that case heard in district court. No case may be assigned to a magistrate unless the plaintiff requests that assignment, and, interestingly, only the plaintiff may do so.[11] The defendant can neither object to a case being heard by the magistrate, nor request that it be heard in district court, nor seek to have a case filed in district court moved to the magistrate's court.

The plaintiff need not, however, make a specific formal request to have the matter assigned as a small claim. It is sufficient to file the claim on one of the standard Administrative Office of the Courts (AOC) complaint forms, which specify that the action is being brought in "the district court division–small claims division."

Filing a Small Claims Action

A small claims case is initiated when the plaintiff files a complaint with the clerk of superior court. The complaint gives notice to the defendant (the person being sued) of who is suing, the reason for the suit, and what relief the plaintiff wishes to recover. A complaint must be made in writing and signed by the plaintiff or the plaintiff's attorney. In a summary ejectment action or back-rent action, a plaintiff's agent who handles the rental also may sign it.[12] The complaint

---

10. G.S. 7A-211.1.
11. G.S. 7A-210(3).
12. G.S. 7A-216, -223.

should be a simple, brief statement easily grasped by a person of common understanding. No particular form is required, although most plaintiffs use the standard small claims complaint forms prepared by AOC.

Where Action Is Filed

Unlike a district or superior court action, a small claim action must be filed in the county where the defendant resides.[13] If there are multiple defendants who live in different counties, one action against all of them may be filed in a county in which one of them resides. In most cases, the county where a lawsuit is filed (the *venue*) is considered a procedural, not a jurisdictional matter—which means that a defendant who raises no objections before trial waives the matter of venue. The small claims statute, however, is more directive than a typical venue statute. Because the general rule by which most chief district court judges assign cases to magistrates specifies that one defendant must reside in the county, a magistrate who determines that none of the defendants is a county resident may send the case back to the clerk because the case was not assigned by the judge. (See discussion below on "Motion Objecting to Venue or Jurisdiction.")

Residence is the defendant's actual place of abode, whether permanent or temporary.[14] A person may have more than one residence.[15] If the defendant is a domestic corporation (that is, is incorporated in North Carolina), its residence is the registered or principal office of the corporation or wherever the corporation maintains a place of business. If the corporation has neither a principal office nor a place of business, its residence is "any place where the corporation . . . is regularly engaged in carrying on business."[16] This same rule applies to "foreign corporations" (those incorporated in another state) that have qualified with the North Carolina Secretary of State to transact business in the state.[17]

> *Example 6.* Franklin Office Supply Inc., a North Carolina corporation, has its principal office in Forsyth County. It also has a store in Stokes County. Beatrice buys a chair from Franklin Office Supply Inc. and is unhappy because she believes the corporation breached the warranty of merchantability. Beatrice can file a small claims action in either Forsyth County or Stokes County.

If a foreign corporation has not been granted authority to transact business in North Carolina, the statute does not specify how to determine the corporation's residence. Although the general venue law provides that a corporation may be sued in any county in which it usually does business,[18] its residence apparently is in the state where it is incorporated. Therefore, it appears

---

13. G.S. 7A-211.

14. Sheffield v. Walker, 231 N.C. 556, 559, 58 S.E.2d 356, 359 (1950).

15. *Cf.* Van Buren v. Glasco, 27 N.C. App. 1, 217 S.E.2d 579 (1975). *See* Glover v. Farmer, 127 N.C. App. 488, 491, 490 S.E.2d 576, 578 (1997) (Whether a person is a resident of a particular place is not determined by any given formula but rather depends significantly on the facts and circumstances surrounding the particular issue.).

16. G.S. 1-79.

17. Hill v. Atlantic Greyhound Corp., 229 N.C. 728, 51 S.E.2d 183 (1949); Moore Golf, Inc. v. Shambley Wrecking Contractors, Inc., 22 N.C. App. 449, 206 S.E.2d 789 (1974).

18. G.S. 1-80.

that a foreign corporation not granted authority to transact business in North Carolina must be sued in district or superior court, not in magistrate's court.

Residence is determined at the time the complaint is filed.[19] If a case is filed in the county in which the defendant resides and the defendant moves to another county before trial, the magistrate in the county where the case was filed should hear the case.

The one exception to the requirement that a defendant reside in the county where the case is filed is an action to enforce a motor vehicle mechanic-and-storage lien. Such a case must be filed in the county where the claim arose (that is, where the motor vehicle was towed or repaired) rather than in the defendant's county of residence.[20]

District Judge Assigns Case

If the plaintiff files a complaint requesting assignment to a magistrate, the chief district judge has the discretion to decide whether to assign the case to a magistrate. The assignment may be made by specific order or general rule.[21] No chief district court judge reads every complaint and determines assignment on a case-by-case basis; all make assignments by means of administrative orders to the clerk. Such orders usually authorize the clerk to assign to the magistrate "any case within the magistrate's jurisdiction for which the plaintiff requests assignment as a small claim" or "any case with an amount in controversy of $5,000 or less for which the plaintiff requests assignment as a small claim."[22] Based on this administrative or general order, the clerk assigns the case to a magistrate as soon as it is filed.

The clerk then issues a *magistrate's summons*, which officially commences the court action.[23] The summons notifies the defendant of the date, time, and location of the trial. After service of the summons, according to the statute, the clerk gives the plaintiff written notice of the assignment.[24] Although some counties follow the statutory procedure, most notify plaintiffs when they file their complaint that the case has been assigned to a magistrate and inform them of the date and time of the trial.

If the complaint does not fall within the district judge's general order of assignment, the clerk issues a *civil summons* rather than a magistrate's summons and gives the plaintiff notice of non-assignment. The clerk also informs the plaintiff that the action will be heard in district court and that those court costs must be paid. Even when a case falls within the chief district judge's general rule, a case may not be assigned to a magistrate if the clerk brings to the judge's attention some particular aspect of a complaint filed as a small claim: for example, that a magistrate is a party to the action or that it includes a very unusual claim.

If the judge assigns a case to a magistrate, the magistrate's judgment is valid and is not subject to challenge on the basis that the action was not properly assignable to a magistrate. The sole

---

19. Bass v. Bass, 43 N.C. App. 212, 215, 258 S.E.2d 391, 393 (1979).
20. G.S. 7A-211.1.
21. G.S. 7A-211.
22. A model general rule is attached as Appendix I at the end of this chapter.
23. G.S. 7A-213.
24. AOC-CVM-300, "Notice of Assignment/Service" is the form used to notify the plaintiff of assignment.

remedy for improper assignment is appeal.[25] However, it is unlikely that a case assigned according to the judge's general order would ever be assigned improperly. Moreover, if a clerk did send a magistrate a case that is not within the judge's order, that case probably would fall under the rule that the magistrate's judgment is invalid because the chief district court judge did not assign the case to the magistrate.[26]

Small Claim for More Than $5,000

Occasionally a plaintiff, usually through an attorney, will try to file a claim for more than $5,000 in small claims court. In doing so, the attorney will argue that there is no jurisdictional limitation based on the amount in controversy and that a defendant who objects can move to transfer the case to district court. That analysis would be accurate with regard to cases filed in district or superior court, where there is no jurisdictional limitation based on amount in controversy between those two divisions[27] and where the statute provides for transfers of a case filed in the improper division.[28] However, small claims are unique. First, the magistrate is part of the district court division, so that such a transfer would not be between different divisions.[29] Moreover, because the $5,000 is jurisdictional, any proceeding before the magistrate would be void.[30] Finally, as mentioned above, a small claims action must be assigned to the magistrate by the chief district court judge. Since judges assign cases through an administrative or general order, a case that does not comply with the order but is sent to the magistrate has not been assigned by a judge; the magistrate's judgment would therefore be invalid.[31]

A magistrate who receives a case in which the amount in controversy at the time the complaint is filed exceeds $5,000 should not hear the case but should return it to the clerk, indicating that he or she lacks jurisdiction to hear it. Sometimes the plaintiff may choose to reduce the amount prayed for to $5,000 and forgive the remainder of the amount owed in order to have the case heard in small claims court. In that situation the magistrate may allow the plaintiff to amend the complaint to ask for only $5,000 and proceed with the case. The magistrate can either allow the plaintiff to amend the copy of the complaint in the file by noting the reduced amount prayed for and signing and dating the complaint where the amount is reduced or can orally request the amendment; in the latter case the magistrate should indicate in the "findings" portion of the judgment that the plaintiff in open court reduced the amount prayed for to $_____.

---

25. G.S. 7A-212.

26. *Id.*

27. G.S. 7A-243 specifies that the district court is the "proper" division for cases of $10,000 or less and the superior court is proper for cases over $10,000.

28. G.S. 7A-257, -258.

29. N.C. Const. art. IV, § 10.

30. *See* Falk Integrated Technologies, Inc. v. Stack, 132 N.C. App. 807, 513 S.E.2d 572 (1999).

31. G.S. 7A-212.

Splitting Claims to Reduce Amount in Controversy

Occasionally a plaintiff will attempt to divide a claim for more than $5,000 and bring two or more actions, each for $5,000 or less. The general rule is that for the breach of an entire and indivisible contract, more than one action for damages is not sustainable.[32] If a plaintiff tries to split one contract into separate claims, the defendant may raise the affirmative defense of res judicata (the matter has been adjudicated) to the second or subsequent action and the magistrate will have to dismiss that action. The question for the magistrate is whether the contract was indivisible. Early cases indicate that when an account consists of several items, either for goods sold or services provided at different times, the plaintiff may sue for each transaction separately before a magistrate even though the aggregate amount exceeds $5,000.

However, if the debt is for one item, it cannot be split;[33] nor can it be split if several items were purchased in one continuous shopping spree.[34] Moreover, if the plaintiff has rendered a statement for the entire amount due and the defendant has accepted the account or not responded within a reasonable time, a new contract to pay the entire amount as one debt has been created.[35] Thus, if transactions were originally separate but the plaintiff has sent the defendant a statement for the full amount due to which the defendant has not objected within a reasonable amount of time, the account has become one debt and may not be split.

Time for Trial

The clerk must set the time for trial not more than thirty days after the summons is issued[36]—except that for summary ejectment cases, in which the clerk must set the time of trial within seven business days after the summons is issued.[37] In counties where small claims court is held only once or twice a week, it may be impossible for the clerk to set all summary ejectment cases within that period; in that case, the clerk should schedule the cases for the first small claims court held after seven days.

Service of Process

The magistrate acquires jurisdiction to hear a case when copies of the complaint and summons are served on that defendant. Four methods of subjecting a defendant to the jurisdiction of the court apply in all small claims cases; a fifth applies in summary ejectment cases only; and a sixth applies in motor vehicle lien cases only.

---

32. Gaither Corp. v. Skinner, 241 N.C. 532, 536, 85 S.E.2d 909, 912 (1955).

33. Mayo v. Martin, 186 N.C. 1, 118 S.E. 830 (1923); Simpson v. Elwood, 114 N.C. 528, 19 S.E. 598 (1894); Boyle v. Robbins, 71 N.C. 130 (1874).

34. T.J. Magruder & Co. v. W.H. Randolph & Co., 77 N.C. 79 (1877).

35. Copland v. Wireless Telegraph Co., 136 N.C. 11, 48 S.E. 501 (1904); D. Marks & Son v. Ballance, 113 N.C. 28, 18 S.E. 75 (1893).

36. G.S. 7A-214.

37. G.S. 42-28.

These methods of service are as follows.

1. The sheriff, or in some instances a private process server, serves a defendant by delivering a copy of the summons and complaint to the defendant personally.[38]
2. The sheriff, or in some instances a private process server, serves the defendant by leaving a copy of the summons and complaint at the defendant's dwelling with a person of suitable age and discretion who also resides in the dwelling.[39]
3. The plaintiff serves the defendant by mailing a copy of the summons and complaint by certified or registered mail, return receipt requested, addressed to the defendant, and the post office delivers the copies to the addressee.[40]
4. Even if the defendant is not served by one of the first three methods, the court has jurisdiction to proceed against the defendant if he or she signs a written acceptance of service or makes a voluntary appearance in the case.[41]
5. In summary ejectment cases only, the sheriff may serve the defendant by mailing a copy of the summons and complaint to the defendant by first class mail at the premises from which the defendant is to be evicted *and* by posting a copy of the summons and complaint in a conspicuous place on the premises.[42]
6. In motor vehicle lien cases only, a defendant can be served by any method authorized by Rule 4 of the Rules of Civil Procedure. This means that in addition to the first four methods listed above, the defendant may be served by (a) depositing with a designated delivery service copies of the complaint and summons addressed to the defendant, to be delivered to the addressee; (b) mailing a copy, signature confirmation required, via the U.S. Postal Service; or (c) if the defendant cannot with due diligence be served by any of the above methods, by publishing a notice of service of process in a newspaper qualified for legal advertising and circulated in the area where the defendant is believed be located, or in the county where the action was filed. [43]

---

38. Except in actions for summary ejectment, if the sheriff returns a summons unserved the plaintiff may select anyone 21 years of age or older who is not a party to the action and not related by blood or marriage to a party to the action to serve the *alias and pluries* (second or subsequent) *summons*. G.S. 1A-1, Rule 4 (h1).

39. G.S 7A-217, which sets out methods of service of small claims actions, speaks only to serving defendants who are natural persons. If the defendant is a corporation, partnership, or local government, G.S. 1A-1, Rule 4 (j)(6) specifies the manner of service. A corporation may be served (a) by delivering a copy to an officer, director, or managing agent; (b) by leaving a copy at the office of an officer, director, or managing agent with the person who is apparently in charge of the office; (c) by delivering a copy to the registered agent of the corporation; (d) by mailing a copy by certified mail, return receipt requested, to an officer, director, managing agent, or registered agent; or (e) by delivery by a designated delivery service to an officer, director, managing agent, or registered agent.

40. G.S. 7A-217(2) and G.S. 1A-1, Rule 4(j)(1)c.

41. G.S. 7A-217(3).

42. G.S. 7A-217(4) and 42-29. If service is by posting, no monetary damages may be awarded. See discussion in Chapter VI, "Landlord–Tenant Law," page 150.

43. G.S. 7A-211.1; G.S. 1A-1, Rule 4(j)(1) and (j1).

Proof of Service

Service by Sheriff

The sheriff's return of the summons showing the place, time, and manner of service is sufficient to prove service.[44] A sheriff's return is presumed to be correct; therefore, if it indicates that the process was left with a person of suitable age and discretion, the plaintiff need not offer any further proof of service.[45] A defendant who wishes to challenge the service must file a motion objecting to jurisdiction over his or her person. A district court judge, not a magistrate, must hear this and other pretrial motions (which are discussed below on page 25).

Service by a Private Process Server

A private process proves service by filing an affidavit (1) showing the place, time, and manner of service; (2) stating the server's qualifications to make service under Rule 4 of the Rules of Civil Procedure; (3) declaring that the server knew the person served to be the defendant and that he or she delivered to and left with the defendant a copy of the summons and complaint; and (4) if the defendant was not personally served, stating when, where, and with whom such copies were left.[46]

Service by Certified Mail

If the plaintiff serves the defendant by certified mail, the plaintiff must file an affidavit showing proof of service and must attach to the affidavit the signed postal return receipt. An *affidavit* is a statement that is sworn to before a person authorized to administer oaths—usually a notary public but sometimes a magistrate. The affidavit must indicate that a copy of the summons and complaint was deposited in the post office for mailing by registered or certified mail, return receipt requested, and that it was in fact received—as evidenced by the attached postal receipt or other evidence of delivery.[47] If the postal receipt is signed by someone other than the defendant, the person signing is presumed to be an agent authorized to accept service or a person of suitable age and discretion residing in the house, subject to rebuttal by the defendant.[48]

Written Acceptance of Service

A defendant may also sign a written acceptance of service, which obviates the need to prove proper service by the sheriff or by certified mail.[49] Acceptance of service is rarely used in small claims cases.

---

44. Williams v. Burroughs Wellcome Co, 46 N.C. App. 459, 265 S.E.2d 633 (1980).

45. Guthrie v. Ray, 293 N.C. 67, 235 S.E.2d 146 (1977); Harrington v. Rice, 245 N.C. 640, 97 S.E.2d 239 (1957).

46. G.S. 1-75.10(1)b.

47. G.S. 1-75.10(4).

48. G.S. 1A-1, Rule 4 (j2)(2). If the defendant wishes to challenge service, he or she must file a motion before trial; the motion must be heard by a district court judge.

49. G.S. 7A-217(3) and G.S. 1A-1, Rule 4 (j5).

Voluntary Appearance

A voluntary appearance dispenses with the need for valid service of process. Voluntary appearance is an appearance "whereby the defendant submits his person to the jurisdiction of the court by invoking the judgment of the court in any manner on any question other than that of the jurisdiction of the court over his person."[50] In other words, a defendant who was not served or was not served properly but makes a voluntary appearance can be treated for all purposes as if he or she were properly served. Generally, in a small claims case the defendant makes a voluntary appearance by appearing at trial. However, a defendant also may make a voluntary appearance by seeking a continuance or filing a motion other than a motion objecting to jurisdiction over the person. To establish that the court had jurisdiction because the defendant made a voluntary appearance, the magistrate should note on the "findings" portion of the judgment form that the defendant was present at trial or, if the defendant makes a voluntary appearance by some other method such as by filing a motion, the magistrate should indicate that fact as a finding on the judgment in the "Other" block.

> ***Example 7.*** Bert Jones sues William Smith for money owed. When the case is called for trial, the magistrate notes that the summons indicates that Smith was not served. Smith is present in the courtroom and participates in the trial. The magistrate may issue a judgment against Smith because he made a voluntary appearance in the case. The same result would occur if Smith were absent at trial but had requested a continuance two weeks before trial.

Service by Publication

Service by publication is not allowed in most small claims cases.[51] If a defendant cannot be served by one of the methods discussed above, the plaintiff cannot go forward with the small claims case. The plaintiff may, however, take a voluntary dismissal in the small claims case and refile the case as a district court case where service by publication is authorized. As mentioned earlier, the one exception to the rule regarding publication in small claims cases is motor vehicle lien cases. In an action to enforce a motor vehicle lien, a plaintiff who after a due and diligent search is unable to serve the defendant by personal service—including leaving the process with the defendant personally or leaving it at the defendant's dwelling with a proper person—or by certified or registered mail, may serve the defendant by publication.[52] Service by publication is discussed in detail in Chapter VII, "Motor Vehicle Mechanic and Storage Liens."

Determining Proper Service

Before hearing a case, the magistrate must determine whether he or she has jurisdiction over the defendant. Fundamental due process requires that a defendant be notified of the lawsuit and date of the trial, and North Carolina courts require strict compliance with the service statutes.[53]

---

50. *In re* Blalock, 233 N.C. 493, 504, 64 S.E.2d 848, 856 (1951).
51. G.S. 7A-217, which lists methods of service in small claims cases, does not include publication.
52. G.S. 7A-211.1.
53. *See* Guthrie v. Ray, 293 N.C. 67, 235 S.E.2d 146 (1977); Roshelli v. Sperry, 57 N.C. App. 305, 291 S.E.2d 355 (1982).

The magistrate must (1) see either the sheriff's return of service on the summons indicating that the sheriff served the defendant or the private process server's affidavit that service was carried out; (2) see the plaintiff's affidavit indicating service by registered or certified mail and the postal receipt indicating receipt of service; (3) see the defendant's written acceptance of service; (4) see that the defendant is present at trial or made an earlier voluntary appearance by seeking a continuance or filing a motion other than one challenging jurisdiction over the defendant; or (5) in motor vehicle lien cases when publication is used, see the plaintiff's and publisher's affidavits.

If the defendant has not been served or the magistrate does not have documented evidence of service (for example, the sheriff's return or plaintiff's affidavit of service by certified mail) that the defendant has been served, the magistrate should not hear the case. Rather, the magistrate should continue the case to allow the plaintiff further time to try to serve the defendant. A summons is valid for only sixty days and cannot be served after that time. However, if the defendant is not served within the sixty-day period, the plaintiff may ask the clerk to issue another summons (called an *alias and pluries summons*), which will give plaintiff a new sixty-day period to try to serve the defendant.[54] A plaintiff could have the clerk issue successive alias and pluries summonses indefinitely, thus keeping the lawsuit alive while he or she attempts to locate the defendant. As a practical matter, most plaintiffs give up after two or three unsuccessful attempts at service and take a dismissal of the case. If a summons is unserved and no new alias and pluries summons is issued within ninety days after issuance of the preceding summons, the case is discontinued automatically.[55]

Multiple Defendants and Service

Should a magistrate proceed in a case where there are multiple defendants and at least one but not all of the defendants have been served? If so, against which defendants may the magistrate proceed? The rules regarding service of process apply to each individual defendant; the court has no jurisdiction over a particular defendant unless he or she has been properly served or makes a voluntary appearance. Therefore, if one defendant has been served but another has not, the magistrate cannot hear the case and enter judgment against both defendants.

When some, but not all, of the defendants have been served, the decision whether to proceed to trial rests with the plaintiff. As the magistrate cannot hold separate trials for multiple defendants in the same case, he or she should require the plaintiff to decide whether to proceed against all of the defendants or against only those served. If the plaintiff wishes to proceed against all the defendants, the magistrate should continue the case to give the plaintiff time to

54. G.S. 1A-1, Rule 4(d). Some clerks use a method called "endorsement" instead of issuing an alias and pluries summons. An endorsement is a notation on the original summons giving it a new sixty-day period for service. Endorsements have the same effect as alias and pluries summonses.

55. G.S. 1A-1, Rule 4(e). Under the computerized civil tracking system developed by the Administrative Office of the Courts the case is automatically discontinued and moved to a closed status. A plaintiff can reopen the discontinued case by asking the clerk to issue an alias and pluries summons. However, when an alias and pluries summons is issued after the case has been discontinued, the case is commenced for statute of limitations purposes when the new summons is issued and not when the original summons was issued.

attempt to serve the other defendants. When all of the defendants have been served, the trial can be held against all defendants. A plaintiff who chooses to proceed against only those defendants who have been served may file a voluntary dismissal against the unserved defendants. When the only defendants remaining in the lawsuit are those who have been served, the magistrate may proceed to trial against them.

> **Example 8.** Watertown Supply sues Ben James and Samuel James on a contract for goods delivered. The trial is scheduled for September 5. At that time the summons indicates that Ben has been served but the sheriff has been unable to locate Sam. As Watertown wants a judgment against both defendants, it can ask for a continuance and then seek an alias and pluries summons from the clerk so that the sheriff can try again to serve Sam (or Watertown can mail the alias and pluries summons by certified mail, return receipt requested). When Sam is served, the trial may be held against both Ben and Sam.

> **Example 9.** But suppose that when Watertown Supply comes to court on September 5, the sheriff's return indicates that Ben has been served but Sam has not been served because he has moved to California. Watertown therefore decides it doesn't want to pursue its case against Sam; even if Sam were served and Watertown obtained a judgment against him, it would be too expensive to try to collect the judgment in California. The firm can file a voluntary dismissal against Sam and ask the magistrate to proceed to trial against Ben. The magistrate can proceed because at this point the only defendant in the case is Sam, who has been served.

Defendant's Answer and Counterclaim

Answer

After being served with the plaintiff's complaint and a summons, the defendant may file a written response to the complaint, which is called an *answer*. In district or superior court actions, a defendant must file a written answer to the complaint or a default judgment will be entered against him or her without a trial. The law for small claims cases is very different. Default judgments are not allowed, and defendants are not required to file written answers, though they may do so. If the defendant does not file an answer, the court assumes that the defendant denies everything the plaintiff says in the complaint.[56] If the defendant chooses to file an answer, it must be written in a manner enabling a person of common understanding to know the nature of the defense and must be filed with the clerk before the time set for the trial. Like a complaint, an answer merely gives other party notice of what the defense claims; it is not evidence. The defendant must appear at trial to offer any defense he or she might have.

Counterclaim

A defendant might also want to file a counterclaim, initiating a counter suit against the plaintiff. Essentially, a counterclaim requires the magistrate to hear two lawsuits in one case, one in which the plaintiff is suing the defendant, and the other in which the defendant is suing the plaintiff.

---

56. G.S. 7A-218.

There are two types of counterclaims—compulsory and permissive. A *compulsory* counterclaim is one that arises out of the same transaction or occurrence that is the subject matter of the complaint.[57] For example, plaintiff might sue defendant for automobile negligence, and defendant's counterclaim might allege that plaintiff's negligence, not defendant's, caused the accident. A *permissive* counterclaim is any other claim the defendant might have against the plaintiff. If, for example, the plaintiff files a summary ejectment action against the defendant for failure to pay rent, the defendant may file a counterclaim against the plaintiff for failing to repay a loan. Under Rule 13 of the Rules of Civil Procedure, if a compulsory counterclaim is not asserted in a pending action, it is barred from being asserted later in an independent action. However, G.S. 7A-219 and G.S. 7A-220 set out special rules for counterclaims in small claims cases; they make it clear that Rule 13 provisions regarding compulsory counterclaims do not apply in small claims court.

Filing a Counterclaim

A counterclaim is asserted by filing a written answer alleging it. Usually the defendant designates the filing as an "Answer and Counterclaim," although this description is not required. Sometimes a defendant will use a standard AOC complaint form and strike through "complaint" and write in "counterclaim." The only statutory requirements are that a counterclaim must be written and must be filed with the clerk of court before the time set for trial.[58] The Rules of Civil Procedure, on the other hand, require a counterclaim to be served on the plaintiff or the plaintiff's attorney by delivering a copy to one of them personally or by mailing a copy by first class mail;[59] the defendant also must file a certificate showing the date and method by which the counterclaim was served on the plaintiff.[60] The small claims procedure statute does not specify that the defendant must serve a copy on the plaintiff.[61] Therefore, if the defendant has filed a counterclaim with the clerk before the time set for trial but has not served a copy on the plaintiff, the counterclaim is properly filed. When calling a case for trial, the magistrate should indicate that the defendant has filed a counterclaim; then, if plaintiff indicates that he or she never received a copy, the magistrate may consider continuing the case (both the claim and counterclaim) to give the plaintiff time to prepare evidence on the subject of the counterclaim.

---

57. G.S. 1A-1, Rule 13. A counterclaim is compulsory when (1) it is in existence when the defendant serves the answer on the plaintiff; (2) it arises out of the transaction or occurrence that is the subject matter of the plaintiff's claim; and (3) it does not require the presence of third parties over whom the court cannot acquire jurisdiction. Faggart v. Biggers, 18 N.C. App. 366, 370, 197 S.E.2d 75, 78 (1973).

58. G.S. 7A-218.

59. G.S. 1A-1, Rule 5.

60. The defendant usually serves the answer and counterclaim on the plaintiff and then files the answer and counterclaim with the certificate of service attached in the clerk's office. A certificate of service usually includes language like "the undersigned hereby certifies that a copy of the foregoing Answer and Counterclaim was served on the following parties to this action, pursuant to Rule 5 of the Rules of Civil Procedure by depositing a copy in the United States mail, postage prepaid and addressed to Jane Doe, 5402 Jones Street, Apartment 6, Merryville, NC 27777."

61. G.S. 7A-218.

Once the defendant files a counterclaim, no further pleading is allowed and any new claim alleged is deemed denied.[62]

If the defendant tries to offer a counterclaim at trial, the magistrate should indicate that the counterclaim was not properly asserted in writing before the time for trial and therefore cannot be considered. In that situation, the defendant may file the counterclaim as a separate action.

Counterclaim Amount in Controversy

G.S. 7A-219 provides that "no counterclaim . . . which would make the amount in controversy exceed the jurisdictional amount established by G.S. 7A-210(1) is permissible in a small claim action assigned to a magistrate." Under this provision, a defendant may file a counterclaim as long as the amount in controversy is not over $5,000. The rules for determining the amount in controversy set out in the amount-in-controversy statute (discussed earlier in this chapter) apply to both a counterclaim and the original claim. The amount in controversy is not determined by adding the amount of the claim and counterclaim together; each is determined separately;[63] if the claim is for $5,000 or less and the counterclaim is for $5,000 or less, both can be heard by the magistrate. If both parties win, the magistrate will offset the claim and counterclaim (reduce the amount of the larger award by the amount of the smaller one if they are not equal), and if only one party wins, the amount awarded will not exceed $5,000.

Counterclaims for more than $5,000 may not be filed in small claims court. G.S. 7A-219 makes it clear that even if the counterclaim is compulsory under the Rules of Civil Procedure, it may not be filed in a small claims case if it is for more than $5,000:

> No counterclaim . . . which would make the amount in controversy exceed the jurisdictional amount . . . is permissible in a small claim action assigned to a magistrate. No determination of fact or law in an assigned small claim action estops a party thereto in any subsequent action which, except for this section, might have been asserted under the Code of Civil Procedure as a counterclaim in the small claim action.

Thus the statute clearly allows a counterclaim for more than $5,000 to be filed as a separate action.[64]

G.S. 7A-219 also makes it clear that even a counterclaim for $5,000 or less that would be a compulsory counterclaim under Rule 13 does not need to be filed in a small claim action but may be filed as a separate action in small claims, district, or superior court.[65]

---

62. G.S. 7A-220.

63. *Cf.* Amey v. Amey, 71 N.C. App. 76, 321 S.E.2d 458 (1984).

64. *See* Chandler v. Cleveland Sav. & Loan Ass'n, 24 N.C. App. 455, 211 S.E.2d 484 (1975). If the small claim action is appealed to district court, a counterclaim for more than $5,000 may be raised at that time, since G.S. 7A-220 provides that "on appeal from the judgment of the magistrate for trial de novo before a district court judge, the judge shall allow appropriate counterclaims."

65. In 2005 the General Assembly amended G.S. 7A-219 to overrule two court of appeals opinions that had required compulsory counterclaims to be raised on appeal of small claims cases to district court. *See* Cloer v. Smith, 132 N.C. App. 569, 512 S.E.2d 779 (1999) (Compulsory counterclaim that can not be asserted in small claim because of the amount in controversy must be filed as counterclaim in district court if small claim is appealed.); Fickley v. Greystone Enter., Inc., 140 N.C. App. 258, 536 S.E.2d 331 (2000) (barring defendant who

Counterclaim for More Than $5,000

When a defendant in a small claims case files an answer and counterclaim, the clerk's role is merely to file the document, not to determine if the amount is appropriate. Therefore, it is not improbable that a magistrate could find a counterclaim for more than $5,000 in a case file. Magistrates who allow plaintiffs who file cases for more than $5,000 to reduce that amount and proceed in small claims court should allow defendants who counterclaim the same opportunity.

Sometimes the defendant asks that both the claim and counterclaim be removed to district court (or superior court if the counterclaim is for more than $10,000), thinking that the entire matter can be postponed by filing a counterclaim for more than $5,000. In this case, the claim and counterclaim are not removed to district court. Rather, the magistrate should try the claim but not the counterclaim.[66] The magistrate should not dismiss the counterclaim but make a finding that the counterclaim was not heard because it was not within the magistrate's jurisdiction. The defendant may request the district court judge to allow the counterclaim to be filed if the magistrate's ruling on the claim is appealed; otherwise, the defendant may file it as a separate claim.

> *Example 10.* Hannah sues Winston for $2,500 for physical damage to the house Winston rented from Hannah. Winston files a counterclaim seeking $3,500 damages for breach of the warranty of habitability. The magistrate should hear the counterclaim as well as the claim because the amount in controversy of the counterclaim—$3,500—is within the allowable jurisdictional amount. If both parties prove they are entitled to the damages they seek, the magistrate will set off the claims and award $1,000 against Hannah. If only Hannah wins, the magistrate will award $2,500 against Winston and if only Winston prevails, the magistrate will award $3,500 against Hannah.
>
> Suppose that Winston files a counterclaim for $6,000. The magistrate should hear Hannah's claim but not Winston's counterclaim. If the magistrate rules in favor of Hannah and Winston decides to appeal, he may seek permission to file the $6,000 counterclaim in district court, or he may file it as a separate action in district court. If Winston is satisfied with the magistrate's decision on Hannah's action, he may accept that decision and then file a new action in district court to assert his claim against Hannah.

Cross Claims and Third Party Claims

Cross claims and third party claims that do not bring the amount in controversy above the jurisdictional amount may be filed in small claims cases.[67] A *cross claim* is a claim by one party against a coparty arising out of the transaction or occurrence that is the subject of the claim

---

does not assert compulsory counterclaim on appeal to district court from asserting it later, thereby placing an affirmative duty on the defendant to appeal the small claim judgment whether an aggrieved party or not).

66. *See* Ervin Co. v. Hunt, 26 N.C. App. 755, 217 S.E.2d 93 (1975) (Court held that magistrate "correctly refused to hear defendant's counterclaim" when magistrate dismissed $300,000 counterclaim.). *But see* Faulk Integrated Technologies, Inc. v. Stack, 132 N.C. App. 807, 513 S.E.2d 572 (1999) (As magistrate lacked subject matter jurisdiction over claim for more than the allowable amount, dismissal of claim was void and does not bar subsequent district court action.).

67. G.S. 7A-219 provides "no counterclaim, crossclaim or third party claim which would make the amount in controversy exceed the jurisdictional limit . . . is permissible in a small claim action assigned to a magistrate"

or counterclaim. For example, Patty sues Adam and Bob for negligence and Adam files a cross claim against Bob, claiming that Bob's negligence caused Adam's injury. A *third party claim* is one in which the defendant brings a new party (called a *third party defendant*) into the lawsuit, claiming that if the defendant is found liable to the plaintiff the third party is liable to the defendant for all or part of the damages. For example, Henrietta sues Big Bob's Towing Inc. for damaging her automobile while towing it from Harry's property. Big Bob's Towing Inc. files a third party claim against Harry, indicating that Harry had signed a contract indemnifying Big Bob's from any liability incurred while towing the car from his property. Although they are authorized, cross claims and third-party claims are extremely rare in small claims court.

Pretrial Motions

Before the trial a party might file one or more of several different motions as described below.

Motion to Name Real Party in Interest

An action can only be brought by the *real party in interest*. In other words, the person or company named in the complaint as the plaintiff must be the person "who is benefited or injured by the judgment"[68] and the person "who is entitled to receive the fruits of the litigation."[69] In summary ejectment cases the owner of the property (the landlord), not the agent handling the property for the owner, is the real party in interest. Sometimes a defendant files a motion objecting to the fact that the plaintiff listed in the complaint is not the real party in interest. Failure to bring the action in the name of the real party in interest is not, however, a basis for immediate dismissal.[70] The magistrate must give the plaintiff a reasonable amount of time after an objection is raised to file an amended complaint substituting the proper plaintiff; this may also be done in open court. If the plaintiff does not substitute the real party in interest within a reasonable time, the magistrate may dismiss the action.

Motion to Perfect Statement

The defendant may bring a motion, in oral or written form, to perfect the statement of the claim in the complaint because it fails to make clear why he or she is being sued.[71] The magistrate assigned to hear the case, the clerk, or a district court judge may rule on the motion without notice to the plaintiff. If the magistrate (or clerk or judge) determines that the complaint is not clearly enough written to enable a person of common understanding to know what is meant—why the defendant is being sued and what remedy is sought—the magistrate must enter an order requiring the plaintiff to amend the complaint to state these matters in clearer and more specific language. The magistrate also may, on his or her own motion, order a plaintiff to perfect the statement of the claim. In either case, the magistrate must mail a copy of the

---

thereby indicating that a claim that is within the limit may be filed.

68. Reliance Insur. Co. v. Walker, 33 N.C. App. 15, 18, 234 S.E.2d 206, 209 (1977).

69. Hood v. Mitchell, 206 N.C. 156, 165, 173 S.E. 61, 66 (1934), Goodrich v. Rice, 75 N.C. App. 530, 537, 331 S.E.2d 195, 199 (1985).

70. G.S. 1A-1, Rule 17(a).

71. G.S. 7A-216.

order to the plaintiff and continue the case to give the plaintiff time to perfect the statement. The plaintiff can perfect the statement by either filing another complaint, entitled, "Amended Complaint," or by merely filing a perfected statement with the clerk of court and mailing a copy to the defendant.

Motion Objecting to Venue or Jurisdiction

At any time before trial, but not after an answer has been filed, a defendant may file a motion objecting that the venue is improper, moving for a change of venue, or objecting to the jurisdiction of the court over him or her.

Venue is the legal term for the location where the lawsuit must be filed and heard. A motion objecting that the venue is "improper" argues that the lawsuit is filed in the wrong county, and a motion to change venue requests that the case be moved to another county. A motion objecting to jurisdiction over the defendant is one that challenges the court's personal jurisdiction over the defendant, which usually entails a complicated legal analysis of whether the State of North Carolina can constitutionally exercise jurisdiction over the defendant.

Both of these motions must be made in writing and, because of their complexity, must be heard by either the chief district court judge or another district court judge the chief judge designates by order or rule.[72] The magistrate has no authority to consider the case or make any rulings about the case while any of these motions are pending. Because some parties may not realize that the law requires the chief district court judge to hear such motions, they may fail to schedule the motion to be heard by that judge. Therefore, at trial the magistrate might find the motion in the case file without a ruling by a judge. In that case, the magistrate should continue the case and ask the clerk to calendar the motion before the chief district judge or another designated district court judge.

Questions about appropriate venue generally are procedural, not jurisdictional, which means they are waived if not raised by the defendant before trial.[73] However, there is some question about whether venue in small claims court is strictly procedural. G.S. 7A-221 seems to indicate that it is procedural by stating (1) that the defendant may object to venue by motion before filing an answer or as part of his or her answer and (2) that the objection is waived if not made before the date set for trial. However, G.S. 7A-211 provides that "[T]he chief district court judge may, in his discretion, ... assign to any magistrate of his district any small claim action pending in his district if the defendant [or at least one of the defendants] is a resident of the county in which the magistrate resides." As explained above, all chief district judges assign cases by general or administrative order, and their orders usually include a statement that the clerk should assign cases within the jurisdiction of the magistrate when one of the defendants resides in the county where the action is filed. The same issue arises, therefore, as in actions filed as small claims for more than the allowable amount in controversy: a clerk who sends a case to a magistrate when none of the defendants is alleged to live in the county is not complying with the judge's order, and therefore, the case is not properly before the magistrate and any judgment rendered is not

---

72. G.S. 7A-221.

73. Gardner v. Gardner, 43 N.C. App. 678, 260 S.E.2d 116 (1979), *aff'd* 300 N.C. 715, 268 S.E.2d 468 (1980).

valid. The best way to read the two statutes together is that G.S. 7A-221 sets out the procedure for defendants who wish to object to venue—by filing written motions or answers before trial and having them heard by a district court judge—while G.S. 7A-212 indicates that a magistrate who discovers that no defendant resided in his or her county at the time the complaint was filed may consider the case as not assigned by the chief district court judge.

Motion to Transfer to Superior Court Division

Another possible, but extremely rare motion, is a motion to transfer the action to superior court because that is the proper division for it. If the defendant files a motion to transfer the case to superior court before the case is assigned to a magistrate, the case may not be assigned, and therefore no magistrate will have authority to hear the matter until a superior court judge has ruled on the motion.[74] The statute assumes that a motion to transfer will be filed before the case is assigned to a magistrate, but this is generally not the case, since in most counties small claims are assigned the moment they are filed. The safest practice for a magistrate is not to hear a case until a superior court judge has ruled on the motion for transfer to superior court.

12(b)(6) Motion

Another motion an attorney representing a defendant might file is called a 12(b)(6) motion—a motion to dismiss the case for failure to state a claim.[75] Essentially, this motion states that even if everything in the plaintiff's complaint is true, it does not state a claim for which the court can grant relief. However, 12(b)(6) motions are not allowed in a small claims action; G.S. 7A-216 provides that "demurrers and motions to challenge the legal and formal sufficiency of a complaint shall not be used." *Demurrer* is the term used before the Rules of Civil Procedure were adopted, and a 12(b)(6) motion is the equivalent motion under the current rules. The magistrate should deny the motion because it is not proper and then hear the case.

Motion for Continuance

The most common motion a magistrate will hear before trial is a motion for a continuance. Any party may move to have the case continued, and the magistrate may grant a continuance "for good cause shown."[76] If all parties consent to change the date and time of the trial, they file a written notice of the change with the clerk. The magistrate may also grant a continuance at the request of one party without getting the consent of or hearing from the other parties.

Nonetheless, "[c]ontinuances are not favored, and the party seeking a continuance has the burden of showing sufficient grounds for it."[77] As the statute does not specify the circumstances that constitute grounds for good cause, the magistrate must determine in each case whether good cause has been met. "In passing on the motion, the trial court must pass on the grounds urged in support of it, and also on the question whether the moving party has acted with diligence and good faith. . . . The chief consideration to be weighed in passing upon the application

---

74. G.S. 7A-258(f)(2). *See* Amey v. Amey, 71 N.C. App. 76, 321 S.E.2d 458 (1984).

75. The motion is set out in G.S. 1A-1, Rule 12(b)(6).

76. G.S. 7A-214.

77. Shankle v. Shankle, 289 N.C. 473, 482, 223 S.E.2d 380, 386 (1976).

is whether the grant or denial of a continuance will be in furtherance of substantial justice."[78] Common situations in which continuances are granted include the illness of a party or witness[79] or insufficient time for one of the parties to prepare for trial.[80] Another frequent reason for requesting a continuance is that one of the party's attorneys must appear in another court at the time the small claim is scheduled. Rule 3 of the General Rules of Practice for the Superior and District Courts sets out the following priority of attendance for attorneys with court conflicts: appellate courts, superior court, district court, and magistrate's court. However, the rules also provide that an attorney who cannot be present in one court because of a conflicting court appearance should make available another member of the law firm who is familiar with the case. When hearing a continuance based on a conflict in another court, the magistrate may ask whether another attorney in the firm can present the case.

There is no limitation on the length of a continuance or the number of continuances a magistrate may grant in a case. Yet, as the purpose of small claims court is to deal with civil cases in an expedient, efficient, and inexpensive manner, it would be contrary to the underlying policy to grant either long continuances or numerous continuances in a case. A motion for a continuance may be made in writing or orally. G.S. 7A-214 specifies that the magistrate to whom the action is assigned may grant the continuance. However, because in many counties the magistrate who will hear the case is not known until the time of trial, in practice any magistrate who hears small claims cases can grant continuances. If a continuance is granted, the magistrate must notify both parties of the new trial date and time.[81] Merely filing a motion for a continuance is not grounds for not appearing at the trial. A party must appear unless the magistrate has granted the continuance.

Dismissal without Trial

Voluntary Dismissal by Plaintiff

Sometimes a case is dismissed without the magistrate ever holding a trial. The most common kind of dismissal is a voluntary dismissal in which plaintiff withdraws the action without approval of the magistrate. As a matter of right, the plaintiff may do so at any time before resting his or her case (that is, completes presenting the evidence).[82] The plaintiff may take a voluntary dismissal by filing a written notice of dismissal before the trial—in which case the dismissal will be found in the case file—or by giving oral notice of dismissal at the trial. If the plaintiff gives oral notice of voluntary dismissal at the time of trial, the magistrate should complete form AOC-G-108, "Order," indicating that the plaintiff has elected not to prosecute the action and has taken a voluntary dismissal. The plaintiff may take a voluntary dismissal for any reason before resting his or her case, and the magistrate cannot prevent the dismissal.

---

78. *Id.* at 483, 223 S.E.2d at 386.
79. Moon v. Central Bldrs., Inc., 65 N.C. App. 793, 310 S.E.2d 390 (1984).
80. Benton v. Mintz, 97 N.C. App. 583, 389 S.E.2d 410 (1990).
81. The proper form to use is AOC-G-108, "Order."
82. G.S. 1A-1, Rule 41(a)(1).

Example 11. Low Cost Furniture Co. sues Susan to recover possession of ten pieces of furniture Susan purchased from the store at various times over a five-year period. At the trial the business manager for Low Cost Furniture Co. begins testifying about the security agreement with Susan. Based on the nature of the magistrate's questions, the business manager believes that the magistrate will not grant him a favorable judgment. Before he finishes his evidence, he tells the magistrate that he is taking a voluntary dismissal. He stops testifying and leaves the courtroom. Even if the magistrate does not believe Low Cost Furniture Co. can win the case, the magistrate cannot prevent the business manager from taking the voluntary dismissal and ending the matter without prejudice at that point.

The most common reason for a voluntary dismissal is that the plaintiff and defendant have settled the case—either the defendant has fully satisfied the plaintiff's claim or the defendant has agreed to make payments satisfactory to the plaintiff.

Without Prejudice
A voluntary dismissal is a dismissal without prejudice unless the plaintiff indicates otherwise. *Without prejudice* means that the plaintiff may refile the lawsuit within one year after dismissal, or longer if the statute of limitations has not run by that time. A second voluntary dismissal bars any further lawsuit in the same case.

Voluntary Dismissal by Court Order
After the plaintiff has lost the right to take a voluntary dismissal (that is, has finished his or her presentation of the evidence), the plaintiff may request the magistrate to grant a voluntary dismissal. In this situation, it is in the magistrate's discretion whether to grant the voluntary dismissal; it is no longer the plaintiff's right. The magistrate should grant the voluntary dismissal upon such terms and conditions as justice requires.[83] The purpose of this provision is to allow the magistrate to give the plaintiff another chance to withdraw in hardship cases when the plaintiff is unable to press his or her claim.[84] In exercising discretion, the magistrate should consider the legitimate interests of both the plaintiff and the defendant and the relative prejudice to each.[85] Thus, under the facts of Example 11 above, assume that the business manager does not take a voluntary dismissal while putting on evidence; Susan then begins testifying and indicates that she had paid for most of the items and that Low Cost Furniture was not, therefore, entitled to recover four of the five items claimed. The business manager indicates that he does not have the records with him to show how the payments were allocated and asks the magistrate to grant a voluntary dismissal. The magistrate must determine whether justice is best served by allowing the voluntary dismissal and then either grant or deny the request.

The magistrate deciding to grant a voluntary dismissal must complete form AOC-G-108, "Order," indicating that the magistrate is granting the motion for voluntary dismissal. This type of voluntary dismissal is also without prejudice, which allows the plaintiff to refile the action

---

83. G.S. 1A-1, Rule 41(a)(2).
84. Gray Wilson, North Carolina Civil Procedure § 41-3 (3d ed. 2007).
85. *Id.*

within one year or until the statute of limitations runs, whichever is longer. If the magistrate denies the request, the magistrate continues to hear evidence and enters judgment.

Involuntary Dismissal

Because the plaintiff initiated the lawsuit, he or she must be present at trial to present evidence or prosecute the case. What happens if the plaintiff (or plaintiff's counsel) is not present when the case is called for trial? "For failure of the plaintiff to prosecute . . . a defendant may move for dismissal of an action . . . against him."[86] Thus, when the plaintiff does not appear but the defendant does appear and asks that the case be dismissed, the magistrate may dismiss the case. The magistrate also may dismiss the case without a motion from the defendant if the failure to prosecute is clear.[87]

With Prejudice

An involuntary dismissal usually is a dismissal *with prejudice*, which means that the plaintiff may not refile the lawsuit. A dismissal with prejudice "ends the lawsuit and precludes subsequent litigation on the same controversy between the parties under the doctrine of *res judicata*."[88] The magistrate, however, has discretion to provide that the dismissal is without prejudice rather than with prejudice and should do so when a judgment with prejudice would defeat the ends of justice.

If neither party appears at trial, an involuntary dismissal is appropriate and would generally be with prejudice unless the magistrate, within his or her discretion, indicates that it is without prejudice. The same principle that applies when the defendant appears but the plaintiff does not also applies when neither party appears: It is the plaintiff who has the responsibility to appear and prosecute the case.

Dismissal When Defendant Files a Counterclaim

The rules regarding voluntary and involuntary dismissals of claims also apply to counterclaims, except that for counterclaims it is the defendant's right to dismiss before resting his or her case and it is the defendant's responsibility to appear and prosecute the counterclaim. But is the plaintiff's ability to take a voluntary dismissal affected by defendant's filing of a counterclaim? Under general law if the defendant has filed a compulsory counterclaim, the plaintiff loses the right to take a voluntary dismissal.[89] But if the counterclaim is permissive, the plaintiff may file a voluntary dismissal and the defendant can proceed with the permissive counterclaim.[90] Small claims procedure, however, makes it clear that the distinctions between compulsory and permissive counterclaims do not apply in small claims court and that any counterclaim may be

---

86. G.S. 1A-1, Rule 41(b).

87. Wilson, *supra* note 84, § 41-6.

88. *Id.* at § 41-5. *Res judicata* means "the thing is adjudicated." Under this doctrine a final judgment on its merits is conclusive as to rights, questions, and facts in issue in subsequent actions involving the same parties. Estate of Graham v. Morrison, 168 N.C. App. 63, 66, 607 S.E.2d 295, 298 (2005).

89. Gardner v. Gardner, 48 N.C. App. 38, 269 S.E.2d 630 (1980).

90. *See* Layell v. Baker, 46 N.C App. 1, 5, 264 S.E.2d 406, 409 (1980).

filed as a separate action.[91] It would therefore follow that a plaintiff can always take a voluntary dismissal in a small claims case, even if a counterclaim has been filed, and that the defendant may proceed with the counterclaim after the plaintiff's dismissal of his or her claim.

Judgment on the Pleadings

In one circumstance the law requires the magistrate to enter judgment without hearing evidence from the plaintiff. In summary ejectment cases the magistrate must give a judgment for possession based solely on the filed pleadings if the following five qualifications are met:

1. The pleadings (complaint) allege defendant's failure to pay rent as a breach of the lease for which reentry is allowed[92] (third block under #3 on "Complaint for Summary Ejectment," AOC-CVM-201);
2. The return on the summons indicates the process was served on the defendant;
3. The defendant has not filed an answer;
4. The defendant fails to appear on the day of court; and
5. The plaintiff requests, in open court, a judgment based on the pleadings.[93]

If all conditions are met, the magistrate must give judgment for possession without asking the plaintiff to offer any evidence. However, all five qualifications must be met; even if the first four are met but the plaintiff does not request, in open court, a judgment on the pleadings, the magistrate cannot give a judgment for possession without hearing the evidence.

If the plaintiff asking for a judgment based on the pleadings also is seeking monetary damages for back rent or physical damage to the property, he or she must prove by a preponderance of the evidence that monetary damages are due. Without such evidence, the magistrate will grant only the possession part of the judgment.

If the plaintiff is seeking possession based on failure to pay rent (first block under #3 on complaint form), holding over after the end of the lease (second block), or criminal activity (fourth block)—and in cases for breaches of condition other than failure to pay rent—G.S. 42-30 does not apply, and the plaintiff must present evidence to prove that he or she is entitled to a judgment for possession.

Trial of the Case

A trial before a magistrate is without a jury, which means that the magistrate acts as the judge in determining the law that applies to the case and as the jury in determining whether the facts are proven. The level of courtroom formality depends on the individual magistrate but is certainly less formal than superior court. Research indicates that citizens prefer to come to small claims

---

91. G.S. 7A-219.

92. This language means the summary ejectment action for failure to pay rent must be based on a condition specifically stated in the lease and the lease must include an automatic forfeiture clause for breach of its conditions.

93. G.S. 42-30.

court rather than to a more traditionally formal court because they feel they can better and more easily tell their story to the magistrate.[94]

No Default Judgment

Perhaps the most important difference in procedure between small claims and other trial courts in North Carolina is that there are no default judgments in a small claims case heard before a magistrate. This means that before judgment may be entered against a defendant, except in the one instance discussed above, the plaintiff must appear at trial and present witnesses who testify, under oath, to all the facts necessary for the plaintiff to prevail. (In most cases the plaintiff is the sole witness.) Even if the defendant does not appear at trial (and often he or she does not), the plaintiff must present the evidence necessary to win the case. It is not uncommon for a plaintiff to have several cases before a magistrate on the same calendar; nonetheless, for judgments to be entered, the plaintiff must present evidence under oath in each case. The complaint filed by the plaintiff is not evidence. Because oral evidence is usually sufficient and introduction of written documents is not required, it is relatively easy for a plaintiff to prevail when the defendant is not present.

> *Example 12.* Landlord Smith sues Tenant Jones for possession and back rent. Jones does not appear at trial. Landlord Smith asks the magistrate to enter judgment. The magistrate may not enter judgment unless Landlord Smith testifies under oath to sufficient facts to be entitled to a judgment.
>
> Assume Landlord Smith testifies that she had an oral lease with Jones; that their only agreement was that Jones was to pay $500 per month rent on the first of each month; that Jones didn't pay the rent on the first of March; and that Smith filed this action on March 12. In this case, the magistrate should find against the plaintiff and dismiss the case (ruling that the plaintiff failed to prove the case by the greater weight of the evidence). The plaintiff didn't prove everything required to win the case because she didn't testify that she had demanded the rent and waited ten days before filing the lawsuit.

Burden of Proof

The burden of proof in civil cases is proof by the greater weight of evidence, sometimes referred to as the *preponderance of the evidence*. That means that the party who bears the burden of proof, usually the plaintiff, must prove, by the greater weight of evidence, the existence of those facts that entitle him or her to a favorable judgment. The greater weight of the evidence does not refer to the quantity of evidence, but rather to its quality and convincing force. The magistrate, after considering all of the evidence, must be persuaded that the facts needed to reach a judgment for the party bearing the burden are more likely than not to exist.[95]

In some rare civil cases a stronger burden of proof applies. The party with the burden of proof must prove each element of the case with evidence that is *clear*, *strong*, and *convincing* as these

---

94. John Conley & William O'Barr, Rules versus Relationships: The Ethnology of Legal Discourse (Chicago: University of Chicago Press, 1990), 36–37; John Ruhnka & Steven Weller, Small Claims Courts: A National Examination (National Center For State Courts, 1978), 21–22.

95. A more detailed discussion of burden of proof is found in Chapter VIII, " Evidence."

words are ordinarily understood. *Webster's* defines *clear* as "free from obscurity or ambiguity: easily understood: unmistakable." *Strong* means forceful, persuasive, presented in a way that brings out pertinent and fundamental points. *Convincing* is "having power to convince of the truth, rightness, or reality of something," persuasive or "plausible."[96] This higher burden of proof is required, for example, when a magistrate chooses not to evict a tenant for criminal activity even though the landlord has proved that criminal activity occurred. In that situation the law requires the magistrate to determine by clear and convincing evidence that immediate eviction would be a serious injustice.

Representing the Parties in Court

Either the party or an attorney must appear in a court proceeding to present that party's case. A plaintiff or defendant cannot designate someone who is not a licensed attorney to appear as his or her agent for purposes of presenting his or her case to the court, except in summary ejectment cases, which are discussed below. The person presenting the case can, however, call witnesses to testify. The reason for limiting persons other than attorneys from acting on behalf of a party is that they would be engaging unlawfully in the practice of law.[97]

However, both parties have the right to represent themselves on their own behalf without an attorney (referred to as *pro se representation*). In small claims court a corporation may represent itself pro se through an employee acting as the agent of the corporation.[98]

In summary ejectment or back rent cases, an agent of the landlord who has personal knowledge of the facts alleged in the complaint may sign the complaint.[99] The agent must be someone, like a real estate broker, who handles the rental of the premises for the landlord—not a person the landlord appoints as agent solely for the purpose of bringing the summary ejectment action. There are no cases specifically indicating whether an agent authorized to sign the complaint may appear at trial on behalf of the plaintiff instead of an attorney. The most logical reading of the statute, however, is that the agent may appear and present the plaintiff's case because the agent, not the landlord, has actual knowledge of the transaction.

Another prohibition important for the magistrate to understand involves collection agencies. Such agencies are prohibited from engaging in the practice of law and may not appear in court on behalf of a creditor except when summoned by court order or subpoena.[100] A *collection agency* is defined as any person, firm, or corporation directly engaged in soliciting from more than one creditor delinquent claims due the creditor, or asserting, enforcing, or prosecuting these claims. The statute specifically excludes from the definition of collection agency a business that is collecting it own debts, regular employees of a single creditor, a licensed real estate

---

96. *Merriam-Webster's Collegiate Dictionary*, 11th ed. (Springfield, Mass.: Merriam-Webster, Inc., 2003).

97. G.S. 84-4 makes it unlawful for any person other than a person licensed to practice law in North Carolina to appear as an attorney or counselor-at-law in any action before a judicial body, give legal advice, or prepare legal documents.

98. Lexis-Nexis, Div. of Reed Elsevier, Inc. v. Travishan Corp., 155 N.C. App. 205, 573 S.E.2d 547 (2002); Duke Power Co. v. Daniels, 86 N.C. App. 469, 358 S.E.2d 87 (1987). However, in other civil proceedings a corporation must appear through an attorney. *See* G.S. 84-5 and *Lexis-Nexis* at 209, 573 S.E.2d at 549.

99. G.S. 7A-216; G.S. 7A-223.

100. G.S. 58-70-120.

agent when accounts are handled as part of the business, persons who purchase accounts when they are not delinquent, and attorneys. The statute also provides that people who purchase an account from the creditor after it becomes delinquent are categorized as collection agencies and must hire an attorney to represent them at trial. The new owner of an account purchased or assigned before default on the debt could bring an action to collect the debt pro se.

What if an unauthorized person appears before the magistrate on behalf of one of the parties? A pleading filed by someone other than a party or an attorney licensed in North Carolina is not null and void,[101] so that the magistrate may choose whether to hear the case or not. If an improper person appears on behalf of a party, the magistrate has several choices. (1) He or she can ignore the improper representation unless the opposing party makes a motion objecting to the representation; in that case the magistrate should either continue the case until a proper person can appear or, if the party seeking relief is improperly represented, the magistrate can dismiss the case without prejudice. (2) Acting on his or her own motion, the magistrate can continue the case until an appropriate person is present to represent the party or dismiss it. (3) A third option is to notify the North Carolina State Bar that an improper person is appearing on behalf of a party. (4) Finally, if a collection agency appears as a plaintiff without an attorney, the magistrate can notify the North Carolina Department of Insurance, which regulates collection agencies.

Hearing Evidence

Order of Presentation

The formal order of presentation of evidence in a civil case is that the plaintiff, the party with the burden of proof, puts on evidence first. The plaintiff determines the order in which his or her witnesses are called to testify. Before testifying, each witness is sworn or affirmed by the magistrate. After the plaintiff has finished questioning each witness, the defendant has a chance to examine the witness. The magistrate also may put questions to the witness. Then the next witness for the plaintiff testifies and the same procedure is followed. When the plaintiff has finished putting on all of his or her evidence, the magistrate may dismiss the case if the plaintiff has failed to establish a case.[102] If the plaintiff has proved a prima facie case—meaning that if the defendant offers no contrary evidence the plaintiff has proved enough to be given a judgment— the proceedings continue and the defendant presents his or her witnesses. The same procedure is followed with the defendant's witnesses, each of whom is sworn beforehand.

Frequently, however, magistrates do not follow this formal presentation of evidence. In many cases there is no formal witness stand from which the witness testifies, and often the only witnesses are the plaintiff and the defendant. Sometimes it is difficult for the parties to understand the difference between asking questions of the opposing party and testifying themselves. Thus, the defendant tells his or her side of the story when "questioning" the plaintiff; or the parties speak to each other or back and forth to the magistrate about what happened. To deal with this

---

101. Theil v. Detering, 68 N.C. App. 754, 315 S.E.2d 789 (1984). *Cf.* North Carolina Nat'l Bank v. Virginia Carolina Builders, 307 N.C. 563, 299 S.E.2d 629 (1983).

102. G.S. 7A-222.

reality, many magistrates swear both parties before beginning any testimony so that all of the evidence can be considered even though it is not presented in an orderly fashion.

If the defendant has filed a counterclaim, the magistrate should first hear all of the evidence from both parties on the plaintiff's claim and then hear all of the evidence on the defendant's counterclaim. On a counterclaim, the defendant has the burden of proof and puts his or her witnesses on first, to be followed by the plaintiff's witnesses.

Oath

The magistrate must administer an oath to every witness in a small claims trial. The witness is required to place his or her hand on the Bible and take the following oath: "You swear that the evidence you shall give to the court in the case of *(name plaintiff)* versus *(name defendant)* shall be the truth, the whole truth, and nothing but the truth; so help you, God."[103] Courts have held that non-Christians may take an oath on their holy book or according to the form of their religion.[104] Although the statute does not specify any method other than placing a hand on the Bible, the custom is to have the witness place his or her left hand on the Bible and raise the right hand while taking the oath. A person who has conscientious scruples against taking an oath may be affirmed.[105] To affirm the witness does not place his or her hand on the Bible, but raises his or her right hand and the magistrate gives the same oath except the word "affirm" replaces the word "swear" and the language "so help you, God" is deleted.

Applicability of Evidence Laws

Small claims procedure provides that "the rules of evidence applicable in the trial of civil actions generally are observed."[106] That sentence can be interpreted in two ways depending on whether the word "generally" modifies "civil actions" or "are observed"—the former requiring the rules to be followed and the latter allowing them to be observed generally. As a practical matter, evidence rules are not routinely applied in magistrate's court; however, a chapter covering the evidence rules magistrates are most likely to encounter in small claims cases is included in this book.

---

103. G.S. 11-11.

104. In *Shaw v. Moore*, 49 N.C. 25 (1856), the North Carolina Supreme Court pointed out that under common law Jews could swear upon the Old Testament or Tanach and other non-Christians could swear "according to the form which they hold to be most sacred and obligatory on their consciences." The court then determined that the sole object of the statute requiring swearing on the Holy Scriptures (which means the Christian Bible) was "to prescribe forms, adapted to the religious belief of the general mass of the citizens, for the sake of convenience and uniformity." If, the court said, the legislature's intent in adopting the statute had been to alter the common law so as to exclude persons of other religions, the statute would be void because it would violate the provision in the North Carolina Constitution affirming that "all persons have a natural and inalienable right to worship Almighty God according to the dictates of their own consciences." N.C. CONST. art. I, § 13. Therefore, the court held, the common law still applies in North Carolina. A recent superior court case reaffirmed the law set out in *Shaw* in a case challenging a Guilford County judge's ruling prohibiting a Muslim from swearing on the Quran. American Civil Liberties Union of North Carolina v. North Carolina, Wake County Superior Court 05 CVS 9872, May 24, 2006.

105. G.S. 11-4.

106. G.S. 7A-222.

Amending the Complaint

G.S. 1A-1, Rule 15 provides that "a party may amend his pleading once as a matter of course at any time before a responsive pleading is served, or if the pleading is one to which no responsive pleading is permitted and the action has not been placed on the calendar, he may so amend it at any time within 30 days after it is served." It is not clear how that rule applies to small claims cases since a responsive pleading is permitted but not required and since cases are "placed on the calendar" immediately upon filing. Presumably, a party may amend his or her pleading at any time before trial and serve a copy of the amended pleading on the other party. However, because the trial is held so soon after the complaint is filed, a party would rarely have a chance to file an amended pleading before trial.

It is more likely that questions about amending the complaint (or the answer and counterclaim) will arise at trial. At that stage a party may amend the pleading with the approval of the magistrate, and the magistrate must freely allow such amendments when justice so requires.[107] More importantly, in many instances, issues not raised in the complaint are brought up at trial and heard without requiring an amended pleading. "When issues not raised by the complaint and answer are tried by the express or implied consent of the parties, they shall be treated in all respects as if they had been raised in the pleadings."[108] Thus, as occurs in many instances, when evidence presented at trial relates to a claim not set out in the complaint, the plaintiff may amend the complaint but need not do so. The magistrate may decide the case on the basis of the evidence given at trial. If the defendant is present and objects that such evidence is not within the issues raised by the complaint (or the plaintiff raises the same objection with regard to a counterclaim), the magistrate may allow the party to amend the pleading and, if necessary, may grant a continuance to enable the objecting party to prepare to prepare a response to the new issue.

The defendant's failure to appear at trial sometimes raises an issue about how much the proof at trial can vary from the complaint without requiring the plaintiff to serve an amended complaint on the defendant. It really is a fairness issue. If a defendant who is sued for possession of a refrigerator does not appear at trial, is it fair to allow the plaintiff to recover a monetary judgment instead, without serving an amended complaint on the defendant? On the other hand, if a plaintiff brings a summary ejectment action against a defendant based on failure to pay rent but provides evidence at trial that the action is actually based on the defendant's breach of a condition of the lease, the magistrate may go forward with the hearing because the defendant was on notice that the suit was for eviction.

If the plaintiff files an amended complaint, the plaintiff must serve it on the defendant by sending a copy to the defendant by first class mail or by personally delivering a copy.[109]

Sometimes a party wishes to amend a pleading to correct the name of another party. An amendment correcting the name of a party who has been properly served is effective as of the

---

107. G.S. 1A-1, Rule 15(a).
108. G.S. 1A-1, Rule 15(b).
109. G.S. 1A-1, Rule 5.

original date the lawsuit was commenced.[110] For example, the plaintiff sues John James but means Johnnie James. As the correct Mr. James was served, no prejudice results in this case from correcting the misnomer. However, if the wrong defendant is named and served, the amended complaint must be served under the regular rules for service on a new defendant and the action commences (for statute of limitations purposes) when the summons for the amended complaint is issued.[111]

> **Example 13.** Jeannie Customer talks to Harry Hustler about repairing a driveway. Harry oper-ates Harry's Blacktar Resurfacing Inc. Jeannie is upset about the quality of the work and has to hire another company to repair the driveway properly. She files an action to recover money from Harry Hustler for the amount she had to pay the second company. Although Jeannie had all of her conversations with Harry, it is the business that is liable for the damages, not an employee, officer, or even the owner of a wholly owned corporation. Because a business that is incorporated is a sepa-rate legal entity, the corporation is the proper defendant. Jeannie Customer discovers this before trial. She must amend the complaint to name Harry's Blacktar Resurfacing Inc. as the defendant, and the magistrate should continue the case to give her time to serve the amended complaint on the new defendant. For statute of limitations purposes, the lawsuit begins when the summons to Harry's Blacktar Resurfacing Inc. is issued by the clerk.

Asking Questions

No statute governs whether and to what extent a magistrate may ask questions of the parties. However, since parties are rarely represented by attorneys in small claims cases and parties are often unaware of what facts are important, most magistrates do ask questions of the parties to elicit the facts needed to make a decision. Magistrates should treat both plaintiff and defendant fairly and equitably by eliciting important facts from both sides. If a magistrate asks questions of the plaintiff to find facts that will help the plaintiff's case, he or she should also ask the defendant questions that will obtain facts related to the defense. Also the magistrate's questions should elicit facts rather than conclusions. For example, a magistrate should ask "Tell me what, if anything, you did to make the defendant aware that the rent was overdue," rather than "Did you demand the rent from the tenant at least ten days before the lawsuit was filed?"

Even when the parties are represented by attorneys, the magistrate is free to ask the witnesses questions.

Rendering Judgment

After both parties have presented their evidence and answered all questions, the magistrate renders a decision. The judgment must include findings of fact, specify the party against whom judgment is entered, and specify the relief granted. In small claims cases, detailed findings of

---

110. *See* Pierce, v. Johnson, 154 N.C. App. 34, 571 S.E.2d 661 (2002) (naming deceased driver instead of personal representative of driver's estate was misnomer and amended pleading related back to date of original complaint); Jones v. Whitaker, 59 N.C. App. 223, 296 S.E.2d 27 (1982) (amending complaint to "Shirley" instead of "Sherrie" when Shirley was served was a misnomer and related back).

111. WILSON, *supra* note 84, § 15-12.

fact are not necessary. The only required finding is either that the plaintiff proved the case by the greater weight of evidence or that the plaintiff failed to prove the case by the greater weight of evidence. In summary ejectment cases the magistrate also must make a finding of the amount of rent in arrears that is not in dispute between the parties, and should make a finding whether the defendant is present at trial.

Announcing the Judgment at Trial

Although there is no prescribed form for announcing the judgment to the parties in open court, most magistrates' judgments consist of four parts: notice, judgment, explanation, and advice.[112] The *notice* merely lets the parties know the magistrate is about to render a decision. The *judgment* portion tells the parties of the magistrate's decision (who wins and what is awarded), and the *explanation* segment explains the specific facts and law on which the decision is based. *Advice* is the part of rendering a judgment in which the magistrate answers the parties' questions about the judgment or its effect.

If there is a counterclaim, the magistrate enters one judgment that disposes of both claim and counterclaim. If both parties win, the magistrate should indicate in the judgment that the plaintiff has proved his or her case by the greater weight of the evidence and that the defendant has proved his or her counterclaim by the greater weight of the evidence. The judgment should then identify the relief to which each is entitled and, if both are entitled to money, should offset the two amounts and award the difference to the party entitled to the greater amount.

Signing the Judgment at Trial

If the magistrate announces the judgment at the end of the trial, the magistrate should also reduce the judgment to writing and sign it at that time. If the judgment is signed in open court at the conclusion of the case, the magistrate should check the block on the judgment form so indicating. In that case, the magistrate is not required to mail copies to the plaintiff and defendant, even if the defendant is not present at the trial. In addition to announcing the judgment and reducing it to writing, the magistrate should make sure that all parties understand the judgment. He or she should then file the judgment with the clerk of superior court.

Reserving Judgment

The magistrate may decide not to announce and enter judgment at the end of the trial and may reserve judgment for up to ten days.[113] In that instance, the magistrate should announce at the end of the trial that he or she is reserving judgment and will make a decision and enter a written judgment within ten days. The magistrate may reserve judgment for any reason. Some common reasons for not entering judgment at the end of the trial are that the case is unusual and the magistrate wishes to research the law on the subject or that the trial was hotly contested and the magistrate thought it would exacerbate the parties' anger to announce judgment at that time. The magistrate can reserve judgment for up ten days after the trial; he or she must then reduce

---

112. John M. Conley & William M. O'Barr, *Fundamentals of Jurisprudence: An Ethnology of Judicial Decision Making In Informal Courts,* 66 N.C. L. Rev. 467, 479–81 (1988).

113. G.S. 7A-222.

the judgment to writing, sign it, mail copies to all parties, certify on the original judgment that copies have been mailed,[114] and file the original judgment with the clerk of superior court.

Effect of Magistrate's Judgment

Once a magistrate's judgment is filed with the clerk, it is treated like any judgment from district or superior court. The clerk records and indexes the judgment, and it becomes a lien on any real property losing party (the "judgment debtor") owns in the county where judgment is rendered.[115] The judgment is valid for ten years and may be renewed for one additional ten-year period.[116] It can be enforced during the ten-year period by asking the clerk to issue a writ of execution. If the judgment is for money, the execution writ orders the sheriff to seize the defendant's property and sell it to satisfy the judgment. If the judgment orders the defendant to return specific personal property to the plaintiff, the execution (called a *writ of possession personal property*) orders the sheriff to take the property from the defendant and turn it over to the plaintiff. If the judgment is for summary ejectment, the execution (called a *writ of possession real property*) orders the sheriff to remove the tenant and the tenant's personal property from the landlord's premises.

Appeal

An aggrieved party may appeal a magistrate's decision for a trial de novo in district court. "An *aggrieved party* is one whose rights have been directly and injuriously affected by the action of the court."[117] *Trial de novo* means a completely new trial—as if no action whatsoever had been instituted in the court below and the suit was being filed for the first time in district court.[118] The party appealing must give notice of appeal in one of two ways: (1) by giving oral notice in open court when the magistrate announces the judgment or (2) by filing a written notice of appeal[119] with the clerk within ten days after the judgment is entered. A party who appeals by filing a written notice also must serve a copy of the notice of appeal on all other parties by either giving copies of the notice to the other parties or their attorneys or by mailing copies to the parties or their attorneys by first class mail.[120] The ten-day period for appeal is governed by Rule 58 of the Rules of Civil Procedure, which provides that judgment is entered when it is reduced to

---

114. G.S. 1A-1, Rule 58.

115. G.S. 7A-225.

116. A judgment is renewed by filing a new lawsuit, but the lawsuit's claim is the prior judgment, not the underlying contract or tort in the original action. The amount sued for is the principal amount still owing on the original judgment, plus interest. At trial, the plaintiff must prove the existence of the original judgment (by introducing a certified copy of the judgment) and the amount currently due (by affidavit from the clerk where the original judgment was entered).

117. Culton v. Culton, 327 N.C. 624, 625, 398 S.E.2d 323, 324 (1990) (emphasis added).

118. Caswell County v. Hanks, 120 N.C. App. 489, 462 S.E.2d 841 (1995). *See* First Union Nat'l Bank v. Richards, 90 N.C. App. 650, 369 S.E.2d 620 (1988).

119. AOC-CVM-303, "Notice of Appeal to District Court," is the preprinted form that can be used to give written notice of appeal.

120. G.S. 1A-1, Rule 5. *See* Ball Photo Supply Co. v. McClain, 30 N.C. App. 132, 226 S.E.2d 178 (1976).

writing, signed by the magistrate, and filed with the clerk of court.[121] In counting the ten days, the day the judgment was entered (that is, filed with the clerk) is not counted; and if the tenth day falls on a weekend or on a holiday when the courthouse is not open for business, the party has until the end of the next workday to file the appeal.[122]

In addition to giving oral notice in open court or filing a written notice of appeal, the appellant must pay the court costs for appeal to the clerk within twenty days after entry of the magistrate's judgment. The court costs for appeal are the same amount as the costs for filing a new action in district court.[123] The appeal is perfected upon giving notice but is automatically dismissed if the appellant fails to pay the costs of appeal within twenty days.[124]

If the magistrate does not announce and sign the judgment in open court at the end of the case, the time for appeal is extended until three days after the magistrate mails a copy of the judgment to the parties or a maximum of ninety days after judgment is entered.[125]

Appealing as an Indigent

An appellant who does not have the money to pay the court costs for appeal may file a petition to appeal as an indigent;[126] if petition is granted, he or she may appeal without paying court costs. The petition to appeal as an indigent must be filed within ten days after the magistrate's judgment is entered and is usually considered by a clerk, though it may be handled by a magistrate, district court judge, or superior court judge.[127] A person is indigent if he or she is (1) receiving food stamps, Work First Family Assistance, Supplement Security Income (SSI), or (2) is represented by a legal services organization that has as its primary purpose the furnishing of legal services to indigent persons or by a private attorney working on behalf of a legal services organization.[128] If an appellant meets one of those criteria, the magistrate or clerk must authorize the person to appeal as an indigent. In other cases, a magistrate or clerk must determine whether the particular appellant is unable to pay the costs of appeal by considering all the relevant circumstances, including the party's assets, income, and expenses.

> Reliance solely upon home ownership has been held to be error. . . . It is not required that the litigant deprive himself of the daily necessities of life to qualify to appear in forma pauperis. . . . The courts of North Carolina are not going to require a litigant to become absolutely destitute before being granted permission to appear as a pauper. Such would destroy the dignity of our people.[129]

121. Provident Fin. Co. v. Locklear, 89 N.C. App. 535, 366 S.E.2d 599 (1988).
122. G.S. 1A-1, Rule 6(a).
123. G.S. 7A-305(b).
124. G.S. 7A-228(b).
125. G.S. 1A-1, Rule 58.
126. G.S. 7A-228(b1). AOC-G-106, "Petition to Sue/Appeal As An Indigent" is the preprinted form used to appeal as an indigent.
127. G.S. 7A-228(b1).
128. G.S. 1-110.
129. Atlantic Ins. & Realty Co. v. Davidson, 320 N.C. 159, 162, 357 S.E.2d 668, 670 (1987) (finding indigent a sixty-five-year old woman who receives Social Security benefits of $340 per month, is unable to work, and has monthly expenses for necessities of $362, a $50 television set, furniture worth $200, her home—valued at $27,150—$10 in cash, and debts amounting to $300).

Stay of Execution Bond

Appealing a case does not necessarily stop enforcement of the trial court's decision. Usually, a defendant who loses at trial and appeals his or her case must sign a bond, called a *stay of execution bond*, to keep the judgment from being enforced while the case is on appeal. The stay of execution bond has a different purpose from the payment of court costs to appeal (appeal costs), which the appellant must pay to have the district court hear the case. The purpose of the stay of execution bond is to protect the plaintiff from the effects of delaying enforcement of the judgment he or she has won. In small claims cases a judgment for money damages is automatically stayed upon appeal until the case is heard in district court.[130] Thus a defendant who receives such a judgment need not post a stay of execution bond.

However, appeal does not stay execution of a judgment for possession of specific personal property or for summary ejectment.[131] To stay execution of a summary ejectment judgment until the case is heard in district court, a defendant must post an undertaking in compliance with G.S. 42-34.[132] To stay execution of a judgment for possession of specific personal property, the defendant must post a bond with the clerk of superior court, executed by one or more sufficient sureties, "to the effect that if judgment be rendered against the appellant the sureties will pay the amount thereof with costs awarded against the appellant." The statute is odd because judgment against the defendant would require him or her to give the property, not to pay money, to the plaintiff. The bond form, however, correctly specifies that the sureties agree to pay all damages that the plaintiff might sustain by the defendant's failure to comply with the order.[133]

The requirements for appeal of small claims cases may be summarized as follows. (1) In cases where the magistrate has awarded money, the party appealing must post court costs (appeal costs) unless he or she is appealing as an indigent; but the money judgment is automatically stayed and cannot be enforced until the district court judge rules. (2) A plaintiff who appeals a judgment for possession of personal or real property, must pay court costs; but if the defendant appeals the judgment and wishes to keep possession of the property until the district court's decision, he or she must pay court costs and also post the stay of execution bond.

Although an appellant has twenty days after the judgment is entered to pay the court costs of appeal, there is no similar provision for posting a stay of execution bond. A defendant who is appealing (*appellant*) must post the bond to stay execution within ten days after the judgment is entered, since the automatic stay of execution ceases at that time.[134] But a defendant's failure to post a bond to stay execution does not remove the right to appeal; it merely gives the plaintiff the right to have the clerk issue a writ to enforce the judgment while the case is on appeal. If after ten days the plaintiff has not sought to have the judgment executed, the defendant can post the stay of execution bond. Essentially, after the tenth day it becomes a race to the courthouse

130. G.S. 7A-227.

131. *Id.*

132. AOC-CVM-304, "Bond to Stay Execution on Appeal of Summary Ejectment Judgment" is the preprinted form available for use. The bond is discussed in detail in Chapter VI, "Landlord–Tenant Law."

133. AOC-CVM-906M, "Bond to Stay Execution on Appeal of Judgment to Recover Possession of Personal Property."

134. G.S. 1A-1, Rule 62(a).

between the plaintiff seeking issuance of a writ of possession and the defendant posting a stay of execution bond.

> ***Example 14.*** William brings an action for summary ejectment and back rent against George. The magistrate announces and signs a judgment in open court on January 16, awarding $450 back rent and possession of the property to William. George states in open court that he wishes to appeal, and the magistrate notes the appeal on the judgment and files the judgment with the clerk that day.
>
> On January 29 William asks the clerk to issue process to enforce the judgment. George has not paid the costs to appeal the case; nor has he signed an undertaking to stay execution of the judgment.
>
> The clerk should not issue a writ of execution for the money judgment since that part of the judgment was automatically stayed when George gave notice of appeal on January 16. The clerk should, however, issue a writ of possession to enforce the possession part of the judgment, since the request was made more than ten days after the judgment was entered and George has not posted a bond to stay execution of the judgment. However, he has twenty days from January 16 to post the costs of appeal with the clerk. If he does so, his appeal will be heard in district court even though he has already been removed from the premises. If George fails to pay the costs of appeal by the end of the day on February 5 (the twentieth day), the appeal is automatically dismissed.

Setting Aside Judgments or Orders

One question frequently asked is whether a magistrate may correct a mistake in an order or judgment. There are several types of mistakes: clerical errors by the magistrate; errors by the parties that are not based on fault; the magistrate's error in hearing a cases when the defendant was not served; and errors of law (when the magistrate incorrectly applies the law in the case). The last type of error, a legal error, is not correctable by the magistrate. The purpose of a right to appeal is to correct magistrates' errors of law. Rule 60 of the Rules of Civil Procedure provides a mechanism in certain situations for relief from judgments or orders based on errors other than errors of law.

Clerical Errors

A magistrate may correct clerical mistakes in a judgment or order at any time, on his or her own initiative or on a motion from a party.[135] He or she has the authority to correct a clerical error without giving notice to the parties. Examples of clerical errors in a judgment are a misnomer, an incorrect mathematical computation, and transposition of principal and interest.[136] Rule 60 may not, however, be used to make small but substantive changes that affect the underlying legal rights of the parties.[137] To correct a clerical error the magistrate should enter an order stating that the original judgment or order contained a clerical error and that the magistrate is therefore

---

135. G.S. 1A-1, Rule 60(a). Snell v. Washington County Bd. of Educ., 29 N.C. App. 31, 222 S.E.2d 756 (1976).

136. WILSON, *supra* note 84, § 60-1.

137. Food Services Specialists v. Atlas Rest. Mgmt., Inc., 111 N.C. App. 257, 431 S.E.2d 878 (1993) (Changing the date of entry of judgment to date not actual date judgment entered is not correcting a clerical error.).

amending the judgment to correct that error. The magistrate should sign the new judgment, which is marked as an amended judgment, date it as of the date it is signed, mail copies to the parties, and file the order and amended judgment with the clerk.

Excusable Neglect, Mistake, or Surprise

G.S. 1A-1, Rule 60(b) authorizes setting aside judgments and orders on the grounds of excusable neglect, surprise, or mistake; newly discovered evidence; or fraud; or because the judgment is void or has been satisfied, released, or discharged; or for other good cause. Generally, a district court judge must hear a Rule 60(b) motion to set aside a magistrate's judgment. However, G.S. 7A-228 allows the chief district court judge to authorize magistrates to hear Rule 60(b)(1) motions to set aside a magistrate's judgment or order because of a mistake, excusable neglect, or surprise. A motion to set aside a magistrate's judgment or order on other grounds must be heard by a district court judge.

Definitions

Excusable neglect arises when a party does not appear at trial to prosecute the case or defend the case through no fault of his or her own. "[W]hat constitutes excusable neglect depends upon what, under all the surrounding circumstances, may be reasonably expected of a party in paying proper attention to his case."[138] A party in a lawsuit is required to give the case "such attention as a man of ordinary prudence usually gives to his important business affairs."[139] If the party fails to meet that standard, the neglect is not excusable. A party who is without fault may also be relieved of a judgment entered as a result of negligence on the part of the party's attorney. For example, when a defendant has conferred with attorneys and kept in touch about the case, but the attorneys have failed to notify the defendant of the trial date, the party's failure to appear at trial would be excusable neglect.[140] However, a party who hires an attorney and never follows up with the attorney would not meet the standard. Examples of excusable neglect include a case in which a defendant relied on her husband's assurances that he would take care of the defense of a suit against both of them;[141] a case in which the party never received notice of the date and time of the trial;[142] or one in which a defendant did not respond to a complaint because the agent on whom the summons and complaint were served did not give the papers to the defendant.[143] However, parties may not assert excusable neglect because they are preoccupied with business

138. Thomas M. McInnis & Assoc., Inc. v. Hall, 318 N.C. 421, 425, 349 S.E.2d 552, 555 (1986).
139. Norton v. McLaurin, 125 N.C. 185, 190, 34 S.E. 269, 270 (1899). *See, e.g.*, Jones v. Statesville Ice & Fuel Co., 259 N.C. 206, 130 S.E.2d 324 (1963); Norton v. Sawyer, 30 N.C. App. 420, 227 S.E.2d 148 (1976).
140. *See* Mayhew Elec. Co. v. Carras, 29 N.C. App. 105, 223 S.E.2d 536 (1976).
141. Hickory White Trucks, Inc. v. Greene, 34 N.C. App. 279, 237 S.E.2d 862 (1977).
142. Callaway v. Freeman, 71 N.C. App. 451, 322 S.E.2d 432 (1984).
143. Townsend v. Carolina Coach Co., 231 N.C. 81, 56 S.E.2d 39 (1949).

or other duties at the time of the lawsuit[144] or because they are so old that they forgot they had been served.[145]

A *mistake* that warrants relief from a judgment is a mistake of fact not of law. For example, in a partition proceeding, partition of a tract of land was set aside on the grounds of mistake when counsel for plaintiffs used an incorrect land description given to him by a third person and the description referred to a tract already owned solely by petitioner.[146]

A *surprise* is "some condition or situation in which a party is unexpectedly placed to his injury, without any fault or negligence of his own, which ordinary prudence could not have guarded against."[147] It is not surprise when a party has a mistaken view of the law.[148] Examples of surprise are when counsel withdraws from a case when the case is called for trial without telling the client[149] or when plaintiff's counsel is detained in another court but does not notify the court about the conflict.[150]

Hearing a Rule 60(b)(1) Motion

As noted above, the chief district court judge may authorize a magistrate to set aside judgments and orders on the grounds of excusable neglect, surprise, or mistake. A party who wishes to have a magistrate's judgment or order set aside must file a written request with a magistrate—the magistrate who issued the judgment or any other magistrate in the county authorized by the judge to hear Rule 60(b)(1) motions. In an unusual case the magistrate may act to set aside his or her own motion in the interest of justice.[151]

A motion to set aside a judgment for excusable neglect, mistake, or surprise cannot be heard ex parte.[152] A hearing must be set and the magistrate must give notice of the date and time of the hearing to all parties. At the hearing, the party seeking to set aside the judgment or order must appear and has the burden of showing that there was excusable neglect, mistake, or surprise on his or her part and—if the moving party is the defendant—that there is a meritorious defense. The magistrate must enter a written order either granting the motion to set aside the judgment or denying it. If the judgment or order is set aside, the magistrate, in the written order, should set the date and time for the case to be retried in small claims court.

---

144. *E.g.* Johnson v. Sidbury, 225 N.C. 208, 34 S.E.2d 67 (1945); Engines & Equip., Inc. v. Lipscomb, 15 N.C. App. 120, 189 S.E.2d 498 (1972); Rawleigh, Moses & Co. v. Capital City Furniture, Inc., 9 N.C. App. 640, 177 S.E.2d 332 (1970).

145. Pierce v. Eller, 167 N.C. 672, 83 S.E. 758 (1914).

146. Mann v. Hall, 163 N.C. 50, 79 S.E. 437 (1913).

147. Townsend v. Carolina Coach Co., 231 N.C. 81, 85, 56 S.E.2d 39, 42 (1949). *See* WILSON, *supra* note 84, § 60-6.

148. Crissman v. Palmer, 225 N.C. 472, 35 S.E.2d 422 (1945).

149. Roediger v. Sapos, 217 N.C. 95, 6 S.E.2d 801 (1940). *See* WILSON, *supra* note 84, § 60-6.

150. Endsley v. Wolfe Camera Supply Corp., 44 N.C. App. 308, 261 S.E.2d 36 (1979).

151. WILSON, *supra* note 84, § 60-12.

152. Doxol Gas of Angier, Inc. v. Barefoot, 10 N.C. App. 703, 704, 179 S.E.2d 890, 892 (1971).

Meritorious Defense

It would not make sense for the defendant to bring a motion to set aside a judgment or order against the defendant if his or her absence or neglect would have made no difference in the outcome. For that reason, the defendant must show not only that there was excusable neglect, mistake, or surprise but also that the defendant has a meritorious defense. The defendant need not prove the meritorious defense by offering evidence at the hearing as if it were a trial on the merits but must plead that a real or substantial defense on the merits exists.[153]

> **Example 15.** The owner of the Acme Store brings an action against a customer, Charles, for money owed on an account, but Charles does not appear at trial. The store owner testifies that Charles owes him $157.30, and the magistrate enters judgment against Charles. Charles moves to set aside the judgment on the basis of excusable neglect. At the hearing, he testifies that he missed the trial because he unexpectedly had to fly to California the night before the trial because his son was involved in an automobile accident and was hospitalized. He says he was so upset, he forgot about the trial and failed to call the court the next day. He brings an affidavit from the hospital emergency physician and a copy of the police accident report to verify his account. The magistrate believes Charles's evidence and finds this to be excusable neglect. However, that evidence is not enough to set aside the judgment. Charles would also have to prove that he had a meritorious defense he could have presented at the trial. If he also testifies that he had paid the store owner two months before the suit was filed, the magistrate could set aside the judgment on the basis of excusable neglect and reschedule the case for trial.

Effect of Bankruptcy

The purpose of bankruptcy is to relieve the honest debtor from the weight of oppressive indebtedness and permit the debtor to start afresh. When a debtor files a petition for bankruptcy, the bankruptcy court takes jurisdiction over all the debts that person owes and all his or her property and handles payment of those debts. For individuals, there are two kinds of bankruptcy. In straight bankruptcy (Chapter 7) the trustee in bankruptcy takes possession of the bankrupt's property, liquidates it, pays off as much of the debt as possible, and discharges the remaining debt. In wage earner or debt adjustment bankruptcy (Chapter 13), the court extends the time allowed for payment of the debt and may reduce the total amount of the debt. Most bankruptcy provisions apply to both Chapter 7 and Chapter 13 bankruptcies, but some special provisions apply only to Chapter 13 bankruptcies. Under the Bankruptcy Abuse Prevention and Consumer Protection Act of 2005,[154] individual debtors can no longer choose which kind of bankruptcy to file. Consumers must file under Chapter 13 unless they meet a specific means test set out in the law.

153. Dollar v. Tapp, 103 N.C. App. 162, 165, 404 S.E.2d 482, 484 (1991).
154. Pub. Law No. 109-8.

The federal bankruptcy law provides that the filing of a petition for bankruptcy operates to stay

1. the commencement or continuation—including the issuance or employment of process—of a judicial action against a debtor that was or could have been begun before the filing of the bankruptcy petition or an action to recover a claim against a debtor that arose before the filing of the petition.
2. the enforcement against the debtor or property of the estate, of a judgment obtained before the bankruptcy case was filed.
3. any act to obtain possession of property of the estate or to exercise control over property of the estate.
4. any act to create, perfect, or enforce any lien against property of the estate.
5. any act to collect, assess, or recover a claim against the debtor that arose before the commencement of the bankruptcy case.[155]

What this means is that if the defendant in a case filed in small claims court has filed a bankruptcy petition, the magistrate may not hear or enter judgment in the case.

In Chapter 13 bankruptcies the stay also operates to prevent a creditor from commencing or continuing an action to collect all or part of a debt incurred by the debtor primarily for personal, family, or household purposes from any co-debtor unless the co-debtor became liable in the ordinary course of business.[156] A co-debtor is someone who incurred the debt along with the bankrupt debtor or who gave security for the debt. For example, a husband and wife have a joint VISA card, which is in default. The husband files Chapter 13 bankruptcy. The stay applies not only to the husband, but also to his wife.

The general bankruptcy stay remains in effect until the case is closed or dismissed or a discharge is granted or denied; but the specific Chapter 13 stay for co-debtors operates until the bankruptcy case is closed, dismissed, or converted to a Chapter 7 bankruptcy.

A defendant in a small claims case is not required to file any federal court document with the magistrate to prove that he or she has filed a bankruptcy petition; therefore a magistrate should not go forward with the case if told that the defendant has filed for bankruptcy. However, the magistrate can take steps to verify that the petition has actually been filed by telephoning the bankruptcy clerk[157] or checking the website;[158] or he or she may continue the case for a couple of days to ask the debtor to bring in some documentation of the filing or to ask the plaintiff to determine whether the defendant has filed for bankruptcy. If the magistrate determines that the stay applies, he or she must enter an order placing the case on inactive status because the

---

155. 11 U.S.C. § 362.

156. 11 U.S.C. § 1301.

157. The telephone numbers for the bankruptcy clerks in North Carolina are: Eastern District—(252) 237-0248; Middle District—(336) 333-5647; and Western District—(704) 350-7500.

158. Eastern District—www.nceb.uscourts.gov; Middle District—www.ncmb.uscourts.gov; Western District—www.ncwb.uscourts.gov. These websites may require a PACER account and password and may charge a fee for information.

defendant has filed for bankruptcy.[159] The magistrate should not, however, dismiss the case because, as discussed below, in some circumstances the bankruptcy court will allow the plaintiff to proceed with the state court action.

There are a several ways in which the state court can continue an action after a bankruptcy petition has been filed, but all require the creditor to seek relief from the bankruptcy court. The most common way is for the creditor to seek to have the bankruptcy court lift the stay as to particular property or a particular claim. In that case the order from the bankruptcy court lifting the stay will allow the creditor to proceed to enforce his or her claim in state court. Also the trustee in a Chapter 7 bankruptcy may abandon (i.e., release) certain property from the bankrupt's estate and allow creditors who have security interests in that property to enforce those interests in state courts; the trustee signs an order abandoning specific property, and the creditor can proceed in state court to satisfy the debt out of that property.

> **Example 16.** Sam purchases a refrigerator from Sears and signs a security agreement for the $2,000 extension of credit from Sears to purchase the refrigerator. Six months later Sam files Chapter 7 bankruptcy. At that point, the refrigerator has a fair market value of $1,000, but Sam still owes Sears $1,500 on it. Sears can seek to have the trustee abandon the refrigerator since it has no equity (value in excess of the amount owed under the security agreement) that could be used to pay any of Sam's other debts. Sears can then bring an action in small claims court to repossess the refrigerator as authorized by the security agreement, although it cannot sue Sam for any deficiency remaining after repossessing and selling the refrigerator.

Special Provisions for Residential Leases

Judgment for Possession before Bankruptcy

The new bankruptcy code provides that the filing of a petition does not stay enforcement of an eviction involving residential property on which the debtor resides as a tenant if the landlord has obtained a judgment for possession of the property before the filing date of the bankruptcy petition.[160] This provision applies for thirty days after the bankruptcy filing. The bankruptcy petition must indicate that a judgment for possession of residential premises was entered against the debtor before the filing of the petition and must list the name and address of the landlord. The debtor then has thirty days after filing the petition to file with the bankruptcy court a certification that would allow the stay to prevent enforcement of the eviction. If the debtor does not file a certification within the allowable time period, the stay is lifted and the clerk may issue a writ of possession.

The landlord can challenge the certification by filing an objection. The bankruptcy court must then hold a hearing to determine whether to authorize relief from the stay.

159. Form AOC-G-108, "Order" should be used.
160. 11 U.S.C. § 362(b)(22).

Evictions for Criminal Activity

The new bankruptcy code[161] also provides an exception to the automatic stay for an eviction action that seeks possession of the residential property in which the debtor resides as a tenant based on endangerment of the property or illegal use of controlled substances on the property. The landlord must file a certification with the bankruptcy court—and serve a copy on the tenant—that a summary ejectment action had been filed at the time the tenant filed bankruptcy or that the conduct justifying the eviction occurred within the thirty days preceding the certification filing. The stay is lifted fifteen days after the landlord files the certification unless the tenant objects to the certification. If there is an objection the bankruptcy court holds a hearing to determine whether the stay applies; that is, whether the situation giving rise to the certification existed or—if it existed—whether it has been remedied.

If the debtor does not file an objection, the bankruptcy clerk must serve upon the tenant and landlord a certified copy of the docket indicating that no certification was filed. The landlord may use that certified copy to prove to the magistrate that the summary ejectment action in the state court may proceed. The bankruptcy act does not define "endangerment of property." Until the bankruptcy court rules on that issue, a landlord who has grounds for bringing an eviction on the basis of criminal activity might qualify for the exception to the automatic stay.

Stays to Other Bankruptcy Actions

The automatic stay provision prohibits any act to obtain possession of property in the bankrupt debtor's estate, and the debtor's leasehold interest is considered property of the estate.[162] Therefore, if a debtor files a bankruptcy petition before a summary ejectment judgment has been entered, the magistrate may not proceed with the case and must handle it like any other small claims case in which the defendant has filed bankruptcy. The landlord must seek relief in the bankruptcy court, and the bankruptcy court is likely to lift the stay and allow the landlord to proceed with the eviction unless the tenant provides adequate assurance of future compliance with the lease. Past rent that was *in arrears* when the judgment was entered will not be collected, but the debtor must pay future rent.

Effect of Bankruptcy on Judgment

What is the effect of the bankruptcy proceeding when it is completed? The most common result of a bankruptcy proceeding is that the debts covered by the proceeding are discharged; in other words, creditors may not continue to collect debts or file legal action against the debtor seeking money owed them before the bankruptcy filing, *with one exception*: if the debtor had signed a security agreement securing the debt and the debtor remains in possession of the secured property after the discharge in bankruptcy, the creditor may bring an action for possession of the secured property[163] but may not sue for a deficiency. Sometimes a bankruptcy case is dismissed without discharge of the debts because the debtor has not complied with the bankruptcy rules.

---

161. 11 U.S.C. § 362(b)(23) and (m).

162. Property of the estate includes all legal and equitable interest of the debtor in property as of the commencement of the bankruptcy case (the filing of the petition). 11 U.S.C. § 541.

163. 11 U.S.C § 524(a). *See* Chandler Bank of Lyons v. Ray, 804 F.2d 577 (10th Cir. 1986).

In that case, the creditor may pursue any actions it had against the debtor before the latter filed for bankruptcy.

Procedural Issues in Appeals to District Court

If the appellant fails to appear in district court and prosecute the appeal, the presiding judge may dismiss the appeal; in such a case the magistrate's judgment is affirmed.[164] Because the failure to appear and prosecute applies only if the appeal is docketed and regularly set for trial,[165] the district court judge's order of dismissal should indicate that the case was set for trial and proper notice was given. The statute specifies that the judgment of the magistrate "be affirmed," but since the appeal is dismissed for failing to appear, the magistrate's judgment becomes the final judgment. As a consequence, the judgment may be enforced immediately, since it was entered more than ten days before the appeal was dismissed. The same result would occur if the appellant had withdrawn or dismissed the appeal.[166]

Upon appeal for a de novo trial, a plaintiff may take a voluntary dismissal under G.S. 1A-1, Rule 41(a) and terminate the lawsuit[167] no matter which party appealed. In that situation the magistrate's judgment is not reactivated, because a de novo appeal is, by its nature, a case originally brought in district court—as if the trial in the magistrate's court never happened.

One question that has not been answered is whether a plaintiff who files a small claim action for $5,000 but actually had a claim for $7,000 and subsequently appeals the small claims judgment to district court may amend the complaint in district court to seek the full $7,000.

When a small claims case is appealed to district court, the district court, on its own motion, may either order the party to replead or may try the case on the pleadings as originally filed;[168] and, upon the request of a party, the judge must allow appropriate counterclaims, cross-claims, third-party claims, and other pleadings.

---

164. G.S. 7A-228(c). *See* Brown v. County of Avery, 164 N.C. App. 704, 596 S.E.2d 334 (2004) (dismissal rule applies even if there was intervening arbitrator's award because award is a nullity if party seeks trial de novo rather than accepting award).

165. Fairchild Properties v. Hall, 122 N.C. App. 286, 468 S.E.2d 605 (1996).

166. First Union Nat'l Bank v. Richards, 90 N.C. App. 650, 369 S.E.2d 620 (1988).

167. *Id.* at 653–54, 369 S.E.2d at 622.

168. G.S. 7A-229 *See* Don Setliff & Assoc., Inc. v. Subway Real Estate Corp., 178 N.C. App. 385, 631 S.E.2d 526 (2006) (Defendant can raise affirmative defense in district court because not required to be pled in small claims court.).

Appendix 1

Model General Order regarding Small Claims Assignments and Magistrates' Authority

(*Language in parentheses is optional. Language in brackets gives alternatives, and only one should be selected.*)

Pursuant to G.S. 7A-211 the undersigned judge issues this general order to the Clerk of Superior Court and the magistrates of _____ County regarding the assignment of cases to small claims court within the county.

The undersigned hereby assigns to small claims court cases which meet all of the following four requirements and requests the Clerk to calendar those cases for the regular small claims court: Cases in which the amount in controversy at the time of the filing of the complaint is $5,000 or less; the plaintiff is seeking monetary damages, recovery of specific personal property, summary ejectment, or any combination of these remedies; the plaintiff requests that the case be assigned to a magistrate; and at least one of the defendants is a resident of the county in which the complaint is filed. The filing of a complaint on a regular AOC-CVM complaint form is a request for assignment to small claims court.

The Clerk is also ordered to assign to the regular small claims court cases in which the plaintiff seeks to enforce a motor vehicle lien pursuant to G.S. 44A-2(d) or 20-77; the amount in controversy is $5,000 or less; the plaintiff requests assignment to a magistrate; and the claim arose in the county in which the complaint is filed.

(Cases filed on small claims complaints but not meeting the criteria set out above are not assigned and should be sent to district court.)

In determining whether the amount in controversy is within the allowable limit, the clerk shall apply the following rules: [In complaints for money owed, the "total amount owed" is the amount in controversy, except if the complaint alleges an unfair trade practice the amount in controversy is triple the total amount owed.] [In complaints for money owed, the "principal amount owed" is the amount in controversy, except if the complaint alleges an unfair trade practice, the amount in controversy is triple the principal amount owed.][169] In summary ejectment cases, the amount in controversy is the "total amount due." In actions to recover possession of personal property, the amount in controversy is the "total value of the property to be recovered" plus the "total amount of damages," if any. In motor vehicle lien cases, the amount in controversy is the "total lien claimed to date."

---

169. The chief district judge must decide which interpretation of the amount-in-controversy statute to follow and choose one of the two bracketed sections as appropriate. G.S. 7A-243(1) specifies that the amount in controversy is computed without regard to interest and costs, while G.S. 7A-243(2) states that where monetary relief is prayed, the amount prayed for is in controversy. In trying to read the two sections together, it raises the question whether "interest and costs" refers to post-judgment interest and costs that are not known at the time of trial and are added by the clerk as opposed to prejudgment interest in a contract case. There are no cases that answer the question so the chief judge must decide for purposes of assignment. One policy argument for the "total amount" reading is that the legislature wished to limit the dollar amount of cases that were heard by magistrates.

When complaints for expedited summary ejectment under vacation rental agreements are filed with the clerk, the clerk shall assign the cases to any magistrate in the county who is available. If such an action is filed at a time when the clerk's office is closed, it shall be filed with the criminal magistrate's office and any magistrate who is on duty shall schedule the case for a hearing and issue a summons pursuant to G.S. 42A-24. Any magistrate within the county is hereby authorized to conduct expedited eviction hearings for vacation rental agreements, whether or not regularly assigned to hold small claims court.

(Pursuant to G.S. 7A-228 the undersigned judge authorizes [the following magistrates: (*name magistrates*)] [all magistrates assigned to hold small claims court] to hear motions to set aside an order or judgment entered in small claims court pursuant to G.S. 1A-1, Rule 60(b)(1) and order a new trial before a magistrate.)

Issued the _____ day of _____, 20__. _____

Chief District Judge, _____ District Court District

Chapter III

Contracts

A contract is a promise between two or more parties that the law recognizes as legally binding and for breach of which it provides legal remedies. Several cases have defined a *contract* as "an agreement, upon sufficient consideration, to do or not to do a particular thing."[1]

The law of contracts comes from two sources: court decisions (case law) and statutes. The sale of *real property* (land and anything permanently attached to the land) and of *services* (for example, repairing a boat or providing medical care) are primarily governed by case law. The Retail Installment Sales Act [Chapter 25A of the North Carolina General Statutes (hereinafter G.S.)] also regulates the sale of some services. Two major statutes govern the sale of *goods* (moveable personal property): the Uniform Commercial Code[2] (hereinafter UCC)—found in Article 9 of G.S. Ch. 25 and the Retail Installment Sales Act. *Personal property* is all property other than real property and includes both *tangible property*, such as goods and animals, and *intangible property*, such as accounts receivable.

Many of the cases in small claims court, such as actions for failure to pay an account or a loan and breaches of warranty cases, are based on contract law. In a breach of contract case, the court addresses the following four questions:

1. Is there a contract?
2. What are the contract's terms?
3. Is the contract enforceable?
4. What damages should be awarded for its breach?

---

1. *E.g.,* Williams v. Jones, 322 N.C. 42, 48, 366 S.E.2d 433, 437 (1988); Arndt v. First Union Nat'l Bank, 170 N.C. App. 518, 522, 613 S.E.2d 274, 278 (2005).

2. The Uniform Commercial Code (hereinafter UCC) is the North Carolina statute governing all aspects of commercial transactions; Article 2, which regulates the sale of goods, is found in N.C. GEN. STAT. §§ 25-2-101 through -725 (hereinafter G.S.). The National Conference of Commissioners on Uniform State Laws was created to work for consistent state laws, particularly in areas where issues cross state lines. The conference, which includes lawyers from every state, drafts and proposes uniform laws on various topics. One of its earliest recommendations was a uniform law governing the sale of goods and other commercial transactions to facilitate business transactions across state lines. The conference can only recommend legislation; individual states must adopt the statutes, and many alter the recommended statute. The UCC has been adopted in all states, except that Louisiana has not adopted Article 2, regarding the sale of goods.

This chapter discusses these questions and some miscellaneous contract issues that arise in small claims cases.

Is There a Contract?

A contract is an agreement between two or more parties that consists of an offer and an acceptance and is supported by consideration. The first question that arises in determining whether a contract exists is whether there is a mutual agreement between at least two parties—sometimes referred to as a meeting of the minds.[3] Mutual assent is usually satisfied by evidence of an offer and an acceptance of the offer.

Offer

An offer invites acceptance; it creates in the mind of the *offeree* (the person to whom the offer is made) a reasonable expectation that the *offeror* (the person making the offer) is willing to enter into a contract on the terms offered. For a reasonable expectation to arise an offer must (1) express a definite intent to sell or do some other act, (2) be communicated to the person to whom the offer is being made, and (3) be reasonably certain and definite in its terms.

> *Example 1.* Xander says to Yvonne, "I will sell you my lawnmower for $300." This is an offer. However, if Xander merely tells Yvonne "I plan to sell my lawnmower for $300," he has not made an offer: this language may invite an offer to buy, but does not indicate an intent to enter into a contract with Yvonne.

> *Example 2.* Dick places an advertisement in the neighborhood newsletter offering to sell his old Honda Accord for $500 to the first person who arrives at his door. His neighbor Sam, who is unaware of the advertisement in the newsletter and thinks the Honda sitting in Dick's yard is an eyesore, decides to offer Dick $750. Sam arrives at Dick's door and completes the sale for $750. When Sam later sees the advertisement he demands that Sam give him back $250 since he (Sam) was the first person to arrive at Dick's door. Since Sam did not know of Dick's offer, he cannot claim that Dick made him the offer.

> *Example 3.* Jane says to Sue, "I will give you a fair share of the profits of the company I am forming if you will come to work for me." Sue agrees. No contract has been formed because the statement includes no definite offer of payment and there is no way to tell what a "fair share" is.

Because mutuality of agreement is necessary to form a contract, the parties must consent to the same thing. Therefore, an offer should be definite in its terms so that the parties will know what their obligations are and the contract can be enforced. Historically, North Carolina law has required that the parties agree on all the terms; if any of the proposed terms remained unsettled and there was no agreed-upon mode by which it might be settled, there was no con-

---

3. *E.g.,* Creech v. Melnik, 347 N.C. 520, 495 S.E.2d 907 (1988); Quantum Corporate Funding, Ltd. v. B.H. Bryan Bldg. Co., 175 N.C. App. 483, 623 S.E.2d 793 (2006); Harrison v. Wal-Mart Stores, Inc., 170 N.C. App. 545, 613 S.E.2d 322 (2005).

tract. Current contract law is somewhat more relaxed, yet there are still some required terms, depending on the type of contract involved. In contracts for services, the parties must agree to the "material" or "essential" terms.[4] In contracts for the sale of goods, the UCC is quite liberal about when an offer is sufficiently definite. The UCC is based on the proposition that if both parties show intent to create a contract, then one exists: "A contract for sale of goods may be made in any manner sufficient to show agreement. . . . Even though one or more terms are left open a contract for sale does not fail for indefiniteness if the parties have intended to make a contract and there is a reasonably certain basis for giving an appropriate remedy."[5] As long as the offer is clear enough so that the parties can agree to the contract, it is sufficient. The UCC also has provisions, which are discussed later in this chapter, to determine contract terms not mentioned in the agreement.

By way of review, an offer must (1) express a definite intent to sell or do some other act, (2) be communicated to the person for whom the offer is intended, and (3) be reasonably certain and definite in its terms. What constitutes *reasonable*, *certainty*, and *definiteness* in terms depends on the specific kind of contract involved.

Terminating an Offer

Once an offer is made, the offeror can (in most circumstances) terminate that offer at any time before it is accepted.

> **Example 4.** Abby sees Lisa and offers, "I will sell you my refrigerator for $150." The next evening Abby telephones Lisa and says, "I've changed my mind. I'm going to keep my refrigerator." There can be no contract, even if Lisa wants to accept, because Abby has made a valid revocation of her offer. But there would be a different result if, when Abby phones Lisa, the conversation had progressed as follows: Abby says, "Hello Lisa, I'm calling about my offer to sell the refrigerator. How are you today?" Lisa replies, "I'm fine, thank you, and I'm glad you called. I accept your offer." At this point Abby can no longer revoke the offer, since Lisa has already accepted it.

Termination of the offer does not have to occur directly; it can happen when the offeree learns information from a reliable source that would lead a reasonable person to believe that the offer is no longer open.[6] For instance, in the example above, if Lisa learned from Cindy that Abby had sold the refrigerator to their friend Lou, the offer would be effectively terminated.

In some circumstances the offeror's right to revoke his or her offer may be limited. One such instance involves *firm offers* by merchants—those who deal in the type of goods involved in the transaction. If a merchant makes a written offer to buy or sell goods that states it will be held open for a certain or reasonable period of time, the offer cannot be revoked before the end of that time period even though no consideration has been given for holding the offer open.[7] This is true, however, only up to a maximum of three months. For firm offers that are made by

---

4. John N. Hutson, Jr. & Scott A. Miskimon, North Carolina Contract Law § 2-30 (2001).
5. G.S. 25-2-204.
6. Normile v. Miller, 313 N.C. 98, 109, 326 S.E.2d 11, 18–19 (1985).
7. G.S. 25-2-205 See p. 57 below for discussion of consideration.

persons other than merchants or that are not written (called *options*), the common law provides that the offer may be revoked if no consideration has been given for holding it open.[8]

An advertisement in a newspaper can be revoked before acceptance if the offeror publishes the revocation in a manner commensurate with the original advertisement.[9]

The precise time that an offer terminates is important because it cancels the offeree's power to accept it. As a general rule, an offer is terminated when

- it has been rejected;
- it specifies a time during which it will remain open and that time lapses;
- it does not specify a time and a reasonable time has elapsed;
- a person necessary to carry out the contract dies;
- a condition on which the offer depends does not occur; for example, when a buyer offers to buy a seller's house for a certain price contingent on obtaining appropriate financing but does not obtain financing;
- in some cases, something necessary to carry out the contract is destroyed; or
- the offeror revokes the offer before the offeree has accepted it.

Acceptance and Counteroffers

An offer must be accepted before a valid contract can be formed. There are two kinds of contracts—bilateral and unilateral. *Bilateral contracts*, the most common, are formed by the exchange of mutual promises; acceptance is indicated by a promise to perform according to the terms of the offer.

> *Example 5.* Bob says to Kathy, "I'll sell you my car for $300." Kathy says to Bob, "I accept. I'll buy your car for $300." This is a bilateral contract; a promise to sell has been given in exchange for a promise to buy. The agreement becomes binding when Kathy promises to pay $300 for the car. Thus, the contract is formed by two promises—Bob's promise to sell the car to Kathy for $300 and Kathy's promise to buy the car for $300. A refusal by either party to make good his or her promise constitutes a breach of the contract, and the injured party can sue for the damage resulting from the breach.

A contract is said to be *executed* when both parties have performed their respective obligations under it. When elements of the contract remain to be performed by either party, the contract is said to be *executory*. In the example above, the contract is executory when Bob has promised to sell his car and Kathy has promised to buy it, and is executed when Bob has given the car to Kathy and Kathy has paid him the $300. When the contract is executory, either party may bring a lawsuit to make the other party comply with the contract. However, forcing a person to comply with a contract to deliver goods, called *an action for specific performance*, must be brought in district court, not in small claims. In the example above, if Kathy pays Bob the $300 and Bob refuses to deliver the car, Kathy can enforce the contract and receive the car by suing in district court for specific performance—that is, a court order requiring Bob to deliver the car.

---

8. Hutson & Miskimon, *supra* note 4, § 2-27.
9. *Id.* at § 2-20.

A *unilateral contract* is one in which performance must be given in exchange for a promise. The performance is the necessary form of acceptance.

> **Example 6.** Adam loses his wallet and runs an ad in the paper offering a reward for its return. Joel reads Adam's ad and returns the wallet. This is a unilateral contract, a promise being given for an act. The one making the offer does not seek a promise in return, but performance of a specific act. Joel, by performing it, has accepted the offer and thus created a contract.

A distinction between these first two illustrations should be carefully noted. In Example 5, if either party later refuses to perform, a breach of contract has occurred. In Example 6, Joel is under no contractual duty to return the wallet. Only after he performs the act are the parties bound by contract; until that time, the failure of either to perform does not constitute a breach of contract.

Who Can Accept the Offer

Acceptance must come from the person to whom the offer was directed; it cannot be accepted by anyone else. For example, Bob offers to sell Kathy his car for $300, and Maria overhears the offer and agrees to buy the car from Bob for that price. No contract has been made because the acceptance was not made by the one to whom the offer was directed.

Acceptance Conforms to Offer

In contract cases not governed by the UCC, acceptance generally must conform to the terms of the offer. If the offeree varies the terms of the offer, there has been no acceptance but simply what the law considers a *counteroffer*. The original offer by the offeror has been rejected, and the party to whom the offer was made (the offeree) has instead made an offer. The original offeror has the choice of accepting the counteroffer or ignoring it, in effect is rejecting it. Once a counteroffer has been made, the original offer terminates and cannot later be accepted by the party who made the counteroffer.

> **Example 7.** Milo offers to paint Laurel's car for $300. Laurel replies, "I'll accept your offer if you'll also install my new stereo system for me." There is no contract at this point. Milo has made an offer. Laurel has made not an acceptance but a counteroffer. If the negotiations cease at this point, neither party has an obligation to do anything. If Milo says, "It's a deal," then a contract is formed because he has accepted the counteroffer and is now bound to paint the car and install the stereo system. If Milo replies, "Sorry, no deal," and then Laurel says, "O.K., I'll pay you $300 to paint my car," there is still no contract. Laurel's counteroffer regarding the stereo was a rejection of Milo's original offer and therefore terminated it. Laurel can accept the original offer now only if Milo renews it.

The UCC has altered the concept of counteroffer to some extent, based on the reality of modern business transactions. It is now common to see a "battle of forms" in which the parties to the contract send each other forms of the contract with conflicting provisions or provisions found only in one party's form.[10] Under the UCC an offeree's proposal of new or additional

---

10. *See* James J. White & Robert S. Summers, 1 Uniform Commercial Code § 1-3 (5th ed. 2006).

terms is not a rejection of the offer; it is an acceptance as long as it includes a definite expression of acceptance and is not made expressly conditional on assent to the new terms.[11]

>*Example 8.* Jan, a retailer of paint, wants to buy 1,000 gallons of house paint manufactured by the Hansen Company. Jan initiated the buying process by completing and mailing to Hansen a printed order form. The form contained a number of printed clauses and had several blank spaces in which the buyer wrote the seller's name, the description of the goods she wanted, the quantity and price of the goods—1,000 gallons at $4 a gallon—and the date and method of delivery. Two days later Hansen received this offer and sent the paint to Jan. Along with paint, Hansen sent a printed acknowledgment that also contained a number of printed clauses as well as blank spaces. The blank spaces were filled in with the same terms as those on the buyer's form offer. A comparison of the two forms shows that they were substantially alike. Hansen's form, however, had a clause requiring the parties to submit any dispute to an arbitration panel and another clause fixing a reasonable time for the parties to enter complaints. Jan's form was silent on these subjects. Hansen's form also had a clause limiting the warranty on the paint's quality, whereas Jan's form had a clause requiring full warranty of the product. Is there a contract? Yes, Hansen has made a definite response to Jan's offer.

Implied Contracts

We have been considering offer and acceptance as if particular forms of words were required to create valid contracts. Actually in a great many valid contracts it is impossible to recognize a specific offer or acceptance. In these cases the agreement between the parties is not spelled out in words but is instead apparent from their behavior. The type of contract we have been discussing is called an *express contract* and the second type is known as an *implied contract*. "An express contract is one in which terms of the agreement are declared or expressed by the parties, orally or in writing, at the time the contract was entered into. An implied contract arises when the intention of the parties is not expressed but an agreement in fact creating an obligation is implied or presumed from their acts and words, when and where there are circumstances which, according to the ordinary course of dealings and common understanding of men, show a mutual intent to contract."[12] An implied contract is as valid as an express contract. Except for the method of proving that both parties agreed, there is no legal difference between them.[13]

>*Example 9.* Edna goes to the office of Christine, a dentist, to have a tooth filled. Christine does the work. Even though neither party has mentioned a fee, there is a contract for the price of the service to which Edna has given implied assent.

>*Example 10.* Lars receives a catalog from Peter, a retail merchant, that shows Peter's merchandise and includes order forms. Lars fills out a form and orders some merchandise. Peter sends the goods

---

11. G.S. 25-2-207(1).

12. Penley v. Penley, 314 N.C. 1, 15, 332 S.E.2d 51, 60 (1985).

13. Creech v. Melnik, 347 N.C. 520, 526–27, 495 S.E.2d 907, 911 (1998). *See also* Hutson & Miskimon, *supra* note 4, § 2-5.

by mail. There is a contract, and Lars must pay for the goods sent since he has by implication offered to pay the catalog price when he sent in his order. Moreover, Peter is offering to sell the merchandise for the price listed in the catalog; if Lars orders the merchandise, Peter has to sell it to him for that price.

Consideration

Once the magistrate determines that the parties have entered into a mutual agreement, he or she must decide whether the plaintiff has proven that the agreement is supported by adequate consideration. *Consideration* means something of value— usually money, goods, or services. But consideration can also be a promise to satisfy one party's desire or to forbear from exercising a right to which he or she is legally entitled.[14] Most promises are made with the hope of getting some benefit in return. An agreement based on an exchange of mutual promises is supported by adequate consideration if the performance of both promises would constitute adequate consideration. Consideration requires that the one who makes a promise will gain a benefit or advantage or that the other party will suffer some loss or detriment.[15] "There is consideration if the promisee [one who receives the promise], in return for the promise, does anything legal which he is not bound to do, or refrains from doing anything which he has a right to do, whether there is any actual loss or detriment to him or actual benefit to the promisor [one who makes the promise] or not."[16]

> *Example 11.* Bill promises his son Edward, who is twenty-two years old, $10,000 if Edward will abstain from drinking alcohol for five years. If Edward agrees, a contract has been made. There is an exchange of mutual promises: Bill promises to give Edward $10,000 and in return Edward agrees to give up drinking. Edward (the promisee) suffers a detriment. And Bill, in exchange for Edward's promise to Bill to give up alcohol, gives up something too—$10,000.[17]

> *Example 12.* Jack promises to give Anne $100, and Anne immediately replies, "I accept this offer." This promise does not constitute an enforceable contract, and Anne cannot force Jack to make good his promise, because Anne suffers no detriment to get the payment, nor has she promised anything to benefit the promisor (Jack). A promise to make a gift, although perhaps a moral obligation, cannot be enforced as a contract because without consideration it is not a legal obligation.

> *Example 13.* John borrowed $100 from Ignatius, promising to repay the loan on January 1. Later Ignatius offers to refrain from demanding payment before January 1 for an additional $10. There is no consideration for the extra $10. John had until January 1 to pay the loan anyway; Ignatius

---

14. HUTSON & MISKIMON, *supra* note 4, § 3-14.

15. E.g., Penley v. Penley, 314 N.C. 1, 14, 332 S.E.2d 51, 59 (1985); Carolina Helicopter Corp. v. Cutter Realty Co., 263 N.C. 139, 147, 139 S.E.2d 362, 368 (1964).

16. Spencer v. Bynum, 169 N.C. 119, 123, 85 S.E. 216, 218 (1915); *Penley* at 14, 332 S.E.2d at 59.

17. *See* Greensboro Bank & Trust Co. v. Scott, 184 N.C. 312, 114 S.E. 475 (1922).

has no right to demand early payment. Therefore John gains nothing from Ignatius's offer and Ignatius gives up nothing. John can pay the $100 on January 1.

However, if Ignatius had said, "I'll give you until February 1 to pay the loan for an extra $10," and John had agreed, then the agreement would be binding. Both parties contributed consideration to the modification of the contract. Ignatius gave up his right to collect on January 1 and benefited by receiving an additional $10. John gave up $10 but also benefited by acquiring an additional month pay the loan.

Generally a promise to perform an act that the promisor is already obligated to perform is not consideration.[18]

> **Example 14.** John agrees to build a deck for Joan for $2,500. Joan pays John $1,000 as a partial payment to buy the supplies, and John begins the work. After working for two days, John doesn't come back. Joan calls John, and he says he will come back and finish the work for an additional $500 (in other words for a total of $3,000). Joan, who wants the work completed, says she will pay what is fair (the same would be true if she agreed to pay the additional amount). John comes back and completes the work. Joan pays him $1,500. John sues for the additional $500. John was already legally obligated to build the deck for $2,500, therefore no consideration was given for the additional $500.[19]

The UCC makes a change to the general rule requiring consideration for contract modifications for sales of goods. It provides that an agreement modifying a contract for the sale of goods needs no consideration to be binding;[20] however, the modification must be made in good faith.

Often two parties have an honest dispute about whether a debt exists; or, if they agree that there is a debt, they disagree about the amount. To avoid the expense of a court suit, the parties may agree to a specified sum as the amount one owes the other. This agreement is supported by consideration: the creditor is giving up his or her right to sue, and the debtor is giving up his or her claim to the full amount of the debt. The law encourages compromises of disputes.[21]

> **Example 15.** Beverly gets $100 from Violet; time passes, and Violet demands the return of that sum. Beverly claims (and believes) that the $100 was a gift. The parties decide to settle the matter for $50. The agreement is supported by consideration since each party is giving up some right that she had before the settlement. (Beverly had the right to claim that the money was a gift and that nothing was due, and Violet had the right to claim that the amount due her was $100.)

It should be noted that a genuine dispute must exist as to the amount due. Otherwise the settlement is not supported by consideration and the creditor can demand full payment.

---

18. Virmani v. Presbyterian Health Servs. Corp., 127 N.C. App. 71, 76, 488 S.E.2d 284, 287 (1997).
19. *See* Festerman v. Parker, 32 N.C. 474 (1849).
20. G.S. 25-2-209(1); *See* Bone Int'l, Inc. v. Johnson, 74 N.C. App. 703, 329 S.E.2d 714 (1985).
21. *See* G.S. 1-540, which provides that "In all claims, or money demands, of whatever kind, and howsoever due, where an agreement is made and accepted for a less amount than that demanded or claimed to be due, in satisfaction thereof, the payment of the less amount according to such agreement in compromise of the whole is a full and complete discharge of the same."

Example 16. Sam loans Richard $100. There is no dispute over the amount due, but Richard tells Sam he only has $75 and does not know when he will have the other $25. Sam takes the $75 and says, "I'll take this in full satisfaction of the debt. We'll just wipe the slate clean." Richard still owes Sam $25 because he gave no consideration for making a smaller payment. Sam received nothing that he was not already entitled to. If Sam should later change his mind and demand the $25 from Richard, he would be entitled to it.

Adequacy of Consideration

So long as some consideration is given in exchange for the promise, courts do not ordinarily consider the adequacy of consideration. The fact that one party made a poor deal or gets the worst of the deal to the enrichment of the other does not enable that party to decline to keep his or her promise to sell, buy, or perform. However, on the rare occasions when fraud or unconscionability is involved, the courts will look at adequacy of consideration.[22]

No Consideration Required

Certain contracts do not require proof of consideration to be enforceable. Perhaps the most common type is the sealed instrument. If a contract is reduced to writing and signed under seal, the seal is a substitute for consideration. An instrument is under seal if the word "SEAL" or letters "LS" is found next to the signatures of the parties. However, the UCC provides that a seal is inoperative (that is, has no effect) in contracts for the sale or lease of goods.[23]

What Are the Contract Terms?

Terms That Must Be Specifically Agreed On

As mentioned earlier, in the past contracts had to include all important or material terms to be enforceable. This continues to be true of contracts for services. The UCC, however, reduces the formality of contracts formation by providing that a contract for the sale of goods may be made in any manner that is sufficient to show an agreement; some terms may be left open "if the parties have intended to make a contract and there is a reasonably certain basis for giving an appropriate remedy.[24]

Determining the Contract's Terms

A contract for the sale of goods is binding even if the acceptance adds new terms or varies the terms of the offer as long as it is clear that the parties mutually agree to the contract. Whether the contract includes the additional terms depends on who the parties to the contract are. If either party is not a merchant, the additional terms are considered proposals to modify the contract and do not become part of the contract unless the parties so agree. However, if both

---

22. *See* discussion on unconscionability clauses at p. 76.

23. G.S. 25-2-203; 25-2A-203. G.S. 25-2-203: "The affixing of a seal to a writing evidencing a contract for the sale or an offer to buy or sell goods does not constitute the writing a sealed instrument and the law with respect to sealed instruments does not apply to such a contract or offer."

24. G.S. 25-2-204.

parties are merchants, the additional terms may become part of the contract unless (1) the offer states that acceptance is limited to the terms of the offer; (2) the additional terms materially alter the contract; or (3) the offeror notifies the offeree of his or her objection to the additional terms.[25] The UCC defines a "merchant" as one who deals in goods of the kind involved in the transaction or holds himself or herself out as knowledgeable about the goods involved in the transaction.[26]

> **Example 17.** (assuming the same facts as Example 8, in which two merchants entered into a contract to buy and sell 1,000 gallons of house paint) The seller's written acceptance adds provisions not found in the buyer's written offer; the new terms fix a reasonable time limit for complaints and require the parties to submit disputes to arbitration. The seller's form also contains a clause limiting the warranty of the quality of the goods, whereas the buyer's form required a full warranty. Do the new clauses in the seller's acceptance become terms of the contract?
>
> The clause fixing a reasonable time for registering complaints becomes part of the contract because both parties are merchants and the term is a minor addition to the contract that does not change the basis of the bargain. However, the arbitration and limitation-of-warranty clauses do not become part of the contract because they materially alter it.

If a buyer and seller have a continuing relationship, their usual pattern of behavior (called *course of dealing*) may supply the unstated terms or give meaning to unclear provisions. Similarly, when there is a normal practice in the trade (referred to as the *usage of trade*), that practice may be used in interpreting the contract.[27] The UCC itself supplies some terms—which apply unless the parties agree otherwise—relating to price, delivery of goods in single lots, place and time of delivery, and time for payment.[28]

In contracts for the sale of goods, parties sometimes come to court with evidence showing that a contract was made but certain terms were left open. If those terms are not specified in the UCC, the magistrate should determine what is fair and reasonable based on the normal custom and usage in the trade, prior dealings between the parties, and market price quotations.

In contracts for services that omit important terms, the courts also will find that reasonable terms are implied in those contracts when it is clear that the parties intended to enter into a contract and understood that the law would supply the omitted term.[29] For example, when a time for performance is not specified, the courts have inferred that the contract implies a reasonable time.[30]

---

25. G.S. 25-2-207(2).
26. G.S. 25-2-104.
27. G.S. 25-1-303.
28. G.S. 25-2-305, 307 through 310.
29. HUTSON & MISKIMON, *supra* note 4, § 2-30.
30. *E.g.,* Digh v. Nationwide Mut. Fire Ins. Co., 187 N.C. App. 725, 654 S.E.2d 37 (2007); Phillips & Jordan Inv. Corp. v. Ashblue Co., 86 N.C. App. 186, 357 S.E.2d (1987).

However, a contract for the sale of real property must be in writing, be signed by all parties, contain an adequate description of the real property, recite a sum of consideration, and contain all key terms and conditions of the agreement.[31]

The party seeking to enforce a contract has the burden of establishing and proving the terms of the contract. When the contract is in writing, the writing itself is the best evidence of the terms. In fact, when the contract is in writing, the parties may not present evidence of prior or contemporaneous oral agreements that differ from the terms of the written contract. This is known as the *parol evidence rule*.[32] As mentioned above, the UCC modifies the parol evidence rule in contracts for the sale of goods by allowing oral testimony of normal custom and usage in the trade to be used to explain or supplement the terms of the contract[33] and to allow evidence of consistent additional terms.[34] If, however, the parties reached an oral or written modification of the agreement *after* the written contract was created, the parties may introduce evidence about that.[35] An agreement to modify a contract for the sale of goods is binding without consideration;[36] but the modification of a contract for services must be supported by consideration to be enforceable.[37]

Many contracts are never reduced to writing; they are oral. These contracts are just as valid as written contracts, but the evidence of their terms will be oral testimony and the party seeking to enforce the contract must prove the terms of the oral contract that he or she is seeking to enforce.

Warranties

Contracts may contain warranty terms. In most contracts, warranties will not be implied as terms; they must be specifically enumerated—that is, they must be express warranties. In contracts for the sale of goods under the UCC, however, the magistrate must be aware of the possibility of implied as well as express warranties.

Express Warranties

An *express warranty* is an affirmation of fact or promise by the seller as to the quality of the goods. Secondhand goods as well as new products may be the subject of an express warranty, and the seller may be any person—not only merchants.[38] For instance, a retailer who is selling a water pump states to the buyer, "The pump is guaranteed to pump 300 gallons of water per minute." This statement is an express warranty; if the pump does not pump this much water, the buyer can sue the seller for breach of contract. However, as the seller's opinions or a mere commendation of the goods does not create a warranty, the magistrate must distinguish between

---

31. Rawls & Assoc. v. Hurst, 144 N.C. App. 286, 290, 550 S.E.2d 219, 223 (2001).

32. G.S. 25-2-202. See section "Parol Evidence Rule" below for a more complete discussion of the rule.

33. G.S. 25-2-202.

34. First Commerce Bank v. Dockery, 171 N.C. App. 297, 303, 615 S.E.2d 314, 318 (2005).

35. Acme Mfg. Co. v. McPhail, 181 N.C. 205, 106 S.E. 672 (1921).

36. G.S. 25-2-209(1).

37. Watson Electric Constr. Co. v. Summit Companies, 160 N.C. App 647, 655, 587 S.E.2d 87, 94 (2003); Brumley v. Mallard, 154 N.C. App. 563, 567–68, 575 S.E.2d 35, 38 (2002).

38. Pake v. Byrd, 55 N.C. App. 551, 552, 286 S.E.2d 588, 589 (1982).

express warranties and "puffing of wares." Statements like "this is the best blender ever made," or "this is wonderful lotion and will beautify your hands" are sales talk or puffing and not express warranties; hence the buyer cannot sue for breach of contract if the product does not live up to the commendation. The line between puffing and warranting often is difficult to determine; however the more specific the statement, the more likely it is to be a warranty.[39] "The distinction between an affirmation or a description . . . from mere sales talk, or opinion, or puffing is so hazy that the courts in the final analysis will often rely on their own sense of fair-play, thereby evaluating the intentions of the parties to create an express warranty."[40]

A second way for a seller of goods to create an express warranty is by showing a buyer a sample or model of the goods that leads the buyer to believe that the product he or she is buying will conform to the sample or model.

> **Example 18.** Susanna goes to Best Buy to purchase a refrigerator. The salesman shows her several refrigerators on the floor. She selects a Maytag refrigerator that has a water and ice dispenser on the front of the door. When the refrigerator arrives it looks like the one on the floor except it does not have the external water and ice dispenser. Best Buy has breached its express warranty that the refrigerator delivered would be the same as the sample it showed Susanna.

In neither type of express warranty must the specific words *warranty* or *guarantee* be used; nor must the seller have a specific intent to make a warranty.[41]

For a seller's statements of facts or promises about the quality of goods sold to form an express warranty, the plaintiff must show that these statements were part of the basis of the bargain. The problem is in determining what the language "basis of the bargain" means. If the affirmation of fact is given while a bargain is being struck, no reliance on the statement need be shown.[42] If the written contract refers to written documentation that is found separately and that documentation includes representations about the product, the documentation becomes part of the contract.[43] But what if the warranty is given after the sale? North Carolina case law indicates that postsale affirmations or promises do not create a warranty.[44]

> As the essential ingredient for this determination [creating a warranty] is whether the seller's affirmation became a basis of the bargain, we may look to certain objective criteria. The first is whether the statements were made before or after the sale was consummated. The second is whether the buyer knew of the seller's statements. Finally, where the buyer relies on his own skill and judgment,

---

39. Russell G. Donaldson, *Affirmations or Representations Made After the Sale is Closed as a Basis of Warranty Under UCC § 2-313(1)(a)*, 47 A.L.R. 4th 200 (1986) at § 2[b].

40. *Pake* at 553, 286 S.E.2d at 589–90.

41. G.S. 25-2-313(2).

42. *See* G.S. 25-2-313, Official Comment No. 3.

43. Smart Online, Inc. v. Opensite Tech., Inc., 2003 W.L. 21555316, 1 U.C.C. Rep. Serv.2d 47 (2003) (unpublished business court decision).

44. Byrd Motor Lines, Inc. v. Dunlop Tire & Rubber Corp., 63 N.C. App. 292, 298, 304 S.E.2d 773, 777–78 (1983); Pake v. Byrd, 55 N.C. App. 551, 286 S.E.2d 588 (1982).

thereby essentially disclaiming any warranty, the seller's statements cannot be viewed as the basis of the bargain.[45]

That the affirmation was not part of the basis of the bargain was clear to the court in a case in which the seller of tires to a trucking company recommended several changes to correct problems with the tires over two years after the buyer started buying tires from the defendant.[46] But the answer might not have been so clear if the affirmation had not been so far removed from the sales agreement. For example, what if the seller's warranty was in the box with the product sold? Apparently courts from other states disagree on the answer: some say no warranty exists. On the other hand, one could argue that the consumer bargain must be construed more broadly and that the question is whether the language used in the warranty rather than the precise time the buyer reads it make it part of the bargain.[47]

Implied Warranties

In addition to an express warranty, the UCC also recognizes two implied warranties—the warranty of merchantability and the warranty of fitness for a particular purpose—unless the seller expressly disclaims such warranties.

A *warranty of merchantability* means that the seller guarantees that the goods are of such generally good quality that they (1) are fit for the ordinary purpose intended, (2) pass without objection in the trade, (3) are adequately contained and packaged, and (4) conform to any promises of fact made on the container or label.[48] For example, a pair of running shoes that fall apart when the buyer runs two miles the day after purchasing them would not be fit for the ordinary purpose for which they were intended. Likewise, an order for 10,000 widgets in which 5 percent of the widgets are unusable might pass without objection in the widget trade, where it is expected that up to 7 percent of the widgets delivered may be imperfect.

The warranty of merchantability requires no affirmative statement on the part of the seller: it is implied, even if the seller says nothing or praises the product to the sky. However, only merchants who regularly sell the type of product involved in the transaction are subject to this implied warranty.[49] A neighbor selling a used car does not make an implied warranty of merchantability but a used-car dealer would. For purposes of the warranty of merchantability only, definition of the word *sale* includes the serving of food or drink for value;[50] so, for example, a foreign object in the food served in a restaurant would be breach of implied warranty.

The *warranty of fitness for a particular purpose* is an implied warranty that the goods will be fit for their intended purpose if (1) the seller has reason to know, at the time of contracting, the particular purpose for which the goods are required and (2) that the buyer is relying on the seller's skill or judgment to select or furnish suitable goods.[51] Again no affirmative statement by

45. *Pake* at 553, 286 S.E.2d at 590.
46. *Byrd Motor Lines* at 298, 304 S.E.2d at 777–78.
47. WHITE & SUMMERS, *supra* note 10, § 9-5.
48. G.S. 25-2-314.
49. G.S. 25-2-314.
50. G.S. 25-2-314(1).
51. G.S. 25-2-315.

the seller is necessary; the warranty is implied and arises by virtue of the buyer's trust. The warranty of fitness for a particular purpose applies to all sellers, not just to merchants.

> **Example 19.** Andrew, a slick used-car salesman, sold Mrs. Lilac, a little old lady with no knowledge of mechanics, a "lemon" for $300. The contract was not in writing. Andrew, using high-pressure tactics, said: "This car has been thoroughly overhauled from top to bottom. We completely rebuilt the motor. You'll probably get 20 miles to the gallon because of the new carburetor, and it won't use much oil because of new rings and valves."

None of these things Andrew had stated as facts—the car has been overhauled, has a rebuilt motor, new carburetor, and new rings and valves—had in fact been done. Formerly, under the common law, Mrs. Lilac got exactly what she bought—a lemon—plus a good lesson in the art of buying a used car. Today she is protected by the UCC, which requires a seller to live up to all express warranties. Mrs. Lilac may sue for damages arising out of the breach of warranty.

> **Example 20.** Steve orders lunch at Sarah's cafe. He eats some of it and gets sick because the food is spoiled. Steve can sue Sarah for breach of the implied warranty of merchantability because Sarah is a merchant and the product was not fit for its ordinary purpose.

> **Example 21.** Hazel sells refrigeration equipment. Mortimer, a butcher, comes to Hazel and explains that he is opening his first butcher shop and needs a refrigeration unit large enough to freeze all the meat in a large locker he is installing. Mortimer says that he doesn't have any idea what size unit he needs and asks Hazel to figure it out. Hazel measures the locker and decided that a 13,000 BTU refrigeration unit would be "just the thing." She sells it to Mortimer for $5,000 and installs it herself. Two weeks later the unit, which was too small for the locker, burns out and all the meat in the locker is spoiled. Hazel breached the warranty of fitness for a particular purpose—it was clear that Mortimer was relying on Hazel, an expert, to provide a cooling unit adequate for that particular locker. The warranty of merchantability would not have been breached because the refrigeration unit cooled property; it simply was not adequate for cooling a locker of the specific size to the required temperature. Although Hazel is a merchant, the warranty of fitness for a particular purpose would also apply if she were a private seller.

Exclusion or Disclaimer of Warranties

Express Warranties

Sellers may exclude or disclaim warranties by specifying that there are no warranties in the contract. If the seller gives the buyer an oral warranty and then the parties sign a written contract that excludes all express warranties, the parol evidence rule prevents the buyer from introducing evidence of the prior oral warranty because it would change the terms of the written contract. But if the parties sign a written contract excluding express warranties and the seller later gives the buyer an oral warranty, that warranty can be considered a modification of the earlier contract and may be introduced.[52] Although in a breach of warranty suit the rule prohibits intro-

---

52. Bone Int'l, Inc. v. Johnson, 74 N.C. App. 703, 706, 329 S.E.2d 714, 716–17 (1985). *See also* Muther-Ballenger v. Griffin Elec. Consultants, Inc., 100 N.C. App. 505, 511, 397 S.E.2d 247, 250 (1990).

duction of evidence of an oral express warranty modifying the terms of a later written contract, that evidence can be introduced to support a claim of fraud or unfair trade practice.[53]

What if the contract for the sale of goods (either written or oral) has both words creating an express warranty and words tending to negate the warranty? The magistrate must read the two provisions as consistent with each other when that is reasonable to do so; but to the extent that it is unreasonable to construe the two together, the provision excluding the warranty must be ignored.[54]

> *Example 22.* Herman buys a used BMW from Reynolds Used Cars, Inc. While negotiating the sale, Herman asks the sales manager whether the car had ever been involved in an accident. The manager replies, "No, the car has never been involved in an auto accident," which is an express warranty that the car has not been in an accident. Herman buys the BMW, signing a written purchase agreement indicating that the car was being sold without any warranties. Three weeks later Herman discovers that the car had been damaged in an accident and that it would cost $2,500 to repair it. Herman sues Reynolds Used Cars for unfair and deceptive practices. If Herman had sued for breach of warranty, the express warranty could not have been considered, but it can be considered to determine whether Reynolds Used Cars committed an unfair trade practice.
>
> If the written contract had provided that the car had not been in an accident and a later provision disclaimed all warranties, the express warranty would be enforceable.

A specific statute provides that if a seller gives an express warranty in a consumer credit sale, that warranty may not be waived;[55] but it is not clear whether that statute overrides the parol evidence rule in a breach of warranty claim or whether the only remedy is an unfair trade practice claim. The only case in which violation of the statute was raised was in the context of an unfair trade practice claim.[56]

Implied Warranties

A merchant may exclude implied warranties by explicit language. To exclude the warranty of merchantability the merchant must make specific reference to merchantability in the exclusion; if the exclusion is in writing, the exclusion provision must be conspicuous; that is, it must be written so that a reasonable person (the buyer) should notice it.[57] A printed heading in capital letters or language in the body of the form set in larger or contrasting type is conspicuous.

A seller may also exclude the implied warranty of fitness for a particular purpose, but only in writing, and, here too, the exclusion must be conspicuous. The statement does not need to

---

53. Torrance v. AS & L Motors, Ltd., 119 N.C. App. 552, 459 S.E.2d 67 (1995) (Oral warranty that vehicle had not been in an accident followed by written disclaimer of express warranties constituted unfair and deceptive trade practice.).

54. G.S. 25-2-316(1).

55. G.S. 25A-20. *See* below, section "Retail Installment Sales Act," which includes a definition of *consumer credit sale.*

56. *Cf.* Simmons v. C.W. Myers Trading Post, Inc., 56 N.C. App. 549, 290 S.E.2d 710; *modified,* 307 N.C. 122, 296 S.E.2d 294 (1982).

57. G.S. 25-1-201(10).

refer to the warranty by name and may simply refer to "implied warranties." The following is an example of an explicit disclaimer:

> EXCLUSIONS OF WARRANTIES, NO WARRANTIES. The implied warranties of MER-CHANTABILITY and fitness for a particular purpose and all other warranties, express or implied, are EXCLUDED from this transaction and shall not apply to the goods sold.[58]

Another common method of excluding implied warranties is by using expressions like "as is" or "with all faults" or other language in common usage that makes it plain there are no warranties.[59]

> **Example 23.** Tamika goes to Acme Appliances to purchase a refrigerator. There is a large sticker stating "SOLD AS IS" on the front of the used refrigerator she decides to buy. Two weeks after purchasing the refrigerator, the compressor dies. The implied warranty of merchantability was excluded, and therefore Tamika is stuck with the refrigerator and does not have a claim for breach of warranty against Acme.

A second method of waiving implied warranties occurs when the buyer inspects the goods before buying or refuses to do so at the seller's request. In either case, the buyer waives the implied warranties only to the extent that any defects are discoverable through inspection.

> **Example 24.** Roberto buys a used car from Fast Eddie Used Cars. Fast Eddie makes no statements about the quality of the car but asks Roberto to look over the car and drive it for at least twenty minutes before finalizing the sale. Roberto looks over the car and then drives it around the neighborhood and on the highway. He returns and purchases the car. Three weeks later, Roberto discovers that he needs to replace the tires because they are oversized and that the transmission needs replacing. He believes that Fast Eddie has breached the warranty of merchantability. Roberto's inspection of the vehicle should have discovered the oversized tires, so no warranty of merchantability applies to them. However, because the transmission problem was latent and would not be apparent to an ordinary layperson while driving the car, Roberto's inspection of the car would not waive the warranty of merchantability on the transmission.

A third situation in which implied warranties are waived occurs when the prior course of dealing or course of performance between seller and buyer or the usage of trade suggests that both parties assume that exclusion or waiver of warranty is part of the contract.[60] Essentially, the statute says, the parties know best what they mean when they enter into a contract, and their own performance shows that meaning best.[61] So, for example, the court found that warranties were excluded when the buyer of a truck who sued for breach of implied warranty of fitness for a particular purpose testified that the truck was purchased "as it was" at the time of sale even though the written contract did not disclaim warranties.[62]

---

58. WHITE & SUMMERS, *supra* note 10, § 12-5.

59. G.S. 25-2-316(3).

60. G.S. 25-2-316(3)(c). See subsection "Determining the Contract's Terms," above.

61. WHITE & SUMMERS, *supra* note 10, § 1-J, at 39.

62. Robinson v. Branch Moving & Storage Co., 28 N.C. App. 244, 221 S.E.2d 81 (1976).

Is the Contract Enforceable?

Many factors can affect the enforceability of a contract. The law uses three different terms in describing these factors. Sometimes a contract is said to be *void*, which means that the agreement was never validly assented to, lacked consideration, or violates a statute.[63] Void means that even if all parties to the contract want to have it enforced, a court cannot enforce it because there is no contract. In other words, factors such as the absence of consideration, mistake, and illegality touch on the validity of the contract's formation. For example, when Joe promises to give Jane his car, there is no contract because there is no consideration.

Some factors make a contract *voidable*, which means that although a valid agreement has been formed, one party is permitted to avoid it. The most common reason for voidable contracts is lack of capacity to consent to the contract on the part of one of the parties. Still other factors, such as the statute of frauds, statute of limitations, or unconscionability, provide defenses to enforcement of a contract. A final group of factors, including impossibility, may excuse a party's nonperformance of a contractual duty.

A special topic to be considered under this heading is the issue of agency or contracts that are made on behalf of a third party by his or her (alleged) representative.

Defenses to Formation

As mentioned above, the absence of consideration in contract formation renders a contract void. The illegality of the subject matter of the contract and a mistake made by both parties also make a contract void.

Illegality

Illegality arises when either the consideration or the subject matter of a contract violates federal or state law or public policy. Contracts that are illegal are void.

> *Example 25.* Jeff offers Johnny $1,000 to lie in court and testify that he did not see Jeff's wife Bunny steal a diamond necklace from a jewelry store. This contract is void because it suborns perjury.

> *Example 26.* Jeff sues Johnny for $250. At trial Jeff indicates that he sold Johnny some marijuana and Johnny did not pay him the agreed-upon price of $250.[64] This contract is void because it is a contract for the sale of illegal drugs.

Mistake

Sometimes a party will argue that the contract is void because it contains or is based on a mistake. A mistake will not excuse a party from performance under the contract unless it is a mutual mistake regarding the subject matter of the contract. One party may be mistaken in his or her estimate of the market value of the item purchased or of the effect of the contract on

---

63. Hutson & Miskimon, *supra* note 4, § 1-7.
64. Believe it or not, a magistrate in Cumberland County had this case many years ago.

his or her business, but this kind of mistake does not make the contract void. If both the buyer and seller are mistaken about the actual subject matter of what is being sold, however, they are consenting to an imaginary set of facts and there is no meeting of the minds on the contract. The party seeking to avoid the contract must prove that (1) the mistake concerns a past or existing material fact; (2) this fact enters into and forms a basis of the contract; and (3) both parties have the same mistaken belief.[65]

> ***Example 27.*** Beverly sees a stone in Bob's shop and asks what kind of stone it is. Bob says he is not sure, but it is either a topaz or a diamond. Beverly likes the stone and wants to buy it. Bob charges her $500, which is more than a topaz would cost and less than a diamond would cost. Beverly takes the stone to a jeweler who tells her it is a diamond worth $1,000. May Bob cancel the contract and demand return of the stone? No. The parties were not mistaken about the subject matter of the contract; they entered the contract knowing that the stone was either a topaz or a diamond, and the price was set accordingly. Bob, in accepting $500, took a risk that the stone was a diamond and worth more than $500, and Beverly took the risk that it was a topaz and worth less than $500.

> ***Example 28.*** Nancy runs a small gift and souvenir shop on the Cherokee reservation. Angela, a tourist, discovers among Nancy's merchandise an odd stone priced at $1 (both Nancy and Angela consider the stone worthless except as a souvenir from the reservation). Angela goes home and immediately shows it to a friend, a jeweler, who tells her that the stone is a gem worth $10,000. This fact is widely publicized, and Nancy reads about it. May Nancy cancel the contract and demand return of the stone on the basis of mistake? Yes. Both parties were mistaken as to the actual subject matter of the contract. In this case, they both thought it was a worthless stone when in fact it was a valuable gem.

Lack of Consent Defenses

Consent is essential to the validity of any contract. If a party can show that he or she did not consent to enter into a contract or that he or she did not have the legal capacity to give consent, the agreement will not be enforced against that party. A related issue involving consent concerns agency: that is, a situation in which a party consents (either expressly or impliedly) to have an agent represent him or her in contracting with a third party.

Lack of Consent

A party who has entered into an agreement as a result of fraud (deception by the other party as to a material fact) or duress (undue coercion) is not considered to have consented to the agreement and can avoid the contract. In the case of fraud, the party has consented only because he or she has been deceived; and in the case of duress, he or she has not consented at all.

To avoid a contract on the basis of fraud, the injured party must prove (1) that the other party made a false representation of or concealed a material fact; (2) that the false representation or concealment was intended to deceive; (3) that the injured party was in fact deceived by

---

65. McKay v. McIntosh, 270 N.C. 69, 73, 153 S.E.2d 800, 804 (1967).

the false representation or concealment; (4) that the injured party entered into the contract as a result of his or her reliance on the false representation or concealment; and (5) that that reliance was reasonable.[66] Fraud can also occur when one party to the contract tricks the other party into signing the contract by inducing him or her to sign a document that is different from the agreed-to document.[67]

Duress occurs when a wrongful act, threat, or coercion is used to force a person to enter into a contract against his or her will.

Example 29. Terry knows that his elderly uncle, Sam, is having trouble taking care of his financial affairs. Terry tells Sam that he would be happy to take care of Sam's financial matters, but Sam must sign a power of attorney to allow Terry to act for him. Sam is thankful for the offer and says he will sign the papers. Terry has Sam sign a promissory note instead of a power of attorney. Sam may cancel the promissory note because he was deceived by Terry's fraud.

Example 30. Keith and Rachel enter into a contract for Keith to build a house for Rachel. One week before the scheduled closing, Keith demands that Rachel meet with him. During the two-hour meeting Keith confines Rachel in his office while a co-worker guards the door. Keith accuses Rachel of fraud and informs her that he will not sign the waiver of lien allowing the closing to go forward unless Rachel agrees to pay him a substantially greater amount than they had agreed in the contract. According to Rachel, Keith tells her they can settle the matter in court, which would mean that the closing would be cancelled, or Rachel can sign a promissory note and deed of trust for the additional amount. Rachel, who had already given notice to vacate her rental unit, signs the note and deed of trust believing that it was the only way she could close on the house. The signing of the note and deed of trust occurred under duress—Rachel's consent was not of her own free will.[68]

Minors and Mental Incompetents

Minors (those under the age of eighteen) and persons who are mentally incompetent are legally incapable of consenting to a contract (that is, they lack capacity to contract). The courts define mental competence as follows:

A person has sufficient mental capacity to enter a contract if he is possessed of the ability to understand the nature of the act in which he is engaged and its scope and effect, or its nature and consequences, not that he should be able to act wisely or discreetly, nor to drive a good bargain, but that he should be in such possession of his faculties as to enable him to know at least what he is doing and to contract understandingly.[69]

---

66. *See* "Contracts—Issue of Formation—Defense of Fraud" N.C.P.I.—Civil 501.45 (May 2004), NORTH CAROLINA PATTERN JURY INSTRUCTIONS, GENERAL CIVIL VOLUME.

67. Nixon v. Nixon, 260 N.C. 251, 132 S.E.2d 590 (1963).

68. *See* Radford v. Keith, 160 N.C. App. 41, 584 S.E.2d 815 (2003).

69. Ludwig v. Hart, 40 N.C. App. 188, 191, 252 S.E.2d 270, 273 (1979).

A lack of that ability is mental incompetence. A person does not have to have been adjudicated incompetent to lack capacity; however an adjudication raises a presumption that the person lacks the capacity to contract.[70]

A minor or person who is mentally incompetent can avoid contracts they enter into with others. This rule is rather one-sided, because the minor or incompetent can, at his or her option, enforce the contract against the other party; thus the contract is not absolutely void but is voidable only at the option of the party who lacks capacity to contract.

> **Example 31.** Xavier, age 17, is a college freshman far from home and parental supervision. He contracts with Hank, an auto dealer, to buy a $7,000 sports car that has to be specially ordered because he wants all the extras plus pink paint. A week later the car arrives, and Xavier refuses to take it. Hank can't find another buyer for the car. Can Hank successfully sue Xavier? No. Xavier is a minor and can avoid the contract.
>
> However, if Xavier had gone to pick up to the car and Hank would not deliver it, Xavier could have successfully forced Hank to perform his duties under the contract since the contract is voidable only at the option of the party who lacks capacity.

Exceptions to Minor's or Mental Incompetent's Lack of Capacity. There are, however, some exceptions to the ability of minors and incompetents to avoid a contract.

The first exception to the general rule that minors and incompetents lack capacity to contract is that such a person does have capacity to consent to *a contract for the provision of necessities* (food, clothing, shelter, medical care, and such articles of property and services as are reasonably necessary to enable to him or her to earn a living). Such a contract may not be avoided.[71] The minor or mentally incompetent person is not responsible for the contract value of the necessities but only for the reasonable value of the goods and services involved.

> **Example 32.** Sixteen-year-old Whit seeks help from ServiTemps, an employment agency, in finding a job. He tells the ServiTemps representative that he desperately needs a job to support his mother and siblings. He signs a contract with the agency agreeing to give it 10 percent of any paycheck he earns with one of their employers for the first three months of his employment. Whit gets a permanent job with one of ServiTemps' employers after his first interview. Feeling that ServiTemp expended very little energy in helping him obtain employment, Whit refuses to honor his contract obligation.
>
> Can ServiTemp enforce the contract? In a similar case, the North Carolina Supreme Court held that the contract could be enforced as one for necessities.[72] Whit would only be held liable, however, for the reasonable value of the agency's services which the magistrate would establish based on evidence presented.

Another situation in which a contract cannot be avoided is when there is *statutory authorization* for the minor or incompetent to enter into a binding contract. For example, a specific statute allows seventeen-year-olds to enter into written contracts for loans for postsecondary

---

70. *In re* Pendergrass's Will, 251 N.C. 737, 745, 112 S.E.2d 562, 568 (1960).
71. Gastonia Pers. Corp. v. Rogers, 276 N.C. 279, 172 S.E.2d 19 (1970).
72. *Id.*

education, and another allows minors to contract with banks for deposit accounts or safe-deposit boxes.[73]

The third exception involves *emancipated minors*—that is minors who are considered adults in the eyes of the law. Emancipation can occur in only one of two ways: first, a minor may be declared emancipated by a judge;[74] and second, a minor may become emancipated by virtue of marriage.[75] In both instances, G.S. 7B-3507 specifies that the minor has the same ability to make contracts as an adult.[76]

The law treats minors and mental incompetents differently in one important way. It places an absolute burden on a person entering into a contract to make sure that the person with whom he or she is contracting is not a minor. Even if the minor looks eighteen or older or falsely represents his or her age, the minor can avoid the contract.[77] However, a different rule applies to mentally incompetent persons, perhaps because it is not as easy to determine whether a person meets that criterion. If the party seeking to avoid the contract proves that he or she lacked the mental capacity to enter into the contract, the contract may still be enforced. In this situation the party seeking to enforce it must prove that (1) he or she did not know or should not have reasonably known of the other party's mental incapacity; (2) he or she gave full and fair consideration for the agreement (in other words the court looks at the adequacy of consideration) and took no unfair advantage of the incompetent person; and (3) the incompetent has not restored the consideration nor made adequate compensation for it.[78]

Example 33. Joseph goes to Friendly Furniture Store and states that he needs a dining room table to seat six to eight people. Fred Friendly sells him a table for $500. Joseph pays $100 down and agrees to pay the rest of the money over the next six months with interest at 1.5 percent per month. Joseph makes no payments, and Friendly Furniture sues him for $400. At the trial, Joseph's wife testifies that Joseph was adjudicated incompetent about a year before the purchase and she was appointed his guardian. She indicates that she cannot return the table because Joseph told her he had given it away to someone he did not know. Fred counters that he had no way of knowing that Joseph did not have the capacity to contract; they carried on a normal conversation regarding the purchase. Moreover he gave Joseph a 40 percent discount on the list price—which is what he does for all his customers—and $500 is a fair price for the table. If the magistrate believes Fred's evidence, he or she will enforce the contract.

73. G.S. 116-174.1; G.S. 53-43.5.
74. G.S. 7B, Art. 35.
75. G.S. 7B-3509.
76. At common law, emancipation by marriage relieved the minor's parent of responsibilities toward the minor but did not remove the minor's incapacity to contract for nonnecessaries. Kowalski v. Liska, 397 N.E.2d 39 (Ill. 1979). *See* Gastonia Pers. Corp. v. Rogers, 276 N.C. 279, 172 S.E.2d 19 (1970); Eubanks v. Eubanks, 273 N.C. 189, 194, 159 S.E.2d 562, 566 (1968); G.S. 39-13.2 (married minor can execute note, deed, etc. with regard to real or personal property held with spouse if spouse is adult).
77. Greensboro Morris Plan Co. v. Palmer, 185 N.C. 109, 116 S.E. 261 (1923); Gillis v. Whitley's Discount Auto Sales, Inc., 70 N.C. App. 270, 319 S.E.2d 661 (1984).
78. Carawan v. Clark, 219 N.C. 214, 216, 13 S.E.2d 237, 238 (1941).

A minor who avoids a contract that the other party has already performed, is obligated to return any consideration that he or she received and still possesses. However, if the minor no longer has the goods, he or she need not return them. If the minor has given money to the other party, the minor is entitled to recover the entire amount paid.

> **Example 34.** Sixteen-year-old Billy goes to Frank's Used Cars the day after he gets his driver's license and buys a 1998 Corvette. He pays $1,000 down and signs a note for an additional $3,000. Two days later while Billy is seeing whether the car will really go over 100 miles an hour, he loses control and ends up in a ditch. Fortunately, he is not seriously injured, but the car is totaled. Billy has the Corvette towed to Frank's Used Cars and sues Frank for $1,000 when Frank refuses to return his money. Frank counterclaims for $3,000 because Billy has defaulted on the note. Billy is entitled to void the contract and recover the consideration he paid. Not only that, he only needs to return the wrecked car and is not liable for the damage.

The final exception to the general rule that minors may avoid contracts they make occurs after the minor becomes an adult and is called *ratification*. A minor may disaffirm a contract before he or she becomes eighteen or within a reasonable time after reaching eighteen;[79] but if he or she fails to disaffirm the contract within a reasonable time after becoming an adult, the contract will be treated as if the person has ratified (approved) it. An unconditional promise to pay after reaching the age of majority ratifies the contract,[80] as does retaining possession of the property and making payments or receiving payments after reaching eighteen.[81]

> **Example 35.** Sally, who was then seventeen, bought a stereo set and sound system from her neighbor, Mrs. Tilley. She agreed to pay Mrs. Tilley $100 a month for six months for the equipment. One month later Sally turned eighteen without making any payments. Mrs. Tilley asked her to pay, and Sally replied she would pay whenever it was convenient for her to do so. Three months later Sally paid $100 to Mrs. Tilley, but then did not pay any more. Mrs. Tilley sued Sally for the remaining $500. Is Mrs. Tilley entitled to recover the money?
>
> Yes. Although Sally was entitled to void her contract with Mrs. Tilley before she turned eighteen and for a reasonable period thereafter, when Sally made the $100 payment after she turned eighteen she ratified the contract. Her promise to pay whenever it was convenient did not ratify the contract because it was not an unconditional promise to pay.

Defenses to Enforcement

Arguments falling into this category focus on a defect in the contract that makes it legally unenforceable. However, these defenses are *affirmative defenses*, meaning that the plaintiff is not required to prove the negative of nonviolation—that is, that the plaintiff did not do some act that would negate the contract; rather, the defendant has the burden of proving that it is the plaintiff who violated the provision.[82]

---

79. Baggett v. Jackson, 160 N.C. 26, 31–32, 76 S.E. 86, 88 (1912).
80. Bresee v. Stanly, 119 N.C. 278, 25 S.E. 870 (1896); Armfield v. Tate, 29 N.C. 258 (1847).
81. Dewey v. Burbank, 77 N.C. 259 (1877).
82. G.S. 1A-1, Rule 8(c).

Statute of Frauds

Most oral contracts are valid, but certain agreements are unenforceable unless they are supported by written evidence. The purpose of this statutory requirement is to prevent fraud by requiring the parties to present some concrete evidence showing the existence of their contract and its terms. This requirement decreases the problems of proof involved in establishing the existence of an oral contract.

In North Carolina the following contracts must be in writing and signed by the parties to the contract:

1. Any contract for the sale of land and any lease of property for a period longer than three years[83]
2. A promise to pay the debt of another person[84]
3. All retail consumer credit installment contracts (dated, and signed by the buyer)[85]
4. All contracts for the sale of goods costing $500 or more (with one important exception)[86]

The important exception to the requirement that a contract for the sale of goods costing $500 or more must be written to be enforceable is for goods that have already been accepted or paid for or are specially manufactured and not suitable for sale in the ordinary course of the seller's business.[87]

> **Example 36.** If Steven contracts to sell his car to Mack for $300 cash, the courts will enforce this contract regardless of whether there is a bill of sale or some other writing proving that the contract exists. It must be kept in mind that although an oral contract for a cash sale of goods for a price of less than $500 is enforceable under state law, the existence of such a contract must still be proven. Thus, to enforce the contract, Steven would have to testify to the terms of the contract; the magistrate would find the testimony either credible or implausible and so determine whether the parties had entered into a contract.
>
> If Steven contracts to sell his car for $500 and fails to have Mack sign a written contract stating the terms of their agreement, he cannot later get a court to enforce the terms of the contract should Mack decide not to buy the car. However, if Steven gives the car to Mack, who accepts it, Mack is bound by the oral contract. Similarly, if Mack gives Steven $500, Steven is bound by the oral contract.

Parol Evidence Rule

In conjunction with the law requiring certain contracts to be written, the parol evidence rule requires that writing to accurately reflect the terms of the contract. Therefore the law forbids the parties to introduce into evidence any agreement between the parties to a written contract made

83. G.S. 22-2.
84. G.S. 22-1.
85. G.S. 25A-28.
86. G.S. 25-2-201.
87. *Id.*

before or at the time the contract was executed that varies or contradicts the terms of the writing. The law considers the written contract to be more reliable than the recollection of either party as to what the two parties agreed to. However, the law does allow the parties to introduce evidence of additional terms on which the written version is silent, as such evidence does not vary or contradict the writing but simply amplifies it to show more fully what the parties actually intended in their agreement. The law also allows additional evidence to explain ambiguities in the written contract. Finally, the parol evidence rule does not apply to contract modifications (either oral or written) agreed to after the written contract is signed.

> ***Example 37.*** Roy agrees in writing to sell Laura 100 bushels of apples at $5 a bushel and deliver them on January 1. Roy may not show at the trial that the parties made an oral agreement that the price would be $6 if delivery was made on December 1, since such evidence differs from the written terms of the contract. He may show, however, that the parties intended that a certain grade of apples was to be delivered, since the written contract makes no mention of the type of apples to be sold.

Statute of Limitations

Statutes of limitations are laws passed to limit the time in which an action may be brought. Their purpose is to prevent stale claims from being brought when witnesses are no longer available or have long forgotten the facts. The statute of limitations, like the statute of frauds, is an affirmative defense, not an element of the plaintiff's case. If the defendant raises the defense and shows that the action is time-barred, the magistrate must dismiss the suit. Conversely, the defendant's failure to assert the statute of limitations constitutes a waiver of the defense.[88] Because parties generally are not represented by attorneys in small claims court, some magistrates choose to ask defendants if they wish to raise the defense or, sometimes, raise it themselves on behalf of defendants.

The statute of limitations on a suit to enforce a contract for the sale of services or real property is three years after the contract is breached.[89] A suit on a sealed instrument, except a contract for sale of goods, must be brought within ten years.[90] A seal on a contract formalizes its execution. As mentioned earlier, an instrument is under seal if the word "SEAL," or the letters "LS" are found next to the signatures of the parties.

Under the UCC an action for any breach in a contract for the sale of goods must be commenced within four years after the breach.[91] This four-year statute of limitations applies to both sealed and unsealed contracts because the UCC makes the use of a seal inoperative in a contract for the sale of goods.[92] However, if the buyer purchases goods on credit and executes a sealed security agreement, the ten-year statute of limitations applies to the security agreement because

---

88. Mrozek v. Mrozek, 129 N.C. App. 43, 46, 496 S.E.2d 836, 839 (1998).
89. G.S. 1-52.
90. G.S. 1-47(2).
91. G.S. 25-2-725.
92. G.S. 25-2-203.

the UCC provision applies only to the pure sales aspects of the transaction, not to the security agreement.[93]

> *Example 38.* Bill agrees to sell Samuel a used car for $2,500. The parties sign a contract under seal. Bill delivers the car to Samuel, but Samuel does not pay. The statute of limitations is four years from the date payment became due; the contract is for the sale of goods; thus the seal does not extend the statute of limitations. If, however, Bill extends credit to Samuel to buy the car and Samuel signs a security agreement and a promissory note that is under seal, the statute of limitations would be ten years from default on payment.

In a sale of goods, the cause of action accrues when the breach occurs, even if the aggrieved party does not know about it.[94] The date of the breach is the payment due date, which is either set by agreement between the parties or otherwise arranged when credit is extended. For example, a credit card account agreement might provide that payment is due within thirty days after any purchase; but if there is no agreement, payment is due on the date the goods are purchased.

Acknowledgment of debt. In an action to obtain payment on an account, the statute of limitations begins to run from the date of each purchase. But part payment will toll (stop) the running of the statute. The general principle is that the part payment is intended by the debtor to acknowledge and admit the total debt due. Nothing else appearing the statute of limitations begins to run anew on the date of the part payment for the entire amount of the debt, not merely for those charges that accrued within the applicable statute of limitations.[95] Unlike payments, additional charges added to the account do not toll the statute of limitations.

> *Example 39.* Timothy had an account with XYZ Hardware on which he charged the following items: in June 2001, a hoe for $15; in August 2002, a saw for $20; in December 2003, a hammer for $15; and in September 2004, a garden hose for $20. By inadvertence, XYZ failed to bill Timothy until 2008, when it billed him $70 for these items. Timothy did not pay the bill, and in April 2008 XYZ filed a small claim action against Timothy for $70. Timothy asserts that because XYZ waited too long to file the lawsuit, he should not have to pay anything. The magistrate should enter judgment for $20, the garden hose—the only item purchased by Timothy within the four-year statute of limitations.
>
> Suppose, however, that in 2004 Timothy was sent a bill for the current balance of $70 and made a payment of $20 on May 1, 2004. Since XYZ filed the lawsuit in April 2008, Timothy would have been liable for the entire remaining balance. Part payment would have tolled the statute of limitations and started it running anew for the entire debt.
>
> However, if in response to the 2004 bill, Timothy had specified that the $20 payment was for the garden hose, the statute of limitations would not have begun anew for the balance of the account because in this case Timothy's limitation to the specific item indicated that he did not intend to recognize the entire debt.

93. G.S. 25-2-201. *See* N.C. Nat'l Bank v. Holshouser, 38 N.C. App. 165, 247 S.E.2d 645 (1978).
94. G.S. 25-2-275(2). See Neugent v. Beroth Oil Co., 149 N.C. App. 38, 54, 560 S.E.2d 829, 839 (2002).
95. Whitley's Elec. Serv., Inc. v. Sherrod, 293 N.C. 498, 238 S.E.2d 607 (1977).

An acknowledgment of debt that stops the running of the statute of limitations can take several forms. As above, it may consist of part payment of an outstanding balance. It may also take the form of an unconditional, written acknowledgment of debt signed by the debtor and directed to the creditor or the creditor's agent.[96]

The statute of limitations does not begin to run if, at the time the claim comes into existence, the injured party is a minor, insane, or mentally incompetent.[97] In that situation the statute of limitations begins to run when the minor becomes an adult or the mentally incompetent person is restored to competency. This general rule does not apply, however, if the injured party becomes insane or mentally incompetent after the statute begins to run.

Mixed contracts. What statute of limitations and what other law applies if the contract includes the sale of both goods and services? The test is "whether their predominant factor, their thrust, their purpose, reasonably stated, is the rendition of service, with goods incidentally involved . . . or is a transaction of sale, with labor incidentally involved."[98] The magistrate must look at the entire contract to determine whether it is predominantly a contract for the sale of goods or one for services. For example, a contract to purchase new tires, to install them, and to balance the tires is predominantly the sale of tires—a contract for goods—and the services to put them on the car and balance them are incidental to the sale. If the contract is predominantly a sale of goods, the statute of limitations is four years from the date of breach and the UCC provisions for the sale of goods apply. On the other hand, if it is primarily a contract for services, the statute of limitations is three years and the UCC does not apply.

Unconscionability

In North Carolina the court may find as a matter of law that a contract or any of its clauses is unconscionable. The court will refuse to enforce a contract or the clause on the ground of *unconscionability* "when the inequality of the bargain is so manifest as to shock the judgment of a person of common sense, and where the terms are so oppressive that no reasonable person would make them on the one hand, and no honest and fair person would accept them on the other."[99] A court must consider all of the facts and circumstances; and if the court determines that the provisions are so one-sided that the person being held to the contract has no opportunity for a meaningful choice, the contract or provision should be found unconscionable.[100] Unconscionability also can include "'bargaining naughtiness' in the formation of the contract, such as fraud, coercion, undue influence, misrepresentation, or inadequate disclosure."[101] It means more than a bad deal; it is identified by such factors as an extremely one-sided contract,

---

96. G.S. 1-26. *See* Phillips v. Giles, 175 N.C. 409, 95 S.E. 772 (1918).

97. G.S. 1-17.

98. Hensley v. Ray's Motor Co. of Forest City, Inc., 158 N.C. App. 261, 265, 580 S.E.2d 721, 724 (2003) (quoting Bonebrake v. Cox, 499 F.2d 951, 960 (8th Cir. 1974)). *See also* Mack Fin. Corp. v. Harnett Transfer, Inc., 42 N.C. App. 116, 121, 256 S.E.2d 491, 495 (1979).

99. Brenner v. Little Red School House, Ltd., 302 N.C. 207, 213, 274 S.E.2d 206, 210 (1981). *See also,* Tillman v. Commercial Credit Loans, Inc., 362 N.C. 93, 655 S.E.2d 362 (2008).

100. *Id.*

101. Weaver v. Saint Joseph of the Pines, Inc., 187 N.C. App. 198, 652 S.E.2d 701, 712 (2007).

superior bargaining power on the part of one of the parties, ignorance of the weaker party, and high-powered selling techniques.

Example 40. (A real case from New York[102]) Husband and wife, who both spoke Spanish and did not understand English, went into the Frostifresh Co. A salesman, speaking in Spanish, tried to sell them a combination refrigerator–freezer. The wife told the salesman that they could not afford the refrigerator–freezer because the husband's job would end the following week. The salesman told them that was okay because the appliance really wouldn't cost them anything—they would receive a $25 bonus for each similar sale made to their neighbors and relatives. The salesman then prepared a contract that was written in English. The contract was neither translated nor explained to the customers. It provided for a cash price of $900 and a credit charge of $245.88

In court, the seller admitted that the cost of the refrigerator to him was only $348. The court said that this contract was too hard a bargain and was unconscionable. Note that the contract did not contain just one unfair element. Rather, a series of factors—a one-sided contract in which the seller had superior bargaining power, high-powered selling techniques, and the buyer's ignorance and inability to read the contract—taken together caused the court to declare the contract unconscionable.

Defenses for Nonperformance

In some cases, a magistrate must refuse a party legal relief, not because the contract itself is void or voidable but because there is some reason to excuse the party who has breached the contract for not performing his or her legal duty under it.

When an unforeseen event makes it impossible to perform a contractual duty, the promisor may be excused from performing. This situation often occurs when parties contract with reference to specific property and the property is accidentally destroyed.[103] For instance, if Madeline contracts to deliver 200 tons of potatoes to be grown on her farm but a disease destroys the crop, Madeline will be excused from performance. But if Madeline merely promises to deliver 200 tons of potatoes, not identifying any particular potatoes, and her crop is destroyed, she must still deliver 200 tons of potatoes.

Another closely related doctrine relieving parties of the legal duty to perform is *frustration of purpose*. When one party's ability to achieve a certain objective is the basis on which both parties contract, the duty to perform is conditioned upon the attainment of that objective. The doctrine does not apply, however, if the parties took the risk of failing to reach the objective into account when the contract was formed, or if the risk of failure was reasonably foreseeable. This doctrine is rarely applicable, and no North Carolina cases mentioning it found for the defense. For example, a father, who was divorced, paid a year's tuition for his child. The contract stated that the tuition was payable in advance and that no portion was refundable. The mother refused to send the child to the school, and the father contended he should not be liable under the contract based on the defense of frustration of purpose. The court refused to recognize the father's

---

102. Frostifresh Corp. v. Reynoso, 52 Misc.2d 26, 274 N.Y.S. 2d 757 (1966).
103. *E.g.,* Steamboat Co. v. Transp. Co., 166 N.C. 582, 82 S.E. 956 (1914).

defense, however, because the possibility that the child might not attend was foreseeable, particularly in light of the contract provision that advance payment was nonrefundable.[104]

The classic example of frustration of purpose taught to law students is an old English case[105] in which a person contracted to lease an apartment from which to watch the king's coronation. The king became ill, and the coronation was postponed. The person who had contracted for the apartment was excused from paying. Performance was not impossible: the room was available, and the person could pay. However, both parties had contracted with the understanding that the room would be used to watch the coronation, and as the coronation was postponed, the purpose of the contract was frustrated.

Agency

Another issue that might arise in deciding whether a contract is enforceable is identification of the parties to the contract. This question can arise when a person makes a contract on behalf of someone else and the plaintiff seeks to hold the person on whose behalf the contract was entered into liable for breach. The issue is one of *agency*, that is, the relation that results when one person, called the *principal*, authorizes another person, called the *agent*, to conduct one or more transactions with third parties for him or her. Under the grant of authority from the principal, the agent represents the principal and acts in the principal's place. For example, if a person buys an item from a clerk at a department store and later discovers a problem, a lawsuit for breach of contract would be against the department store, not the clerk, because the clerk was acting as an agent for the store.

Actual and Apparent Authority

An agency relationship may be created in two different ways: actual and apparent authority.

Actual authority occurs when the principal actually grants authority to the agent to act on his or her behalf, and it may be express or implied. In *express authority* the two discuss and agree on specific authority. For example, John, who lives in Georgia, wants to buy a car that is located in Winston-Salem. He calls his sister, Susan, who lives in Winston-Salem and asks her to buy the car for the best deal she can get but to pay no more than $20,000. Susan agrees, and when she goes to buy the car she indicates that she is acting as agent for her brother, who is the purchaser. In *implied authority* the principal and agent convey by their words and conduct that the agent will act for the principal but the authority is not specifically granted, either verbally or in writing. In both cases the principal and agent must have had a meeting of the minds regarding the authority.

Apparent authority occurs when there has been no authorization, but the principal has given others the impression that the agent acts for him or her. The authority results from the principal's statements or conduct, on the basis of which third persons are justified in believing that the agent is acting for the principal. If the principal passively permits the agent to give a third person the impression that he or she acts on behalf of the principal, the principal might be held liable for the contract on the basis of apparent authority.

---

104. Brenner v. The Little Red School House, Ltd., 302 N.C. 207, 274 S.E.2d 206 (1981).
105. Krell v. Henry, 2 K.B. 740, 1903 WL 12966 (1903).

Example 41. Robert and his wife, Samantha, go to Sears. Robert indicates to the salesman that his wife wants to buy a new dryer and has asked him to negotiate the sale on her behalf. In fact, Samantha could care less whether they get a new dryer since Robert does all the laundry. However, Samantha says nothing and Robert buys the dryer and signs Samantha's name to the purchase agreement. Sears can look to Samantha to pay for the dryer; by not saying anything when Robert told the salesman he was acting as her agent, she made it appear that Robert had the authority to act on her behalf.

It is important to note that apparent authority is determined by the acts of the principal, not the agent. Therefore, apparent authority is not shown by a person telling a third party that he or she is acting as agent for a principal. Nor can apparent authority be used if the third person deals with the agent is if he or she is the principal.[106]

Example 42. Tate, who wanted to move his mobile home, entered into discussions with Ross. Tate stated that his primary concern was getting an experienced and licensed mover. Ross assured him that he moved mobile homes all the time and that he was insured. Tate relied on Ross's representations, and they agreed on a price and a moving date. When Ross came to move the mobile home, he was wearing the shirt with "Chambers Home Movers" insignia and had a "Chambers Home Movers" magnetic sign on his truck (Ross was an employee of Chambers Home Movers.). When the mobile home was damaged in the moving, Ross told Tate he wouldn't pay for the damage and that he worked for Chambers. In this situation, Tate dealt with Ross as a principal and so Ross could not assert a claim that he was an agent of Chambers Home Movers.[107]

Appendix I to this chapter provides a chart that might help the magistrate analyze whether an agency relationship was created in this case.

Example 43. Robert is the general manager of Burton Office Supply, Inc. Under the corporation's bylaws the general manager is authorized to act on its behalf. When the store needed some additional shelving, Robert called a local carpenter, Benjamin, and said, "I am general manager of Burton Office Supply. The company needs shelves built on one wall to store heavy boxes. Can you come and build those?" Benjamin builds the shelves and then sends a bill addressed to both Burton Office Supply and Robert. Who is liable? In this situation Robert is only an agent. Burton Office Supply Inc. is responsible for paying. Robert had express actual authority to act as the store's agent and indicated to Benjamin that he was doing so.

Example 44. Wendy and Herb were co-owners of "Wendy and Herb's," an interior design firm, for many years. When Wendy discovered that Herb had been embezzling money for several years, she bought out his interest in the firm and told him in no uncertain terms that he was forever barred from the premises. Wendy did not, however, remove the word "Herb's" from the firm's name. Despite being banished, Herb enters into a contract for some new work. with one of his favorite clients. He contracts for supplies with many of the same merchants he used when he was with Wendy but neglects to tell them that the partnership has been dissolved. The merchants,

106. Tate v. Chambers, 94 N.C. App. 154, 379 S.E.2d 681 (1989).
107. *Id.*

assuming that nothing has changed, bill Herb's purchases to the "Wendy and Herb's" account. Can Wendy be held liable on these contracts?

Yes. Herb once had authority to act as Wendy's agent, and although he no longer has that authority Wendy has never bothered to notify anyone. In fact, by failing to remove Herb's name from the firm's logo, she maintained the impression that Herb was her authorized agent. Wendy may, however, seek reimbursement from Herb for any contracts she is held responsible for as a result of his actions.

In cases involving agents, the following rules apply:

1. If the agent acts with the principal's consent and the identity of the principal is known to the other contracting party, the principal is liable and the agent is not. In these cases, if the contract is written, the agent usually signs the contract "as agent for named principal" or signs only the principal's name.
2. If the agent acts with consent but the identity of the principal is not known, either the agent or the principal can be sued. If the contract is written, the agent signs his or her own name.
3. If the agent acts without consent but the actions of the principal create apparent authority, the third party can sue the principal and the principal can sue the agent.
4. If the agent acts without any authority, the third party can sue only the agent.

Ratification

However, even if the agent acted without authority, the principal may create an enforceable contract by ratifying the agreement. A valid ratification requires that the agent has represented himself or herself as the agent of the principal and that the principal, upon discovering the relevant facts, signifies his or her intent to fulfill the contract.[108] Ratification requires an unambiguous confirmation by word or deed of the principal's intention to accept or be bound by the contract.

The most important point for a magistrate to know is that marriage does not create an agency relationship. If a third party seeks to hold liable a spouse who was not party to the contract, the third party must show that the contracting spouse was an agent for the noncontracting spouse in the same manner as he or she would prove any other agency relationship. The one exception to this rule involves unpaid medical bills, which one spouse can be required to pay for the other; this rule is not, however, based on agency theory but on spouses' legal obligation to provide necessaries for each other. When a couple is separated, the spouse seeking to avoid payment of medical bills on the basis of separation must show that the provider of the necessary goods or services was on notice of the couple's separation when the goods or services were provided.[109]

Example 45. Bill contracted with Ace Heating and Cooling Co. to install a new heating system in the house he owned with his wife, Muriel. All of the negotiations regarding the installation

108. Gen. Air Conditioning Co. v. Douglas, 241 N.C. 170, 173–74 , 84 S.E.2d 828, 831 (1954); Flowe v. Hartwick, 167 N.C. 448, 453, 83 S.E. 841, 844 (1914).
109. Forsyth Mem'l Hosp., Inc. v. Chisolm, 342 N.C. 616, 467 S.E.2d 88 (1996).

were between Bill and the manager of Ace Heating. In fact, the manager of Ace Heating testified that he never met Muriel. Bill did not pay for the heating system, and Ace Heating and Cooling Co. sued Bill and Muriel, claiming that Muriel ratified the contract by accepting the benefit of the new heating system. There was no evidence that Bill had actual or apparent authority to enter into the contract as an agent for Muriel. Muriel could not have ratified the contract because Bill never represented that he was acting as her agent.

But what if Bill had called the manager of Ace Heating and Cooling and said he and his wife wanted Ace to install a heating system? And, when Ace came to the door and told Muriel they had come to install the heating system she and her husband had ordered, she had answered "That's right. Come on in and begin the work"? Because there was no evidence that Muriel had authorized Bill to act as her agent, no agency relationship existed between them. However, when Muriel said "That's right; come on it and do the work" when told that Bill had indicated she wanted it, she ratified the agency. In this circumstance, both Bill (who acted on both his own behalf and as Muriel's agent) and Muriel would be liable for the contract.

Retail Installment Sales Act

The Retail Installment Sales Act, G.S. Ch. 25A (hereinafter RISA), enacted in 1971 as a consumer protection statute, regulates the credit terms of contracts for the sale of goods and services. As the act is long (forty-five sections), no attempt is made here to detail all its specifics. This section discusses some of its most important provisions.

RISA governs *consumer credit sales*, which are defined as the sale of goods or services in which

1. the seller is one who in the ordinary course of business regularly extends or arranges for the extension of credit;
2. the buyer is a natural person (not a corporation);
3. the goods or services are purchased primarily for a personal, family, household, or agricultural purpose;
4. either the debt representing the price of the goods or services is payable in installments (more than four), or a finance charge is imposed; and
5. the amount financed does not exceed $75,000.[110]

There are two major exceptions to the act's coverage: it does not apply to bona fide direct loans (for example, loans to individuals from a bank or finance company) or to a sale on a credit card issued by someone other than the seller (for example, American Express or Visa).[111] In some cases the seller extends credit by arranging for financing with a bank, and in that situation the contract is covered by RISA.

Example 46. Lydia goes to Appliance City to purchase a new flat screen television set. Appliance City advertised that there would be no interest for nine months, so Lydia asks to open an account with Appliance City to purchase the television set. Appliance City gives Lydia an application, and

110. G.S. 25A-2(a).
111. G.S. 25A-2(c). A VISA or MasterCharge card is a loan from a bank backing the card.

she is approved for credit. Lydia buys the television set and when she looks at her credit papers and gets her first bill, she sees that payments are to be sent to Fidelity Bank, which actually extended the credit. RISA applies to this contract because Appliance City offered and arranged for the credit. If Lydia had paid for the television set with her MasterCharge card or had gone to a local finance company to borrow money to purchase the television, the contract to purchase it would not have been covered by RISA.

One of the major provisions of RISA sets the maximum finance charge and other fees that can be charged in a consumer credit sale: 1.5 percent per month on a revolving charge account.[112] On other consumer credit sales, such as the purchase of a refrigerator in which the buyer signs a promissory note and security agreement to pay $100 per month for twenty-months, the maximum finance-charge rate is 24 percent per year if the amount financed is less than $1,500; 22 percent if the amount financed is at least $1,500 but less than $2,000; 20 percent if the amount financed is at least $2,000 but less than $3,000; and 18 percent if the amount is $3,000 or greater. These rates can be higher when the purchase being financed is a used car.[113] The finance charge is not merely interest; it is "the sum of all charges payable directly or indirectly by the buyer and imposed by the seller as an incident to the extension of credit."[114] It includes such charges as interest, time price differential (different prices for paying and buying on credit), loan fees, credit reports, and appraisal fees. It does not include transfer of equity fees or default or deferment charges, although the act also sets maximum rates for these extra charges.[115]

Every consumer credit installment sale contract must be in writing, dated, and signed by the buyer.[116]

Certain clauses and provisions are forbidden or restricted in consumer credit sales contracts.

- Balloon payments (one very large payment at the end) are forbidden. No scheduled payment may be more than 10 percent larger than earlier payments except the last payment, which may be 25 percent larger than the average of scheduled payments.[117]
- The contract may not modify or exclude any express warranty given by the seller.[118]
- Referral sales contracts are void.[119] (In referral sales the seller promises to give the buyer a rebate of a certain amount contingent on the buyer's finding other persons to whom the seller might sell the product.) This provision applies to all contracts, not just consumer credit sales.

112. G.S. 25A-14; 24-11(a).

113. Appendix II at the end of this chapter sets out the allowable finance charges on sales of consumer goods or services as well as the allowable charges on loans.

114. G.S. 25A-8(a).

115. G.S. 25A-8.

116. G.S. 25A-28.

117. G.S. 25A-34.

118. G.S. 25A-20.

119. G.S. 25A-37.

- A buyer's authorization for another person to confess judgment on his or her behalf is void.[120] (A *confession of judgment* is when a debtor authorizes a judgment to be entered against him or her without a court hearing.)
- The types of property that may be taken to secure a debt are limited.[121]
- When payments for separate purchases are consolidated, new payments must be applied to the first item purchased.[122]

The act also provides extra protection for the buyer in a home-solicitation sale—that is, when the seller solicits the sale at the buyer's home and the buyer signs the contract there. These provisions permit the buyer to cancel such a sale at any time within three days after signing the agreement. For the three-day cancellation limitation to apply, the agreement signed by the buyer must conform to certain specifications set out in the statute: it must designate the date of the sale and include a conspicuous statement of the method of cancellation. If the agreement does not comply with the statute, the buyer need not cancel within the three-day limit but may cancel in any manner he or she chooses.[123]

Finally, RISA provides certain remedies and penalties for charges in excess of those allowed:

1. If the finance charge is over the allowable rate but not more than double that rate, the seller cannot recover any finance charge and the seller is liable to the buyer for twice the amount of any finance charge the buyer has already paid.

2. If the finance charge is more than twice the allowable finance charge, the contract is void. The buyer may retain the goods without any liability, and the seller is not entitled to recover anything under the contract (which implies that the buyer can recover any money already paid under the contract).

3. If the seller does not make a rebate that is due or assesses and receives excess or non-authorized fees or charges other than the finance charge (for example, default fees), the buyer can demand, and receive, the amount of the rebate due or the excess charges he or she paid. If the seller does not comply with the buyer's demand, the seller is liable to the buyer for three times the amount due.[124]

Example 47. Pedro enters the First Rate Furniture Store to purchase a living room couch for his new home. He finds one for $250, but he only has $50 to pay down that day. The salesman says, "That's okay. We normally extend credit to our customers and will allow you to pay off the other $200 over the next year." Pedro then decides to buy the couch. The salesman prepares an installment sales contract and a promissory note. In addition to the $200 principal due, the following

---

120. G.S. 25A-18.

121. G.S. 25A-23. See discussion in Chapter V, "Actions to Recover Possession of Personal Property" at p. 128.

122. G.S. 25A-31. See discussion in Chapter V, "Actions to Recover Possession of Personal Property" at p. 132.

123. G.S. 25A-39.

124. G.S. 25A-44.

fees are charged: 15 percent interest ($30), $4 credit report, $10 loan fee. The total finance charge is $44. On the day of the sale Pedro pays the $50 down payment and $14 for the credit report and loan fee. He makes payments on the couch for six months and then defaults. First Rate Furniture Store brings an action for the amount due on the note ($100 and 15 percent interest). This is a consumer credit sale and falls under the Retail Installment Sales Act. It therefore appears that First Rate can recover the full amount due because the finance charge of 22 percent is within the allowable maximum limit of 24 percent.

Suppose, instead, that the contract required Pedro to pay 22 percent interest ($44), $4 for a credit report, and a $10 loan fee, for a total finance charge of $58. The seller would be charging more (29 percent) than the maximum allowable finance charge and, as a result, would not be entitled to receive any finance charge in the judgment. The magistrate would award recovery of only the $100 principal due to First Rate.

Suppose that Pedro filed a counterclaim because of the overcharge on the finance charge. First Rate would be liable to Pedro for twice the amount of the finance charges it had already received from him. In six months Pedro would have paid the furniture company $36 ($14 in fees; $22 in interest) and would be entitled to a judgment of $72 against First Rate. In that case, the magistrate's judgment would be for First Rate on the claim ($100) and for Pedro on the counterclaim ($72). The magistrate would then offset the two and award a judgment of $28—the difference between the two awards—to First Rate.

Finally, suppose that First Rate had two prices for the couch—$200 for cash customers and $250 for customers buying on credit. Since Pedro bought the couch on time, he had to pay $250. He made a $50 down payment; in addition to the remaining $200 principal, he was charged 15 percent interest ($30), $4 for a credit report, and a $10 loan fee. Are these charges within the allowable 24 percent finance charge rate? No. Finance charges include any time price differential as well as any charges for interest, loan fees, or credit reports. In this situation, the time price differential of $50 and the other charges of $44 totaled $94, or a finance charge of 47 percent. Since the finance charge is more than twice the allowable charge, the contract is void. The magistrate should not allow First Rate to recover anything. If Pedro wishes, he can retain the couch without any liability. In addition, although the act is vague on this point, he should be able to file a counterclaim against First Rate for the $186 ($50 down, $100 principal, $36 interest and fees) he had already paid the store.

What Damages Should Be Awarded for Breach of Contract?

Parties injured by a breach of contract are entitled to a remedy to compensate them for the loss involved in the other party's failure to perform under the contract. *Compensatory damages* are the most common remedy for breach of contract. *Rescission*—that is, invalidating the contract and placing the parties in the positions they occupied before the contract—is another remedy. Interest on damage awards may also be awarded from the date of the breach of contract. In limited situations, as discussed below, the magistrate may also award attorney fees. *Specific performance*, another remedy that might be available in district or superior court, is not available in small claims court. Specific performance requires the party that breached the contract to carry out his or her part of the bargain. For example, Bill promises to paint Janet's living room; he begins the job but stops when the job is one-fourth completed. Janet wants Bill to finish the job—specific performance of the contract—but magistrates do not have the authority to award that remedy.

Monetary Damages

A breach of contract entitles the injured party to sue for *damages*—compensation for losses suffered as a result of the other party's failure to perform. The terminology used in the UCC for breach of contracts for the sale of goods differs from that used in the common law for breach of contracts for services, but the overall concept of damages is the same.

The person damaged by a breach of contract is entitled to be placed, insofar as this can be done by money, in the same position he or she would have occupied if there had been no breach of the contract.[125] *Direct damages* are measured by the difference between the value of the performance that had been promised and what acquiring such performance will now cost the plaintiff. The plaintiff has the burden of proving the damages, just as he or she has the burden of proving that the defendant breached the contract. The plaintiff must prove with reasonable certainty the amount of actual damages suffered as a result of the breach. The magistrate cannot award damages based upon mere speculation or conjecture.[126] In addition to direct damages suffered, *actual damages* includes any incidental and consequential damages suffered. *Incidental damages* include reasonable costs incurred by the injured party preparing to perform his or her obligations under the contract, amounts reasonably incurred in response to the breach, and amounts reasonably incurred for the purpose of minimizing the injury resulting from the breach. *Consequential damages* include any losses resulting from the circumstances of the breach that the injured party suffered of which the breaching party knew or should have known and which the injured party could not have prevented.

If the plaintiff cannot prove any actual damages, he or she is entitled to recover *nominal damages*—some trivial amount, such as one dollar, in recognition of the technical damage resulting from the breach.[127]

In the most common breach of contract case brought in small claims court—failure to pay on an account—the damages are usually straightforward and easy to prove. The plaintiff is entitled to the amount owed on the account (plus interest). In other breach of contract cases, damages are more difficult to prove.

> *Example 48.* Yuri, a baker, anticipated that a bad hurricane season might damage peach crops, thereby raising the price of fresh peaches. With this in mind, he contracted with George, a peach grower, to sell him 1,000 bushels of peaches at harvest time. The price agreed on was $3 per bushel, a good price at the time.

---

125. Lee Cycle Center, Inc. v. Wilson Cycle Ctr, Inc., 143 N.C. App. 1, 9, 545 S.E.2d 745, 750 (2001) (quoting Perfecting Serv. Co. v. Product Dev. & Sales Co., 259 N.C. 400, 415, 131 S.E.2d 9, 21 (1963)).

126. *See* "Contracts—Issue of Common Law Remedy—Damages Mandate" N.C.P.I. Civil 503.79 (May 2003) NORTH CAROLINA PATTERN JURY INSTRUCTIONS, GENERAL CIVIL VOLUME.

127. Bowen v. Fid. Bank, 209 N.C. 140, 183 S.E. 266 (1936); Waynick Constr., Inc. v. York, 70 N.C. App. 287, 319 S.E.2d 304 (1984).

Yuri's prediction was right. At harvest time the market value of fresh peaches was $5 per bushel. The temptation was too great for George. He breached his contract and sold all his peaches to other buyers for $5 per bushel. What are Yuri's damages? To place himself in a position he would have been if George had performed according to the contract, Yuri will have to go out into the market and buy 1,000 bushels of peaches at $5 per bushel. His damages are the difference between the contract price of $3 per bushel and the replacement price of $5 per bushel. Thus Yuri is entitled to recover $2,000 ($2 per bushel times 1,000 bushels) from George because Yuri had to pay $5,000 for peaches instead of the $3,000 contract price.

Example 49. Selma and Reese enter into a contract for Reese's bull, which he will sell to Selma for $2,000. The contract provides that Reese will deliver the bull on June 1. On May 25 Selma calls Reese and tells him not to deliver the bull. She found another bull she liked better for only $1,500 and bought it. Reese cannot find another buyer for the bull until July 1, and that buyer will only pay $1,000 for it. Reese sues Selma for breach of contract.

What are Reese's damages? He is entitled to $1,000 for the difference between the contract price and the price he was able to get for the bull (direct damages). In addition, Reese is entitled to the costs of keeping the bull for the period between the date of delivery under the contract and the date he was able to sell the bull (incidental damages). So if, as Reese testifies, feed for the bull costs $5 per day, he would be entitled to an additional $150. Finally, Reese testifies that to sell the bull he had to place an advertisement in an animal husbandry magazine, and he shows the magistrate the ad and the bill for $200 for running it. Reese would thus be entitled to the cost of running the ad (incidental damages) and a total judgment of $1,350.

In a case in which the contract breach is that the defendant failed to return plaintiff's property, allowable damages are the fair market value of the property, not the replacement cost. For example, a plaintiff who sues a dry cleaning establishment for the loss of a suit must prove how much he paid for the suit and how long he had worn it so that the court can estimate its present value. The plaintiff is not entitled to recover the full cost of buying a new suit, only the fair market value of the suit that was lost. Damages for breach of contract are intended only to compensate for monetary loss that can be measured or estimated. If the plaintiff sues a moving company for the loss of a letter that had great sentimental value, or a picture of his mother, the plaintiff can recover only a token sum because the property has little or no monetary value.

Verified Itemized Statement of an Account—A Rule of Evidence

In an action upon account for goods sold and delivered, for rents, for services owed, or for money lent, the plaintiff is entitled to submit—and the magistrate must admit into evidence—a verified itemized statement of the account. A verified itemized statement of the account is sufficient evidence, absent evidence to the contrary, that it is correct and that the defendant owes the amount of money it states.[128] The statement must itemize each charge. *Verification* means that the account is accompanied by an affidavit (sworn statement) that the account is a true and accurate statement of the account signed by a person who has personal knowledge of the

128. G.S. 8-45.

account or is familiar with the books and records of the business and is in a position to testify to the correctness of the records. Typically the account is verified by the bookkeeper or, in a small business, by the owner. Verification of the account by the plaintiff's attorney probably would not be appropriate since the attorney would not be a person with personal knowledge of the account or familiarity with the books and records of the business.

Breach of Warranty Damages

In an action for breach of warranty, the party suing is entitled to recover the difference between the fair market value of the goods as warranted and the fair market value of the goods as received.

> *Example 50.* Amelia goes to Sears to buy a refrigerator. She looks at all the samples on the floor and decides on a 20-cubic-foot GE refrigerator–freezer with a water and ice dispenser on the door. Amelia orders the refrigerator and agrees to pay $1,100 for it. The refrigerator delivered to Amelia does not have the water and ice dispenser. Amelia is desperate for the refrigerator and cannot wait to have the correct one delivered so she accepts the refrigerator. She then sues Sears because it breached an express warranty to deliver a refrigerator identical to the sample on the floor. Amelia offers evidence (by showing an advertisement in the local newspaper) that a similar refrigerator without a water and ice dispenser sells for $950. Sears is liable to Amelia for $150, the difference between the fair market value of the refrigerator as warranted ($1,100) and the fair market value as delivered ($950).

Check Returned for Insufficient Funds

Special damages are allowed for civil actions brought on checks returned because the maker does not have sufficient funds on deposit or does not have an account at that bank. In civil actions brought against a person who pays with a check that is refused by the bank for any reason, the plaintiff is entitled to the amount owing on the check plus the bank's service charge and a processing fee the plaintiff imposes. The bank's service charge is the actual amount the bank charges the person who receives the check and deposits it in his or her account. The amount differs depending on the bank's contract with the depositor. For example, a bank is more likely to charge a depositor a higher fee for depositing a worthless check in an individual bank account than in a commercial account. The processing fee imposed by the plaintiff is the fee the receiver of the check charges the maker of the check for giving him or her a worthless check. The statute authorizing that fee sets it at a maximum of $25.[129]

If a civil action is brought on a check returned for insufficient funds or because no such account exists, special (or additional) damages are allowed.[130] To be entitled to the special damages, however, the payee must first send a demand letter to the maker of the check stating that

---

129. G.S. 25-3-506. Formerly the statute required merchants to post a conspicuous sign indicating that they would impose a fee of a specified amount—but not more than $25—for checks returned for insufficient funds. In 1997 the statute was amended to delete the notice requirement and provide that merchants may now merely claim a fee of up to $25 for a check returned for insufficient funds or no account.

130. G.S. 6-21.3.

if he or she does not pay the face amount of the check, the service charge from the payee's bank, and the payee's processing fee within thirty days after the written demand is mailed, the payee will file a civil action seeking additional damages of three times the amount of the check but not less than $100 nor more than $500. The statute provides a model with which the payee's letter must substantially conform. The demand letter must be sent by certified mail to the defendant at his or her last known address. The statute specifies that a second demand letter may be sent seeking the additional damages, but by using "may" for the second letter and "shall" for the first letter, the statute seems to indicate that the second letter is optional and that the plaintiff may be entitled to the additional damages if he or she sends only the first demand letter. If the charges are not paid within thirty days, the payee may file a lawsuit.

At the trial the plaintiff must prove that the check was returned for insufficient funds; that the check was issued with knowledge that there were insufficient funds in the account or that no credit existed with the bank with which to pay the check; and that a proper demand letter was sent to the defendant. The magistrate may waive the additional damages if he or she finds that the defendant did not cover the check because of economic hardship. In certain bad check cases, the magistrate may also award attorneys' fees (see p. 92 below).

> **Example 51.** Harry wrote a check to Food Lion for $75.50 for groceries. The check was returned for insufficient funds. Food Lion's bank charges Food Lion $5 for every dishonored check it deposits in its account. Food Lion sends a certified letter to Harry that complies with G.S. 6-21.3(a1). Two months later, when Food Lion had heard nothing from Harry, the manager files a small claim action against Harry. At trial, Food Lion proves that the check was returned for insufficient funds and offers evidence to show that Harry did not have more than $50 in his account during the month preceding the date he wrote the check. The manager shows the magistrate a copy of the demand letter sent to Harry and indicates that it was sent by certified mail more than thirty days before the lawsuit was filed. Food Lion is entitled to the following damages: $105.50 ($75.50, the face amount of the check + $5.00, the bank processing fee + $25.00, the payee's processing fee) plus additional damages of $316.50 (three times the face value of the check). Thus, Food Lion is entitled to a judgment for $422.00.
>
> If the face value of the check was $25, Food Lion would be entitled to recover $155 ($25 + $5 + $25 + $100—because three times $25 is less than the $100 minimum for additional damages). Similarly, if the check was for $175, Food Lion would be entitled to $705 ($175 + $5 + $25 + $500—because three times $175 is more than the maximum additional damages of $500).
>
> Suppose Harry testifies (and the magistrate believes) that he lost his job a month before he wrote the check and had to buy groceries for his family. He still has not been able to find a job and, although he has made timely applications for unemployment benefits and food stamps, he has not yet received them. The magistrate may waive the additional damages—but not the face amount of the check, bank processing fee, and payee's processing fee—because the defendant's failure to cover the check was due to economic hardship.

Duty to Mitigate Damages

A party damaged by a breach of contract must minimize the losses caused by a breach and cannot simply let the losses pile up, thinking that the party who committed the breach will have to pay anyway. The injured party is obligated to avoid or minimize his or her loss by a reasonable effort and cannot recover for losses that might have avoided. He or she has a duty to use ordinary care to reduce, minimize, or avoid damages resulting from the breach. Plaintiff's failure to mitigate must be raised by the defendant. If the defendant proves that damages would have been avoided or reduced if the plaintiff had used ordinary care to mitigate them, the defendant will be entitled to a credit of the amount that damages could reasonably have been mitigated.

> *Example 52.* Quick Framing Inc. rents a commercial space from Acme Mall, Inc. The parties sign a one-year lease that provides for a monthly rent of $700 and specifies that the rent for the entire year is due if the tenant vacates early. Quick Framing Inc. isn't doing well and notifies the landlord that it is vacating the premises at the end of the eighth month.
>
> Five months after Quick Framing vacates the store, Acme Mall files a small claim action seeking $2,800 under the contract provision requiring payment of the entire year's rent. Quick Framing offers testimony that Acme Mall made no attempt to advertise and re-rent the premises and proves that the mall occupancy was at 99 percent and that the space it rented was the only vacancy. Moreover, Quick Framing showed that two other comparable spaces in the mall renting for $700 a month had been re-rented within a month of being vacated and that Acme could easily have rented the space within a month if it had tried. Acme says it just had not gotten around to trying to re-rent the premises. If the magistrate determines that Acme could have re-rented within a month, Acme is entitled to recover only for that month. Quick Framing would then be entitled to a credit for three months' rent, and Acme Rental would only be entitled to recover $700.
>
> But what if Acme proves that the occupancy rate of the mall is only 55 percent, that it only has filled two spaces in the last six months, that it advertised Quick Framing's space within three weeks but has not been able to re-rent the space? In that situation, the magistrate might find that Acme had used ordinary diligence to mitigate damages and was entitled to $2,800 (four months rent).

Joint and Several Liability

A final issue, joint and several liability, should be noted with respect to monetary damages. When two or more people agree to pay an amount of money, each one is *jointly liable*, which means they can be sued together for the full amount of the debt. And they are *severally liable*, which means they can be sued individually or separately, each for the full amount. If one debtor is successfully sued for the full amount of the debt, he or she may then sue the co-debtors for their share of the debt. Thus if Mary and John borrow $2,500 from Friendly Finance and default after paying $1,000, Friendly Finance can either sue both of them, or it can sue one of them for the full amount.

Rescission

Instead of collecting money damages, a plaintiff may prefer to be restored to the position he or she was in before the contract was made. This remedy has many names. It is sometimes called *rescission* or *cancellation*; in cases of contracts for the sale of goods, it may be referred to as *rejection* or *revocation of acceptance* by the buyer. For example, if Sarah purchases a dryer from Sears and when it is delivered notices that the top is badly damaged, she may reject it and rescind the contract and get back any money she paid to Sears. But what if when the damaged dryer is delivered Sarah accepts it before she calls Sears and the manager promises to replace the entire top of the dryer? Two weeks later, after several telephone calls from Sarah, the manager says he will order a new part when he gets around to it. The law permits Sarah to revoke her acceptance and sue to recover the money already paid to the seller. In both situations the magistrate will hear an action to recover money based on breach of contract.

Allowable Interest

In breach of contract cases the magistrate awards prejudgment interest at the rate established in the contract; if no interest rate is specified, the contract draws interest at the legal rate of 8 percent per year from the date of breach.[131] The magistrate is required to distinguish principal from interest in the award because interest awarded on the judgment (post-judgment interest) is assessed only against the principal, not on interest awarded in the judgment (prejudgment interest). If credit was extended for personal, family, household, or agricultural purposes, the judgment draws interest (post-judgment interest) at the legal rate. In commercial extensions of credit, post-judgment interest is charged at the contract rate if the parties agreed in the contract that that rate of interest would also apply after judgment; otherwise it draws interest at the legal rate.

Several statutes govern the maximum allowable interest rates for various transactions, but interest rates for transactions governed by RISA are different from those under other statutes. Transactions covered by RISA, are subject to a monthly maximum rate for goods or services sold under revolving charge accounts and a maximum annual rate for other consumer credit contracts; the rates depend on the amount financed and whether the goods sold are used motor vehicles or other goods.

The (non-RISA) statutes governing money lent by lending institutions or by private individuals set separate interest rates for finance companies. There are two types of finance companies—small-loan lenders and optional-rate lenders—and the rates differ depending on the type: If the finance company is a *small-loan lender*, it may lend up to $3,000 to any one person and charge interest at a rate of 36 percent per year on the first $600 of the unpaid balance and 15 percent per year on the remaining unpaid balance.[132] If the finance company is an *optional-rate lender*, it can lend up to $10,000 to any one person. For loans up to $7,500 it may charge 30 percent per year for the first $1,000 of the unpaid balance and 18 percent interest per year on the remainder;

131. G.S. 24-1; G.S. 24-5(a).
132. G.S. 53-173(a).

and for loans of more than $7,500 the finance company may charge 18 percent per year on the outstanding balance.[133]

If the lender is someone or something other than a finance company—for instance, a bank, credit union, or private individual—and the principal amount of the loan is $25,000 or less, the lender may charge up to the maximum rate of interest set monthly by the North Carolina commissioner of banks: the greater of the latest noncompetitive rate for U. S. Treasury bills plus 6 percent or 16 percent.[134]

Damages for Usury

Two statutes also provide specific damages if money is lent at a higher rate of interest than allowed by law— called *usury*. A lender other than a finance company that knowingly charges a greater rate of interest than allowed is not entitled to recover any interest, and the borrower is entitled to recover twice the amount of interest he or she has already paid.[135]

If a finance company charges more than the allowable interest rate, the loan contract is void unless the error is a result of an accidental or bona fide error of computation. The finance company is not entitled to collect any principal, interest, or other charges under the loan, and the borrower is entitled to recover any moneys already paid.[136]

A defendant must raise the affirmative defense of usury when he or she is challenging the amount of interest charged in an action on the debt. The debtor may file a usury claim to recover money already paid as an action for money owed or as a counterclaim to an action against the defendant for the debt.

Attorneys' Fees

In North Carolina attorneys' fees may not be awarded to a party unless there is specific statutory authority to do so.[137] Thus the party seeking award of attorneys' fees must show the magistrate the specific statute that authorizes the award. Some of these statutes are discussed below.

Evidences of Indebtedness

In small claims courts award of attorneys' fees most often arises when the plaintiff is suing to collect a debt and the note or other evidence of indebtedness provides for payment of attorneys' fees. G.S. 6-21.2 provides that obligations to pay attorneys' fees in a note, conditional sale contract, or other evidence of indebtedness are valid, enforceable, and collectable as part of the debt when the debt is collected by or through an attorney. *Evidence of indebtedness* means "any printed or written instrument, signed or otherwise executed by the obligor(s), which evidences

---

133. G.S. 53-176(a).

134. G.S. 24.1.1. If the principal amount of the loan is more than $25,000, the interest rate may be any rate the parties agree upon. For a chart of allowable interest rates in North Carolina, see Appendix II at the end of this chapter.

135. G.S. 24-2.

136. G.S. 53-166(d).

137. *E.g.*, Hicks v. Albertson, 284 N.C. 236, 200 S.E.2d 40 (1973); *In re* King, 281 N.C. 533, 189 S.E.2d 158 (1972); Southland Amusements Vending, Inc. v. Rourk, 143 N.C. App. 88, 545 S.E.2d 254 (2001).

on its face a legally enforceable obligation to pay money."[138] If an attorney represents a plaintiff at trial to collect on a note, conditional sale contract, or other instrument of indebtedness, the attorney is entitled to have an attorney's fee awarded if (1) the attorney has given the debtor the required notice and (2) the contract or note evidencing the debt provides for payment of attorneys' fees. The creditor or the creditor's attorney must notify the debtor after default of the obligation that the provisions of the evidence of indebtedness relating to attorneys' fees will be enforced unless the debtor pays the full amount of the outstanding balance within five days after the notice is mailed. There is no time limit on when the notice must be mailed, and it can even be mailed after the complaint is filed.[139] However, serving a complaint that seeks attorneys' fees is not sufficient notice.[140]

If the evidence of indebtedness provides for payment of a certain percentage of the outstanding balance (not in excess of 15 percent) as attorneys' fees, that provision is enforceable. If, for example, the note provides for the payment of attorneys' fees of 12 percent of the outstanding balance, the magistrate will award attorneys' fees of 12 percent of the outstanding balance. But if the instrument provides for attorneys' fees of more than 15 percent, if it does not specify an amount or percentage, or if it specifies only payment of "reasonable" attorneys' fees, the magistrate must award attorneys' fees of 15 percent of the outstanding balance.

A question that may arise is whether a lease for real property is an evidence of indebtedness. Several cases have answered the question affirmatively when commercial leases for a definite period of time included attorneys' fee provisions.[141] The awards were made when landlords were seeking monetary damages under the lease agreement, not when seeking solely possession of the premises. The ruling in these cases would probably also apply to cases involving residential leases for a definite period of time in which (1) the plaintiff seeks monetary damages as well as possession, (2) the lease contains a clause stating that if the tenant violates the lease the rent for the entire period is due, and (3) the lease includes an attorneys' fee clause. However, if the action seeks only possession, the landlord seeking to collect attorneys' fees must show that the summary ejectment action is reasonably related to the collection of the debt.[142]

Action on a Check

Another statute allows attorneys' fees in small claim actions to collect on a bad check.[143] In an action to recover on a check in which payment has been refused by the bank because the maker has no account or has insufficient funds in the account, the magistrate must award a reasonable

---

138. Stillwell Enter., Inc. v. Interstate Equip. Co., 300 N.C. 286, 294, 266 S.E.2d 812, 817 (1980). *Also see* State Wholesale Supply, Inc. v. Allen, 30 N.C. App. 272, 227 S.E.2d 120 (1976) (sales receipt and invoice after sale not evidence of indebtedness).

139. Binning's Inc. v. Roberts Constr. Co., 9 N.C. App. 569, 177 S.E.2d 1 (1970).

140. Blanton v. Sisk, 70 N.C. App. 70, 74–75, 318 S.E.2d 560, 564 (1984).

141. N.C. Indus. Capital v. Clayton, 185 N.C. App. 356, 649 S.E.2d 14 (2007); WRI/Raleigh v. Shaikh, 183 N.C. App. 249, 644 S.E.2d 245 (2007); RC Assoc. v. Regency Ventures, Inc., 111 N.C. App. 367, 432 S.E.2d (1993).

142. *See* Coastal Prod. Credit Ass'n v. Goodson Farms, Inc., 70 N.C. App. 221, 227–28, 319 S.E.2d 650, 655–56 (1984).

143. G.S. 6-21.3.

attorneys' fee to a licensed attorney representing the plaintiff if (1) the plaintiff mailed written notice of intent to file suit to the defendant at his or her last known address at least ten days before suit was filed and (2) the defendant did not make payment or provide evidence of bank error within ten days after the notice was mailed. As this statute does not limit reasonable attorneys' fees to any specific percentage, the magistrate determines what is reasonable in each case. He or she will consider the kind of case involved, the complexity of the legal issues, the time and amount expended by the attorney, fees customarily charged for similar services, and the skill and experience of the attorney.[144]

Miscellaneous Attorneys' Fee Statutes

In a suit alleging an unfair and deceptive practice, a magistrate has the discretion (as the presiding judge) to award a reasonable attorneys' fee, taxed as court costs, against the losing party upon finding that

1. the party charged with the violation willfully engaged in the act and demonstrated an unwarranted refusal to pay the claim that was the basis of the suit, or
2. the party who brought the action knew, or should have known, that the action was frivolous and malicious.[145]

The difficulty in awarding attorneys' fees under this statute in small claims court is that the plaintiff, to be entitled to an award, must prove not only that the defendant engaged in an unfair and deceptive practice but also that he or she exhibited an unwarranted refusal to resolve the matter. Because the trial date in magistrate's court is set within thirty days after the lawsuit is filed, parties have less time than they do in other courts to engage in the kind of discussions that show an unwarranted refusal. In any case, under this statute it is the magistrate who has discretion to decide whether to award an attorneys' fee and to determine the amount of the award.

G.S. 25A-21 provides for award of attorneys' fees in actions to recover under consumer credit sales contracts. If the plaintiff sues for default on a consumer credit sale and obtains a money judgment, the magistrate, as the presiding judge, must award a reasonable attorneys' fee when requested. The attorneys' fee award is taxed as court costs. As in the case of attorneys' fees for collecting on a bad check, the magistrate determines the amount of a reasonable fee. If the seller loses, the magistrate must award a reasonable fee to the attorney representing the defendant. This statute overlaps with G.S. 6-21.2 in some ways. If the consumer credit sale contract specifically provides for attorneys' fees, G.S. 6-21.2 governs the award, whereas if the credit contract does not provide for attorneys' fees, G.S. 25A-21 controls. In either instance, an attorney who successfully represents a plaintiff attempting to collect on a default of a credit sale will be entitled to an attorney fee if the plaintiff asks for it.

---

144. Redevelopment Comm'n v. Hyder, 20 N.C. App. 241, 246, 201 S.E.2d 236, 239 (1973).

145. G.S. 75-16.1. In two instances, recitation of the facts of the case indicates that the magistrates awarded attorneys' fees under this statute though the magistrate's ruling was not an issue in either court decision. *See* Riverview Mobile Home Park v. Bradshaw, 119 N.C. App. 585, 459 S.E.2d 283 (1995); Mills v. Stallings, 2004 WL 26535 (N.C. App. 2004) (unreported case).

G.S. 25-9-615(a)(1) authorizes the award of reasonable attorneys' fees as part of the costs of retaking, holding, and selling collateral under the UCC. This provision is likely to arise in the situation in which a party sells repossessed goods, deducts attorneys' fees from the sale proceeds, and then sues for a deficiency. (See Chapter V, "Actions to Recover Possession of Personal Property," for a detailed discussion of this topic.)

Appendix 1

Agency

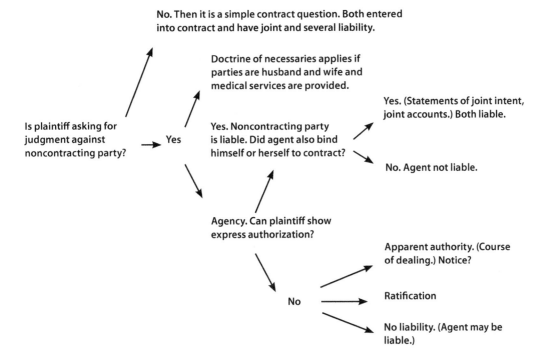

No. Then it is a simple contract question. Both entered into contract and have joint and several liability.

Doctrine of necessaries applies if parties are husband and wife and medical services are provided.

Yes. (Statements of joint intent, joint accounts.) Both liable.

Is plaintiff asking for judgment against noncontracting party?

Yes

Yes. Noncontracting party is liable. Did agent also bind himself or herself to contract?

No. Agent not liable.

Agency. Can plaintiff show express authorization?

Apparent authority. (Course of dealing.) Notice?

No

Ratification

No liability. (Agent may be liable.)

Appendix 2

Table 1. Maximum Allowable Interest Rates on Loans in North Carolina

Type of Lender (Statute)	Amount Lent	Security	Interest Rate	Other Allowable Charges
Bank, credit union, savings and loans, and individual (G.S. 24-1.1, -2, -10.1)	$25,000 or less	Any property (but not home loan secured by first deed of trust)	Greater of 16% or noncompetitive rate for six-month U.S. Treasury bills plus 6%. Rate set monthly by N.C. Commissioner of Banks.	Late payment charge: up to 4% of outstanding balance. Prepayment fee: 2% if prepaid within 3 years of 1st payment for contract loan. Fee for modification of loan: ¼% of 1% of balance.
Bank, credit union, savings and loans, and individual (G.S. 24-11)	Extension of credit on open-end credit or revolving credit charges	Any property if charge 1.25% or less. No property if over 1.25%.	1.5% per month (18% per year) on unpaid balance	Annual charge: no more than $24. Late payment fee: $5 for unpaid balance less than $100; $10 for balance of $100 or more.
Finance company—small-loan lender (G.S. 53-173, -177, -189)	$3,000 or less	Any personal property	Prejudgment: 36% per year on unpaid principal up to $600; 15% per year on remainder. Post-judgment: 8% on unpaid principal	Processing fee: 5% but max $25. Charges for credit life, accident and health, or property insurance: must comply with Truth in-Lending Act
Finance company—optional-rate lender (G.S. 53-176, -177, -189)	$10,000 or less	Any personal property	Prejudgment: 30% per year on unpaid principal to $1,000; 18% per year on the remainder on loan of $7,500 or less; 18% per year on loan of more than $7,500. Post-judgment: 8%	Processing fee: not to exceed $25 for loans up to $2,500; 1% for loans over $2,500, but not over $40. Charges for credit life, etc. (as indicated above)

Penalties

- Banks, credit unions, individuals: Knowingly charging greater rate of interest than allowable forfeits entire interest on loan; borrower may recover twice the amount of interest actually paid. (G.S. 24-2)

- Finance companies: Misdemeanor punishable by fine of $500 to $2,500 and/or imprisonment for four months to two years. Also contract is void unless violation the result of accidental or bona fide error of computation. Lender has no right to collect or retain any principal or interest with respect to the loan. Borrower could bring an action against the lender to recover any principal or interest paid. (G.S. 153-166)

Table 2. Maximum Allowable Finance Charges on Sale of Consumer Goods or Services in North Carolina: G.S. 25A-14 THROUGH -15

Property Sold	Security Taken	Amount Financed	Allowable Finance Charge[a]	Other Allowable Charges
Any personal property or services to be used for personal, household, family, or agricultural purposes	Property sold or property previously sold by seller to buyer in which seller has existing security interest	Less than $1,500	24% $5 minimum	Damage to property; credit, life, accident insurance charges if comply with truth-in-lending
		$1,500–$1,999	22% $5 minimum	Official fees paid to public officials for perfecting, releasing, etc., security interest or, in lieu thereof, premiums for insurance to protect seller if not more than official fees charged
		$2,000–$2,999	20% $5 minimum	
		$3,000–$25,000	18% $5 minimum	
Motor vehicle 1 or 2 model years old[b]	Property sold or property previously sold by seller to buyer in which seller has existing security interest	$25,000 or less	Higher of 18% or amount allowable under personal property category (above)	Default charge for installment past due at least ten days of 5% of past due installment or $6, whichever less. Written, dated deferral agreement may provide for charge of 1.5% of each installment for each month from date installment would have been due.
Motor vehicle 3 model years old			Higher of 20% or amount allowable under personal property category (above)	
Motor vehicle 4 model years old			Higher of 22% or amount allowable under personal property category (above)	
Motor vehicle 5 model years old or older			29%	
Personal property to be affixed to real property	Real property to which property sold is affixed	$1,000 or more	16%	
Personal property on revolving charge account	Property sold or property previously sold by seller to buyer in which seller has existing security agreement for which case price was $100 or more.		1.5% per month (18% per year)	Damage to property; credit, life, accident insurance charges if comply with truth-in-lending. Late payment fee of $5 for unpaid balance less than $100 and $10 for balance of $100 or more

a. Finance charge is the sum of all charges payable directly or indirectly by the buyer and imposed by the seller as an incident to the extension of credit. It includes interest, price differential, service charge, loan fee, finder's fee, appraisal report, investigation report, credit report, and any nonexcluded insurance fees.

b. A motor vehicle is one model year old on January 1 of the year following the designated year model of the vehicle.

Penalties (G.S. 25A-44)

1. If contract requires payment of not more than twice the permitted finance charge, seller cannot recover any finance charge, and seller is liable to buyer for twice the amount of finance charges already paid, plus reasonable attorneys' fees.
2. If contract requires payment of more than twice the permitted finance charge, contract is void. Buyer can keep goods and seller is not entitled to recover anything.
3. If charges for authorized fees (default etc.) are in excess of allowable rate, buyer can demand a refund in writing; if seller fails to refund excess within 10 days, seller is liable for three times the amount of overpaid fee.
4. Knowing and willful violation constitutes unfair and deceptive practice.

Chapter IV

Torts

The broad category of the law known as *torts* deals with civil wrongs for which the injured person may bring a private lawsuit seeking damages for his or her injury. Unlike contract law, which arises from an agreement between the parties, liability for tort grows out of the violation of a legal duty. The usual legal remedy for a tort is money damages to compensate the victim for property damage or personal injury arising from the tort. A tort victim seeking damages must file suit in civil court because torts are *private* wrongs (or wrongs against the individual) rather than wrongs against the state, which the state itself prosecutes in criminal court. There are several categories of torts, most of which involve either negligent or intentional interference with another person or another person's property. Although the primary subject of this chapter is negligence, the next section briefly addresses intentional torts. The chapter ends with brief discussions of the statute of limitation, liability laws, and attorneys' fees in tort cases.

Intentional Torts

Intentional torts are those in which a harmful act is done purposefully, as opposed to accidentally or negligently. To prevail in a suit for an intentional tort, the plaintiff must prove (1) that the defendant committed an act, (2) that he or she did so intentionally, and (3) that the act caused the plaintiff harm. An intentional tort may be interference with a person or his or her property, but no actual damages is required for a finding of intentional tort. The essence of an intentional tort is not that the defendant intended the harm but that he or she intended to do the act that resulted in harm. The language the court uses is that "one who intentionally engages in conduct knowing that particular results are substantially certain to follow also intends those results for purposes of tort liability."[1]

> *Example 1.* Nancy, who is 6 feet tall and weighs 190 pounds, is a baseball coach. In friendly greeting, she slaps one of her players, Hall, on the back. Hall is 5 feet tall and weighs 95 pounds. The slap bruises Hall's shoulder. Nancy's slap is the tort called battery: even though she did not intend to bruise Hall, she did intend the act that resulted in the harm and that is the intent necessary for an intentional tort.

1. Mickles v. Duke Power Co., 342 N.C. 103, 110, 463 S.E.2d 206, 211 (1995).

Examples of intentional torts include false imprisonment, intentional infliction of emotional distress, trespass, libel, slander, and conversion. This chapter discusses only assault, battery, and trespass because they are the intentional torts a magistrate is most likely to hear. Conversion is discussed in Chapter V, "Actions to Recover Possession of Personal Property."

Assault and Battery

Assault and battery are two separate torts, although they are frequently spoken of as one. *Assault* is the "intentional placing of a person in reasonable apprehension of an imminent harmful or offensive conduct;"[2] *battery* is making actual, unwanted, physical contact with another person. As the following examples show, a defendant can commit the tort of battery without committing the tort of assault, and vice versa.

> *Example 2.* Mary is asleep. Her sister Jane comes into the bedroom and slugs her in the arm. Jane is guilty of battery because she touched Mary without Mary's consent. Jane is not guilty of assault, however, because Mary was not aware of Jane's punch before it happened.

> *Example 3.* Mary is sitting in front of the television. Jane enters the room, stands in front of Mary with her arm raised and says "I'm going to punch you." Jane then brings her arm down but hits the couch instead of Mary. Here Jane is guilty of assault, because Mary was aware of the threatened punch. Jane is not guilty of battery because no physical contact occurred.

If, in Example 3, Jane had actually punched Mary, then she would have committed both torts, assault and battery.

The civil torts of assault and battery should not be confused with criminal assault. *Criminal assault*, as defined by Section 14-33 of the North Carolina General Statutes (hereinafter G.S.), means striking another person (battery), attempting to strike another person (assault), or both. Although called simply *assault*, this single criminal offense covers conduct that in the civil context would be two torts—assault and battery. Put another way, under the criminal statute a defendant may be guilty of assault whether or not he or she committed an assault, a battery, or both. Magistrates must keep in mind that in the civil tort context assault and battery are not interchangeable—each tort is separate, has its own elements, and can support a damage award.

These examples also illustrate that the same conduct can constitute both a crime and a tort. When Jane hits Mary, she can be charged with the crime of assault and she can also be sued by Mary for assault and for battery. The criminal charge is intended to protect society as a whole from conduct judged to be criminal, and the tort is to recompense Mary for the wrong done to her.

To prevail in an assault action, the plaintiff must prove that (1) the defendant, by an intentional act or display of force or violence, threatened the plaintiff with imminent bodily harm, and (2) the act caused the plaintiff to have a reasonable apprehension that harmful or offensive contact was imminent.[3] The defendant must have done something, like clench a fist or point a gun, to cause the plaintiff apprehension of imminent physical contact. Words alone generally

---

2. Charles E. Daye & Mark W. Morris, North Carolina Law of Torts § 2.20 (2d ed. 1999).
3. North Carolina Pattern Jury Instructions, N.C.P.I.—Civil 800.50.

do not constitute an assault.[4] The plaintiff's apprehension need not amount to fear; *apprehension* in this context means expectation of imminent contact. Generally, apprehension is reasonable when the defendant is within striking distance of the plaintiff. However, if the defendant makes a statement indicating that he or she does not actually intend to strike the plaintiff, the plaintiff's apprehension may be unreasonable.[5] In any event, if the plaintiff's apprehension is reasonable, he or she will recover damages whether or not physical contact actually occurred.

Nonetheless, an action for assault alone rarely occurs; more frequently, assault is coupled with an action for battery because there has been harmful or offensive physical contact. *Harmful contact* is contact that causes injury or pain, while *offensive contact* is contact that a reasonable person would find offensive.[6] As Example 1 indicates, the defendant need not intend that the contact harm the plaintiff; contact is harmful when a reasonable person of ordinary sensibilities would consider it so, or when a person has not consented to it. Direct physical contact between the defendant and the plaintiff is not necessary for battery; indirect contact with the plaintiff that is caused by some force that the defendant set in motion—such as might occur if the defendant intentionally smashed a plate and a flying shard of glass cut the plaintiff—also constitutes battery.[7] Some cases indicate that touching another person even lightly may constitute a battery,[8] but usually a more substantial contact is involved. Contact with the plaintiff may include contact with anything connected to the plaintiff—for example, a purse or a tote bag.[9]

To recover damages for battery, a plaintiff must prove that (1) the defendant intentionally caused bodily contact with the plaintiff, (2) the bodily contact actually offended a reasonable sense of personal dignity or caused physical pain and injury, and (3) the bodily contact occurred without the plaintiff's consent.[10]

> *Example 4.* Dawson is attempting to repossess a car belonging to Holloway that was parked in front of a laundromat. Holloway comes out of the shop before Dawson hooks up the car; Holloway gets in her car, holding her infant son, and her niece gets in the back seat. As she attempts to start the car, Dawson points a gun at her and reaches his other hand into the window to try to grab the keys. In the process, Dawson's elbow touches the infant's back. The niece testifies that she saw the gun pointed at her aunt and she was afraid both she and her aunt would be shot.
>
> Dawson committed the tort of assault against Holloway and her niece, but not against the infant. The baby, according to testimony, was either asleep or too young to understand what was going on and therefore experienced no apprehension of imminent contact. Dawson did, however,

4. State v. Daniel, 136 N.C. 571, 574, 48 S.E. 544, 545 (1904).

5. State v. Crow, 23 N.C. 375 (1841) (Defendant's statement "were you not an old man I would knock you down" could show no present purpose to strike.).

6. DAYE & MORRIS *supra* note 2, § 2.34.

7. McCracken v. Sloan, 40 N.C. App. 214, 216, 252 S.E.2d 250, 252 (1979).

8. Andrews v. Peters, 75 N.C. App. 252, 330 S.E.2d 638 (1985) (tapping plaintiff's knee from behind was offensive conduct).

9. Kirkpatrick v. Crutchfield, 178 N.C. 348, 100 S.E. 602 (1919).

10. North Carolina Pattern Jury Instructions, N.C.P.I.—Civil 800.51.

commit the tort of battery against the infant. The gist of the action for battery is not that Dawson's intent was hostile, but rather the absence of consent to the contact on the part of the child.[11]

A defendant sued for assault or battery or both has a number of defenses. First, the defendant may argue that the plaintiff consented to the act in question. Consent eliminates the harmful aspect of the defendant's act so long as the act does not go beyond the scope of the plaintiff's consent. Normally, the plaintiff's consent is understood from the way he or she behaves or from the circumstances, rather than from anything he or she says aloud. For example, a plaintiff who is playing football must expect, and impliedly consents to, bodily contact. Because a certain amount of contact is inevitable, "consent is assumed to all those ordinary contacts which are customary and reasonably necessary to the common intercourse of life."[12] For example, a reasonable person expects bodily contact in a crowded elevator. Consent can also be implied by law in emergency situations when the plaintiff is unable to consent and a reasonable person would conclude that some action is necessary to save the plaintiff's life or prevent serious bodily injury.[13] An obvious example of consent implied by law is when the plaintiff is unconscious after an automobile accident and needs mouth-to-mouth resuscitation.

Another defense is self-defense or the defense of others. If the defendant has reasonable grounds to believe that he or she is about to be attacked, and actually does so believe, he or she may use such force as is reasonably necessary to protect against possible injury.[14] Self-defense is only available as a defense, however, if the defendant is not the aggressor in the situation. And the defendant must use only as much force as is necessary to prevent harm. The defendant may also justify the use of force in defense of a third person if he or she had reason to believe that the third person would have been entitled to use force in self defense.

A plaintiff who proves assault or battery or both may recover damages for personal injury. A plaintiff who proves assault or battery or both but cannot prove that the defendant caused actual physical injury may recover nominal damages—for example, one dollar. Finally, if the plaintiff shows that the defendant acted with malice or displayed willful and wanton conduct, he or she may recover punitive damages. A later section of the chapter discusses the difference between these types of damages and how to calculate them.

Actions for both assault and battery tort must be brought within one year of the occurrence.

Trespass to Land

Another intentional tort magistrates might hear is *trespass to land*, which is "any unauthorized entry onto land in the . . . possession of the plaintiff."[15] The intention is to enter another person's land. Entry onto the land can be authorized by permission from the possessor or by an implied

11. Holloway v. Wachovia Bank & Trust Co., 109 N.C. App. 403, 415, 428 S.E.2d 453, 460 (1993).

12. McCracken v. Sloan, 40 N.C. App. 214, 217, 252 S.E.2d 250, 252 (1979).

13. Kennedy v. Parrott, 243 N.C. 355, 90 S.E.2d 754 (1956).

14. State v. Marsh, 293 N.C. 353, 354, 237 S.E.2d 745, 747 (1977). Young v. Warren, 95 N.C. App. 585, 588, 383 S.E.2d 381, 383 (1988) (Defenses of self-defense and defense of others available in criminal actions are also available in civil actions.).

15. DAYE & MORRIS, *supra* note 2, § 6.20.

consent based on customs in the community. It is also an intentional tort to refuse to leave another person's land when asked to do so. For example, unless there is a fence and no trespassing signs are posted, most home owners impliedly authorize anyone to come to the door for any legitimate purpose. Therefore, it is not trespass for a solicitor to come to the front door and ring the doorbell; but if the owner or possessor of the property asks the solicitor to leave, the solicitor commits a trespass if he or she does not leave. Unauthorized entry can also occur through objects, substances, or forces—such as blasting—rather than through the defendant's physical presence on the land.[16] For example, the intentional tort of trespass occurs if the defendant, while on a public street, shoots a pellet gun at plaintiff's mailbox.

The law may also give a person the right to enter on another's land for specific purposes, but that right ceases if the specific purpose is not strictly followed. For example, a secured party has the right to go onto a debtor's land to repossess personal property after the debtor is in default if the secured party can accomplish the repossession peacefully; however, if the secured party acts in a way that creates a breach of the peace, he or she is liable for trespass.[17]

To recover damages for trespass to land, the plaintiff must prove that (1) he or she was in possession of the property, (2) the defendant voluntarily entered or remained upon the plaintiff's property, and (3) the defendant's entry or presence was unauthorized—that is, that it occurred without the plaintiff's express or implied consent, that the defendant refused to leave after having been asked to do so, or that the defendant's conduct exceeded that which had been authorized.[18]

Negligence

A second, very broad, area of torts is negligence. *Negligence* is liability for unintentional injury. A person may be liable to another for causing injury, even though the harm was unintentional, if his or her action or inaction is found to be negligent. The law says that a person who does not behave with the same care that is expected of everyone else and, as a result, harms another, must pay the injured person for the harm done.

The most important rule in the law of negligence is as follows: a person who fails to act as a reasonably prudent person would act under the same or similar circumstances is negligent. In other words, the standard being applied is one that most people should be able to follow. The duty of care imposed by tort law flows from each individual to all persons—known and unknown—who foreseeably could be injured if that individual behaves negligently.

The particular conduct that breaches this duty of care and creates an unreasonable risk of harm to others depends on the facts of each case. Perhaps two examples will illustrate the concept.

16. Wilson v. McLeod Oil Co., 327 N.C. 491, 398 S.E.2d 596 (199) (seepage of gasoline from underground tank).

17. Freeman v. General Motors Acceptance Corp., 205 N.C. 257, 258, 171 S.E. 63 (1933) ("It may be, he was not at first a trespasser, but he became such as soon as he put himself in forcible opposition to the [debtor].").

18. North Carolina Pattern Jury Instructions, N.C.P.I.—Civil 805.00.

Example 5. Menny loved to cook out on breezy summer days. His grill was located on his own property but close to an empty shed on his neighbor Vaughn's land. Vaughn noticed that flames from the grill came dangerously close to the shed and repeatedly asked Menny to move the grill. Menny said he would just "keep an eye on it" rather than moving it. One evening while he was grilling, Menny's wife called him to the phone; while he was talking Vaughn's shed caught fire and burned to the ground. Menny was negligent and is liable for the cost of replacing the shed because a reasonable person would have realized the risk of fire and moved the grill.

Example 6. Sarah was driving to work one day when she suffered a seizure and lost control of her car. Her car crashed into a parked car on the side of the road. Whether Sarah behaved reasonably under the circumstances depends on whether she knew or had reason to know she was susceptible to seizures. If Sarah did not know, no amount of care could have prevented the accident and she was not negligent. If she did know, it may have been negligent for her to drive at all.

As these examples show, negligence is a relative term and the magistrate must look at the particular facts in each case to determine whether negligence is present.[19]

Four Elements of Negligence Action

A plaintiff must prove four elements to recover damages in a negligence action. The plaintiff must show that

1. the defendant had a duty of reasonable care to the plaintiff,
2. the defendant breached that duty (that is, was negligent),
3. the defendant's negligence was a proximate cause of the plaintiff's injury, and
4. the defendant's negligence injured the plaintiff or damaged the plaintiff's property.

Each of these elements is discussed below.

Defendant Owed Plaintiff a Duty of Reasonable Care

What is the legal duty of care? As a general rule, every person is under a legal duty to act as a reasonably prudent person and take precautions against creating an unreasonable risk of injury to others. For example, all drivers of automobiles owe a duty to all others along their route and so must drive with care to avoid injuring any of them. Prudent drivers know—the automobile being a powerful and dangerous instrument—that negligent driving endangers everyone along their route.

A defendant's action creates an unreasonable risk of injury when it is foreseeable that his or her action may result in harm to people in the plaintiff's position; a plaintiff who makes this showing has established that the defendant owed him or her a duty of care. If the defendant could not have reasonably foreseen the events that caused the plaintiff's injury, the plaintiff has not established a duty of care. Most cases that come before a magistrate present no problem in finding the duty to avoid negligent injury of the plaintiff, because the defendant usually owes that duty to the general public.

19. Daye & Morris, *supra* note 2, § 16.20.

When is there a duty to act? Besides the duty *not* to act so as to injure another, we must consider the duty to come to another's assistance. With certain exceptions, the law recognizes no such duty. Generally there is no duty to act to help another.

Example 7. Three-year-old Joey falls into his parents' swimming pool and cannot keep afloat. McNasty, a former Olympic swimming star and next-door neighbor, looks on. Without making a move, he watches Joey drown. McNasty is not liable; he owed the child no legal duty to come to his rescue.

Although there is no legal duty to come to the rescue of another, a person who does undertake a rescue or other assistance must carry it out in a reasonable manner. For example, if McNasty had undertaken to rescue Joey and then had negligently let him fall and hit his head on the concrete next to the pool, McNasty would be liable for the harm resulting from his negligence. By undertaking the rescue, the rescuer creates a duty to the person assisted: that duty is to act with reasonable care in carrying out the rescue, and the rescuer is liable for failure to meet this standard.

There are several exceptions to the general rule that there is no duty to come to the assistance of another. The most important exception is that a person who is at fault and so causes injury to another person is obliged to aid that person.[20]

Example 8. Lawrence is throwing rocks at tin cans. He throws one rock wildly and negligently hits Virginia, who is standing at the side. Virginia slumps to the ground. At this point Lawrence has a duty to help Virginia. If Virginia is seriously injured, Lawrence should see that she gets immediate medical attention.

Lawrence's duty to help Virginia arose because he was at fault: he was negligent in hitting Virginia with a rock.

Sometimes a person has a duty to act because of the relationship between the two parties. Parents have a duty to exercise ordinary care to protect their children, and a person who contracts to provide services to another has a duty to protect that person from harm. For instance, in Example 7, if McNasty had been hired to give Joey swimming lessons and during a lesson had left Joey in the pool while he answered his cell phone and Joey drowned, McNasty would be liable because he owed Joey a duty of care to not be negligent while teaching him to swim.

Finally, North Carolina law provides a duty to act in another situation, even though the person who has the duty may not have been at fault. According to G.S. 20-166 the driver of a vehicle involved in an automobile accident must stop and give assistance to any other person injured in the accident, no matter whose fault the accident was. The same statute provides that anyone who gives assistance at the scene of an automobile accident is not liable for any harm that he or she does unless the harm is the result of "wanton conduct or intentional wrongdoing."

---

20. Parrish v. Atlantic Coast Line R.R., 221 N.C. 292, 300, 20 S.E.2d 299, 304–05 (1942).

Defendant Must Have Failed to Meet the Standard of Reasonable Care

Once the plaintiff has established that the defendant owed him or her a duty of care, the plaintiff must show that the defendant breached that duty—that is, that the defendant was negligent. Generally, the defendant's actions are judged against what a reasonably prudent person, acting with due care and diligence, would do under the same circumstances. In determining whether the defendant exercised reasonable care, a magistrate must judge the actions of the defendant according to the situation facing the defendant at the time he or she decided on a course of action.

> *Example 9.* Sean is driving his automobile one very dark and rainy night. A dog runs in front of his car, about twenty feet ahead. He puts on his brakes and turns to avoid hitting the animal. The car goes into a skid. Before Sean can correct for the skid, the car hits Paul's car, which is parked on the shoulder of the road.
>
> Whether Sean was negligent, whether he failed to exercise reasonable care, should be determined in light of all the circumstances: the wet road, the low visibility, the need for a quick decision, and the desirability of not hitting the dog.

The fact that the defendant's actions should be judged according to the circumstances at the time of the incident means that a lesser standard of care is required in emergency situations. As an emergency allows little time to think about what should be done, Sean could not be expected to make as good a decision as he might have if there were time to think about applying the brakes and swerving to avoid the dog. His actions should be judged by what he could do with only a few seconds to react. In other words, the magistrate should keep second-guessing to a minimum.

Nevertheless, a defendant whose actions created the emergency cannot assert that emergency to get a finding that he or she owed the plaintiff a lower standard of care.

Characteristics of the reasonably prudent person. The magistrate should compare the defendant's actions to those of a person with ordinary mental skills; the defendant's own intellectual ability is not to be taken into account. Whether or not the defendant has normal intelligence, he or she will be judged according to what an ordinary, sane person of average intelligence would have done in those circumstances. In addition, the defendant is presumed to know things that the average member of the community would know. For example, driving on slick or icy roads requires extra care.

Although the defendant's intellectual shortcomings are not to be taken into account, his or her physical limitations are. If the defendant is physically disabled, his or her actions are judged by what a reasonably prudent person with the same disability would have done under the same circumstances. The issue of whether a defendant with a mental disability should receive similar consideration is unsettled.

> *Example 10.* Gorman has been totally blind since he was eight years old. While walking along the sidewalk without a cane or seeing-eye dog, he bumps into Watkins, knocking him to the ground and giving him a concussion. Whether Gorman was negligent depends on whether a reasonably prudent blind man would have been walking abroad without a cane or a dog.

Particular standards of conduct. Some persons are held to standards of conduct different from the reasonable-person standard because of special knowledge, youth, or status in relation to others. Among the most important of these are professionals, children, and bailees (that is, people who, like dry cleaners or airline baggage carriers, hold another person's property for a specific purpose with a promise to return it). In addition, statutes may establish standards of care for particular individuals.

PROFESSIONALS. Professionals or people with special skills (for example, doctors, lawyers, airplane mechanics) are expected to possess and exercise the same level of skill, training, and experience as a practitioner in good standing in the same or similar community. A professional who possesses superior knowledge must use it. Under this standard, an oncologist would be held to a higher degree of care with regard to the treatment of cancer than, say, a country doctor.

CHILDREN. Magistrates should judge a child by what a reasonably prudent child of the same age would do, with a few exceptions. For one thing, the law considers children younger than seven years old incapable of negligence: they are simply is not mature enough to be held responsible for their actions. Children between seven and fourteen are also presumed incapable of negligence, but that presumption may be refuted by evidence that the child failed to exercise the degree of care that can be reasonably expected of a child of like age, discretion, knowledge, and experience under the same circumstances.[21] Thus a twelve-year-old could be held negligent if the plaintiff shows that children of twelve have sufficient intellectual and physical maturity to be held accountable for the kind of act this child committed and therefore that this child failed to behave like a reasonable twelve-year-old.

> *Example 11.* Twelve-year-old Jimmy was playing baseball with some neighborhood kids in his front yard. One of the kids hit a long fly ball and Jimmy, keeping his eyes on the ball, ran into the middle of the street to catch it. Janice, who was driving at a normal rate of speed when Jimmy suddenly appeared in the road, was forced to veer off into a ditch to avoid hitting him. If a normal twelve-year-old child could reasonably be expected to look for cars before running into the street, then Jimmy could be held responsible for any costs incurred by Janice (for example, towing) when she drove into the ditch.

When a child engages in an activity normally reserved for adults, the child will be required to conform to the same standard of care as an adult engaging in the activity. Examples of such activity would be driving an automobile or operating a motorboat.

Questions about a child's responsibility for his or her actions arise most often when a defendant argues that the child–plaintiff was contributorily negligent—that is, when the defendant seeks to prevent recovery by showing that the child's negligence contributed to the accident. Contributory negligence will be discussed more fully below, but one example involving a child will be presented here:

> *Example 12.* The same circumstances as in Example 11, except that Janice was daydreaming and did not turn in time to drive into the ditch; she hit Jimmy, breaking his leg. When Jimmy brings suit against Janice to recover the costs of his medical bills and damages for pain and suffering,

---

21. Allen v. Equity & Investors Mgmt. Corp., 56 N.C. App. 706, 709, 289 S.E.2d 623, 625 (1982).

Janice will not be held responsible if a normal child of Jimmy's age could reasonably be expected to look for cars before running into the street. Jimmy's contributory negligence bars recovery from Janice for her negligence.

BAILEES. A *bailee* is someone who receives possession of another person's property for a specific purpose and promises to return it when the purpose is ended; a *bailor* is the person who entrusts the property to the bailee; delivery of property to the bailee is called *bailment*. Most situations involving bailments are commercial transactions: dry cleaners, appliance repair services, and pet groomers are all bailees. Nonetheless, noncommercial bailments also exist—for example, when Sam borrows his neighbor's lawnmower he is a bailee.

A plaintiff establishes a case of negligence against a bailee by showing that (1) the property was delivered to the bailee, (2) the bailee accepted it and therefore had possession and control of the property, and (3) the bailee failed to return the property or returned it in a damaged condition.[22] That evidence establishes a *prima facie case,* which means that in the absence of evidence to the contrary the magistrate can infer that a negligent act or omission occurred. For example, if the plaintiff shows that the sweater she brought to the dry cleaners was returned to her six sizes smaller, she has established enough for the magistrate to decide the dry cleaners was negligent. To avoid liability in these circumstances the defendant usually must offer some evidence to show that he or she was not negligent—in other words that he or she exercised due care in handling the property.

As it does in other negligence cases, what constitutes due care depends on the circumstances.[23] The law formerly distinguished the level of care needed according to whether the bailment was for the sole benefit of the bailor (a gratuitous bailment), for the bailee's sole benefit, or for the benefit of both. That classification has been discontinued, and the court has held that for all bailments, the standard is "the care of the man of ordinary prudence as adapted to the particular circumstances of the case. The care must be 'commensurate care' having regard to the value of the property bailed and the particular circumstances of the case."[24]

In an action for negligence by a bailee, the plaintiff is entitled to recover the fair market value of the property lost or the difference between the value of the property when delivered to the bailee and its value when it was returned.[25]

> **Example 13.** Nan agrees to hold Sam's lawnmower in her garage as a favor while Sam builds a shed for it in his back yard. Nan does not normally lock her garage door and one night someone breaks in and steals Sam's lawnmower as well as Nan's snow blower. Sam probably would not recover from Nan in a negligence action for the loss of his mower: Nan took the mower as a favor to him, and it is probably not reasonable under these circumstances to ask Nan to take better care of Sam's property than her own.

---

22. Clott v. Greyhound Lines, Inc., 278 N.C. 378, 388, 180 S.E.2d 102, 110 (1971).

23. *Id.* at 384, 180 S.E.2d at 107.

24. *Id.* at 388, 180 S.E.2d at 110.

25. Wilson v. Posey, 219 N.C. 261, 13 S.E.2d 416 (1941).

Example 14. Nan is a lawnmower mechanic. Sam brings his lawnmower in for a tune up. Nan doesn't get to Sam's mower the first day and stores it overnight in her garage, from which it is stolen. Sam will recover from Nan unless she can show that she exercised due care in storing the mower. Nan might show, for example, that she locked the garage door, that she had the same kind of lock as other merchants in the area who store the property of others, that all other means of access to the garage were closed and inaccessible, that nothing had ever been taken from her garage before, or that she had a state-of-the-art security system.

Defendant's Negligence Must Be a Cause of the Plaintiff's Injury

The third requirement for a negligence action is proof that the defendant's negligence was the proximate cause the plaintiff's injury. In other words, what the defendant did wrong must be a cause of the harm to the plaintiff. The North Carolina Supreme Court has defined "proximate cause" as "a cause that produced the result in continuous sequence and without which it would not have occurred, and one from which any man of ordinary prudence would have reasonably foreseen that some injury or harm would probably result from his act or omission under all the facts as they existed."[26]

A close look at the court's definition shows that causation depends on two elements: (1) *but for* causation, that is, the plaintiff's injury would not have occurred but for the defendant's negligent conduct; and (2) *foreseeability*, that is, the defendant should have foreseen that the plaintiff might be harmed if the defendant did not act with reasonable care.

Example 15. Turner is daydreaming while driving down the street. Because of his lack of concentration he rams into Rule's car, which is parked on the side of the road. Turner will be found liable to Rule for his negligence. The damage to Rule's car would not have occurred but for Turner's negligence; and it was foreseeable that if Turner did not drive with reasonable care, he might damage someone else's car. Thus, Turner's actions can be said to be the proximate cause of the damage to Rule's property.

Foreseeability is not very important in most cases; in fact, it seems to be a concept that the courts use only when, as a matter of policy, it seems unfair to hold the defendant liable for particularly remote and unexpected consequences of his actions. North Carolina courts generally consider a wide range of consequences to be foreseeable; even so, situations may occur in which the cause of injuries is so remote that the courts do not hold the defendant liable.

Example 16. Pace is driving his own car down the street. He negligently runs off the side of the road and hits a telephone pole. Edison is inside his house, just opposite the pole, talking on the telephone to his friend Sullins. The noise of the crash startles Edison's pet parrot, which flies into him in panic. When the bird hits him, Edison screams and Sullins, frightened drops the phone at the other end of the line. The phone hits his dog, Rover. Rover jumps up and runs straight into Sullins's Aunt Sally, knocking her over and injuring her. Although Aunt Sally would not have been injured but for Pace's negligence, it is unlikely that he will be held liable for her. The injury

---

26. Boone v. North Carolina R.R., 240 N.C. 152, 155, 81 S.E.2d 380, 383 (1954).

to Aunt Sally was not a foreseeable result of Pace's negligence; it is too remote a consequence for Pace to be held liable.

The defendant need not be able to foresee the particular injury that occurs; he or she need only be able to foresee that some injury might occur. For example, if the defendant shoots at the plaintiff, it is clearly foreseeable that the plaintiff might be injured, which satisfies the foreseeability requirement. For recovery, it does not matter that the plaintiff was in fact injured not by a bullet but by falling when he jumped to avoid it.

Plaintiff Must Have Suffered Actual Loss or Damage

Finally, in an action based on negligence, the plaintiff must show some actual loss or injury. This differs from intentional torts, such as assault or battery, in which the plaintiff is entitled to a nominal sum as damages just for showing that the tort was committed, without proving that he or she was harmed. In a negligence action, the plaintiff must show actual physical injury or property damage, or that he or she was harmed in some other way that caused an out-of-pocket loss. It is not enough to show that the defendant ran into his or her car; the plaintiff must show that the car was dented (or otherwise harmed) as a result of the defendant's act.

Summary

The four elements of a negligence action can be summarized (1) duty, (2) breach, (3) causation, and (4) damages. Except for actions brought against a bailee or under a safety statute, a plaintiff in a negligence action must prove all four elements.

Negligence *per se*—Violation of Safety Statutes

If a defendant has violated a safety statute or ordinance, the magistrate can find him or her negligent without having to determine what a reasonably prudent person would have done in the circumstances. Safety statutes establish standards of conduct for various situations, and everyone is expected to meet those standards; in other words, the General Assembly has established what the reasonably prudent person should do. A defendant who violates the standard established in a safety statute is said to be *negligent per se*, or negligent without question—thus the plaintiff does not have to establish the first two elements of a negligence action—duty and breach of duty.

> ***Example 17.*** Jennifer was driving on the wrong side of the road when she hit Jonathan's car, which was coming in the opposite direction. Driving on the wrong side of the road is a violation of G.S. 20-146, a motor vehicle safety statute. To prove negligence, Jonathan only has to show that Jennifer was driving on the wrong side of the road. He does not have to show that a reasonably prudent person under the circumstances would not have been driving the wrong way on that side of the road, or that Jennifer could have foreseen that driving on the wrong side of the road was likely to cause injury to someone like Jonathan.

A safety statute imposes a duty on each person for the protection of others. Therefore the magistrate must determine the purpose of the statute that has been violated to determine whether negligence per se applies. The magistrate must look at the legislative intent to determine whether it is a safety statute.[27] North Carolina courts have found that the statute prohibiting the use of dealer license plates on personal vehicles is a safety statute,[28] whereas the statute prohibiting the sale of alcoholic beverages to minors is not.[29]

In an action based on negligence per se, the plaintiff must still show that he or she is within the class of people the statute is designed to protect and that the statute was designed to prevent the kind of harm the plaintiff suffered.

> *Example 18.* Lanny owns and manages a newly constructed apartment building that is in violation of a fire safety statute regulating the construction of residential buildings. The regulation requires that each residential unit have two separate exits, but Lanny's units each have only one exit. One night a thief in the process of stealing jewelry from a tenant's apartment was surprised by the sound of a key in the door. Lacking another avenue of escape, the thief jumped through the bathroom window and landed in the alley two stories below, breaking his leg. The thief cannot recover under the fire safety code because its purpose is to protect rightful residents of rental properties, not trespassers. Nor was the harm suffered by the thief the kind the statute was designed to prevent.

In a negligence per se case, the plaintiff must prove that the defendant's negligence (violation of the statute) was a cause of the plaintiff's injury and that the plaintiff suffered damages.

> *Example 19.* Gillman is driving a truck that has several long rods extending more than four feet past the rear of the truck. He has no flag or light on the end of the rods, in violation of G.S. 20-117. Gillman does a bad job of making a left turn and the front end of his truck collides with the front end of an oncoming car belonging to Nichols. Although violation of G.S. 20-117 is negligence per se, Nichols cannot recover against Gillman on those grounds as violation of the statute was not the cause of the accident. (It might have been if Nichols had been following Gillman and the rods pierced his windshield.)

Finally, the plaintiff must also prove that violation of the statute resulted in some injury to the plaintiff or the plaintiff's property.

> *Example 20.* Mrs. Wimpy is walking down the sidewalk when Tommy, a teenage driver showing off for a friend in the car with him, "scratches off" from the corner; he drives down the street at a very high rate of speed that clearly exceeds the posted speed limit of 25 miles per hour. The car startles Mrs. Wimpy and momentarily frightens her. Mrs. Wimpy sues Tommy and shows that he was negligent in violating the speed limit statute and that his violation caused her to be frightened and startled. Mrs. Wimpy is not entitled to a judgment because she cannot show any actual loss or damage.

---

27. Gregory v. Kilbride, 150 N.C. App. 601, 610, 565 S.E.2d 685, 692 (2002).

28. Johnson v. Skinner, 99 N.C. App. 1, 392 S.E.2d 634 (1990).

29. Estate of Mullis v. Monroe Oil Co., 127 N.C. App. 277, 488 S.E.2d 830 (1997) (Purpose is not to protect the driving public from intoxicated drivers but rather to restrict the consumption of alcohol by minors.).

Contributory Negligence

What if, after the plaintiff proves the defendant's negligence, the defendant can show that the plaintiff was also negligent? In North Carolina, if the plaintiff was at all negligent and that negligence contributed to the injury, the plaintiff may not recover. It does not matter that the defendant's negligence was much greater than the plaintiff's; the plaintiff still may not recover.

Contributory negligence is an affirmative defense, which means that the defendant must raise the issue and prove the plaintiff's negligence by the greater weight of the evidence. (However, some magistrates raise affirmative defenses on their own.) The plaintiff does not have to claim lack of negligence as part of his or her case but only has to prove that the defendant was negligent. If, after that, the defendant proves that the plaintiff was also negligent (contributory negligence), the plaintiff then must offer evidence to rebut that claim.

> **Example 21.** Greer is crossing the street in the middle of the block when Cooper, who is driving 30 miles per hour over the speed limit, crashes into him and breaks one of Greer's arms. Greer sues Cooper for hitting him and proves that Cooper was negligent: Cooper violated a safety statute (speed limit law), the violation was a cause of Greer's injury, and Greer suffered injury. Cooper, however, argues that even if he was negligent, Greer's negligence contributed to his injury because he crossed the street in the middle of the block with no crosswalk. Greer was found contributorily negligent and was not entitled to recover from Cooper.

An exception to the contributory negligence rule is the doctrine of "last clear chance." Even if the defendant proves that the plaintiff was contributorily negligent, the plaintiff may still recover damages against the defendant. If the defendant could have, or should have, seen that the plaintiff had placed himself or herself in peril and could have, by using reasonable care, avoided injuring the plaintiff but did not do so, the defendant is liable—even though the plaintiff was contributorily negligent—because he or she had the last clear chance to avoid the accident. To recover damages under last clear chance in Example 21, Greer, the plaintiff, must prove the following: (1) by his own negligence, he placed himself in a position of peril from which he could not escape; (2) the defendant, Cooper, knew, or by the exercise of reasonable care should have recognized, the plaintiff's position of peril and his inability to escape from it; (3) Cooper had the time and the means to avoid the accident and failed to use reasonable care to do so; and (4) that failure proximately caused Greer's injury or damage.[30]

Damages

A magistrate may award three kinds of damages in intentional torts cases—compensatory, punitive, and nominal—and two kinds in negligence cases—compensatory and punitive.

Compensatory Damages

Plaintiffs seeking any damages in negligence cases must show actual damage. In intentional torts cases, plaintiffs are also entitled to any actual damages they show. The purpose of actual damage awards is to make plaintiffs as whole as money can make him or her—thus the official

---

30. Williams v. Lee Brick & Tile, Inc., 88 N.C. App. 725, 728, 364 S.E.2d 720, 721 (1988).

name of these damage awards is *compensatory damages*. Compensatory damages should reimburse the plaintiff for both personal injury and property damage caused by the defendant's conduct, and the total of all damages should be awarded in one lump sum.

Compensatory Damages in Personal Injury Cases

A plaintiff who has suffered physical or mental harm due to the defendant's negligence or intentional tort may seek compensatory damages for personal injury. *Personal injury damages* include medical expenses, loss of earnings, pain and suffering, scars or disfigurement, permanent injury, and loss of future earnings. The kind of personal injury claims magistrates will hear most often are claims for medical expenses, pain and suffering, and loss of earnings.

Medical expenses include hospital, doctor, drug, and other reasonable bills relating to treatment of personal injury. The plaintiff does not have to prove that he or she has already paid these bills to be entitled to reimbursement for them[31]—it is enough that the plaintiff has incurred the expenses because of the harm done by the defendant. Also, the fact that some or all of the plaintiff's medical expenses were paid by an employer, medical insurance, or some other source does not deprive the plaintiff of the right to recover the expenses.[32] In fact the defendant cannot even introduce evidence that the plaintiff has received payment from some other source. This doctrine, called the *collateral source rule*, is based on the idea that the wrongdoer's liability should not be reduced by compensation the plaintiff receives from an independent source.[33] Essentially, the law takes the attitude that the wrongdoer, the defendant, cannot assert someone else's rights (e.g., the employer's or insurer's) to relieve himself or herself of the duty to pay for the damage that he or she caused.

The plaintiff bears the burden of proof to show the amount or value of his or her damages. Generally any manner of proof that tends to establish the amount of the damages inpermissible unless it specifically violates the rules of evidence (and the defendant raises an objection to the evidence). For example, a plaintiff may prove the amount that he or she has spent on medical bills by producing actual bills, receipts, or canceled checks or by orally testifying to the amount.

Generally a plaintiff who suffered a personal injury will have experienced physical pain, mental suffering, or both. For example, if the defendant hit the plaintiff in the face causing a wound that required stitches, the injury would probably hurt for several days; and the plaintiff may have suffered mental anguish worrying about whether the injury will leave a scar. Concrete proof of pain or suffering may be difficult to come by; in most cases plaintiffs simply testify about the nature and extent of the pain they suffered or the effect the injury had on their peace of mind.

The difficulty with pain and suffering claims is determining what amount to award the plaintiff. The plaintiff should be reimbursed for this kind of damage, but it is very difficult to put a fixed monetary value on something as individual as pain and mental anguish. There is no specific formula for figuring out the appropriate amount; the magistrate just has to use common sense to arrive at a figure.

31. Williams v. Charles Stores Co., 209 N.C. 591, 601, 184 S.E.2d 496, 502 (1936).
32. Cates v. Wilson, 321 N.C. 1, 5, 361 S.E.2d 734, 737 (1987).
33. White v. Lowery, 84 N.C. App. 433, 436, 352 S.E.2d 866, 868 (1987).

An award for loss of earnings, on the other hand, is more straightforward. It should give fair compensation for time actually spent away from work because of the injury. The award does not include worktime the plaintiff may lose in the future; nor does it include time away from work for court appearances.

Compensatory Damages for Property Damage

Magistrates can calculate damages for harm to property in two different ways: diminution in market value and recovery of intrinsic value.

The plaintiff shows the diminution in value by proving the difference in fair market value of the property immediately before and after the defendant damaged it. *Fair market value* is the amount that an owner who wishes to sell—but is not compelled to do so—and a buyer who wishes to buy—but is not compelled to do so—would agree is a fair price. Evidence on the fair market value of property before it was damaged might include records of sales of similar property in the plaintiff's local area, pricing information from books (like the NADA Guides) that give estimated retail values for used property, testimony from someone with experience selling property like the plaintiff's, or testimony by the property owner of the property's value. In determining the diminution in value, the magistrate may consider the cost of repairs.

> ***Example 22.*** The door to Bob's 1990 Amana refrigerator was dented by Jerry, who ran into it head first after having too many beers. Bob presents evidence from the local paper's classified section that two 1990 Amana refrigerators are for sale for $500, and another two are for sale at $600. He then presents evidence that he sold the damaged refrigerator, via the classified ads, for $350, which he says was it's fair market value as damaged. In this case, the magistrate would award Bob $200 in damages because Bob's evidence showed that Jerry's action diminished the value of the refrigerator by $200.
>
> But what if Bob testifies that rather than sell the refrigerator, he had the dent repaired for $100? In that situation, the magistrate could consider the $100 repair cost as evidence of the refrigerator's diminution in value.

The second method of calculating damages is used for personal property—such as clothing or architectural drawings—that has no market value. In these circumstances, "the actual value is the property's intrinsic value, that is, its value to its owner."[34] The magistrate may consider the item's original cost, the age of the property, the degree to which it has been used, its condition before it was damaged, the cost of replacing it (taking into account the degree to which it had been worn out), and the owner's opinion of its value.

Punitive Damages

Most cases in which a plaintiff seeks punitive damages are filed in superior or district court because of the higher allowable amount in controversy. Nonetheless, magistrates are authorized to award punitive damages when appropriate. Punitive damages may be awarded in both intentional tort and negligence cases, but they are much more common in intentional tort cases

---

34. William F. Freeman, Inc. v. Alderman Photo Co., 89 N.C. App. 73, 76, 365 S.E.2d 183.

because proof of more than ordinary negligence is required for such awards. *Punitive damages* are awards of money greater than the amount necessary to compensate the plaintiff for his or her loss or injury. The purpose of punitive damages is not, in fact, related to compensating the plaintiff for injury at all; they are intended to punish the defendant for egregiously wrongful acts—in other words, they are designed to teach the defendant a lesson and to deter others from committing similar acts.[35]

Punitive damages may be awarded only if the plaintiff proves that the defendant is liable for compensatory damages and that fraud, malice, or willful or wanton conduct was present and was related to the injury for which the compensatory damages were awarded. Compensatory damages include nominal damages, so it is possible for a plaintiff to be awarded punitive damages even when the compensatory damages award was only a dollar. *Malice* means that the defendant's personal ill will toward the plaintiff caused him or her to undertake the act that resulted in harm to the plaintiff. *Willful or wanton conduct* is the conscious and intentional disregard of and indifference to the rights and safety of others, which the defendant knows, or should know, are reasonably likely to result in injury, damage, or other harm. To recover punitive damages, the plaintiff must prove fraud, malice, or willful or wanton conduct by clear and convincing evidence, a standard higher than the usual greater-weight-of-the-evidence standard.

If the plaintiff proves that he or she is entitled to punitive damages, the magistrate, in determining the amount of damages, must consider the purposes of punitive damages and may consider any evidence showing the reprehensibility of the defendant's conduct, the degree of his or her awareness of the probable consequences of that conduct, the actual damages suffered by the plaintiff, the existence and frequency of any similar past conduct by the defendant, and the defendant's ability to pay punitive damages as evidenced by his or her revenues or net worth.

> *Example 23.* Aunt Elizabeth knows that her niece Emma has been taunted by bullies at school all year long; and every night she has nightmares in which the bullies shake their fists in her face and threaten to punch her. Her constant fear of the bullies and inability to sleep restfully because of the nightmares have made Emma very jumpy. Yet one day when Aunt Elizabeth is visiting the family, she sneaks up behind the child, puts her fist in front of Emma's face, and says in a disguised voice, "I'm gonna get you, little girl." Emma faints and breaks her glasses when she falls. A magistrate might award Emma punitive damages for her aunt's assault as Elizabeth knew about Emma's very sensitive state and her conduct was willful or wanton.

Whether or not to award punitive damages in cases in which the evidence of the defendant's conduct meets the clear and convincing standard is entirely up to the magistrate hearing the case. A plaintiff never has a *right* to punitive damages.

Nominal Damages

Nominal damages are available only in intentional tort cases (for example, for assault or battery). Nominal damages are trivial monetary awards, usually of a dollar, designed to give the plaintiff a symbolic victory when he or she cannot show any actual injury. Nominal damages reflect

---

35. N.C. Gen. Stat. § 1D-1 (hereinafter G.S.). North Carolina's punitive damages law is statutory and found in G.S. Ch.1D.

society's judgment that intentional interference with a person or a person's property should be punished and that, even though the purpose of nominal damages is not compensation, the plaintiff who shows that the defendant committed an intentional tort is entitled to collect damages in some fashion—even if the tort resulted in no actual damages.

Statute of Limitations

The plaintiff in a negligence action must file a complaint within three years of the time the cause of action arose.[36] The three-year statute of limitations also applies to most intentional torts—for example, assault, battery, conversion, fraud, and trespass. The statute of limitations for libel and slander, however, is one year.[37]

Strict Liability

In some cases, liability is strict liability, or liability without fault. *Strict liability* means that the defendant has an absolute duty to the plaintiff that, if breached and the plaintiff is injured, results in liability. The plaintiff is not obligated to show that the defendant behaved negligently. Most frequently, strict liability applies to activities that, while tolerated, pose a great risk of harm to others. For example, dangerous activities like blasting are not prohibited outright because they are socially useful; but the risk of harm they create is so great—even when they are done with every reasonable precaution—that a person engaging in them will be held to answer for any damage they cause.

Magistrates will almost never encounter strict liability cases except for violations of the dangerous dogs statute.[38]

Parents' Liability for Children's Acts

In certain cases, one person injures another but a third person is held liable to the injured party. This kind of liability, called *vicarious liability*, rests not on the third person's direct involvement in the tort but, rather, on a special relation between the third party and the person who committed the tort. The most important point about this doctrine for magistrates is that, as a general rule, parents are *not* vicariously liable for the torts of their children.

G.S. 1-538.1 does, however, make parents liable for the willful and intentional torts of their children and imposes liability of up to $2,000 dollars for a child's willful injury of another person or destruction of another's real or personal property. To recover damages under this statute, the plaintiff must show that the defendant's child was under the age of eighteen, that the child maliciously or willfully injured the plaintiff or destroyed the plaintiff's property, and that actual damages resulted. If the actual damages are more than $2,000, the parents are liable

---

36. G.S. 1-52. The statute provides that in personal injury or property damage cases, the cause of action accrues (in other words, the statute of limitations begins to run) when the injury or damage becomes apparent or should reasonably have been discovered. However, the plaintiff must bring the action within ten years of the last act of the defendant that gave rise to the suit.

37. G.S. 1-54.

38. G.S. 67-4.4.

for only $2,000. The statute does not apply if the parents' custody and control of the child have been removed by court order before the act complained of; in other words, if the child is in the custody of the county department of social services and has been placed in a foster home or group home when the act occurs, the parents are not liable under G.S. 1-538.1. Moreover, if the father has primary custody of the child and the mother has visitation only on weekends, the mother is not liable under the statute unless the cause of action occurred during the periods of visitation.

> **Example 24.** Eleven-year-old Johnny was out in the front yard pitching a baseball to his friends. One of his pitches went wild and crashed through the window of the house next door.
>
> Johnny's parents are not liable for the damage to the window because it was caused by Johnny's negligent, not intentional, act. (Although remember that if Johnny did not exercise the degree of care that could be reasonably expected of a child of the same age and like discretion, knowledge, and experience under the same circumstances, he could be held liable.)
>
> If, on the other hand, Johnny was angry at the owner of the house next door for not giving him any candy on Halloween, and he intentionally threw the baseball through the window, his parents may be held liable for damages up to $2,000. Johnny's act was intentional, done expressly for the purpose of breaking the window, and with fairly certain knowledge that his action would achieve that result.

Parents can also be held liable for their own negligence in relation to their children. This liability, following traditional negligence principles, is independent of G.S. 1-538.1 and is therefore not limited to $2,000. The parents' liability arises out of a duty to adequately supervise and control their child. A plaintiff injured by a child can recover from the child's parents under a theory of the parent's negligence if he or she can show that (1) the child's parents knew or should have known that the child was engaging in—or on past occasions had engaged in—conduct dangerous to others or their property; (2) the parents had the ability and opportunity to control the child; (3) in the exercise of ordinary care under the same or similar circumstances, a reasonable parent would have exercised sufficient control over the child to prevent such misbehavior; and (4) the parents failed to exercise sufficient control or supervision over the child, which failure was a proximate cause of the injury.[39]

Attorneys' Fee Awards in Tort Cases

G.S. 6-21.1 provides that

> [i]n any personal injury or property damage suit . . . instituted in a court of record, where the judgment for recovery of damages is ten thousand dollars or less, the presiding judge may, in his discretion, allow a reasonable attorney fee to the duly licensed attorney representing the litigant obtaining a judgment for damages in said suit, said attorney's fee to be taxed as a part of the court costs.

---

39. Moore v Crumpton, 306 N.C. 618, 295 S.E.2d 436 (1982).

As there is no appellate case indicating whether or not this statute applies to magistrates, two issues of definition arise: Is small claims court a "court of record"? Does the term "presiding judge" include a magistrate?

Court of record does not have a universal meaning. Blackstone defines it as a court "where the judicial proceedings are enrolled in parchment for the perpetual memorial and testimony, which rolls are called the record of the court and are of such high and preeminent authority that their truth is not in question."[40] A record of a court's proceedings does not refer only to a court that keeps a verbatim transcript a court that maintains a permanent record of its acts and judicial proceedings is a court of record.[41] Minutes of small claims proceedings are kept;[42] the clerk keeps and microfilms records of the proceeding;[43] and the magistrate's judgment is a district court judgment that is recorded and indexed and enforced in the same manner as other district court and superior court judgments.[44] Therefore, small claims court is a "court of record."

G.S. 6-21.1 provides that the presiding judge may award attorneys' fees, which raises the question of whether the magistrate is a "presiding judge" in small claims cases. Most of the statutes provide that the "presiding judge" awards attorneys' fees. The exceptions are G.S. 6-21.3 (the worthless check statute), which specifically applies to the presiding judge *or* magistrate; and G.S. 6-21.2 (attorneys' fees provisions in notes, conditional sale contracts, or other evidences of indebtedness), which simply makes the contract enforceable and does not mention "presiding judge." One might argue that since G.S. 6-21.3 specifically mentions magistrates and none of the other statutes do, only a judge can award attorneys' fees in the other statutes. However, that does not make sense, because magistrates are, in fact, presiding judges over small claims cases. Moreover, the court has held that the purpose of G.S. 6-21.1 is "to provide relief for a person who has sustained injury or property damage in an amount so small that, if he must pay his attorney out of his recovery, he may well conclude that it is not economically feasible to bring suit on his claim."[45] That purpose should apply equally to parties who choose to file suit in small claims and district courts. Even though this question is not the issue in appellate cases, it is clear from the facts stated in some opinions that magistrates are in fact awarding attorneys' fees in cases in which the statute authorizes the "presiding judge" to do so.[46] Thus, it is probable that magistrates may award attorneys' fees, upon request, in property damage or personal injury cases (for, example automobile accidents or assaults) before them. The decision to award

---

40. Newman v. Basch, 89 Misc. 622, 627–28, 152 N.Y.S. 456, 459–60 (1915). *See also* State v. West, 31 N.C. App. 431, 439, 229 S.E.2d 826, 830 (1976) (quoting 3 Blackstone, COMMENTARIES § 24).

41. *In re* Marriage of Case, 856 P.2d 169 (Kan. App. 1993); *In re* Interest of Mainor T., 674 N.W.2d 442, 461 (Neb. 2004). *See* 20 AM. JUR. 2D, *Courts* § 10 (2005).

42. *See* Provident Fin. Co. v. Locklear, 89 N.C. App. 535, 366 S.E.2d 599 (1988); Rules of Recordkeeping, Rule 4.7 Comment (Raleigh: Administrative Office of the Courts, 2001).

43. Rules of Recordkeeping, Rule 4.10.

44. G.S. 7A-224 and -225.

45. Hicks v. Albertson, 284 N.C. 236, 239, 200 S.E.2d 40, 42 (1973).

46. Mills v. Stallings, 162 N.C. App. 180, 590 S.E.2d 332 (2004) (unpublished opinion); Friday v. United Dominion Realty Trust, Inc., 155 N.C. App. 671, 575 S.E.2d 532 (2003); Riverview Mobile Home Park v. Bradshaw, 119 N.C. App. 585, 459 S.E.2d 283 (1995).

attorneys' fees in such cases is discretionary, and the magistrate who decides to award fees must determine a reasonable amount.

Summary

As a rule, the bulk of tort cases magistrates hear are based on negligence. In the rare cases that are based on intentional torts, magistrates must keep in mind that the intention to do the act that causes the harm, not the intention to cause harm, is key to his or her finding. Another thing to remember is that nominal damages can be awarded in intentional tort cases, even if the plaintiff cannot show that he or she sustained actual damages.

To be successful in a negligence action, the plaintiff must prove (1) that the defendant owed him or her a duty of care, (2) that the defendant breached this duty of care, (3) that the defendant's breach was a cause injury, and (4) that the plaintiff suffered damage.

Breaking the negligence action down into those four elements makes it easier to decide the more complicated cases. That same purpose can be accomplished in most negligence small claims actions by the magistrate asking himself or herself several simple questions.

1. Could the defendant reasonably expect that that his or her negligent conduct could cause harm to another person?
2. Did the defendant act less carefully than a reasonably prudent person would under the same circumstances?
3. Did the defendant's actions cause the plaintiff's injury?
4. Was the plaintiff actually hurt in some way?

If the answer to each of these questions is yes, the defendant is liable to the plaintiff.

The defendant can avoid liability by showing that the plaintiff also was negligent (contributory negligence), but the defendant must raise that argument and prove the plaintiff's negligence.

Once the plaintiff has proved his or her case and the defendant has been found negligent, the magistrate must determine the amount of damages to award. That determination generally will not be difficult because the plaintiff must show actual damages. He or she should recover a sum of money adequate to pay for the losses shown, such as the cost of repairing a car, or the sum of his or her doctor bills, or lost wages while away from work. The magistrate should rely on these proven costs of injury and avoid guessing at the damage done to the plaintiff.

Chapter V

Actions to Recover Possession
of Personal Property

When personal property is wrongfully taken from its owner or is taken with permission but wrongfully detained, an owner has a choice of legal actions to bring against the person holding the property. He or she can bring a lawsuit for the tort of conversion or an action to recover possession of the property.[1] This chapter begins with a consideration of these two choices and the distinctions between them; it then looks in detail at the process of bringing an action to enforce a security agreement.

Conversion and Actions to Recover Possession By a Nonsecured Party

Action for Conversion

Conversion is defined as "an unauthorized assumption and exercise of the right of ownership over goods or personal chattels belonging to another, to the alteration of their condition or the exclusion of the owner's rights. . . . The essence of conversion is . . . a wrongful deprivation of [the property] to the owner."[2]

Conversion is sometimes called a "forced sale" because if the plaintiff succeeds in the lawsuit, the defendant is in effect forced to buy the property from the plaintiff. The plaintiff does not seek to recover the property but to recover its value from the defendant. Therefore, in an action for conversion, the plaintiff sues the person who wrongfully took or wrongfully retained the property for the fair market value of the property at the time it was taken or not returned.[3] *Fair market value* is the amount that would be agreed upon as a fair price by an owner who wishes to sell, but is not compelled to do so, and a buyer who wishes to buy, but is not compelled to do

---

1. Both of these present-day actions come from common law actions. At common law, today's action for conversion was called a *writ of trover*, and an action to recover possession of personal property was *replevin* or *detinue*. The magistrate might see old North Carolina cases that use those terms rather than the present-day ones.

2. State *ex rel.* Pilard v. Berninger, 154 N.C. App. 45, 57, 571 S.E.2d 836, 844 (2002). Although the cases that define conversion state that the plaintiff must be the owner of the property, in *Wall v. Colvard, Inc.,* 268 N.C. 43, 149 S.E.2d 559 (1966), the plaintiff was someone entitled to immediate possession, which could be a bailee or a senior lienor seeking to recover the property from a junior lienor.

3. The complaint form used to file for conversion is "Complaint for Money Owed," AOC-CVM-200.

so.[4] The owner's testimony of the property's worth is sufficient to uphold a judgment for that amount.[5] The magistrate may also award interest at the legal rate of 8 percent per annum from the date of the wrongful taking.[6]

A plaintiff is not required to demand return of the property if the defendant wrongfully took possession of the property; but he or she must make such a demand if the property came into the defendant's possession lawfully but was not returned.[7] For example, if the defendant leased the property from the owner but failed to return it, the property is not converted until the plaintiff demands its return. This principle applies even when the lease specifies a time to return the property and the defendant does not return it at that time.[8]

In an action for conversion the plaintiff must prove the following three things:

1. The plaintiff is the lawful owner of the personal property taken and is entitled to repossess it immediately.
2. The defendant converted the property by
   a. wrongfully taking it from the plaintiff, or
   b. rightfully taking the property from the plaintiff but wrongfully retaining it after a demand to return it.
3. The fair market value of the property at the time it was wrongfully taken or wrongfully retained.

Action to Recover Possession

When a person has personal property wrongfully taken from him or her, or rightfully taken but wrongfully retained, he or she may—instead of bringing a complaint for conversion—bring an action to recover possession of the personal property. In doing so, the plaintiff is asking the court to require the defendant to return the property to its rightful owner, pay the owner for any damage done to the property while it was in the defendant's possession, and pay compensation for the plaintiff's loss of use of the property while it was wrongfully held by the defendant. The plaintiff is entitled to monetary damages as well as recovery of the property when money damages are necessary to put the plaintiff in the position he or she would have been in had the wrong never occurred.[9] Sometimes the plaintiff cannot discover whether there has been any physical damage to the property until he or she recovers possession; in that situation, the plaintiff may later file a separate action for damages.[10]

---

4. *E.g.*, Huff v. Thornton, 287 N.C. 1, 12, 213 S.E.2d 198, 206 (1975); City of Hillsborough v. Hughes, 140 N.C. App. 714, 720, 538 S.E.2d 586, 589 (2000).

5. Yeargin v. Spurr, 78 N.C. App 243, 336 S.E.2d 680 (1985) (Owner's testimony that his two cows were worth $1,000 was sufficient for jury to award those damages.).

6. Phelps v. Duke Power Co., 324 N.C. 72, 77, 376 S.E.2d 238, 241 (1989).

7. Porter v. Alexander, 195 N.C. 5, 7, 141 S.E. 343, 344 (1928); Hoch v. Young, 63 N.C. App. 480, 482, 305 S.E.2d 201, 203 (1983).

8. Griffith v. Glen Wood Co., 184 N.C. App. 206, 213, 646 S.E.2d 550, 556 (2007).

9. The complaint form used for this action is "Complaint to Recover Possession of Personal Property/Plaintiff A Secured Party/Plaintiff Not A Secured Party," CVM-202. The bottom half of the form—Plaintiff Not A Secured Party—is to be completed by the plaintiff in this type of action.

10. *Cf.* Coulbourn v. Armstrong, 243 N.C. 663, 667, 91 S.E.2d 912, 915–16 (1956).

The action to recover possession must be brought against the person who is actually in possession of the property, even if that is not the person who wrongfully took it or wrongfully retained it.[11] However, if the action is brought against the person who wrongfully took the property and the plaintiff discovers that the defendant has sold or otherwise disposed of the property, the magistrate may allow the plaintiff's request to amend the complaint to an action for conversion.[12]

In an action to recover possession of personal property (as a nonsecured party), the plaintiff must prove the following four things:

1. The plaintiff is the lawful owner of the personal property and is entitled to repossess it immediately.
2. The property was wrongfully taken from the plaintiff, or the property was lawfully taken but wrongfully retained after demand for its return.
3. The defendant is in possession of the property.
4. The amount of damages, if any, for loss of use of the property and physical damage to it.

Claim and Delivery

There is one other difference between an action in conversion and an action to recover possession by a nonsecured party. In the action to recover possession, the ancillary remedy of claim and delivery is available.[13] *Claim and delivery* is a procedure by which the plaintiff who files an action to recover possession of personal property can gain possession of the property immediately to protect it and hold it until the magistrate determines at the trial who is entitled to the property.[14] The claim and delivery proceeding is heard before the clerk of court, not the magistrate, and is rare in small claims cases. The magistrate will know it has occurred because the case file will contain a copy of the clerk's order of seizure with a return of service indicating that the sheriff has seized the property and turned it over to the plaintiff.[15] Claim and delivery does not decide ownership of the property; it is only a provisional remedy allowing the plaintiff to acquire temporary possession. Therefore, even though the plaintiff has physical possession of the property, at the trial for action to recover possession the plaintiff must still prove that he or she is entitled to possess the property. The magistrate's determination and judgment are the same as those in any other action to recover possession. If a plaintiff who has gained possession by claim and delivery fails to prove in the main action that he or she is entitled to possess the property, the magistrate must order the plaintiff to return it to the defendant.

11. Bowen v. Harris, 146 N.C. 385, 389, 59 S.E. 1044, 1046 (1907).
12. Craven v. Russell, 118 N.C. 564, 24 S.E. 361 (1896).
13. N.C. Gen. Stat. § 7A-210 (hereinafter G.S.), G.S. 7A-231.
14. The procedure for claim and delivery is set out in G.S. 1-472 through -484.1.
15. The form the clerk uses is "Order of Seizure in Claim and Delivery," AOC-CV-203. The file also might contain the following other preliminary forms in the claim and delivery proceeding: "Affidavit and Request for Hearing in Claim and Delivery," AOC-CV-200; "Notice of Hearing in Claim and Delivery," AOC-CV-201; "Findings on Application for Claim and Delivery Order," AOC-CV-202.

Who Decides Which Action to Bring

The choice between an action for conversion or an action to recover possession of the personal property lies solely with the owner of the property. Once the property has been converted, the defendant cannot prevent the owner from bringing an action for conversion by offering to return the property.[16]

Examples of Conversion versus Action to Recover Possession

Examples of the difference between an action to recover possession and an action in conversion may be useful.

> ***Example 1.*** Anna and Greg are next-door neighbors. While Anna is on vacation, Greg goes to her house and takes Anna's new riding lawn mower (value: $550) and uses it to cut his own grass. When Anna returns, she discovers that Greg has the lawn mower. Not only that, Greg ran over a large rock while cutting his grass and damaged the blade. It will cost $150 to repair. Because she does not have the lawn mower, Anna rents one for $25 to cut her grass.

What legal remedies does Anna have? She can bring an action against Greg to recover possession of the personal property, the lawn mower. If she prevails, her relief will include return of the mower plus $175 monetary damages ($150 for damage to the mower blade and $25 for loss of use of the mower). Or Anna could bring action in conversion against Greg. If she prevailed in that action, she would recover from Greg damages of $550 (the value of the mower at the time it was wrongfully taken) plus interest of 8 percent per year on $550 from the time Greg took the mower until judgment was entered. (The clerk would also add 8 percent interest on the $550 from the date of judgment until the judgment is satisfied.)

Generally, these two actions are brought by private individuals unconnected with any business enterprise. However, either action can also be brought in a business situation, as the following example shows.

> ***Example 2.*** Dave rents a television from Furniture Rental Inc. on April 15. He pays the rent in advance and agrees to return the television at the end of May. When he does not return it on May 31, the manager calls him on June 3 and asks him to return the television. Dave does not. Furniture Rental Inc. has two options: if it wants the television back, it can bring an action to recover possession of personal property; or it can force Dave to buy the television by bringing an action in conversion.

Notice that in Example 1 the property taken—the lawn mower—was wrongfully taken. In Example 2 the television was not wrongfully taken but was wrongfully retained after being rightfully taken. Either way, the true owner is denied use of his or her property and so is entitled to bring an action against the person holding the property. However, the time when the action accrues is different in the two situations. When property is wrongfully taken, the conversion or wrongful act occurs when the property is taken, whereas when the property is taken with permission but wrongfully retained, the conversion or wrongful act occurs when the property

16. Wall v. Colvard, Inc., 268 N.C. 43, 49, 149 S.E.2d 559, 564 (1966).

is not returned after the owner demands its return. In Example 2 the wrongful act occurs on June 3, not May 31, and the magistrate may award interest at 8 percent per year from that date until judgment.

Action Brought to Enforce a Security Agreement

Most actions to recover possession of personal property a magistrate hears result from commercial transactions in which different provisions of the law come into operation. The most important of these is Article 9 of the North Carolina General Statutes, Chapter 25 (hereinafter G.S.). That chapter contains North Carolina's version of the Uniform Commercial Code (hereinafter UCC), a set of laws governing commercial transactions that has been adopted by almost all states. Article 9 contains the provisions regulating *secured transactions*—that is, transactions in which a debt is created and payment of the debt is secured by personal property.[17] These transactions are for personal property what mortgages and deeds of trust are for real property.

A creditor must consider two main risks when he or she sells goods on credit or lends money. One is that the debtor will stop making the payments, in which case the creditor will want to be able to gain possession of some of the debtor's property in order to sell it and satisfy the remaining debt. The other risk is that the debtor will default and that a third party will claim the property sold to the debtor: for example, the debtor might sell the property, the property might be seized under a judgment against the debtor, or the debtor may file bankruptcy. In these situations the creditor will have to defeat third parties' claims to the property. The UCC contains provisions that protect the creditor against both these risks. By taking a security interest in the property, the creditor obtains the right to repossess the goods if the debtor defaults; if certain filing requirements are met, the security interest also protects the creditor's right of possession against third parties. Because the first situation—relating to the rights of creditor and debtor in cases of default on the debt—is more likely to come before a magistrate, it is discussed in detail. A briefer explanation of the creditor's rights against third parties appears at the end of the chapter.

First, some definitions are in order. A *secured party* is the person who has advanced money or extended credit and taken a security interest in personal property (collateral) in return. The secured party is either a seller who sells goods, at least partly on credit, or a lender who advances money for either the purchase of specific goods—in that case taking a security interest in the goods purchased—or for some other purpose—in which case the lender takes as collateral personal property already owned by the debtor. The same rules apply to both types of secured parties, whether sellers or lenders. Sometimes the secured party is referred to as the *creditor* and the debtor is called a *buyer* or a *borrower*. In the following discussion, the terms *secured party* and *creditor* are used interchangeably when the law is the same for seller–buyer and lender–borrower transactions. The terms *seller* and *buyer* or *lender* and *borrower* are used when the statement applies only to one type of transaction.

---

17. The UCC provisions have replaced the previous law governing mortgages on personal property (chattel mortgages) and conditional sales.

A *security interest* is an interest in specified personal property that secures payment of the underlying debt or secures some other obligation. *Collateral* is the common term for the property in which a security interest is taken. The secured party takes a security interest in the debtor's personal property or takes the personal property as collateral for an extension of credit or a loan. The term *security agreement* refers to the agreement that creates or provides for a security interest—an agreement between creditor and debtor in which the debtor grants a security interest in personal property to the secured party/creditor.

Why Take a Security Interest?

An example of when a security agreement might be signed is instructive.

> *Example 3.* Tamika and Billy decide they want a new refrigerator. The one they like costs $2,500 from Sears. Unfortunately, they don't have $2,500. However, Sears agrees to sell them the refrigerator on credit if they make a $200 down payment. Sears has Tamika and Billy sign a promissory note indicating that they owe Sears $2,300, plus interest at 18 percent per year. They also ask Tamika and Billy to sign a security agreement indicating that if they default on the payments, Sears is entitled to take possession of the refrigerator.

But why would Sears want to make a security agreement? If Tamika and Billy default, whether or not they signed a security agreement, Sears could always sue for money damages for the remaining balance due on the note. So if they had made payments for six months and then defaulted owing $1,250, Sears could sue for money owed and seek a judgment of $1,250, plus interest at the contract rate until judgment. If Sears were to get a judgment against Tamika and Billy, the sheriff could seize their property and sell it to satisfy the judgment. Debtors, however, are entitled to claim a certain amount of their real and personal property as exempt from judgments. In many instances, debtors do not have sufficient property over and above what they can claim as exempt and creditors are left with uncollectible judgments. But if the creditor takes a security interest in personal property (or a deed of trust in real property), the debtor cannot exempt that property and the creditor can take possession of the property and sell it to satisfy the debt. So if, in Example 3, Tamika and Billy don't have sufficient property above their exemption rights to satisfy the debt, Sears can at least repossess the refrigerator and sell it to satisfy some or all of the remaining debt.

Many people incorrectly believe that when a seller sells something to another person on credit and the buyer does not fully pay for the item, the seller has the right to take it back. That is not the law! A seller who sells goods on credit has no right to take them back if the buyer fails to pay unless the seller has taken a security interest in the property. Once property is sold, the purchaser becomes the owner of the property and it can only be reclaimed if the parties have entered into a security agreement. Similarly, if a lender lends money to a borrower to buy certain personal property and the borrower fails to repay the loan, the lender cannot take possession of the purchased property unless the lender has taken a security interest in the property. The unsecured seller's or lender's only remedy is to sue for the money owed on the underlying debt.

When Creditor Has Rights against Property

To have an enforceable right to repossess property, a secured party must first show proof that the following three requirements have been satisfied:

1. Value has been given.
2. The debtor has rights in the collateral.
3. There is a valid security agreement.

The UCC refers to the time at which a security interest becomes enforceable against the debtor as *attachment*.[18] Value has been given when the debtor makes a down payment, signs a note, or provides other evidence of indebtedness for the purchase. In most cases that come before the magistrate, the debtor's rights in the collateral is proven by the debtor's possession of the property.

The following requirements must be met for a valid security agreement:

- The agreement must be authenticated by the debtor. *Authenticate* means that the debtor has to sign or "to execute, or otherwise adopt a symbol, or encrypt or similarly process a record . . . with the present intent of the authenticating person to identify the person and adopt or accept a record."[19] Use of the word *authenticate* is intended to cover agreements entered into electronically as well as by means of traditional signed, written contracts.
- The agreement must provide a description of the personal property in which a security interest is taken. The description is sufficient, whether or not it is specific, if it reasonably identifies what is described.[20] It need not include serial numbers, but it must be sufficient to make it possible to separate the property from other similar property owned by the debtor.[21] For example a description of "five mules"—when the debtor owned fifteen mules—was insufficient,[22] while a description reading "all dairy cattle including 512 bulls, cows, heifers, calves and all progeny resulting from said cattle on the premises of Jen Hethrington, in the City of Morganton" was sufficient.[23]
- The agreement must indicate the intention of the parties to create a security interest.[24] The writing does not need to be labeled as a security agreement or be a separately executed document, so long as it evinces the intention to create a security interest.[25]
- If it is a consumer credit contract, the agreement must be dated.[26]

---

18. G.S. 25-9-203.

19. G.S. 25-9-102(a)(7).

20. G.S. 25-9-108.

21. Forehand v. Edenton Farmers Co., 206 N.C. 827, 829, 175 S.E. 183, 184 (1934).

22. *Id.* at 830; 175 S.E. at 185.

23. Mountain Farm Credit Serv. ACA v. Purina Mills Inc., 119 N.C. App. 508, 511–12, 459 S.E.2d 75, 78–79 (1995).

24. Evans v. Everett, 279 N.C. 352, 358, 183 S.E.2d 109, 113 (1971).

25. Little v. Orange County, 31 N.C. App. 495, 497–98, 229 S.E.2d 823, 825 (1976); *In re* Murray Bros., Inc., 53 B.R. 281, 284 (Bankr. E.D.N.C. 1985).

26. G.S. 25A-28. A consumer credit contract is a sale of goods or services in which the seller in the ordinary course of business regularly extends credit, the buyer is a natural person, the goods or services are purchased

The Retail Installment Sales Act (RISA),[27] which covers only the seller–buyer relationship, limits the property a creditor may take as collateral. If the security agreement arises out of a consumer credit sale (essentially one in which the seller of the goods extends the credit for consumer purposes), the seller may take a security interest in the following property only:

1. the property being sold to the debtor at the time the security agreement is created;
2. property previously sold by the same seller to the buyer in which the seller still has an existing security interest;
3. personal property to which the property sold is installed (e.g., a new compressor in a heating/air conditioning unit), if the amount financed is more than $300;
4. a self-propelled motor vehicle to which repairs are made, if the amount financed exceeds $100; and
5. property used for agricultural purposes if the property sold is to be used in operating an agricultural business.[28]

A security interest taken in property other than permitted property is void and unenforceable.

Example 4. John buys a Maytag washing machine and dryer from ABC Appliance Company, and the company extends him credit for the purchase. He signs a security agreement listing the Maytag washing machine and dryer, a Westinghouse refrigerator, and a 36-inch Sony television set as collateral for the extension of credit. John defaults, and ABC Appliance brings an action as a secured party to obtain possession of all four items. In court John proves that he bought only the washer and dryer from ABC Appliance; he already owned the refrigerator and television, which he bought from other stores. The magistrate should find that ABC Appliance was entitled to recover possession of the washing machine and dryer only. It could have no security interest in the refrigerator or television because John had not bought them from ABC—either at the same time as the refrigerator or at any earlier time under a still existing security agreement. The provision of the agreement granting a security interest in the refrigerator and television is void and not enforceable.

But what if John had borrowed money from a finance company to purchase the washing machine and dryer? In that situation, RISA does not apply. As no state law limits the collateral lenders can take, a finance company would be able to recover possession of all four items under state law. There is, however, a federal regulation making it an unfair trade practice for a finance company (or some sellers) to take certain household goods as collateral in a security agreement.[29]

---

primarily for personal, family, household, or agricultural purposes, the debt is payable in installments or a finance charge is imposed, and the amount financed is not more than $75,000. G.S. 25A-2(a).

27. The Retail Installment Sales Act (RISA) is discussed in Chapter III, "Contracts."

28. G.S. 25A-23. The statute also allows the seller to take a security interest in real property to which the property sold is affixed if the amount financed is more than $1,000; however, magistrates cannot hear cases in which plaintiffs are seeking to recover real property.

29. 16 C.F.R. § 444.1 to 444.5. The regulation states that it is an unfair trade practice for a lender or seller to take a security interest in household goods other than a purchase money security interest. It defines the following items belonging to the consumer and his or her dependents as household goods: clothing, furniture, appliances, one radio and one television, linens, china, crockery, kitchenware, and personal effects (including

Unless the debtor files a counterclaim for an unfair trade practice, however, the federal regulation will not be at issue in the secured party's action to recover possession. If the debtor does file a counterclaim asserting that the finance company committed an unfair trade practice by taking a security interest in household goods, he or she would argue that North Carolina law— G.S. 53-180(g)—prohibits finance companies from engaging in unfair trade practices. Because North Carolina's law is patterned after the federal unfair trade practice act, North Carolina judges can look to federal decisions interpreting the federal law to aid in determining whether the state's unfair trade practice law has been violated.[30] If the magistrate concludes that that the finance company's agreement giving it a security interest in household goods violates the state unfair trade practices act, another North Carolina law—G S. 53-166(d)—would make the contract void and so prevent the finance company from recovering the property or the amount of the debt.

Another situation a magistrate might face is one in which a seller who sells goods under a revolving charge account takes a security interest in the goods sold. In a revolving charge account the seller and debtor contract to create an account—for example a Belk's or Sears account— allowing the debtor to charge items and be billed monthly. Generally, North Carolina law prohibits a seller or lender from taking a security interest in property sold under a revolving charge account or other open-end credit extension if the interest rate is higher than 1.25 percent per month.[31] However, one exception to this prohibition exists: a seller of goods under a revolving charge account may take a security interest in goods sold on the account but may only seek to repossess commercial units with a cash price of $100 or more.[32] "A commercial unit may be a single article (as a machine) or a set of articles (as a suite of furniture or an assortment of sizes) or a quantity (as a bale, gross, or carload) or any other unit treated in use or in the relevant market as a single whole."[33] Usually security agreements are created in revolving charge accounts by a combination of two documents—the revolving charge account (credit card) agreement and the sales receipt for the specific items purchased. The credit card agreement includes a provision stating that the seller retains a security interest in goods purchased under the agreement, and the sales receipt describes the property purchased. Therefore, if a single unit item, such as a television set, was sold for $250 on a revolving charge account that retains a security interest in property purchased and the buyer defaulted on payments, the seller may bring an action to recover the television set. Similarly, if a dining room suite (table and chairs) was sold under the same circumstances, the seller could bring an action to recover the furniture. However, if two dresses were purchased on a revolving charge account for $60 each (a total of $120), the magistrate could not award possession of the dresses to the merchant because each dress is a separate commercial unit that costs less than $100.

---

wedding rings). The definition of household goods does not include works of art, electronic equipment (except one radio and one television), items acquired as antiques (over 100 years old), and jewelry (except wedding rings).

30. Johnson v. Phoenix Mut. Life Ins., Co., 300 N.C. 247, 262, 266 S.E.2d 610, 620 (1980).

31. G.S. 24-11(c).

32. G.S. 25A-23(d).

33. G.S. 25-2-105(6).

Secured Party's Rights after Debtor Defaults

When a debtor defaults, the secured party has the right to repossess the personal property listed as collateral in the security agreement. The creditor may repossess the property without filing an action in court if he or she can do so without causing a breach of the peace.[34] Clearly, a breach of the peace occurs if there is a confrontation. The courts, however, have adopted a broader standard for determining whether a breach of the peace has occurred; it applies a balancing test of the following five factors:

1. where the repossession took place,
2. the debtor's express or constructive consent,
3. the reactions of third parties,
4. the type of premises entered, and
5. any use of deception by the creditor.[35]

If there is a breach of the peace, the debtor cannot use self-help repossession but must file a lawsuit to recover possession. If the creditor takes the property and causes a breach of the peace, it is an unlawful possession and the creditor can be sued for the damages provided in the UCC, for the tort of conversion[36] and, depending on the circumstances, for trespass[37] and assault.[38] The creditor might also face criminal charges, depending on the circumstances.[39] The creditor remains liable for the breach of the peace even if the creditor hires an independent contractor to undertake the repossession.[40]

The creditor's alternative to self-help repossession is to file an action to recover possession of the property as a secured party and have the court determine if the creditor is entitled to possession. This action may be filed whether or not the creditor has tried to use self-help repossession. However, the creditor cannot be forced by the debtor to take possession of the property[41] and can always choose, instead, to sue the debtor for the money owed on the debt. The main reason a creditor would file an action for money owed rather than seeking possession of the collateral is that the property has so little value it is not worth repossessing.

34. G.S. 25-9-609.

35. Giles v. First Va. Credit Serv., Inc., 149 N.C. App. 89, 560 S.E.2d 557 (2002). For other North Carolina cases discussing breach of the peace, *see* Rea v. Universal C.I.T. Credit Corp., 257 N.C. 639, 127 S.E.2d 225 (1962); Freeman v. Gen. Motors Acceptance Corp., 205 N.C. 257, 171 S.E. 63 (1933).

36. Binder v. Gen. Motors Acceptance Corp., 222 N.C. 512, 23 S.E.2d 894 (1943).

37. *Id.*; *Freeman*, 205 N.C. 257, 171 S.E. 63.

38. Mauro v. Gen. Motors Acceptance Corp., 164 Misc.2d 871, 626 N.Y.S.2d 374 (1995).

39. *Cf.* Girard v. Anderson, 257 N.W. 400 (Iowa 1934); Biggs v. Seufferlein, 145 N.W. 507 (Iowa 1914).

40. *E.g.*, Sammons v. Broward Bank, 599 So.2d 1018 (Fla. App. 1992), *rev'd on other grounds*, 648 So.2d 1264 (1995); Nichols v. Metro. Bank, 435 N.W.2d 637 (Minn. App. 1989); MBank El Paso, N.A. v. Sanchez, 836 S.W.2d 151 (Tex. 1992).

41. N.C. Nat'l Bank v. Sharpe, 35 N.C. App. 404, 406, 241 S.E.2d 360, 361 (1978).

Issues at Trial

When a secured party brings an action to recover possession of personal property in small claims court, he or she seeks return of the property only and is not entitled to any monetary damages.[42]

The plaintiff must prove the following three things to be entitled to recover possession of the property:

1. The existence of a valid security agreement. The security agreement must be in writing, indicate an intent to create a security agreement, include a description of the property to be used as collateral, be signed by the debtor, and if the agreement is a seller–buyer contract for consumer goods, be dated.
2. Under the security agreement, a security interest was taken in the property the plaintiff is seeking to recover.
3. The debtor defaulted. In most cases the default is nonpayment, and the amount of the remaining debt is irrelevant. The plaintiff need only prove that the defendant defaulted. The security agreement also may include other conditions that constitute default, such as the debtor's obligation to maintain insurance on the property. In that situation, the plaintiff must prove that such a default occurred.

In almost all cases, if the plaintiff proves these three things, he or she is entitled to recover all the personal property described in the complaint (that is, all the property listed as security for extension of credit or a loan).[43]

Example 5. After purchasing a new house, Angie goes to Friendly Furniture Store and purchases a couch, two living room chairs, and dining room table and six chairs, and a china cabinet for a total of $5,000. She pays $500 down, and signs a promissory note for $4,500 and a security agreement describing all of the items purchased. She defaults after making her payments for a year. Friendly Furniture sues to recover all of the items listed as security. At the trial, Friendly shows the magistrate a copy of the security agreement signed by Angie, indicates that Angie defaulted on the loan before she finished making all her payments, and asks for a judgment for the couch, two living room chairs, the dining room table and six chairs, and the china cabinet. Friendly Furniture is entitled to a judgment for all of the items listed in the security agreement.

---

42. The complaint form to be used is "Complaint to Recover Possession of Personal Property/Plaintiff A Secured Party/Plaintiff Not A Secured Party," AOC-CVM-202. The top half of the form is used for this action.

In district or superior court, plaintiffs frequently seek, in one lawsuit, to recover possession of the property as well as the amount of money still owed. Sometimes an attorney drafts a complaint for small claims court in this way, seeking both remedies. If, in that situation, the magistrate finds for the plaintiff, he or she should award the plaintiff a judgment for the amount owed on the debt and possession of the property. But the magistrate should also require the plaintiff to sell the repossessed property and apply the proceeds against the monetary award.

43. The magistrate will file the form "Judgment in Action to Recover Money or Personal Property," AOC-CVM-400, and check the block indicating that the plaintiff is entitled to recover possession of the personal property described in the complaint.

What if Angie only owes $500 and the secured property has a fair market value of $3,000? Friendly Furniture is still entitled to a judgment for all of the items listed as collateral. (See Example 7 below and the sentence following it for a discussion of why this is appropriate.)

There are two exceptions under which the plaintiff may not be entitled to recover all the personal property described in the security agreement. First, as indicated earlier, RISA limits the property that the seller can take as collateral in a consumer credit sale. In Example 4, the seller of goods on credit (ABC Appliance) took a security agreement in property sold to debtor but also listed as collateral debtor's property that it did not sell to the debtor. ABC was entitled to recover only the property it sold to the debtor. In that situation, the magistrate's judgment must specifically list the property the plaintiff is entitled to recover.

The second exception arises from RISA's special provision regarding property listed as security for the extension of credit when items are purchased from the seller at different times. As noted above, a seller is entitled to take a security interest in property that he or she is selling on credit, or in property the seller previously sold the debtor on credit with a security agreement that has not been paid off when the later item is purchased. In that situation the law requires payments to be applied in a certain manner.

> **Example 6.** Dave goes to Friendly Furniture on August 5, 2007, and buys a couch for $1,000. He pays $100 down and signs a security agreement listing the couch as collateral and a note indicating he owes $900 with interest at the rate of 18 percent per year and monthly payments of $85. On February 15, 2008, Dave returns to Friendly Furniture and purchases two living room chairs for $500. Since he is still paying for the couch, Friendly Furniture consolidates the loan for the couch and living room chairs into one contract listing the total amount owed, which includes the outstanding balance from the couch and the cost of the living room chairs. The agreement specifies that Friendly Furniture has a security interest in the couch and living room chairs. On August 23, 2008, Dave returns to Friendly Furniture and buys a dining room table and six chairs for $2,500. Again Friendly Furniture consolidates the contracts and prepares a new security agreement listing the couch, living room chairs, and dining room table and chairs as collateral. Dave continues to make payments of $85 per month until he defaults on November 1, 2008. On January 15, 2009, Friendly Furniture files an action to recover all of the secured property and the trial is held on January 31.

Note that the difference between this example and earlier ones is that in this action the property was purchased from the seller at different times rather than all at once. In this situation, RISA requires the seller to apportion the monthly $85 payments in the following manner:

1. The entire amount of all payments made before the subsequent purchase must be applied to the previous purchases.
2. Unless otherwise designated by the buyer, the amount of down payment on a subsequent purchase is applied to the subsequent purchase.
3. All subsequent payments are applied first to finance charges and then to principal. The application of payments to principal must be applied to the various purchases on the basis that the first sums paid in are applied to the oldest purchase until payment

is received in full; other payments are applied accordingly to all other purchases in the order that each obligation is assumed.[44] When the amount owed on the first purchase is paid, the security interest in that property is extinguished. The process continues as each obligation is paid off.

This method is sometimes referred to as "first in-first out." In Example 6, assume that of the monthly $85 payment, $15 is the finance charge. When Dave defaults he has made fourteen payments, which means $980 was applied to principal. Therefore, at the time of default, he had paid the full amount of the couch ($900) and $80 toward the living room chairs. The couch was, therefore no longer security for the extension of credit, and Friendly Furniture is not entitled to recover it, though it is entitled to recover all of the other items.[45]

The creditor has the burden of proving that he or she has apportioned the payments in accordance with the statute.[46] Therefore, when a seller is seeking possession of multiple items of personal property purchased at different times by the debtor and the creditor has consolidated the security agreements, the seller must prove that the payments have been properly apportioned and that none of the items requested in the lawsuit have been fully paid for. If the seller fails to prove that the debtor's payments have been properly allocated and that none of the items claimed have been paid off, the magistrate should find that only the latest items purchased can be recovered. If the security interest is taken in goods purchased on a revolving charge account with interest higher than 1.25 percent per month, the seller loses the security interest on all the property if the payments are not properly allocated.[47] If the plaintiff fails to prove that he or she is entitled to recover all of the items listed in the complaint, the magistrate's judgment must specify the items to be recovered.

What Happens after the Trial?

Although the magistrate's responsibility for the case ends with the judgment, what happens after trial may affect subsequent small claims actions in the matter. If, for example the plaintiff receives a judgment for possession of the property but the debtor does not voluntarily turn over the property within ten days, the plaintiff may ask the clerk of court to issue a writ of possession for personal property. That writ will order the sheriff to satisfy the judgment by taking the property from the defendant and turning it over to the plaintiff.

44. G.S. 25A-27.

45. This example is a simplified because the actual finance charge each month will be different based on the amount of the outstanding balance.

46. *See In re* Beasley, 23 B.R. 404, 406 (Bankr. E.D.N.C. 1982).

47. Sears, Roebuck & Co. v. Vandeusen, 155 B.R. 358 (Bankr. E.D.N.C. 1993). The court based its reasoning on the fact that (1) the general law (G.S. 24-11(c)) prohibits taking a security interest in property when the extension of credit is under an open-end revolving charge account in which the monthly interest rate is greater than 1¼ percent and (2) the exception to the general law for revolving accounts covered by RISA (G.S. 25A-23) applies only if the RISA provision regarding application of payments is followed.

Secured Party's Obligations after Reacquiring Possession

The secured party has certain obligations to the debtor even after the debtor has defaulted and the secured party has taken possession of the property, either by self-help or by going to court. Failure to fulfill these obligations subjects the secured party to liability to the debtor.

After repossessing the property the secured party generally has the choice of keeping the property in full satisfaction of the remaining debt[48] or selling it and bringing a second lawsuit for the amount remaining on the debt after the sale. In one instance, however, the secured party is required to sell the property: This requirement applies only to cases in which the collateral is consumer goods (property used for personal, family, or household purposes). If the debtor has paid at least 60 percent of the amount secured, the secured party may not keep the goods in full satisfaction of the debt but must instead sell the goods within ninety days after taking possession. This time period may be extended if the debtor and other affected parties, after default, enter into a written, signed agreement to that effect.[49]

> **Example 7.** Robert borrows $2,000 from First Finance Co. for a vacation. He signs a note for $2,000 and a security agreement listing several items of property he already owns—a riding lawnmower, a weed eater, a stereo system, and a DVD player. Robert pays for over a year and then defaults while still owing $300. First Finance files an action to recover possession as a secured party. At the trial First Finance shows the magistrate the security agreement listing all the items as security and the note for $2,000 plus interest, both signed by Robert. First Finance testifies that Robert defaulted. Robert agrees with everything First Finance says but argues that since he only owes $300 and the value of the property to be recovered is $1,500, the magistrate should only allow repossession of enough property to satisfy the debt. First Finance agrees that $300 is owed but says it is entitled to a judgment for all of the property. The magistrate should enter judgment to First Financial for all of the property described in the complaint. (Because First Finance Co. is a lender, the agreement is not covered by RISA and First Finance is not limited in the types of collateral it may take, but the same result would apply if Robert buys these items at one time from Sears and gives a security agreement for them.) However, because at least 60 percent of the debt has been paid, once First Finance repossesses the collateral it must conduct a sale within ninety days. After proper written notification to Robert, First Finance sells the property at a public sale to the highest bidders for a total amount of $800. It pays the $300 debt owed on the debt and must send the remaining $450 surplus to Robert.

This example indicates how the UCC deals with a situation in which it is likely that the property to be recovered is worth more than the remaining debt. It protects the creditor by allowing repossession of all of the property listed as collateral, but it also protects the debtor by requiring a timely sale when it is likely that the sale may bring more than the debt and by providing that any surplus goes to the debtor rather than the creditor.

---

48. If the security agreement is not a consumer transaction, the secured party can propose keeping the property in partial satisfaction of the debt. Nonconsumer security agreements are rarely enforced in small claims court, but if the magistrate has such a case, G.S. 25-9-620 specifies the requirements the plaintiff must meet.

49. G.S. 25-9-620(e), (f).

When the secured party is not required to sell the property, he or she may keep the property in full satisfaction of the debt, provided the debtor agrees. This agreement may be manifested in two ways: (1) express consent, shown by the debtor's signature after default; or (2) the debtor's failure to object within twenty days after being notified by the secured party of a proposal to do so.[50] If the secured party receives a written objection from the debtor within the twenty-day period, he or she must sell the property rather than keep it. If there is no objection, the secured party keeps the property and the matter is closed.

Secured Party's Duty to Give Debtor Notice of Sale

A secured party who is selling the property must send the debtor a reasonable, authenticated notification of his or her intent to dispose of the property. The notice of disposition of collateral must be reasonable in the manner in which it is sent, its timeliness, and content. Whether the notification is sent within a reasonable time preceding the sale is a question of fact the magistrate must determine based on the circumstances of the individual case.[51] G.S. 25-9-614 specifies the required content of the notice when consumer goods are being sold:

- identification of debtor and secured party;
- description of the collateral (that is, the subject of the disposition);
- statement of the intended method of disposition (for example, public auction, or private sale);
- notice that debtor is entitled to an accounting of the unpaid indebtedness and the cost, if any, of the accounting;
- the time and place of the public sale or the time after which a private sale will be made;
- statement of liability for any deficiency;
- a telephone number the debtor can call to learn the amount that must be paid to redeem the collateral; and
- a telephone number or address from which additional information concerning the disposition can be obtained.

Although the statute requires no particular phrasing for the notification, it provides a form that, if used, is deemed sufficient. If the creditor's notice departs substantially from the statutory notice, it is probably not a reasonable notice.

The secured party is not required to send a notice to the debtor if the collateral is perishable or is of a type customarily sold on a recognized market.

Debtor's Right to Redeem the Property

G.S. 25-9-623 gives the debtor the right to redeem the property any time before the secured party has sold the property, entered into a contract for its disposition, or accepted the collateral in satisfaction of the obligation. One of the reasons for requiring the secured party to give

---

50. G.S. 25-9-620(c).

51. G.S. 25-9-612. Notification rules for nonconsumer transactions are not discussed because they rarely come up in small claims cases. Formerly, North Carolina's version of the UCC included a statutory sale procedure that, if followed, created a conclusive presumption that the sale and notice were commercially reasonable. However, those provisions were deleted in the 2000 revision of Article 9.

notice of the sale to the debtor is so that the debtor knows how long he or she has to redeem the property. A debtor who wants to redeem the collateral must fulfill all obligations secured by the collateral; pay the reasonable expenses of retaking, holding, and preparing the property for disposition; and, if the security agreement provides for attorney's fees, pay the reasonable attorney's fees incurred by the secured party.[52]

Security agreements and promissory notes almost always include an "acceleration" clause stating that if the debtor defaults on an installment payment, the creditor may declare the remainder of the debt due and owing—thereby making the entire debt due. An example of a fairly standard acceleration clause is "In the event of default in payment of any installment of principal or interest or default under the terms of any instrument securing this note, and if the default is not made good within fifteen days, the holder may, without notice, declare the remainder of the debt at once due and payable. Failure to exercise this option shall not constitute a waiver of the right to exercise the same at any other time."[53]

> **Example 8.** Barbara purchases a refrigerator, stove, and dishwasher from Sears for $6,000. She signs a promissory note and security agreement listing the three items as collateral. The agreement provides that if the creditor notifies the debtor in writing of a default and the debtor does not pay the amount of the default within ten days after the creditor has mailed the notification, the full amount of the obligation is due. Barbara's monthly payments are $100 per month. After making payments for a year, she fails to make her March and April 2008 payments. At that time the total amount of the obligation is $4,800. On April 5, Sears mails Barbara notice of the default, requiring her to pay the missed payments within ten days. When she does not respond, Sears repossesses the property. Barbara now wants to redeem the property. To do so, she must pay the full amount of the debt—$4,800—rather than just the two months' missed payments, plus the reasonable expenses Sears incurred in repossessing the property. In this case no attorney's fees were recoverable since Sears had not hired an attorney.

Sale of the Property

If it decides to sell the property,[54] the secured party must follow the procedure set out in G.S. 25-9-610. The secured party may sell the property in its present condition, or it may make any commercially reasonable preparation of the property for sale. Although the wording of the statute seems to indicate that the secured party always has a choice about selling the property in its present condition or preparing it for sale, the official comment to the section indicates otherwise:

---

52. G.S. 25-9-623.

53. Meehan v. Cable, 135 N.C. App. 715, 716, 523 S.E.2d 419, 420 (1999).

54. G.S. 25-9-610(a) states that the secured party, after default, may sell, lease, license, or otherwise dispose of the collateral. Because it is the most likely disposition in small claims cases, this chapter refers only to disposition by sale. However, it is important to point out that although the language "otherwise dispose of the collateral" is never defined or discussed in a North Carolina appellate case, another court has held that it does not mean permanent retention for the secured party's own use. Lamp Fair, Inc. v. Perez-Ortiz, 888 F.2d 173, 176 (1st Cir. 1989).

Although courts should not be quick to impose a duty of preparation or processing on the secured party, [the statute] does not grant the secured party the right to dispose of the collateral "in its then condition" under all circumstances. A secured party may not dispose of collateral "in its then condition" when, taking into account the costs and probable benefits of preparation or processing and the fact that the secured party would be advancing the costs at its risk, it would be commercially unreasonable to dispose of the collateral in that condition.[55]

Cases from other states have held that washing and cleaning the goods may be required to generate bidder interest and that making minor repairs that would generate a much higher sales price is required to avoid making the sale commercially unreasonable.[56]

Every aspect of the disposition, including the method, manner, time, place, and other terms, must be commercially reasonable. The statute authorizes the secured party to sell the collateral by a public or private sale, by one or more contracts, as a unit, or in parcels, and at any time and place and on any terms. Although the intent is to give the secured party flexibility in disposing of the property, the secured party is still bound by the overarching requirement of a commercially reasonable sale, which essentially places on the secured party the duty to "use his best efforts to see that the highest possible price is received for the collateral."[57] The creditor is required to use fair and reasonable means but not extraordinary means.[58] In determining whether the sale was commercially reasonable, the fact that a better price could have been obtained if the sale had been at a different time or by a different method is not of itself sufficient to establish that it was not carried out in a commercially reasonable manner.[59] A disposition is commercially reasonable if it is made in the usual method on any recognized market (for example, sweet potatoes sold on the sweet potato market or stocks sold on the New York Stock Exchange) or in conformity with reasonable commercial practices among dealers in the type of property that is the subject of the disposition.

Price. Although sale of the collateral at a low price is not in itself sufficient to establish a violation of the requirement for a commercially reasonable sale, it is a factor that could cause the court to look carefully at all aspects of the sale.[60]

Public versus private sale. The property may be sold at either a public or private sale. The question sometimes arises whether the secured party may buy the property "from himself." The rule is that secured party may buy the property at a public sale but may not buy at a private sale unless the property is of a type customarily sold in a recognized market or is the subject of

---

55. Official Comment 4 to G.S. 25-9-610.

56. BARKLEY CLARK, THE LAW OF SECURED TRANSACTIONS UNDER THE UNIFORM COMMERCIAL CODE (Rev. ed. 1993) Publisher: Warren Gorham Lamont § 4.08[1]. *See* Liberty Nat'l Bank & Trust Co. v. Acme Tool Div. of Rucker Co., 540 F.2d 1375, 1381 (10th Cir. 1976) (failing to clean and paint drilling rig); Franklin State Bank v. Parker, 346 A.2d 632 (N.J. Dist. Ct. 1975) (failing to install missing spark plugs, points, condenser, and carburetor air filter to make car operable).

57. Vetter v. Bank of Oregon, 591 P.2d 768, 769 (Or. 1979).

58. First Westside Bank. v. For-Med., Inc., 529 N.W.2d 66, 70 (Neb. 1995).

59. G.S. 25-9-627.

60. Official Comment 10 to G.S. 25-9-610; Fieldcrest Cannon Employees Credit Union v. Mabes, 116 N.C. App. 351, 353, 447 S.E.2d 510, 512 (1994).

widely distributed standard price quotations. A public sale is an auction held by the secured party with notice given to the general public. Any other sale is a private sale. For example, selling repossessed furniture by putting it in a back room of the secured party's store with other used furniture and selling it at a listed price is a private sale. So too is giving a repossessed motor vehicle to a wholesaler who sells at a wholesale auction. A public sale may not always be a commercially reasonable way to dispose of goods. Sometimes, because of the nature of the goods, a better price can be obtained by a private sale or by contacting people in the business who might have an interest in the goods and negotiating a sale price. For example, if the property repossessed is a large lift for repairing motor vehicles, the secured party might determine that the most profitable way to sell the lift is to contact the automobile repair shops in the area to determine whether any of them are interested and, if so, to negotiate for the best price the secured party can get. The magistrate must determine if the method used is commercially reasonable. Apparently no case has struck down a sale solely because it was handled as a wholesale transaction.[61]

Time of sale. With one exception, the statute does not specify any time the sale must be held or any period within which the secured party must dispose of the collateral after repossession. The exception, as noted in connection with the discussion of Example 7, is for the requirement that the property be sold within ninety days after repossession if at least 60 percent of the debt has been paid. However, the time must be commercially reasonable. It may not be reasonable to hold a sale on Sunday morning in a community where most people are in church at that time. Likewise it might not be commercially reasonable to hold for a long period property that depreciates in value.

The sale should be held at the time and place specified in the notice and advertisements. Failure to do so would likely be found commercially unreasonable.[62]

Publicity. There is no specific requirement that the secured party advertise a public sale. However, the comments indicate that a public disposition is "one at which the price is determined after the public has had a meaningful opportunity for competitive bidding."[63] "Meaningful opportunity" implies public notice and public access to the sale.[64] The notice should also adequately describe the collateral to be sold.[65] For a private sale the secured party must take proper measures to find the best markets and buyers.[66]

Presale inspection of goods. Normally prospective bidders should be given an opportunity to inspect the repossessed goods before the sale. If the property is an automobile, it is likely that commercial reasonableness would include allowing a prospective bidder's mechanic to inspect the goods.[67]

---

61. CLARK, *supra* note 56, § 4.08[3].

62. JAMES J. WHITE & ROBERT S. SUMMERS, UNIFORM COMMERCIAL CODE § 34-11 (5th ed. 2002) (*citing* C.I.T. Corp. v. Anwright Corp., 191 Cal. App. 3d 1420, 237 Cal. Rptr. 108 (1987) (sale held several blocks away from location in notice)).

63. Official Comment 7 to G.S. 25-9-610.

64. *Id.*

65. CLARK *supra* note 56, § 4.08[3].

66. WHITE & SUMMERS, *supra* note 62, § 34-11.

67. *Id.* at § 34-11.

Application of Proceeds

G.S. 25-9-615 specifies that the secured party must apply the proceeds from the sale of the goods in the following order:

1. The proceeds must be applied first to the reasonable expenses of retaking the property, holding it, and preparing it for sale; and, to the extent provided for in the agreement and not prohibited by law, to reasonable attorney's fees incurred by the secured party.

A magistrate may have to determine whether the expenses allocated for retaking and holding the property are reasonable or, as discussed above, whether any preparation of the goods for sale was commercially reasonable. With regard to attorneys' fees, two questions must be answered: (1) Does the agreement provide for attorneys' fees and (2), if it does, does North Carolina law allow the award of attorneys' fees in that situation? The first question is easily answered by looking at the security agreement or promissory note to see if it includes an attorneys' fee provision. The second question is more difficult: Under North Carolina law, attorneys' fees may not be awarded unless there is a specific statute authorizing the award.[68] G.S. 6-21.2 provides that an attorneys' fee provision in a note or other evidence of indebtedness is enforceable; but it also provides that "reasonable attorneys' fee" may not exceed 15 percent of the outstanding balance. The statute specifically refers to the holder of a note and security agreement or to the holder of a security agreement that provides evidence of both a monetary obligation and a security interest in goods. Does the statute require that the purpose of the action be recovery of the debt or does it also apply when the debtor has already repossessed the goods?

As a practical matter, the issue for the magistrate arises when the secured party files an action for deficiency against the debtor because the sale proceeds do not to cover the balance of the debt and the attorneys' fees and the secured party's attorney seeks to enforce the attorneys' fee provision of G.S. 6-21.2. (See below, "Secured Party's Action for Deficiency.") If the secured party has already paid the attorneys' fees from the proceeds of the sale, the magistrate cannot award any more attorneys' fees in the action for the deficiency. If no attorneys' fees have been paid from the proceeds of the sale or if the proceeds of the sale are not adequate to fully pay the attorneys' fees, the magistrate will award the full amount or part not yet paid of the fees allowed under G.S. 6-21.2.

2. After paying the expenses, the proceeds are allocated to the satisfaction of the debt owed to the secured party.
3. Under certain circumstances, any remaining funds are applied to any junior or subordinate security interests or liens.
4. Finally, if there is any surplus remaining, it is paid to the debtor. If there is a balance still owing on the debt, the secured party may bring an action for the deficiency.

After the sale in a consumer goods transaction, the secured party is required to send a written explanation to the debtor stating the amount of a surplus or deficiency. The explanation must be sent before or with payment of the surplus, with the first written demand for the deficiency, or within fourteen days of receiving the debtor's signed request for an explanation. G.S 25-9-626 sets out a detailed list of what must be included in the explanation.

68. *F. v. Barrier Explosives De., Inc.*, 52 N.C. App. 496, 499, 281 S.E. 2d 78, 80 (1981)

Examples of Follow-up after Repossession

Several examples of application of the UCC principles following repossession are instructive.

Example 9. As described in Example 8, Barbara purchases a refrigerator, stove, and dishwasher from Sears for $6,000. She signs a promissory note and security agreement listing the three items as collateral. The agreement has an acceleration clause that is activated when Barbara fails to make her March and April 2008 payments. The total outstanding balance of the obligation is $4,800. Sears repossesses the property at a cost of $50 and, after proper notice to Barbara, conducts a public auction at which the three items are sold separately for a total of $2,000. Sears deducts the $50 for its expenses and applies the remaining $1,950 toward the debt, leaving $2,850 still owing on the debt. Sears can then sue Barbara for the deficiency of $2,850.

Example 10. Assume the same facts as Example 9 except that when Sears repossesses the three items, it decides it does not want to worry about complying with the sale provisions or trying to recover all the debt from Barbara. Therefore, Sears mails her a written proposal stating that it will accept the collateral in full satisfaction of the debt unless it receives a written and authenticated notification of her objection within twenty days after the proposal was sent. Forty days later, having heard nothing from Barbara, Sears sells the repossessed property to an employee for $10. In this case Sears cannot sue Barbara for the deficiency because it agreed to keep the property in full satisfaction of the debt. But neither does Barbara have any action against Sears for the manner in which it disposed of the property.

Secured Party's Action for Deficiency

A creditor who sells the goods rather than keeping them in satisfaction of the debt may bring a second lawsuit against the debtor to recover any remaining amount still owed on the debt. This action is referred to as a *suit for a deficiency judgment.*[69] Perhaps the most important thing for the magistrate to note about this action is that the secured party must prove not only the amount of the deficiency but also that he or she conducted a commercially reasonable sale and gave reasonable notice of the sale to the debtor.[70] The magistrate must look at all the factors discussed above in the section "Sale of the Property" to determine whether a reasonably commercial sale was held. Although price alone is not determinative of a commercially reasonable sale, it is a factor that may be considered, and a defendant must be allowed to present evidence of the fair market value of the property at the time it was repossessed.[71] To recover a deficiency, the creditor must prove the following:

1. Proper written notice of disposition was sent to the debtor within a reasonable time before the public sale or a reasonable time before the property was offered for private sale.

---

69. The lawsuit is usually brought on the form for "Complaint for Money Owed," AOC-CVM-200.

70. N.C. Nat'l Bank v. Burnette, 297 N.C. 524, 529, 256 S.E.2d 388, 391 (1979); ITT-Indus. Credit Co. v. Milo Concrete Co., 31 N.C. App. 450, 458, 229 S.E.2d 814, 820 (1976).

71. Fieldcrest Cannon Employees Credit Union v. Mabes, 116 N.C. App. 351, 354, 447 S.E.2d 510, 512 (1994).

2. The sale, whether public or private, was held in a commercially reasonable manner.
3. The amount of remaining debt.

North Carolina does not follow the rule applied in some other states that the creditor's failure to prove a commercially reasonable sale bars all rights to a deficiency judgment. Nonetheless, in North Carolina such a failure does raise a presumption that the collateral was worth at least the amount of the debt. The secured party may overcome that presumption by proving the market value of the collateral with evidence other than the sale price.[72]

Example 11. After Lane defaulted on a loan, Friendly Finance Company repossessed four items of Lane's personal property in which it had a valid security interest. Lane owed $3,545 on the debt. The property had a fair market value of $1,500. Friendly spent $100 cleaning and making minor repairs to the property and then sold it at a public sale for $400. After applying the proceeds to the expenses and debt, Friendly Finance Company sues Lane for a deficiency of $3,245. At the trial Friendly Finance testifies that it mailed notice of a public sale to Lane three days before the public sale, posted the notice of sale on the courthouse bulletin board the same day, and held the sale at the company office at 8:00 P.M. on Friday evening. Only one person came to the sale. Two issues arise from this evidence: (1) Was the notice of sale sent to the debtor within a reasonable time and (2) was the sale commercially reasonable? The magistrate could determine that mailing the notice three days before the sale is not reasonable notice because it is not likely to reach the debtor before the sale, much less give him time to redeem the property. Or the magistrate may determine that posting the notice of sale two days before the sale is not sufficient publicity or that holding the sale at 8:00 P.M. on a Friday evening is unlikely to produce a sufficient number of interested bidders. If the magistrate reaches any of these conclusions, he or she will find that Friendly Finance Co. did not hold a commercially reasonable sale or give reasonable notice. In that case, the presumption is that if Friendly Finance had held a commercially reasonable sale and given reasonable notice, the items would have sold for the amount of the remaining debt—$3,245. Therefore, Friendly Finance is entitled to a judgment for $100—the expenses of repossessing, holding, and preparing the property for sale. (Because it is not clear whether the expenses of sale can be considered part of the debt, some magistrates might determine that Friendly Finance is entitled to recover nothing.)

Example 12. Assume the facts in Example 11 but add the following evidence presented at trial. Lane testifies that the fair market value of the four items was $1,500. Friendly Finance Co.'s witness, Hamilton, a used appliance dealer, testifies that the fair market value of each of the four used appliances was only $150 and that the price bid at the sale is similar to the amount he has received for similar items in his store. In that situation, if the magistrate believes Hamilton's testimony, he or she would find that Friendly Finance Co. has overcome the presumption by proving the fair market value by evidence other than the sale price and therefore is entitled to a judgment for $3,245.

---

72. Nations Bank v. Amer. Doubloon Corp., 125 N.C. App. 494, 500, 481 S.E.2d 387, 390 (1997); Hodges v. Norton, 29 N.C. App. 193, 198–99, 223 S.E.2d 848, 851–52 (1976).

Debtor's Remedies for Creditor's Failure to Comply with Law

The law provides the debtor with certain remedies if the secured party does not follow the rules given above. A secured party who repossesses consumer goods after 60 percent of the purchase price has been paid and fails to sell the goods within ninety days after taking possession of the goods is liable to the debtor for the fair market value of the goods in an action for conversion.

> *Example 13.* Bryant buys a bedroom suite and two lamps for $6,000 from Fabulous Rooms Inc. She pays $200 down and signs a security agreement listing all the items purchased as collateral and a note for $5,800 plus interest. Bryant pays on the furniture for several years and then defaults, with $1,500 still owing. She gives Fabulous Rooms permission to come to her house and take the collateral, which the company does. She hears nothing from Fabulous Rooms until, six months later, she discovers that they are still holding the property. Bryant sues Fabulous Rooms Inc. for $2,500, which she alleges is the fair market value of the collateral. Since at least 60 percent of the principal amount of the debt had been paid when Fabulous Rooms repossessed the goods, they were required to sell them within ninety days or get Bryant's permission to wait longer. By its failure to do so, the company converted Bryant's property and is liable to her for the fair market value of the property at the time it was repossessed.

If the secured party fails to comply with any provision of Article 9 of G.S. Chapter 25, the debtor is entitled to recover any actual damages suffered.

> *Example 14.* Jefferson grows various fruits and has a delivery truck to deliver the fruit to local groceries. The finance company has a security interest in the delivery truck. When Jefferson misses a payment, the finance company hires a repossession man to take the truck. Jefferson sees the repossession man arrive and immediately goes out; he stands in front of the truck, and tells the repossession man not to take it. The repossession man says "tough" and drives off in the truck, almost hitting Jefferson. Three days later the finance company returns the truck to Jefferson. Jefferson sues the finance company and at the trial proves that during those three days he was unable to deliver fruit to four local grocers; he lost the $500 they would have paid him, and the fruit deteriorated so much it could no longer be sold. If the magistrate finds that the property was repossessed with a breach of the peace, he or she would award Jefferson the $500 actual damages he suffered by the breach.

Because it is often difficult for a debtor to prove actual damages, the statute provides for a way of determining what damages the debtor is entitled to in lieu of proving actual damages if the collateral is consumer goods. If the creditor violates any of the provisions regarding default and enforcement of the security agreement, the debtor is entitled to recover an amount not less than the total credit service charges paid (finance charge) plus 10 percent of the principal amount of the obligation (that is, the total amount of the credit extended or money lent).[73] The most likely situations to come before a magistrate are those in which the debtor shows that the secured party failed to give proper notice of the sale of consumer goods or in which the sale of the collateral was not commercially reasonable. In either event the debtor, even without proving

---

73. G.S. 25-9-625(c)(2).

any actual damages, is entitled to recover an amount equal to the credit charge plus 10 percent of the cash price or principal amount of the loan.

> ***Example 15.*** As in Example 11, Friendly Finance is bringing an action for deficiency after selling Lane's repossessed goods. This time, Lane is filing a counterclaim for damages, asserting that Friendly Finance failed to conduct a commercially reasonable sale and give him reasonable notice. Though Lane cannot prove any actual damages, he proves that he has already paid Friendly Finance $260 in finance charges and that the principal amount of the debt was $4,900. If the magistrate finds that the sale was not commercially reasonable or that the notice was not reasonable, Lane will be entitled to statutory damages of $750 ($260 in finance charges paid and $490 as 10 percent of the principal amount of the debt). In that situation the magistrate's judgment would award Friendly Finance $100 on the claim for a deficiency (or $0 if the magistrate includes expenses as part of the debt), award Lane $750 on the counterclaim, and offset the two, granting a final judgment that Friendly Finance owes Lane $650.
>
> If Friendly Finance does not seek a deficiency, Lane can still file a lawsuit for damages for failing to conduct a commercially reasonable sale and failing to give proper notice. The only difference would be that in that situation Lane would have the burden of proving that the sale was not commercially reasonable or that the notice was not reasonable. If he proves his case, the magistrate will award Lane a judgment of $750 against Friendly Finance.

Failure of the secured party to give reasonable notification or to carry out a commercially reasonable disposition of the goods not only gives rise to a cause of action by the debtor under G.S. 25-9-625; under certain facts it might also result in a claim for unfair and deceptive practice under G.S. 75-1.1. If the debtor is successful in proving an unfair trade practice, the resulting damages are trebled; and under some circumstances, attorneys' fees may be awarded as well.[74]

In addition to the damages mentioned above, a debtor may recover $500 in damages from a creditor who (1) without reasonable cause, fails to comply with a written request for an accounting of the unpaid obligation or a list of the collateral covered by the obligation or (2) as part of a pattern or practice of noncompliance, fails to send an explanation of the surplus or deficiency after disposition of the repossessed property.[75]

Secured Party's Rights against Third Parties

The discussion thus far has centered on the rights of the debtor and the secured party. What happens if a third person enters the picture? More specifically, what happens if the debtor defaults in his or her payments but has sold or given the property to a third person before the secured party has an opportunity to repossess the property? Or what happens if two creditors have security interests in the same property? To enforce the security agreement against someone other than the debtor, the secured party must *perfect* the security interest; that is, the secured party must comply with certain requirements of the UCC designed to give that third person

---

74. *Cf.* Parks Chevrolet, Inc. v. Watkins, 74 N.C. App. 719, 329 S.E.2d 728 (1985); Richardson Ford Sales, Inc. v. Johnson, 676 P.2d 1344 (N.M. Ct. App. 1984).

75. G.S. 25-9-625(e).

notice that the secured party has an interest in the property.[76] To perfect the security interest, the secured party usually has to file a notice, called a *financing statement*, with the secretary of state. Filing the financing statement gives the third person notice that the secured party has an interest in the property; this statement is similar to the notice a bank with a lien against real property gives by recording a deed of trust in the register of deeds office. However, there are three exceptions to the need to perfect a security interest by filing a financing statement:

1. A purchase money security interest (one in which credit is extended or money is lent to purchase property that is listed as collateral) is perfected without filing a financing statement.[77]
2. When the collateral is a motor vehicle, the lien must be registered with the Division of Motor Vehicles, rather than filed with the secretary of state.[78]
3. If the creditor takes possession of the collateral when the credit or loan is extended rather than repossessing it after the debtor defaults, no financing statement is required.[79] The most common example of this situation is a pawn agreement: A pawnbroker lends money to a person who gives the pawnbroker personal property to hold as collateral for the extension of credit. Under the pawn agreement if the loan is not repaid within a certain period of time, the pawnbroker is entitled to dispose of the goods without further notice.

Once a security interest is perfected, the creditor can repossess the collateral from third-party purchasers or from other secured parties whose security agreements were perfected after the creditor's. Because the creditor's security interest has been perfected, the reasoning is that other parties with an interest in the collateral knew or should have learned that someone else had an interest in the property. When there are conflicting security interests they are ranked as follows: A purchase money security interest takes priority over other security interests;[80] conflicting security interests are ranked according to their dates of perfection; and unperfected security interests are subordinate to the rights of perfected security interests or lien creditors.[81]

> ***Example 16.*** Samuel is having a hard time paying his bills, so he borrows $1,000 from Friendly Finance Co. and signs a security agreement granting Friendly Finance Co. a security interest in his treasured hunting rifle and binoculars. About two months later Samuel needs money again, and he goes to Fast Cash Pawn Shop and pawns the rifle. Later, Samuel stops paying Friendly Finance Co. and tells them the rifle is now at the pawn shop. Friendly Finance Co. files a financing statement with the secretary of state and then sues Fast Cash to recover possession of the rifle. The magistrate should find for Fast Cash because conflicting security agreements rank according

76. G.S. 25-9-310(a).
77. G.S. 25-9-309(1); G.S. 25-9-310(b)(2).
78. G.S. 25-9-310(b)(3), G.S. 25-9-311(a)(2).
79. G.S. 25-9-310(b)(6), -313(a).
80. G.S. 25-9-324(a).
81. G.S. 25-9-317(a), -322.

to the time of perfection. Fast Cash perfected first when it took the rifle in possession; Friendly Finance Co. perfected second, when it filed the financing statement.

But if Friendly Finance Co. had filed the financing statement when it lent the money, Friendly would prevail because it would have perfected its interest first.

One final important rule deals with consumer goods: A buyer of consumer goods who buys goods from a person who bought them primarily for personal, household, or family purposes may take them free and clear of a security interest—even if it is perfected—if he or she buys them without knowledge of the security interest, for value, and to use primarily for personal, family, or household purposes and does so before a financing statement for the goods is filed.[82] Because a purchase money security agreement for consumer goods is perfected without filing a financing statement, this provision protects an unknowing buyer of those goods from the original buyer unless the secured party has taken the additional step of filing a financing statement. For example, Jared buys a television from Circuit City on credit and signs a security agreement using the television as collateral; he then sells the television to his neighbor, Lloyd, who does not know of the security interest held by Circuit City. Even though Circuit City's purchase money security agreement was perfected without filing a financing statement, it cannot repossess the television from Lloyd unless it had already filed a financing statement when Lloyd purchased the television from Jared.

The whole area of enforcing a security interest against someone other than the debtor is extremely complicated, and a magistrate assigned such a case should consult the chief district judge or some other neutral expert.

Claim and Delivery

The ancillary remedy of claim and delivery, discussed at the beginning of the chapter in the section on "Actions to Recover Possession by Nonsecured Party," is also available to secured parties in actions to recover possession. If the magistrate sees in the file that a claim and delivery proceeding has been filed before the clerk and that the sheriff has seized the property as ordered by the clerk and given it to the creditor, the magistrate must still hear the case to determine who is permanently entitled to the property and make the same determinations that he or she would make if no claim and delivery proceeding had occurred. The only difference would be that if the secured party has possession of the collateral and fails to prove the case by the greater weight of the evidence, the magistrate would have to order the plaintiff to return the property to the defendant.

One point must be strongly emphasized. Once the secured party has acquired possession of that property by claim and delivery, he or she is not entitled to take a voluntary dismissal of the action to recover possession and keep the property. The secured party must either go to trial on the action to recover possession or, if he or she takes a voluntary dismissal, return the property to the defendant. Otherwise, the defendant will suffer an injustice. The secured party will have acquired possession of the property without having proved the right to it.[83]

82. G.S. 25-9-320(b).
83. Manix v. Howard, 82 N.C. 125 (1880); Epps v. Miller, 7 N.C. App. 656, 660, 173 S.E.2d 558, 561 (1970).

This law concerning voluntary dismissal does not prevent a consent judgment. The action to recover possession may be concluded after the plaintiff has taken possession of the property through claim and delivery—but before the trial—if the defendant consents to have judgment entered against him or her.

Chapter VI

Landlord–Tenant Law

The law of summary ejectment is complex and demanding. It encompasses some of the most difficult issues magistrates must face in trying small claims. Although an individual case may deal with only a few of the issues discussed, over a career of trying cases, magistrates will eventually encounter all of these issues.

The basic law governing summary ejectment and other landlord–tenant disputes is contained in Articles 2A through 7 of the North Carolina General Statutes, Chapter 42 (hereinafter G.S.). Procedures for carrying out summary ejectment actions are found in G.S. Chapter 7A. Discussion in this chapter is based on the law as set forth in G.S. Chapters 7A and 42 and as interpreted by North Carolina courts.

The chapter also contains information on North Carolina's Residential Rental Agreements Act, the federal Fair Housing Act, and federal law relating to publicly assisted housing as it affects summary ejectment actions. Discussions about judgments on the pleadings and the effect of bankruptcy on summary ejectment cases are found in Chapter 2, "Small Claims Procedure." This chapter does not include information on the state Vacation Rental Agreements Law because cases enforcing it are rarely heard in small claims court.[1]

Summary Ejectment Actions

Summary ejectment is the legal procedure a landlord must use to evict a tenant. Under North Carolina law, a landlord has the right to evict a tenant from the premises when

1. the lease has expired and the tenant refuses to leave,
2. the tenant has violated some provision of the lease for which eviction is specified as the penalty,
3. the tenant has failed to pay rent, or
4. the tenant has engaged in criminal activity.

---

1. For information about that law, the reader can download Joan G. Brannon, "1999 Small Claims and Miscellaneous Legislation Affecting Magistrates," *Administration of Justice Bulletin* No. 1999/04 at http://shopping.netsuite.com/s.nl/c.433425/it.I/id.344/.f.

Summary ejectment is a statutory remedy of long standing designed to give the landlord a prompt recovery of premises from a tenant unlawfully in possession.

Much of North Carolina's current summary ejectment law was enacted almost three centuries ago as the law of Great Britain.[2] Although much of the statute has remained substantially unchanged, several significant changes have been made to landlord–tenant law in the past thirty years. Among these changes are statutes (1) requiring the landlord to provide and keep premises in a fit and habitable condition, (2) prohibiting retaliatory evictions, (3) forbidding self-help evictions in residential housing, and (4) allowing eviction for criminal activity.

Summary ejectment may be used to remove a tenant from a house, a mobile home, a mobile home space (when the tenant brings the mobile home to the landlord's rental space), an apartment, or a commercial building. The statute regarding eviction of a tenant for criminal activity, however, applies only to residential leases.

Who Brings the Lawsuit?

All lawsuits must be brought in the name of the *real party in interest*[3]—the person who would be benefited by the judgment. In summary ejectment cases the owner of the property is the real party in interest and must bring the action in his or her own name.[4] When residential and commercial rental property is managed by an agent, as it commonly is, the agent, not the owner, usually has actual knowledge of the tenant's breach of the lease; the agent probably negotiated the lease with the tenant and is the person to whom the rent is paid. In this situation, the agent may file the lawsuit and sign the complaint[5] but must name the owner (landlord) as the plaintiff. To sign the complaint, the agent must have personal knowledge of the facts alleged in the complaint.[6] If he or she does not, the landlord or the landlord's attorney must sign the complaint. Sometimes an elderly landlord who has handled the rental but does not want to come to court will appoint a relative or friend as agent to prepare the complaint and come to court on his or her behalf. That person is not an agent under the statute because he or she does not have actual knowledge of the facts.

---

2. The first cite to the law is an English statute—4 George II no. 27—enacted during the session of Parliament held from January 23, 1727, to January 1730 and printed in 1731. This act, entitled "An act for the more effectual preventing frauds committed by tenants, and for the more easy recovery of rents, and renewal of leases," included provisions for (1) damages for holding over after the term of the lease, (2) the landlord's right to re-enter when tenant failed to pay rent, and (3) the tenant's right to tender the full amount of rent and costs to stop the ejectment proceeding. It was the law of the American colonies and was adopted as the common law when North Carolina became a state. The first codification of the summary ejectment law in North Carolina legislation was S.L. 1868–69, chapter 156, found in BATTLE'S REVISION OF CODE OF NORTH CAROLINA ch. 64 (1873).

3. N.C. GEN STAT. § 1A-1, Rule 17(a) (hereinafter G.S.).

4. Home Real Estate, Loan & Ins. Co. v. Locker, 214 N.C. 1, 197 S.E. 555 (1938); Choate Rental Co. v. Justice, 211 N.C. 54, 188 S.E. 609 (1936).

5. G.S. 7A-223.

6. Although G.S. 7A-216 states that an agent may sign the complaint in summary ejectment cases, G.S. 7A-223, the more specific statute, requires the agent to have actual knowledge of the facts in order to do so.

If a summary ejectment action that does not name the real party in interest is filed, the magistrate should not dismiss it. Instead, he or she must allow the plaintiff a reasonable time after an objection is raised to substitute the name of the real party in interest.[7] An objection for failure to bring the action in the name of the real party in interest may be made by the defendant or by the magistrate on his or her own motion.[8] If the plaintiff does not substitute the real party in interest within a reasonable time, dismissal of the lawsuit is appropriate. The change can be made by filing an amended complaint substituting the name of the owner as the plaintiff. The change can also be made in the courtroom; if it is done at the trial, the magistrate should make a finding about the substitution in the judgment so that the clerk will be aware of the new plaintiff.

Service of Process

The landlord may serve the tenant by any of the means for service available in a small claim action:

1. by having the sheriff deliver a copy of the complaint and summons to the defendant in person,[9]
2. by having the sheriff leave a copy of the summons and complaint at the defendant's dwelling with a person of suitable age and discretion who also resides in the dwelling, or
3. by mailing a copy of the summons and complaint by certified mail, return receipt requested, addressed to the defendant.[10]

A defendant who has not been properly served but makes a voluntary appearance in the case is subject to the magistrate's jurisdiction just as if he or she had been served by one of the above-mentioned methods.[11]

In summary ejectment cases only, another method of service is allowed: The sheriff may serve the defendant by mailing a copy of the summons and complaint to the defendant by first class mail and posting a copy in a conspicuous place on the premises from which the defendant is to be evicted.[12] This method frequently is referred to as "service by posting." There is one important difference between service by posting and other methods of service. If the defendant is served by one of the other methods of service used for small claims cases or makes a voluntary appearance, the magistrate can hear a claim by the landlord for monetary damages and enter a money judgment against the tenant for the amount of damages the plaintiff proves. But in cases involving service by posting, it is not clear that a magistrate has jurisdiction to enter a money judgment against the tenant.

---

7. G.S. 1A-1, Rule 17(a).

8. Booker v. Everhart, 294 N.C. 146, 158, 240 S.E.2d 360, 367 (1978).

9. Unlike other small claims cases, a private process server may not serve a summary ejectment complaint and summons that has been returned unexecuted by the sheriff. G.S. 1A-1, Rule 4(h1).

10. G.S. 7A-217.

11. G.S. 7A-217(3).

12. G.S. 7A-217(4).

It is most likely that the North Carolina courts would not uphold a judgment for money damages against a defendant served by posting and would find that the magistrate's jurisdiction is limited to awarding possession of the premises. The supreme court of Georgia, in interpreting an ejectment statute similar to North Carolina's, found that granting a monetary judgment after service by posting and first class mail would be unconstitutional.[13] The North Carolina Attorney General's Office has reached the same result by statutory interpretation.[14] Therefore, a magistrate should not consider a claim for monetary damages in a summary ejectment case when the defendant was served by first class mail and posting. The magistrate should not enter a judgment that the plaintiff is not entitled to a money judgment. Rather, the summons return indicating that the plaintiff was served by posting and the finding that the defendant was not present at trial indicates why no money judgment was considered. If the magistrate wants to explain why there is no judgment for monetary damages, he or she should make a finding that "the claim for monetary damages is not considered because the defendant was served by posting." However, if the defendant was served by posting and makes a voluntary appearance, the magistrate has jurisdiction to enter a money judgment and should indicate in the judgment that the defendant appeared. The record will then indicate that he or she had jurisdiction to enter the money judgment.

Action Limited to Landlord–Tenant Relationship

Certain basic limitations apply to the use of the summary ejectment action. The first of these is that the action may be brought only by a landlord against his or her tenant.[15] An action for summary ejectment may be brought before a magistrate "only in the case when the simple relation of lessor and lessee has existed."[16] If the parties do not bear the relationship of landlord and tenant, there may be grounds for a lawsuit but the suit is not properly called a summary ejectment and cannot be heard by a magistrate. For example, a landlord cannot use summary ejectment to eject a trespasser; nor may a mortgagee use such an action to evict a mortgagor.[17] Neither an heir nor a fiduciary may use summary ejectment to recover property belonging to the decedent or principal.[18] A buyer may not bring a summary ejectment action to oust a seller still in possession,[19] and a seller of real property may not use it to evict a buyer who took possession under a contract of sale.

---

13. Housing Auth. of Atlanta v. Hudson, 296 S.E.2d 558 (Ga. 1982). *See also* Greene v. Lindsey, 456 U.S. 444 (1982); Mullane v. Central Hanover Bank & Trust Co., 339 U.S. 306 (1950).

14. 60 N.C. Op. Att'y Gen. 95 (Feb. 26, 1992) (letter to Hon. Thomas N. Hix).

15. Howell v. Branson, 226 N.C. 264, 37 S.E.2d 687 (1946); Chandler v. Cleveland Sav. & Loan Ass'n, 24 N.C. App. 455, 211 S.E.2d 484 (1975).

16. Hughes v. Mason, 84 N.C. 473, 474 (1881).

17. Hauser v. Morrison, 146 N.C. 248, 59 S.E. 693 (1907). There is a specific statutory procedure— G.S. 45-21.29(k), (l)—to remove a person who will not leave real property after it has been sold in a foreclosure procedure and summary ejectment is not appropriate.

18. Hayes v. Turner, 98 N.C. App. 451, 391 S.E.2d 513 (1990); Jones v. Swain, 89 N.C. App. 663, 367 S.E.2d 136 (1988).

19. College Heights Credit Union v. Boyd, 104 N.C. App. 494, 409 S.E.2d 742 (1991) (Buyer at I.R.S. tax sale cannot use summary ejectment to remove previous owner.).

Seller–Buyer Relationship

One of the more difficult problems for magistrates involves a contract that mixes sale of the land with lease of the land and requires the magistrate to determine which sort of contract is at issue. It is clear that if a person signs a contract to purchase land (an *installment land contract*), the relationship is not landlord–tenant and the seller cannot use summary ejectment to "evict" a buyer who defaults.[20] This principle applies even if the land contract specifies that default creates a landlord–tenant relationship and that the landlord can bring a summary ejectment action.[21] However, if the parties enter into a lease and a contract for the sale of land and the seller completely cancels the contract for sale, the buyer becomes a tenant and the landlord can evict him or her through a summary ejectment action.[22] To end or rescind the contract for sale, the seller must indicate in an unmistakable manner that the contract is canceled and must restore, or offer to restore, the status quo; or he or she must clearly establish the new landlord–tenant relationship in some other way. *Recission* implies the entire abrogation of the contract and a restoration of any benefits received from the other party.[23] In other words, if the seller rescinds the contract for sale of the property, he or she is entitled to keep a reasonable rent for the property during buyer's occupation and an amount to recover for any damage to the property; the seller must, however return any other benefits received, such as the buyer's down payment.

If the parties enter into a lease with an option to purchase the property at some time in the future, the relationship is that of landlord and tenant until the option is exercised.[24] The court has held that the contract is a lease and not a purchase agreement because the lessee acquires no interest in the property itself.

In cases such as these, the magistrate must read the entire contract between the parties to determine whether the underlying agreement is a sale or lease. One factor the magistrate should consider in making that determination is whether the money paid by the defendant is going toward acquisition of the property; if it is, it is not a simple landlord–tenant relationship and the magistrate must then determine whether the contract for sale was terminated.

Employer–Employee Relationship

Summary ejectment is also inappropriate if the parties' relationship is that of employer and employee (also referred to as master and servant). "[A]s a general rule, it is held that a person who occupies the premises of his employer as part of his compensation is in possession as a servant,

---

20. McCombs v. Wallace, 66 N.C. 481 (1872).

21. Hughes v. Mason, 84 N.C. 473, 478 (1881).

22. Marantz Piano Co. v. Kincaid, 108 N.C. App. 693, 424 S.E.2d 671 (1993). In *Marantz* the parties entered into a lease, and later a contract, to purchase the property. When the contract to purchase was breached, the seller filed a summary ejectment action claiming that the relationship returned to landlord and tenant. However, the court found that the seller had not shown an unmistakable intent to cancel the written agreement even though he had asked the buyer to vacate the property.

23. Brannock v. Fletcher, 271 N.C. 65, 155 S.E.2d 532 (1967).

24. Farmville Oil & Fertilizer Co. v. Bowen, 204 N.C. 375, 168 S.E. 211 (1933); Jerome v. Setzer, 175 N.C. 391, 95 S.E. 616 (1918). Once the option is exercised, the seller can cancel for breach and the parties revert to a landlord–tenant relationship. Marantz, 108 N.C. App. 693, 424 S.E.2d 671.

and not as a tenant."[25] However, a defendant may successfully avoid eviction on the ground that rental of the premises arises out of an employer–employee relationship with the plaintiff rather than a landlord–tenant relationship. To do so, the defendant must show that occupancy of the residence is (1) reasonably necessary for the effective performance of the employee's job, (2) inseparable from that job, or (3) required by the employer as essential to the employment.[26] The mere fact that the employer, when hiring the employee, offered the residence to the employee does not establish that occupying it is essential to the employment. For example, when a plaintiff who owned two houses employed the defendant as manager and custodian of the two houses, he allowed the defendant to live in one room while assisting with the rental of the other rooms, collection of rents, and management of the property. The court found that the defendant's occupancy was not critical to his job as managing agent.[27] In other words, the employer–employee relationship did not extend to the defendant's occupancy of the room; for purposes of use of the residence, the defendant was a tenant, and the plaintiff, as landlord, had to bring a summary ejectment action to remove him from the premises.

Only one of the North Carolina cases raising the issue held that an employer–employee relationship existed,[28] which indicates how difficult it is to prove this exception.[29] In the rare case in which the relationship is that of employer and employee, the employee's right to stay in the premises terminates when the employment ends; at that point an employee who does not leave when requested to do so apparently becomes a trespasser.[30]

Innkeeper–Guest Relationship

Occasionally a magistrate must determine whether a landlord–tenant relationship can be based on rental of a motel or hotel room. Generally, when a person rents a motel or hotel room, the relationship is that of innkeeper and guest.[31] Whereas a tenant acquires an interest in real property, the occupant of a hotel does not. Typically, hotel occupancy is transient: a person stays in a hotel for a short period of time while away from his or her regular residence. The occupant does not have exclusive legal possession of the room—the hotel management keeps a key to the room, enters the room daily to clean it, and furnishes sheets and towels.[32] A guest is not entitled to receive legal notice to leave the premises and cannot be removed through a summary eject-

25. Simons v. Lebrun, 219 N.C. 42, 47, 12 S.E.2d 644, 647 (1941). *See also* State v. Curtis, 20 N.C. 363 (1839).

26. *Simons*, 219 N.C. at 49, 12 S.E.2d at 648.

27. *Simons*, 219 N.C. 42.

28. State v. Curtis, 20 N.C. 363 (1839).

29. In *Simons; Tucker v. Park Yarn Mill Co.*, 194 N.C. 756, 140 S.E. 744 (1927); and *State v. Smith*, 100 N.C. 466, 6 S.E. 84 (1888), the court held that a landlord–tenant, not a master–servant relationship, existed as to the dwellings.

30. Ecija v. Paauhau Sugar Plantation Co., 26 Haw. 42 (1921); Crain v. Burnett, 190 Ill. App. 407 (1914).

31. North Carolina cases refer to hotel occupants as "guests." Holstein v. Phillips, 146 N.C. 366, 369, 59 S.E. 103 (1907); Hutchins v. Town of Durham, 118 N.C. 458, 24 S.E.723 727 (1896).

32. *See* 43A C.J.S. *Inns, Hotels, and Eating Places* § 5 (1978). *Hutchins*, at 457, 24 S.E. at 723; State v. McRae, 170 N.C. 712, 86 S.E. 1039 (1915).

ment action.[33] A guest who does not leave when asked to do so by a hotel operator becomes a trespasser and can be charged with criminal trespass.[34]

Sometimes, however, the relationship between the hotel and occupant is more ambiguous. An occupant who lives in a hotel for an extended period of time may have no other residence, and payment for the room may be collected weekly or even monthly. The North Carolina Court of Appeals has made it clear that the fact that a building is licensed as a hotel does not preclude a relationship of landlord and tenant between an owner and a resident: "[T]he fact that a building is identified as a 'hotel' and those who reside in it as 'guests' is not determinative."[35] The magistrate must look at all of the circumstances of the particular case in determining whether the relationship is landlord–tenant or innkeeper–guest.[36] Factors to consider are (1) whether the "hotel" is the sole and permanent residence of the occupant, (2) the length of the occupancy, (3) the method of payment and what the payments are called, (4) whether the rooms contain separate kitchens, (5) whether the rooms are unfurnished, (6) whether the occupant has exclusive possession of the living quarters, (7) whether the occupant has his or her own key or the "hotel" keeps a key to the premises, and (8) whether the owner supplies utilities, and (9) whether the owner provides such services as cleaning or changing sheets.[37]

When a Cohabitant Is a Guest

Another common situation in which there is a question about whether the relationship is one of landlord–tenant is when a tenant or an owner invites his or her girlfriend or boyfriend to live on the premises and later wishes that person to leave. Is the invited girlfriend or boyfriend a lessee of the boyfriend or girlfriend who owns the property?[38] A sublessee of the person renting the property? Or is the invited friend merely a guest of the person in whose residence he or she is living? If the friend is a lessee or a sublessee, summary ejectment is the appropriate method of removing the person from the premises, regardless of whether the original occupant owns or rents the residence. If the friend is simply a guest, criminal trespass or a civil trespass action would be the appropriate remedy. No cases in North Carolina discuss that situation, although in one case the court found that a man whose father-in-law allowed him to live in a vacant house

---

33. Tamamain v. Gabbard, 55 A.2d 513 (D.C. 1947); Jacob v. Jacob, 212 N.Y.S. 62 (1925).

34. *Cf.* Roberts v. Casey, 93 P.2d 654 (Cal. 1939); G.S. 72-1 (providing that at the expiration of time guest is to stay, innkeeper may remove lodger's property and restrain lodger from entering room). G.S. 72-1 reflects the common law regarding inns and guests, which was a public accommodations law: the hotel has a duty to provide lodging to a person who can pay, but at the expiration of the contract to stay the lodger may be restrained from entering without liability to the innkeeper.

35. Baker v. Rushing, 104 N.C. App. 240, 247, 409 S.E.2d 108, 112 (1991).

36. *Id.* In *Baker* some of the occupants had lived in the hotel for as long as six years and none had other residences.

37. *See generally, id.*; City of Mercer Island v. Steinmann, 513 P.2d 80 (Wash. 1973); Stowe v. Fritzie Hotels, Inc., 282 P.2d 890 (Cal. 1955); Hundley v. Milner Hotels Mgmt. Co., 114 F. Supp. 206 (W.D. Ky. 1953), *aff'd per curiam*, 216 F.2d 613 (6th Cir. 1954).

38. This situation applies to any invited friend, but it most commonly occurs in the boyfriend/girlfriend situation.

"so long as he and his family would live there," was a tenant at will.[39] In that case, however, the owner of the property gave exclusive occupancy of the house to his son-in-law. In the invited-girlfriend/-boyfriend situation, the owner or tenant remains in occupancy and invites another person to join him or her, so there is no exclusive occupancy that might make it clear that there is a tenancy.

In a District of Columbia case, a person lived with his girlfriend in her apartment for about two months and refused to leave when asked. The girlfriend had entered into the lease with the landlord, and she paid all the rent. The boyfriend had contributed some furniture and, at times, had bought food. The court found that the boyfriend had become a trespasser and had no right to stay and upheld a criminal charge against him.[40]

In making the determination of whether the person moving in is a subtenant or a guest, the magistrate must consider several factors. The most important determination is the intention of the parties at the time one friend moved in with the other: Was there an agreement that the person moving in would be a tenant or subtenant of the other?[41] Other factors may be considered in determining their original intentions: Did both parties contribute to the living expenses in a significant way (for example, by an agreement to pay or split the rent or utilities), how long did they live together, and (if original resident is a tenant) did the landlord agree to the second person being there—which, depending on the agreement, might indicate that the person moving in has become a co-tenant with the original tenant.[42]

A magistrate sometimes also encounters a situation in which a landlord is trying to evict a person who was either a subtenant or guest of the original tenant who has since moved out. In that situation, summary ejectment is appropriate, but the issue is whether the landlord has entered into a lease with the current occupant (the boyfriend or girlfriend still living there). If so, the action must be brought against that person rather than the original tenant. However, if the landlord has not entered into a lease with the current occupant, the landlord should bring a summary ejectment action against the original tenant; a judgment against the tenant would then authorize the removal of anyone who lives on the property at the invitation of the tenant.[43]

The same consideration of whether a person is a guest or a tenant arises when a parent wishes a child who is living with him or her leave the dwelling. Usually the child is a guest in his or her parents' house because there is no agreement that the child pay rent to live there. However, there are occasions when a child (usually an adult who is working) moves in with his or her parents under an agreement to pay rent. In that situation, the child is a tenant of the parents and can only be removed by summary ejectment.

---

39. Barbee v. Lamb, 225 N.C. 211, 212, 34 S.E.2d 65, 66 (1945) (father offered home to his son-in-law if son-in-law would move his family back to the area).

40. Jackson v. United States, 357 A.2d 409 (D.C. 1976). *See also* Young v. District of Columbia, 752 A.2d 138 (D.C. 2000).

41. *Young*, 752 A.2d. at 143.

42. *Jackson*, 357 A.2d 409.

43. Stone v. Guion, 223 N.C. 831, 28 S.E.2d 510 (1944).

Types of Leases

There are three kinds of leases in North Carolina: tenancy for years, periodic tenancy, and tenancy at will. The characteristics of each must be kept distinctly in mind because the rights and obligations of the parties may vary with each type. Sometimes reference is made to a "tenancy at sufferance," but this is not a separate type of tenancy. Rather, it is the status of the tenant during the time when the tenancy is over—that is, before either a new tenancy is created (under the "holdover" provisions described below) or while the landlord prepares to bring a summary ejectment action against the tenant.

Tenancy for Years

A *tenancy for years* is a tenancy for a definite, fixed term. Despite the name, the period of time need not be for one year or several years; it can be for a year, more than a year, or less than a year, or for any fixed period of time on which the parties agree. For example, a landlord and tenant agree orally that the tenant may rent the mobile home for six months beginning November 1, 2008, or the landlord and tenant enter into a written lease authorizing the tenant to rent the apartment for two years, beginning January 1, 2009. Each of these leases or tenancies is a tenancy for years. In both cases, the lease has a definite ending time—the November lease ends on April 30, 2009, and the January lease ends on December 31, 2010—of which both parties have knowledge.

Periodic Tenancy

A *periodic tenancy* is a lease that does not end on a definite date or last a defined period of time, but one that is renewable from one period to the next; they may run year to year, month to month, or week to week. Although there is no fixed end to this type of lease, the parties do not intend for the tenancy to continue forever. Therefore, either the landlord or the tenant may terminate the lease by giving notice to the other party that the lease will terminate at the end of the current period (year, month, or day). Thus, periodic tenancies "continue to renew themselves indefinitely until they are terminated at the end of one of the periods by proper notice by either the lessor or lessee."[44] A periodic tenancy need not begin on the first day of the year, month, or week. For example, a year-to-year tenancy may run from August through July; a month-to-month tenancy could run from the fifteenth of the month to the fifteenth of the next month, and a week-to-week tenancy could be from Wednesday to Wednesday. Sometimes periodic tenancies are created by express agreement and sometimes they are created by implication. An express agreement would arise when the landlord and tenant agree that the rental period is month to month. An implied periodic tenancy would be created when the agreement states that the tenant may move in on Monday, March 1, if he or she pays the first week's rent before that date. In that situation the parties have agreed to a week-to-week tenancy from Monday through Sunday with the rent being due on the first day of the rental period.

Sometimes a periodic tenancy is created by act of the parties at the end of a tenancy for years. Suppose the parties agree to a tenancy for one year with rent payable monthly. (Five years

44. Goler Metropolitan Apartments, Inc. v. Williams, 43 N.C. App. 648, 652, 260 S.E.2d 146, 149–50 (1979).

would do just as well for this example.) At the end of the year, the tenant "holds over" and remains in possession of the premises, continuing to pay rent monthly, The landlord accepts the rent—rather than bringing a summary ejectment proceeding), and nothing is said. By their actions the parties have created a periodic tenancy. The general rule is that, in the absence of a lease provision to the contrary, when a tenant holds over under a lease for one year or more and the landlord continues to accept rent, a new year-to-year tenancy is created unless there are qualifying facts or circumstances.[45] If the tenancy for years is for a period less than a year, the magistrate must determine the period of the holdover; in that situation, the period in which the rent is paid may be indicative of the period of the tenancy. Two examples of circumstances that might overcome the presumption that a holdover creates a periodic tenancy are instructive: When the parties are negotiating for a renewal or change of the lease when the term ends and the landlord agrees that the tenant can remain on the premises during the negotiations or when the tenant remains in possession solely because of his or her illness or that of some member of his or her family if moving would result in serious danger to the patient.[46]

If the lease itself specifies the period of the tenancy if there is a holdover, that provision must be followed.[47] If the lease includes an option to renew (for example, a one-year lease with an option to renew for successive one-year terms up to a total of five years), the tenant holds over after the end of the first year, and the landlord continues to accept rent, the tenant is presumed to have exercised the option to renew or extend the lease.[48] To complicate matters, sometimes the magistrate must decide whether the holdover provision in the lease or the general holdover rule applies.

> **Example 1.** Landlord and tenant enter into a lease for three years, with rent to be paid monthly at a rate of $500. The lease provided that at the expiration of the original term, the lessee has the option of extending the lease for an additional period of two years and pay rent of $650 per month. The lessee must notify the lessor at least thirty days before termination of the original term of the lease of his or her intention to exercise the option. The tenant held over after the end of the three years and without giving notice to the landlord began paying monthly rent of $650, which the landlord accepted. Eleven months later the tenant gave the landlord notice that he was terminating the lease at the end of the next month (in other words the end of the year). Landlord notified tenant that the lease was a two-year lease and not a year-to-year lease. When tenant moved out, landlord brought a suit against the tenant for damages for the period that the premises were not re-rented. Did the tenant enter into a two-year lease under the terms of the lease or did the

45. *E.g.* Kearney v. Hare, 265 N.C. 570, 144 S.E.2d 636 (1965); Williams v. King, 247 N.C. 581, 101 S.E.2d 305 (1958); Cherry v. Whitehurst, 216 N.C. 340, 4 S.E.2d 900 (1939). *But see* Simmons v. Jarman, 122 N.C. 195, 29 S.E. 332 (1898) (although the facts of this case are somewhat muddled as to whether it was a month-to-month tenancy or a tenancy for a year with rent paid monthly, the case indicates that the holdover periodic tenancy was month-to-month when the rent is paid monthly).

46. Murrill v. Palmer, 164 N.C. 50, 54, 80 S.E. 55, 56 (1913).

47. Coulter v. Capitol Fin. Co., 266 N.C. 214, 146 S.E.2d 97 (1966) (Payment of increased rent indicated an intent to exercise the option for a two-year extension and was not a holdover provision creating a month-to-month lease.).

48. First-Citizens Bank & Trust Co. v. Frazelle, 226 N.C. 724, 40 S.E.2d 367 (1946). *See also Coulter*, 266 N.C. at 218, 146 S.E.2d at 100.

holdover create a year-to-year lease under the general rule? Even though the lease required the tenant to give thirty days' notice to exercise the option to renew the lease for two years, because the tenant paid the higher rent under the option and the landlord accepted it, the landlord waived the requirement for notice. The tenant had entered into a lease for two years and was liable for the damages for breach of the lease.

But what if the tenant had continued to pay monthly rent of $500 after the three-year term expired and the landlord had accepted that amount? In that situation the option in the lease was probably not exercised and the tenant became a year-to-year tenant under the general rule.

Generally, when the tenant holds over, the terms of the original tenancy for years (except for length of the lease) continue to apply.[49]

Tenancy at Will

A *tenancy at will* is created when the landlord and tenant have entered into a void lease or a lease for an uncertain term.[50] Examples of tenancies at will include (1) a lease to the landlord's son-in-law to occupy the house "free of rent and taxes so long as this defendant and his family would live thereon,"[51] (2) an agreement that the tenant may rent this property "as long as it was to be used for hotel purposes unless the [landlord] . . . tore the property down,"[52] or (3) an oral five-year lease.[53] Either party may terminate a tenancy at will at any time. Although the tenancy is immediately terminated by a demand for possession by the landlord, the tenant has a reasonable time to pack up and leave.[54] Tenancies at will are rare.

Grounds for Action

A landlord may bring an action for summary ejectment only when the tenant

1. breaches a condition of the lease for which reentry is specified,
2. fails to pay rent,
3. holds over after the end of the lease, or
4. engages in criminal activity.[55]

---

49. Kearney v. Hare, 265 N.C. 570, 573, 144 S.E.2d 636, 639 (1965); Cherry v. Whitehurst, 216 N.C. 340, 4 S.E.2d 900, 902 (1939).

50. Davis v. Lovick, 226 N.C. 252, 255, 37 S.E.2d 680, 681–82 (1946); Barbee v. Lamb, 225 N.C. 211, 34 S.E.2d 65 (1945).

51. *Barbee*, 225 N.C. at 212, 34 S.E.2d at 66. This case is discussed briefly above at note 39 and related text. *See also* Stout v. Crutchfield, 21 N.C. App. 387, S.E.2d (1974).

52. Choate Rental Co. v. Justice, 212 N.C. 523, 524, 193 S.E. 817, 818 (1937).

53. Kent v. Humphries, 50 N.C. App. 580, 275 S.E.2d 176 (1981).

54. Patrick K. Hetrick & James B. McLaughlin, Jr., Webster's Real Estate Law in North Carolina § 6-46 (5th ed. 1999). *See Barbee*, 225 N.C. 211, 34 S.E.2d 65; Stout v. Crutchfield, 21 N.C. App. 387, 204 S.E.2d 541 (1974). In two earlier cases, *Choate*, 212 N.C. at 525, 193 S.E. at 819 and *Mauney v. Norvell*, 179 N.C. 628, 103 S.E. 372 (1920), the court stated that tenant, if entitled to any notice, is entitled to reasonable notice.

55. Technically, eviction for criminal activity is not a summary ejectment action. The basis for eviction is found in a separate article in Article 7 of G.S. Ch. 42, which provides that eviction for criminal activity is a civil

In each of these situations, a landlord bringing an action for summary ejectment must seek possession of the premises and, perhaps, monetary damages. To be entitled to a judgment for possession, however, the landlord must prove all the elements of one of the grounds above to evict the tenant.

Violating a Condition in the Lease

To prevail in a summary ejectment based on violation of a condition in the lease, the landlord must prove (1) that he or she is the landlord and the defendant is his or her tenant; (2) that the parties agreed, as part of the lease, to the condition the landlord is seeking to enforce; (3) that the parties agreed, as part of the lease, that the lease will terminate if this condition is violated; and (4) that the defendant violated the condition.[56]

Proving the landlord–tenant relationship usually is a simple matter of the plaintiff orally testifying that he or she rented the property to the defendant or showing the magistrate a written lease designating the parties as landlord and tenant. The kinds of relationships for which summary ejectment are not appropriate are discussed above in the section "Action Limited to Landlord–Tenant Relationship."

The second element requires proof that the parties agreed in the lease to the condition the landlord is seeking to enforce—for example, that the rent is payable on the first of the month or that the tenant may not keep pets on the premises. The most common reason for bringing this action is that the tenant has breached the condition in the lease requiring payment of rent by a certain time. If there is a written lease, the condition may be proved by showing the magistrate a copy of the written lease containing the condition that was signed by both parties. If the lease is not in writing, the landlord must prove that the parties orally agreed on the condition when they entered into the lease.

The third element—that the parties also agreed, as part of the lease, that the lease will terminate if these conditions are violated—is critical. It is not sufficient for the parties to have agreed that the tenant must pay rent on time; they also must have agreed that breach of this condition terminates the lease or authorizes the landlord to re-enter the premises.[57] Provisions for forfeiture are not looked upon with favor by the court and are strictly construed against the party seeking to enforce them. Consequently, "the right to declare forfeiture of a lease must be distinctly reserved [in the lease]."[58] In an oral lease a landlord may testify that the parties agreed the landlord could re-enter and evict the tenant if he or she breached a condition in the lease. However, it is much more likely that a summary ejectment for breach of a condition of the lease will be brought when the landlord and tenant have entered into a written lease. In that case, the landlord should bring the lease to the trial and show the magistrate the lease condition he or she is trying to enforce—for example, that the tenant cannot keep pets—and the forfeiture clause

---

action that may be filed in district or small claims court. When the action is heard in small claims court, the summary ejectment procedure is to be followed.

56. G.S. 42-26(2).

57. Morris v. Austraw, 269 N.C. 218, 222, 152 S.E.2d 155, 158–59 (1967); Stanley v. Harvey, 90 N.C. App. 535, 537, 369 S.E.2d 382, 384 (1988).

58. *Morris,* 269 N.C. at 223, 152 S.E.2d at 159.

for violation of that condition. Usually, a lease lists a number of conditions and the forfeiture clause is found at the end of all of those conditions. The following are examples of language that might be used in a forfeiture clause:

- If any provision of the lease is violated, lessor may terminate this lease and demand and receive possession of the premises.
- In default of any of the above agreements, the lessor may re-enter and repossess the premises and remove all persons therefrom.
- If the lessee shall violate any of the provisions of this lease, the lessor, without any other notice or demand, may terminate this lease and require the lessees to vacate the premises, or may enter the premises and expel the lessee therefrom.
- In the event you fail to pay the rent or fail to perform any other promise, duty, or obligation agreed on by you in this lease, we may at our option terminate the lease or terminate your right to possession of the premises without terminating the lease.
- Upon the occurrence of an event of default, landlord has the right, by written notice to tenant, to re-enter the property and remove tenant and his or her belongings from the property; terminate the lease; or terminate defendant's possession of the property.

A forfeiture clause may provide that forfeiture is automatic upon breach of the lease, or it may require the landlord to give the tenant notice of the breach. The landlord must prove that he or she complied with the specific forfeiture provisions in the lease. If notice of termination is required, "the notice must be given in strict compliance with the contract as to both time and content"[59] and must be unequivocal as to the forfeiture.

The fourth element that the landlord must prove is that the tenant violated the condition in the lease—for example, that the tenant did not pay the rent or kept a pet on the premises. Usually, the issue in this element is a matter of proving the violation. Sometimes, however, the condition in the lease is ambiguous, and the magistrate will have to construe the meaning of the provision before determining whether the tenant violated it.

> *Example 2.* McIntyre rents a mobile home space to Sam. At the trial, McIntyre offers the following evidence: He shows the magistrate a written lease between himself, as landlord, and Sam, as tenant, that provides for a one-year lease and requires Sam to pay $200 rent per month by 5:00 p.m. on the first day of the month and to abide by the written regulations posted in the mobile home lot rental office. McIntyre shows the magistrate a copy of the regulations posted in the office; they include a prohibition against parking a motor vehicle heavier than 26,001 pounds on the property. McIntyre testifies that on November 15 he noticed a large hauling truck, which weighs more than 26,001 pounds, parked in front of Sam's lot. On November 17 the truck was still there. McIntyre says that he asked Sam to move it and that Sam replied that he'd move it when he felt like it. McIntyre filed this action immediately and is asking for possession. Sam was served but is not present at the trial.
>
> The magistrate should find that the landlord failed to prove his case and dismiss the action because the landlord did not prove that the lease included a termination provision for breach of

---

59. *Stanley*, 90 N.C. App. at 539, 369 S.E.2d at 385.

the condition—the third element that he is required to prove. Even though the parties agreed that certain vehicles could not be parked on the premises, the landlord cannot evict for that unless the lease also has a forfeiture clause.

If McIntyre had shown the magistrate that the lease contained an automatic forfeiture clause, the magistrate should have ruled for the landlord.

Three cases have mentioned the possibility that a fifth element may exist in cases of breach of condition of the lease—a showing that enforcing the forfeiture is not unconscionable.

> In order to evict a tenant in North Carolina, a landlord must prove: (1) That it distinctly reserved in the lease a right to declare a forfeiture for the alleged act or event; (2) that there is clear proof of the happening of an act or event for which the landlord reserved the right to declare a forfeiture; (3) that the landlord promptly exercised its right to declare a forfeiture; and (4) that the result of enforcing the forfeiture is not unconscionable.[60]

The phrase regarding unconscionability was first used in this context in *Morris v. Austraw*, in which the court quoted it from *American Jurisprudence*.[61] However, as unconscionability was not the basis for the court's decision in any of the three cases, or in any other North Carolina case, it is not clear that the plaintiff has the burden of proving this element in breach-of-condition cases. The issue is more likely to be raised by the defendant in cases in which the defendant argues that enforcing the forfeiture would be unconscionable.

Failure to Pay Rent

The second, and probably most common, ground for summary ejectment is failure to pay rent.

To be entitled to a judgment for possession based on a tenant's failure to pay rent, the landlord must prove (1) that he or she is the landlord and the defendant is the tenant, (2) that the terms of the lease required the tenant to pay a certain amount of rent and to pay it by a certain time, (3) that the tenant breached the lease by failing to pay the rent when it was due, and (4) that the landlord made a demand after the rent was due that the tenant pay the rent and gave the tenant at least ten days after the demand to pay the rent before filing the lawsuit.

The first element, proving the landlord–tenant relationship, is identical to that in an action based on breach of a condition of the lease. The second element, the terms of the lease with regard to the amount of rent and when it is due, is usually proved by oral testimony. The plaintiff will testify either that the parties agreed on those terms when entering into an oral lease or that the terms were established by their actions. (For example, if the landlord allowed the tenant to move in after paying the first month's rent of $400, the parties would have created a month-to-month periodic tenancy, with the monthly rent of $400 being due the first day of each month.) If the lease was written, the magistrate must read the provisions regarding the amount of the rent and when it was payable. For the third element, the landlord must prove that the tenant

---

60. Lincoln Terrace Assoc. Ltd. v. Kelly, 179 N.C. App. 621, 623, 635 S.E.2d 434, 436 (2006). The other two cases are *Morris*, 269 N.C. at 223, 152 S.E.2d at 159, and *Charlotte Hous. Auth. v. Fleming*, 123 N.C. App. 511, 513, 473 S.E.2d 373, 375 (1996).

61. 269 N.C. at 223, 152 S.E.2d at 159 (quoting 32 Am. Jur. 2d § 848).

did not pay the rent. The fourth element—that the landlord made a demand to the tenant for the rent and waited at least ten days after making the demand before filing the lawsuit[62]—is the crucial element in an action based on failure to pay rent. The demand need not be made in any particular form unless the lease specifies a method, in which case the lease provision must be followed. In any case, "a clear, unequivocal statement, either oral or written, requiring the lessee to pay all past due rent, is necessary."[63]

Must the plaintiff prove that the tenant actually received the demand? At common law the landlord was required to prove that a demand was made for payment of "the precise sum due, at a convenient time before sunset on the day when the rent was due, upon the land and in the most notorious place of it, though there be no person on the land to pay."[64] If, at common law, it was not necessary for the tenant to hear the oral demand for the rent, it should be sufficient for the landlord to prove proper mailing of the demand rather than actual receipt by the tenant.[65]

It is important to understand the difference between (1) an action brought for breach of a condition of the lease when the condition breached was a requirement to pay the rent by a certain date and (2) an eviction action based on the tenant's failure to pay rent. If the lease agreement provides for forfeiture of the lease if the tenant breaches the condition regarding payment of rent, the action is based on the tenant's "breach of a lease condition," *not* on the second kind of action called "failure to pay rent." As explained in the preceding section, even if the landlord and tenant agree that the rent must be paid, an action based on breach of a lease condition will be unsuccessful if the lease does not also contain a provision that failure to pay rent when due will result in termination of the lease. Although it may be reasonable to prohibit a landlord from evicting a tenant who violates some condition—for example, not keeping pets on the premises—if the landlord has not included a forfeiture clause in the lease, it is quite another matter to say that a landlord who fails to include a forfeiture clause in the lease cannot evict a tenant who does not pay rent. Therefore, the General Assembly passed the statute authorizing eviction for "failure to pay rent" for less legally sophisticated landlords who fail to include lease provisions providing for forfeiture for nonpayment of rent. Under the statute, when the tenant fails to pay the rent when it is due, the landlord may demand the rent from the tenant; if the rent is not paid within ten days after the demand, the statute provides that the tenant forfeits the lease and the landlord may bring a summary ejectment action for possession.[66] Thus, the action for "failure to pay rent" applies when there is no forfeiture clause in the lease.

---

62. G.S. 42-3.

63. Snipes v. Snipes, 55 N.C. App. 498, 504, 286 S.E.2d 591, 595 (1982) (Landlord telling tenant she "wanted to get all this business settled" does not constitute a demand for past-due rent.).

64. Prout v. Roby, 82 U.S. (15 Wall.) 471, 476–77 (1872); Connor v. Bradley, 42 U.S. (1 How.) 211, 217 (1843); Trakas v. Mitchell, 97 S.E. 245, 248 (S.C. 1918).

65. *Cf.* Main St. Shops, Inc. v. Esquire Collections, Ltd., 115 N.C. App. 510, 445 S.E.2d 420 (1994) (upholding mailed notice to tenant who did not claim letter when lease required written notice of default).

66. G.S. 42-3. *See* Ryan v. Reynolds, 190 N.C. 563, 130 S.E. 156 (1925).

Holding Over after the End of the Term

The third type of summary ejectment action is an action to evict a tenant who remains on the premises (*holds over*) after the end of the term of the lease.[67] In this case the landlord must prove (1) a landlord–tenant relationship, (2) the terms of the lease regarding its length (for example, that the parties had a tenancy for a period of one year ending on a particular date), (3) that the landlord gave the tenant proper notice that the lease would be terminated at the end of the term, and (4) that the tenant did not vacate the premises at the end of the term. To evict a tenant on this basis the landlord does not have to prove any wrongdoing on the part of the tenant other than failure to leave at the end of the term.

The first element—landlord–tenant relationship—is identical to the first element in an action for breach of a condition of the lease; the second element—terms of the lease—is similar to the second element in an action brought for failure to pay rent.

With respect to the third element, the kind of notice the landlord must give to terminate the lease may depend on the kind of lease the parties had. The parties can agree in advance on the manner and amount of notice required and can write this agreement into the lease[68] (or, in an oral lease, simply agree to the terms). In such a case, the lease provisions regarding notice must be followed.[69]

If the tenancy is for years (for a definite period of time) and the lease contains no agreement about notice, the landlord is not required to give any notice to the tenant to end the tenancy. Because the lease is for a definite period of time, both the landlord and the tenant know in advance when it is to end, so that no notice to vacate is required. For example, landlord and tenant enter into a lease agreement that tenant can rent the apartment for six months beginning April 1, 2008, and they did not agree on any provision for notice to terminate the lease. The landlord may file a summary ejectment action on October 1, 2008, without giving tenant notice to vacate because both parties understood when they entered into the lease that it would end on September 30, 2008.

If the lease is a periodic tenancy and it contains no agreement about notice to terminate, the amount of notice depends on the length of the period. If the tenancy is from year to year, the landlord must notify the tenant at least one month before the end of the year that the tenancy will terminate at the end of the year. If the parties have a month-to-month tenancy, the landlord must give the tenant notice at least one week before the end of the month in which the landlord wishes to end the tenancy. For week-to-week tenancies, notice must be given at least two days before the end of the week. If the parties have a periodic tenancy of a mobile home space (tenant provides the mobile home and rents a space on which to put it), the landlord must give the tenant notice at least sixty days before the end of the term that the tenancy is to end, no matter whether the term is year to year, month to month, or week to week.[70] For example, in a week-to-week tenancy of a mobile home space with rent due on Mondays, if the landlord wants to end the tenancy on Sunday, August 15, he or she must give the tenant notice on or before June 16 for

---

67. G.S. 42-26(1).
68. Cherry v. Whitehurst, 216 N.C. 340, 343, 4 S.E.2d 900, 902 (1939).
69. Lincoln Terrace Assoc., Ltd. v. Kelly, 179 N.C. App. 621, 623, 635 S.E.2d 434, 436 (2006).
70. G.S. 42-14.

the tenant to vacate on August 15. But if the lease is for an apartment or mobile home furnished by the landlord, the landlord has to give notice by August 13 to terminate the lease on August 15. In a month-to-month tenancy beginning on the first day of the month, the landlord must give notice by December 28 to end the tenancy of a mobile home space at the end of February, while notice by February 21 would be sufficient for any other kind of premises. Note that the sixty-day notice provision only applies to the notice to terminate a periodic tenancy of a mobile home space. It does not, however, give a tenant of a mobile home space any longer than any other tenant to leave after a summary ejectment judgment is entered; nor does it apply to any demand to pay rent in a failure-to-pay-rent action.

The notice given must terminate the lease at the end of the period (week, month, or year). For example, notice given on February 8 to vacate by February 15 would be improper in a month-to-month tenancy that begins on the first of the month.[71] In other words the notice is not to terminate the lease in a specific number of days, but rather to terminate the lease at the end of the weekly, monthly, or yearly periodic tenancy.

If the landlord does not give notice as required by the lease, statute, or regulation, the tenant is entitled to remain in possession (and is required to pay rent) for the next period; the landlord must then give a new notice at the proper time before the end of the next period that he or she wishes to terminate the lease.

Example 3. Barnes enters into a lease to rent a mobile home (not a mobile home space) to Nobles from month to month, beginning the first of the month. After six months, Barnes decides he does not want to rent to Nobles anymore. On January 15, Barnes notifies Nobles that the lease is ending in seven days on January 22. Nobles does not move out by January 22, so Barnes files his summary ejectment action based on holding over after the end of the term, and the case is heard on January 30.

The magistrate should dismiss the case because Barnes failed to prove the case by the greater weight of the evidence. Notice given seven days before Nobles was to move out is not proper notice. The landlord must give notice at least seven days before the end of the period in which the tenant must leave. Barnes could have given notice on January 15 that Nobles was to leave by the end of the day on January 31 (the end of the period in the tenancy); if Nobles did not leave by then and Barnes waited until February 1 to file the lawsuit, the magistrate would find for Barnes.

If the parties have a tenancy at will, the landlord need not give prior notice to vacate the premises; nonetheless, the tenant has a "reasonable time to pack up and leave."[72]

Any form of notice, verbal or written, is sufficient unless the parties have agreed in the lease to a particular manner of providing it or, as is the case in publicly assisted housing, federal law specifies how notice must be given.[73] The notice must be specific and clearly indicate the intention to terminate the lease at the end of the term. However, notice may also be given by presenting the tenant with an alternative—for example, "Apply for and receive a new lease and

71. Stafford v. Yale, 228 N.C. 220, 222, 44 S.E.2d 872, 873 (1947); Cla-Mar Mgmt. v. Harris, 76 N.C. App. 300, 332 S.E.2d 495 (1985).
72. Hetrick & McLaughlin, *supra* note 54, § 6-46.
73. Poindexter v. Call, 182 N.C. 366, 109 S.E. 26 (1921).

give a security deposit, or vacate this space by June 30."[74] If the tenant has failed to pay rent, the demand for rent and notice to vacate at the end of the term may be given in the same notice: "I demand that you pay the past due rent immediately, and hereby give you notice that the lease is terminated at the end of this month."

The fourth element the plaintiff must prove in a holdover case is that the tenant did not vacate the premises at the end of the term. In an action for summary ejectment based on holding over after the end of the lease, the landlord need not prove any fault on the part of the tenant during the lease period. Even if the tenant paid the rent on time and did not violate any conditions in the lease, the landlord may decide for whatever reason to end the lease at the end of a period in a periodic tenancy. In this case the tenant's breach is not leaving at the end of the term. This general rule may not apply to some publicly assisted housing, where landlords may have to show good cause for not renewing leases.[75]

> **Example 4.** At a summary ejectment trial, the tenant, Frances, does not appear, and the landlord, Betty Lou, testifies to the following facts. Betty Lou and Frances entered into a periodic year-to-year tenancy. The period began on January 1 and ended on December 31. Betty Lou decided that she wanted to rent the house to her cousin and gave notice on December 3 that Frances was to vacate by the end of the month. Frances did not leave by December 31, and Betty Lou filed the summary ejectment action on January 5.
>
> The magistrate should dismiss the case because Betty Lou failed to prove her case by the greater weight of the evidence. Notice given less than one month before the end of the year is not effective to terminate the tenancy, so Frances is entitled to another year's occupancy. The same result would apply to notice given less than one full week before the end of the rental month in a month-to-month tenancy or less than two days before the end of the week in a week-to-week tenancy. If Betty Lou and Frances had agreed to a one-year tenancy ending on December 31, rather than a periodic tenancy, no notice would be required, and the magistrate would grant possession to Betty Lou.

Tender

Many summary ejectment cases are terminated without ordering the tenant to vacate the premises. This is true because most actions are brought for failure to pay rent and G.S. 42-33 provides that the action ceases if, before the magistrate has entered judgment, the tenant tenders the rent due plus court costs. *Tender* means offering, in cash, at a time before judgment, the full amount of rent due plus all court costs. The *rent due* is the amount that should have been paid if it had been paid on time.[76] It does not include other monetary damages claimed for breach of the lease,

74. *Cla-Mar Mgmt.*, 76 N.C. App. at 304, 332 S.E.2d at 497.

75. For further discussion of this topic, see section "Ejectment of Tenants in Publicly Assisted Housing," page 184.

76. *See* Ryan v. Reynolds, 190 N.C. 563, 130 S.E. 156 (1925) (Although the headnote to the case indicates tenant must tender the amount of rent due as of date the action was filed, the tenant tendered all rent due at the time he made the tender.).

such as damages for physical damage to the property;[77] but it is not clear whether a late fee is also part of the rent due for tender purposes. Tender can be made before or during the trial. If the tenant tenders rent before court and the landlord refuses to accept it, the tenant must again tender payment at the trial.[78]

If the eviction is brought for failure to pay rent, the magistrate must dismiss the lawsuit when tender has been made. Thus, even though the landlord does not want to accept the rent and wants a judgment for possession, the magistrate must allow the tenant to hand the money to the landlord and then dismiss the lawsuit.

Tender applies only to an action brought for failure to pay rent. The purpose of the tender statute is to give the tenant a way to counteract the implied forfeiture for nonpayment of rent in G.S. 42-3 when the lease includes no forfeiture clause. "The statutory forfeiture is saved by a statutory right to pay the rent sued for and cost before judgment. The two statutes, G.S. 42-3 and 42-33, must be construed together, in pari materia."[79] If the action is brought for breach of a condition in the lease (for which forfeiture was reserved)—the breach being failure to pay rent—the tenant does not have a right to tender the full amount of rent due and have the lawsuit dismissed.[80] In an eviction based on breach of a lease condition, a landlord may either choose to accept the payment of rent and take a voluntary dismissal in the case or refuse the money and go forward with the lawsuit. The tender also does not terminate the action if the action is being brought for holding over after the lease ends[81] or for criminal activity.

Monetary Damages

In any summary ejectment action, the landlord may have a claim for monetary damages in addition to possession of the premises. The landlord may either file the claim for monetary damages with the action for possession or file two separate actions.[82] However, if the total amount of monetary damages exceeds the maximum allowable amount in controversy for small claims court—$5,000 at the time of publication—the landlord may file only the summary ejectment action seeking possession in small claims court, not the claim for monetary damages; the latter must be sought in a separate action in district or superior court. Of course, a landlord willing to reduce his or her claim to $5,000 and forgive any amount due over $5,000 can file the monetary claim in small claims court.

There are four kinds of monetary damages: (1) unpaid rent, (2) damages for occupancy of the premises after the end of the lease, (3) damages for physical injury to the premises, and (4) contract damages for the remainder of the term. The landlord also may be entitled to recover a late

---

77. *Id.*

78. Ingold v. Phoenix Assurance Co., 230 N.C. 142, 148, 52 S.E.2d 366, 370 (1949).

79. *Ryan*, 190 N.C. at 566, 130 S.E. at 158.

80. Tucker v. Arrowood, 211 N.C. 118, 189 S.E. 180 (1937); Charlotte Office Tower Assoc. v. Carolina SNS Corp., 89 N.C. App. 697, 366 S.E.2d 905 (1988); Couch v. ADC Realty Corp., 48 N.C. App. 108, 268 S.E.2d 237 (1980).

81. Seligson v. Klyman, 227 N.C. 347, 42 S.E. 2d 220 (1947).

82. *Id.* at 349, 42 S.E. 2d at 222; Chrisalis Properties, Inc. v. Separate Quarters, 101 N.C. App. 81, 84, 398 S.E.2d 628, 631 (1990).

payment fee or certain other fees. (See sections below on "Late Fees" and "Other Contractual Fees.")

Unpaid Rent

Damages for unpaid rent is the amount of rent agreed upon by the parties under the lease that has not been paid during the term of the lease. For example, if a tenant has a month-to-month lease, with rent at the rate of $700 a month, and fails to pay rent for the months of November and December, the landlord is entitled to recover the unpaid rent at the agreed-upon rate of $700 for those two months.

Damages for Occupancy after the End of the Lease

Damages for the tenant's continued occupancy of the premises after the term of the lease has ended are not measured by the agreed-upon rate in the lease but by "the fair rental value of the premises."[83] The *fair rental value* is an amount that would be agreed upon as a fair rent by a landlord who wishes to rent but is not compelled to do so and a tenant who wishes to rent but is not compelled to do so. The strongest evidence of fair rental value usually is the amount of rent being paid under the lease, and in most cases the landlord will not distinguish between past-due rent and damages for occupancy after the end of the term. In an unusual case, however, the landlord might be able to prove a higher fair rental value (for example, if the landlord has rented the property to a third party at a higher rental rate effective when the defendant's lease terminates). On the other hand, the tenant might prove that the fair rental value of the premises is less than the rate contracted in the lease because the premises are not in proper repair or because an overabundance of unoccupied apartments has driven down the local market price.

Physical Damage to Property

The third type of damages allowed, referred to as *special damages*, is for physical damage to the landlord's property. The landlord's claim is called *waste* and is available after the lease is terminated. To recover for physical damage to the property, the landlord must prove that the damage was beyond normal wear and tear to the property, for which the landlord is responsible The tenant is liable for damage caused by any willful or negligent conduct by the tenant or family members, other residents of the premises, or guests. The tenant is not responsible for acts of God (for example, damage caused by a tornado). Examples of the type of injury to the leasehold for which the tenant may be liable are removal of plumbing fixtures, knocking big holes in walls, or cutting shrubbery.

The landlord must present evidence of the amount of the damages. The measure of damages is the difference between the fair market value of the property immediately before and immediately after the damage. The actual cost of repairs or an estimate of the cost of repair is

---

83. Martin v. Clegg, 163 N.C. 528, 79 S.E. 1105 (1913). *See Seligson*, 227 N.C. at 349, 42 S.E.2d at 222 (Damages are those that may fairly and reasonably be considered as the natural and proximate result of the breach.); Fairchild Realty Co. v. Spiegel, Inc., 246 N.C. 458, 98 S.E.2d 871 (1957) (damages for wrongful possession, not rent).

not the true measure of damages, although it may be considered in determining the amount of damages.

Example 5. Santee rents a mobile home to Rivers on a month-to-month periodic tenancy for $600 per month. Rivers has lived there two years. Rivers fails to pay the rent on August 1. Santee decides she no longer wishes to rent to Rivers. On August 8 Santee notifies Rivers that the tenancy will end August 31 and that Rivers must vacate by the end of that day. Rivers doesn't pay the August rent, nor does he vacate by August 31. On September 2 Santee enters the mobile home for an inspection and discovers that Rivers has pulled up the carpet in one bedroom and has hung several pictures in the living room, which will require Santee to have the living room repainted. Santee files a summary ejectment action and proves all of these facts at trial on September 15. She also brings an estimate from New York Carpet World indicating that it will cost $550 to replace the carpet in the bedroom and an estimate from Jones Painting Company indicating that it will cost $350 to repaint the living room. She seeks $900 for rent owed (1.5 month's rent) and $900 for physical damage to the property, for a total of $1,800.

Rivers testifies that he was very careful hanging the pictures, used the smallest picture hangers possible, and considers those small marks to be ordinary wear and tear. He shows the magistrate a photograph of the walls, which indicates only two picture hooks in the wall. He also testifies that Santee told him at the inception of the leasehold that the carpet in the bedroom was eight years old at that time. Rivers argues that the carpet he removed was, therefore, ten years old, fairly worn out, and worth no more than $100 at the end of his tenancy. Finally he testifies that Santee had signed two new leases for comparable mobile homes in the park within the last two months and both of them had a monthly rental rate of $400 because there is a surplus of mobile homes for rent in the community. Therefore, the fair rental value of the premises is $400, not $600 per month.

The magistrate believes Rivers's evidence. Santee is entitled to a judgment for possession and for $800 in monetary damages—$600 at the contract rate for unpaid rent for August when the lease contract was in effect, $200 at the fair rental value for occupancy after the end of the term from September 1 through 15, and $100 for replacing the carpet in the bedroom (the fair market value of the personal property at the time of the loss). The small nicks in the wall to hang pictures are judged to be ordinary wear and tear.

The landlord may also sue the tenant for repair costs and other damages when the lease has not yet terminated. Such claims are merely claims for money owed without any claim for possession of the premises and have to be grounded on damage beyond normal wear and tear or based on a violation of the Residential Rental Agreements Act. That act specifies that residential tenants may "not deliberately or negligently destroy, deface, damage, or remove any part of the premises or knowingly permit any person to do so."[84]

---

84. G.S. 42-43(a)(4).

Damages for Remainder of the Term

At common law a lease was solely a property interest, but modern law views leases as possessing both property rights and contractual rights.[85] Damages for the remainder of the term are based on contract, not property, rights. These damages are available only if the tenant breaches a tenancy for years before the term is over; for example, a tenant who has a one-year lease abandons the premises or stops paying rent after three months. The purpose of these damages is to place a landlord in the same position that he or she would have occupied had the contract been performed.

Under North Carolina law a summary ejectment judgment terminates the lease and the tenant's obligation to pay rent; however, that does not mean that a tenant who breaches a tenancy for years during the term has no liability beyond the rent due as of the date of the judgment.[86] At the point the lease is terminated, the landlord becomes entitled to breach of contract damages rather than rent.

Another contract principle at play in breach of contract is that the nonbreaching party to a lease (the landlord in this case) has a duty to mitigate the damages upon breach of the contract. Thus, when a tenant breaches a tenancy for years and is evicted, the landlord is required to use reasonable efforts to re-rent the premises to lessen the liability of the tenant. Although the landlord is the one who has the duty to mitigate the tenant's liability, the burden is on the tenant (the breaching party) to prove that the landlord failed to exercise reasonable diligence to minimize his or her loss.[87] In a claim for damages for the remainder of the term, a landlord who mitigates damages is entitled to recover the amount of rent the landlord would have received for the remainder of the term, less the amount received from a new tenant.[88] If no issue of failure to mitigate is raised, the landlord's damages for future rents are ascertainable and may be awarded at the trial for summary ejectment.[89] In that situation, the plaintiff's damages are the future rent due under the lease reduced to present value. Damages for future rent due under the contract must be reduced to its "present value," because a smaller sum received now is equal to a larger sum received in the future. If the landlord fails to use reasonable diligence to mitigate, his or her damages are limited to the difference between what the landlord would have received under the lease had tenant complied with its terms and the fair market value of what the landlord would have received had he or she used reasonable diligence to mitigate.

Some leases include a specific provision allowing the landlord to terminate tenant's right to possession but not his or her duty to pay rent. However, such a provision does not release the landlord from the duty to mitigate damages. Therefore, the damages for tenant's breach of this condition would be the same as damages when no such specific provision is included in the lease.[90]

---

85. Strader v. Sunstates Corp., 129 N.C. App. 562, 570, 500 S.E.2d 752, 756 (1998).

86. Holly Farm Foods, Inc. v. Kuykendall, 114 N.C. App. 412, 415, 442 S.E.2d 94, 96 (1994).

87. Isbey v. Crews, 55 N.C. App. 47, 51, 284 S.E.2d 534, 538 (1981).

88. *Id.*

89. Chrisalis Properties, Inc. v. Separate Quarters, 101 N.C. App. 81, 88, 398 S.E.2d 628, 633 (1990).

90. Although some states do not allow breach of contract damages unless there is a specific clause in the lease giving residual liability after eviction, North Carolina apparently does not require such a provision. *Holly Farm*

A landlord can also be entitled to breach of contract damages when the lease contains a provision for *liquidated damages*— a specific amount of damages due the landlord if a breach by the tenant results in termination of the lease. Rather than suing for the rent due for the remainder of the term, less the amount received from the new tenant, the landlord merely sues for the specific amount of damages agreed to in the lease. However, to be enforceable a liquidated damages provision must represent a reasonable estimate of the anticipated damages; otherwise, it is a penalty and therefore unenforceable.

Late Fees

The General Assembly has enacted legislation limiting the amount of late fees that may be charged in residential leases.[91] A magistrate may order a residential tenant to pay a late fee only if the landlord proves that (1) the landlord and tenant agreed upon the late fee at the time they entered into the lease, (2) the late fee agreed upon does not exceed the greater of $15 or 5 percent of the rental payment if the rent is paid monthly or the greater of $4 or 5 percent if the rent is paid weekly, and (3) the agreement provides that the late fee is not charged until the rent is at least five days late. If the tenant's rent is subsidized by a federal, state, or local government, the late fee is calculated based on the tenant's share of the rent, not the total rent.

> *Example 6.* Rodriguez rents a Section 8 apartment from Crosswinds with monthly rent of $800. The lease provides for the U.S. Department of Housing and Urban Development to pay Crosswinds $600 monthly and for Rodriguez to pay the remaining $200. The rent is due by the first day of the month, and the lease specifies a late fee of $15 if the rent is not paid by the end of the fifth day of the month. Rodriguez fails to pay rent for July and August and Crosswinds files a summary ejectment action seeking back rent and $30 in late fees ($15 each for missing July and August payments). Crosswinds is entitled to the late fees since the $15 is allowed under the statute.
>
> If the rent were paid weekly and Rodriguez paid $50 a week, the maximum allowable late fee would be $4 (since 5 percent of $50 is only $2.50).

Any late fee agreement contrary to these requirements is against the public policy of North Carolina and is void and unenforceable.[92] Therefore, a lease that calls for payment of a late fee of more than the allowable maximum or authorizes imposition of a late fee before the rent is five days overdue is unenforceable. The magistrate may not merely reduce the late fee to an allowable amount but may not award the landlord any late fee at all. Even if the landlord did not charge the tenant a late fee in excess of the allowable statutory amount, if the lease calls for a higher amount the landlord is not entitled to a late fee. In one case a lease provided for a late fee of $31 on a monthly rental payment of $610—just fifty cents over the maximum allowable amount. The court ruled that the landlord was not entitled to any late fee, even though he actually charged the tenant only $30 when the rent was at least five days late.[93]

Foods, 114 N.C. 412, 442 S.E.2d 94.

91. G.S. 42-46.

92. *Id.*

93. Friday v. United Dominion Realty Trust, Inc., 155 N.C. App. 671, 575 S.E.2d 532 (2003).

Other examples of impermissible late fees would be a lease provision that provides a late fee of a certain amount per day for every day the rent is more than five days late or one stating that the late fee is due if the rent is not paid by the due date. Even if the fee is not called a late fee, it must not exceed the statutory limits if it has the same effect as charging the tenant more for late payment. A questionable practice is a lease providing that the monthly rent of $500 is due on the first of the month but saying the tenant is not in default until the end of the fifth day of the month. Under this lease, the tenant is entitled to a discount of $50 if the rent is paid by the first of the month and incurs a penalty of $50 if the rent is not paid by the fifth of the month. Clearly, the "penalty" charged after the fifth of the month is a late fee and is void because it is more than the allowable amount. But what about the $500 payment that is due by the fifth of the month? It is unclear what a court would do in that situation. If the lease states that the rent is due by the first of the month, it is certainly possible that the magistrate might find that the monthly rent is $450 and the $50 fee for the additional five days is void because it is a late fee in violation of the statute. But what if the lease specifically says the rent is due by the fifth of the month but the tenant would get a $50 reduction by paying by the first? Is this a true benefit or merely a subterfuge for a late fee during the first five days the rent is late? There is no clear answer to this question; however, since the late fee statute provides that any late fee provision that does not comply with the statute is against the state's public policy, magistrates should read lease such lease provisions strictly and against the landlord.

In commercial leases, landlords and tenants may agree on any late fee as long as it is reasonably related to the costs of receiving rent late and is not a penalty.[94]

Other Contractual Fees

Other fees may also be allowed if provided for in a residential lease as long as the fee is not a subterfuge to avoid the late fee statute. The court has upheld a provision in a residential lease providing for an administrative fee of $75 if the landlord files legal papers against the tenant;[95] The court implied it might look more closely if the fee did not reasonably relate to actual expenses: "A lease providing for a fee reasonably related to such an additional expense incurred not solely relating to rent being late does not violate the [late fee] statute."[96] In commercial leases, other fees agreed upon in the lease are allowed.

One final fee a landlord may request if it is provided for in the lease is attorneys' fees. G.S. 6-21.2 provides that provisions to pay attorneys' fees in "any note, conditional sale contract or other evidence of indebtedness" are enforceable if the debt is collected by an attorney. The question is whether a written lease would be considered "other evidence of indebtedness." In a case in which the court applied the statute to a lease of personal property (a road scraper) the court stated that evidence of indebtedness "has reference to any printed or written instrument, signed or otherwise executed by the obligor(s), which evidences on its face a legally enforceable

---

94. *See* Crawford v. Allen, 189 N.C. 434, 127 S.E. 521 (1925). *Cf.* Weinstein v. Griffin, 241 N.C. 161, 84 S.E.2d 549 (1954) (A late fee of 4 percent of the rental payment was imposed under the lease, but the amount of the fee was not at issue in the case.).

95. *Friday,* 155 N.C. App. at 676; 575 S.E.2d at 536.

96. *Id.* at 677, 575 S.E.2d at 536.

obligation to pay money."[97] The North Carolina Court of Appeals has held that a lease of real property is an evidence of indebtedness under G.S. 6-21.2.[98] If the lease includes an attorneys' fee provision, the attorney is entitled to an award of 15 percent of the rent due (unless a lower percentage is set in the lease). However, in order to recover the fee, the landlord, or the landlord's attorney, after default, must notify the tenant that the attorneys' fee provision, as well as the requirement to pay the outstanding balance, will be enforced; the tenant then has five days from the mailing of the notice to pay the outstanding balance without incurring the attorneys' fee.

The cases related to this issue do not, however, answer the question of whether the magistrate can award attorneys' fees under a lease provision in the summary ejectment action when damages for unpaid back rent are not sought or cannot be awarded because the tenant was served by posting. In *Coastal Production Credit Association v. Goodson Farms, Inc.*,[99] the court said that the attorneys' fee provision in an evidence of indebtedness may be applied to an action other than that for the debt when the action is reasonably related to the collection of the debt; but the court put on the party seeking to recover the burden of proving that the summary ejectment proceeding is reasonably related to the monetary debt. Moreover, it is always within the judge's discretion to decide whether to allow attorneys' fees in an ancillary action that is not seeking the debt.[100] However, in a summary ejectment action, because the landlord is specifically allowed to split the claim for possession and back rent, it may make more sense for the attorneys' fee provision to be applied only when the landlord is seeking back rent; otherwise, the landlord might receive attorneys' fees for bringing the summary ejectment action and again for bringing a separate action for the back rent.

Tenant's Defenses against Summary Ejectment

In many instances a tenant will avoid ejectment by negating one of the elements the plaintiff is required to prove. For example, in a failure-to-pay-rent case, the landlord may assert that he or she demanded the rent more than ten days before bringing the lawsuit, while the tenant testifies that the landlord asked him to come to the office to discuss the late rent but never explicitly demanded that he pay it. If the magistrate does not find that the plaintiff has proved by the greater weight of the evidence that a proper demand was made, the landlord's case will fail and the magistrate must dismiss the action.

Waiver of the Breach

In addition to raising factual issues about elements that the plaintiff must prove, a tenant may raise a number of affirmative defenses to ejectment. Perhaps the most common affirmative defense is that the landlord has waived the right to declare the lease forfeited and to sue for

---

97. Stillwell Enter., Inc. v. Interstate Equip. Co., 300 N.C. 286, 294, 266 S.E.2d 812, 817 (1980).

98. N.C. Indus. Capital v. Clayton, 185 N.C. App. 356, 367, 649 S.E.2d 14, 22 (2007); WRI/Raleigh, L.P. v. Shaikh, 183 N.C. App. 249, 644 S.E.2d 245 (2007).

99. 70 N.C. App. 221, 319 S.E.2d 650 (1984).

100. *N.C. Indus. Capital*, 185 N.C. App. at 369, 649 S.E.2d at 23 (upholding lower court's refusal to award attorneys' fees in underlying summary ejectment action).

breach. The general rule is that when a landlord knows the tenant has breached the lease and accepts rent that comes due after the breach, the landlord has waived the tenant's breach and is not entitled to evict the tenant for that breach.[101] The rule applies if the landlord accepts the rent after he or she has filed a lawsuit and even if the landlord indicates that he or she will accept future rent payments without prejudice to the action.[102] However, the rule does not apply to an eviction for criminal activity brought under Article 7 of G.S. 42: collecting rent while knowing about the tenant's criminal activity does not constitute a waiver of the default.[103] The general rule also does not apply to any eviction by a public housing authority (PHA). A PHA that accepts rent after a breach does not waive the right to terminate the tenant's lease based on the breach; the waiver does apply, however, if the PHA expressly agrees to the waiver in writing or fails to take action against the tenant within 120 days after it learns of the breach.[104]

> ***Example 7.*** Wilbur rents a house from Harvey for a year. The lease provides that the tenant can-not keep pets on the premises and includes an automatic forfeiture clause for breach of that condi-tion. Harvey files a summary ejectment action against Wilbur for violating the pet condition in the lease. At the trial on June 8, Harvey testifies that on the mornings of May 20 and 23, he saw Wilbur outside the house walking a large black dog and watched Wilbur go back into the house with the dog. He filed the action to evict Wilbur on June 3. Wilbur admits he did violate the lease but testifies that he paid his June rent on the first day of the month and Harvey accepted it. By accepting the rent after he knew of the breach, Harvey has waived the breach and cannot evict Wilbur. Harvey has failed to prove his case and the magistrate should dismiss the action.
>
> But what if Wilbur did not get rid of the dog and Harvey sees him on September 15 walking the dog. Harvey can then bring a summary ejectment action for the new breach. If he does not accept any future rent, thus waiving the breach, Harvey will be entitled to judgment.

If, however, Wilbur had been renting from the Charlotte Public Housing Authority, the defense of waiver of the breach would not have been valid as long as the housing authority brought the eviction action within 120 days after becoming aware of the breach.

Other Defenses

The tenant may raise several other defenses. As discussed earlier, the tenant's tender of the rent owed is a complete defense to eviction if the action is brought for failure to pay rent but not if the action is brought for a breach of condition of the lease, holding over after the end of the term, or criminal activity. Under G.S. 42-41 the tenant's duty to pay rent is mutually depen-dent on the landlord's duty to provide and maintain habitable premises; however G.S. 42-44(c) provides that the tenant may not unilaterally withhold rent without a judicial determination of

---

101. Winder v. Martin, 183 N.C. 410, 111 S.E. 708 (1922). *See also* Fairchild Realty Co. v. Speigel, Inc., 246 N.C. 458, 98 S.E.2d 871 (1957); Community Hous. Alternatives, Inc. v. Latta, 87 N.C. App. 616, 362 S.E.2d 1 (1987); Mewborn v. Haddock, 22 N.C. App. 285, 206 S.E.2d 336 (1974); Office Enter., Inc. v. Pappas, 19 N.C. App. 725, 200 S.E.2d 205 (1973).

102. Fairchild Realty Co. v. Spiegel, Inc., 246 N.C. 458, 98 S.E.2d 871 (1957).

103. G.S. 42-73.

104. G.S. 157-29(d).

his or her right to do so.[105] The tenant may also raise the defense of retaliatory eviction, which is discussed later in this chapter.

Under common law the tenant's duty to pay rent is mutually dependent on the landlord's duties to deliver possession of the premises[106] and not to breach the tenant' quiet enjoyment of the premises.[107] The covenant of quiet enjoyment is an implied promise that the landlord will not interfere with the tenant's quiet and peaceable possession of the premises during the tenant's term. These defenses usually will not arise in a summary ejectment action because, in the case of failure to deliver possession of the premises, the tenant never takes possession in the first place and, in the case of breach of quiet enjoyment, the tenant usually terminates the lease and moves out. However, the tenant may raise these defenses in an action for money owed if the landlord tries to sue for rent; or the tenant may bring a lawsuit against the landlord for breach of the lease.

The federal Servicemembers Civil Relief Act[108] includes a provision allowing a stay of a summary ejectment proceeding against a member of the armed services for nonpayment of rent if the premises are residential and the monthly rent does not exceed $2,400, as adjusted for inflation each year after 2003.[109] A service member may request a stay on the grounds that his or her ability to pay the agreed-upon rent is materially affected by military service. The magistrate may then stay the eviction for a period of ninety days unless justice and equity require a longer or shorter period of time; or the magistrate may adjust the obligation under the lease to preserve the interests of all parties.

Denying Landlord's Title

In a summary ejectment action, the magistrate may not determine whether the plaintiff has title to the land.[110] Under G.S. 7A-223 if the defendant files a written answer before the trial denying the plaintiff's title to the premises, the magistrate loses jurisdiction and the clerk places the action on the district court judge's docket. If such a defense is offered at trial, the magistrate should not permit it. The plaintiff's remedy, if the magistrate erroneously proceeds to try the issue of title, is to appeal from an adverse judgment. If the landlord proves that the defendant is his or her tenant or if the defendant admits it, the tenant may not then contend that someone else has title to the property. Whether the landlord's title to the property is defective is of no legal concern to a tenant who has a valid lease. This is not to say, however, that the tenant may not, as a defense, deny that the plaintiff is the landlord, that he or she is the tenant, or that there is a lease; to recover possession, the plaintiff must prove all of these elements.

---

105. The tenant's right to offer proof of the landlord's breach of duties under G.S. 42-41 as a defense is discussed below in "Residential Rental Agreements Act."

106. Sloan v. Hart, 150 N.C. 269, 63 S.E. 1037 (1909).

107. Andrews & Knowles Produce Co. v. Currin, 243 N.C. 131, 90 S.E.2d 228 (1955); Huggins v. Waters, 154 N.C. 443, 70 S.E. 842 (1911).

108. This act replaces the Soldiers' and Sailors' Civil Relief Act of 1940.

109. In 2007 the adjusted rate was $2,720.95. 72 Fed. Reg. 1319 (Jan. 11, 2007).

110. Harwell v. Rohrbacher, 243 N.C. 255, 90 S.E.2d 499 (1955).

Magistrate's Judgment

If the magistrate finds that the plaintiff has proved the case by the greater weight of the evidence, the magistrate should enter a judgment giving possession of the premises to the plaintiff. If the magistrate has jurisdiction to consider the landlord's claim for monetary damages, the magistrate also should give the landlord a judgment for rent up to the date of the judgment (or for damages for occupancy after the end of the term, when appropriate).[111] The $5,000 limitation under the amount-in-controversy provision must be distinguished from the amount awarded in a judgment. Amount in controversy is determined at the time the lawsuit is filed with the clerk. Therefore, in a summary ejectment case, a landlord may file an action seeking possession and monetary damages of $5,000 or less (the total amount owed at the time the lawsuit is filed); by the time the case is heard in small claims court nine days later, however, the additional nine days of rent due would make the judgment more than $5,000. In that instance, it is proper for the magistrate to enter a judgment for more than $5,000.

If the landlord seeks damages for damage to the property, the magistrate must determine the amount of those damages and include them in the judgment.

Splitting Monetary Claims

A principle that will arise in determining damages is that all of a party's damages resulting from a single wrong must be recovered in one action. This means that if a landlord sues for possession and part of the back rent in one action, then brings another action for the remainder of back rent owed, the second action must be dismissed because the court has already decided the issue.[112] This doctrine, called *res judicata*, provides that once there is a final judgment, no subsequent action involving the same issues and same parties may be brought; nor may another action be brought for issues that could have been raised in the prior action.[113] In *Chrisalis Properties, Inc. v. Separate Quarters*, for example, the landlord filed a summary ejectment action seeking possession, back rent, and damages for the cost of re-renting the premises. The magistrate's judgment awarded all the damages in the space marked "other damages," leaving the "rent owed" space blank. When the landlord filed a subsequent action for breach of contract damages, the court held that res judicata prohibited a subsequent award because those damages could have been determined at the time the earlier action was brought. To avoid this result, a landlord who wishes to collect monetary damages for more than past-due rent can bring two separate law suits—the first for possession only and a second, separate action—after the tenant has been removed and landlord is able to ascertain all of the damages—for all the money damages.

With regard to damages for physical damage to the property, it is likely that the doctrine of res judicata would not prohibit a landlord from bringing two separate actions: one for possession and back rent and a second for damage to the property because the landlord does not have the opportunity to discover the damage to the premises until after the tenant is evicted.

---

111. The standard complaint form (AOC-CVM-201) includes a prayer for relief of rent up to the date of judgment.

112. *Chrisalis*, 101 N.C. App. at 86, 398 S.E.2d at 632.

113. *Id.*

Appeal and Stay-of-Execution Bond

Notice of Appeal and Costs

Occasionally a dissatisfied party wishes to appeal the magistrate's judgment. Either party may appeal by announcing an appeal in open court at the conclusion of the magistrate's judgment or by filing a written notice of appeal with the clerk of superior court no later than ten days after the judgment is entered. If the appeal is requested in open court, the magistrate must note the name of the party appealing the judgment. Although not statutorily required, the magistrate should inform the appealing party that he or she must go to the clerk's office and pay the costs of the appeal within twenty days after judgment is entered. A defendant who cannot pay the costs of appeal may seek permission from the court within ten days after the judgment is entered to file the appeal as an indigent.

Stay-of-Execution Bond

The appeal does not automatically stay execution of a judgment for possession against the defendant. In addition to paying the costs of appeal, a defendant who wishes to remain on the premises until the district court rules must post a stay-of-execution bond with the clerk within ten days after the magistrate enters judgment.[114] Paying the costs of appeal allows the case to be heard in district court, and the stay-of-execution bond allows the tenant to remain on the premises while the case is on appeal. If a tenant appeals and pays costs but does not stay the execution, he or she can be removed from the premises but is still entitled to have the case heard in district court.

A stay-of-execution bond has three parts.

Rent in arrears. The first part of the stay requires the tenant to post in cash the rent in arrears as of the date of the magistrate's judgment. The magistrate is required to determine the amount of undisputed rent in arrears and make a finding in the judgment so that the clerk will know what amount to assess the tenant. The law specifies that the magistrate must base that determination on the evidence presented at the trial or the amount listed on the complaint.[115] If the defendant is present at trial and disputes the amount of rent in arrears, the magistrate must find that the amount of rent in arrears is the amount undisputed by the defendant. For example, if plaintiff claims the rent in arrears is $650 and defendant claims it is only $200, the magistrate must find that the undisputed amount of rent in arrears is $200. The sole purpose of determining the undisputed amount is to give the clerk the amount to assess the defendant for the stay-of-execution bond. The magistrate must make this finding in all summary ejectment cases in which he or she orders eviction, regardless of whether a money judgment will also be entered. If a money judgment is entered in the case, the amount of rent in arrears in the findings may be entirely different from the magistrate's monetary award.

---

114. G.S. 7A-227, G.S. 42-34.

115. The statute specifies that this requirement applies to situations in which a judgment on the pleadings is authorized. However, the same concerns arise in other summary ejectment actions when the plaintiff has filed an action for possession only and monetary damages are not an issue in the case. The magistrate must still either ask the plaintiff about back rent owed or rely on the complaint to determine the amount of rent in arrears.

Example 8. Billie Jean files an action for summary ejectment against her tenant, Henrietta, on April 30 alleging that Henrietta failed to pay her rent of $600 per month for March and April. At the trial on May 15, Billie Jean asks for $1,500 in back rent: the rent due for March, April, and one-half of May. Henrietta didn't bother to come to court, though she was personally served. The magistrate would make a finding that the undisputed amount of rent in arrears is $1,500 and the judgment would be for possession and $1,500. However, if Henrietta had been served by posting, the magistrate would find an undisputed amount of rent in arrears of $1,500 but would award no monetary damages.

But assume that Henrietta appears at trial and testifies that she paid Billie Jean the rent for March and April in cash and has the money to pay the rent for May at trial. She doesn't, however, have a receipt to show the magistrate. Billie Jean counters that she was never paid for March and April and shows the magistrate her account records indicating no payments for that month. She also testifies that she always gives receipts to tenants for cash payments and that her receipt book shows no record of any receipts to Henrietta. The magistrate believes Billie Jean's testimony. In that situation, the magistrate's finding as to the undisputed amount of rent in arrears would be $0, and the magistrate's judgment would be for possession and back rent of $1,500.

Undertaking to pay future rent. The second part of the bond requires the defendant to sign an undertaking to pay the periodic rent due under the lease to the clerk of superior court as it becomes due after judgment has been entered. If, for example, the rent is due monthly on the first of the month, the tenant must sign a bond to pay the rent to the clerk by the first of each month. If the tenant is in public housing or Section 8 assisted housing—under which the tenant is responsible for paying a portion of the rent and the U.S. Department of Housing and Urban Development (HUD) or another public agency is responsible for paying the remainder of the rent—the tenant must undertake to pay his or her portion of the rent into the clerk's office as it becomes due under the terms of the lease.[116] If the public agency discontinues its payments to the landlord while the case is on appeal, the landlord may request a hearing before the clerk or district court judge to determine whether the tenant's bond should be increased. If the tenant fails to pay the periodic rent to the clerk within five days of its due date, the landlord may seek a writ of possession from the clerk.[117]

Prorated rent. The third part of the bond applies only if the summary ejectment action was based on nonpayment of rent and the magistrate's judgment was entered more than five working days before the next rent is due under the lease. It requires the tenant to pay to the clerk in

---

116. G.S. 42-34(b).

117. There is some question as to whether the five-day requirement means five actual days or five working days. G.S. 1A-1, Rule 6(a) provides that "[i]n computing any period of time allowed by these rules . . . or by any applicable statute, [w]hen the period of time prescribed or allowed is less than seven days, the intermediate Saturdays, Sundays, and holidays shall be excluded in the computation." The question arises because G.S. 42-34, which includes the subsection providing that the bond must be paid "within five days," also includes another subsection requiring an additional cash bond to be paid if the magistrate's judgment is entered more than "five working days" before the next rental period. Thus an argument could be made that the General Assembly intended the bond payment to be made within five actual days.

cash, at the time of signing the undertaking, an amount equal to the prorated rent for the days between the date the magistrate entered the judgment and the next due date for the rent.

Example 9. Baron's rent is $400 a month, due on the first day of the month. He fails to pay for the month of June, and Ginny, his landlord, brings a summary ejectment action against him. Trial is held before the magistrate on June 20, and Baron appears and asks for additional time to pay but does not contest the amount claimed by Ginny. Ginny is awarded a judgment for possession and for $266.67 plus court costs. Baron appeals the decision. He can stay execution (continue living in the apartment) until the case is heard in district court by paying the undisputed amount of rent in arrears, $266.67, in cash to the clerk and by signing an undertaking with the clerk that he will pay each month's rent as it becomes due. He will have to pay $400 to the clerk within five days of July 1 and within five days of the first of each month thereafter until the case is decided. Also, because the judgment was entered on June 20, more than five working days from the date the next rent was due on July 1, Baron will have to pay an additional $133.33 in cash at the time of signing the undertaking; this amount is the prorated rent due from June 21 through June 30. If Baron does not pay his monthly rent to the clerk within five days of its due date, Ginny can have Baron evicted.

If the magistrate's judgment had been entered on June 27, Baron would not have been required to pay the additional prorated amount of the rent from June 27 to July 1, but would only have had to sign the undertaking agreeing to pay $400 on July 1 and each month thereafter. (In that situation, however, the undisputed amount of rent in arrears and the amount in the judgment would have been $360—27 days of rent—instead of $266.66.)

Bond when defendant appeals as an indigent. A defendant who appeals as an indigent must sign the undertaking to pay the future rent to the clerk as it becomes due and, if assessed, pay the prorated rent from date of judgment until the next rental period. Otherwise, the tenant would be allowed to live rent-free for the entire time the case is on appeal and the landlord would suffer significant additional monetary damages. However, if the tenant appeals as an indigent, he or she is not required to post the rent in arrears at the time of the magistrate's judgment.

After a bond is posted. When a tenant pays rent to the clerk under a stay-of-execution bond, the clerk, upon application by the landlord, must give the rent to the landlord as it is paid to the court rather than holding the payments until the action is heard in district court.[118] The clerk also will give the landlord the prorated rent from the date of judgment to the next payment due date but will hold the undisputed rent in arrears until the district court decides the case.

A landlord or tenant who disputes the amount of rent due under the bond or the date on which the payments are due may move for a hearing before the clerk of superior court or the district court judge for a determination of the issue.

---

118. The statute provides that if, in the pleading, the tenant claims part of the rent being paid into the court, only the undisputed portion may be turned over to the landlord. G.S. 42-34(e). However, tenants rarely file pleadings (answers) in small claims cases.

Eviction for Criminal Activity

There are two bases for evicting tenants for criminal activity—the statutory provision for criminal activity and a breach of condition of the lease.

Statutory Provision

In 1995 the General Assembly added the fourth ground for summary ejectment—criminal activity. Article 7 of Chapter 42 of the General Statutes[119] authorizes a landlord to bring an eviction proceeding against any of the following persons involved in criminal activity as defined in the statute: a residential tenant (the person who entered into the lease with the landlord), a member of the tenant's household (including minors), any person who lawfully resides in the leased residential premises but has not signed the lease or does not have a contractual relationship with the landlord, or a guest of the tenant. It specifically authorizes the landlord to list a fictitious name as a defendant if the defendant's true name is not known at the time the action is filed; the plaintiff must also add a description good enough to identify the defendant. An action to evict a tenant for criminal activity may be filed by the landlord or the agent who handles the property and may be filed as a small claim or as a district court action. When the action is heard in small claims court, the regular summary ejectment procedure applies.[120] The Article 7 provisions allow a magistrate to order a complete eviction in certain circumstances and a partial eviction in others. A *complete eviction* is the eviction and removal of a tenant and all members of his or her household; this definition comports with what is normally meant by the term *eviction* or *ejectment*. On the other hand, *partial eviction* means that the landlord may seek to remove specified persons other than the tenant from the premises (for example, removing a member of the tenant's household without evicting the tenant). Partial eviction is only allowed under this statute and not under any other ground for summary ejectment. In certain circumstances the statute also allows the magistrate to issue an order for *conditional eviction*, which puts the tenant on notice that he or she may be evicted in the future if certain conditions in the order are violated.

Complete eviction of the tenant. In a summary ejectment action against a tenant for criminal activity, the landlord must prove, by the greater weight of evidence, one of the following five things:

1. Criminal activity occurred on or within the individual rental unit leased to the tenant. *Criminal activity* is defined as
   (a) an activity that would constitute a drug violation under G.S. 90-95 (except possession of a controlled substance);
   (b) any activity that would constitute conspiracy to violate one of those drug provisions; or
   (c) any other criminal activity that threatens the health, safety, or right of peaceful enjoyment of the premises by other residents or employees of the landlord. This last category must be conduct that would constitute a crime; it may be a felony or a misdemeanor

---

119. G.S. 42-59 through -76.
120. If filed in district court, the statute sets out an expedited trial procedure. G.S. 42-68.

and must be conduct that threatens other residents or their right to peaceful enjoyment of the premises. For example, a tenant who assaults someone in a bar in a part of town distant from his or her apartment would probably not be covered by this definition.

Individual rental unit means an apartment or individual dwelling or accommodation that is leased to a particular tenant. Note that the act applies to tenants in single-family dwellings as well as those in apartments or mobile home parks.

2. The individual rental unit was used in any way in furtherance of or to promote criminal activity.

3. The tenant, any member of the tenant's household, or any guest of the tenant engaged in criminal activity on or in the immediate vicinity of any portion of the entire premises. *Entire premises* means a house, building, mobile home, or apartment that is leased for residential purposes and the entire building or complex of buildings or mobile home park of which it is a part, including the streets, sidewalks, and common areas. Under this provision the criminal conduct can occur anywhere in the apartment complex or mobile home park or in its immediate vicinity, which could be across the street from the complex. Similarly, if the tenant is residing in a single-family dwelling, the conduct could occur anywhere on the lot on which the dwelling sits, the public street in front of the house, or on the next door neighbor's property. A *guest* is "a person entertained in one's house, . . . a person to whom hospitality is extended, . . . one invited to participate in some activity at the expense of another."[121] For example, an adult son who did not reside with his mother (who was the tenant) was not found to be a guest when evidence showed that he came to the apartment complex of his own accord and did not speak to his mother until after he was arrested; moreover, his mother was not aware of her son's presence in front of her apartment until after he arrived, and had not invited him to her apartment or extended any hospitality when she became aware of his arrival.[122]

4. The tenant gave permission to a person to return to the property after that person was removed and barred from the entire premises.

5. The tenant failed to notify a law enforcement officer or the landlord immediately upon learning that a person who was removed and barred from the tenant's individual unit had returned to that rental unit. When the action is based on an allegation that the tenant gave permission to a person barred from the premises to return to any portion of the entire premises or that he or she failed to report a barred person who returned uninvited to the individual unit, the person may have been barred by a proceeding under the criminal activity statute or by the reasonable rules of a publicly assisted landlord.[123]

The landlord must offer evidence proving that one of these five things occurred: for example, testimony from another resident of the apartment complex that he or she saw the tenant's son,

121. Charlotte Hous. Auth. v. Fleming, 123 N.C. App. 511, 514, 473 S.E.2d 373, 375 (1996) (quoting from *Webster's Third New International Dictionary*).

122. *Id.*

123. 24 C.F.R. § 966.4 (f)(4) provides that a public housing tenant must abide by necessary and reasonable regulations promulgated by the public housing authority for the benefit and well-being of the residents of the housing project.

who lived with the tenant, brandishing a gun in the apartment courtyard and threatening to shoot another resident would be sufficient evidence. However, a letter from the police department to the landlord stating that the landlord should evict the tenant because the tenant was selling drugs would not be sufficient unless the officer, or someone else, testified to facts supporting such a conclusion.

The statute specifies that if the magistrate orders a complete eviction, the order is valid against the tenant and all other residents of the tenant's individual unit; but that provision merely restates the general rule that an ejectment order against a tenant is valid to remove anyone on the premises who is in possession by virtue of the tenant.[124] While the ejectment action is pending, a district court judge, but not a magistrate, has the authority to issue a temporary restraining order or preliminary injunction to enjoin the commission of criminal activity on or in the immediate vicinity of the premises while the ejectment action is pending.

Defense to eviction for criminal activity. If the landlord proves one of the five grounds for eviction, the tenant may still avoid complete eviction by proving that he or she did not know or have reason to know that (1) criminal activity was taking place or would likely occur within the individual rental unit, (2) the individual rental unit was being used in any way in furtherance of or to promote criminal activity, or (3) any member of the tenant's household or guest was engaged in criminal activity on or in the immediate vicinity of any portion of the entire premises.[125]

The tenant may also avoid eviction by proving that he or she did everything that reasonably could have been expected under the circumstances to prevent the commission of criminal activity. This might include

1. requesting the landlord to remove the offending household member's name from the lease,
2. reporting prior criminal activity to appropriate law enforcement authorities,
3. seeking assistance from social service or counseling agencies,
4. denying permission, if feasible, for the offending household member to reside in the unit, or
5. seeking assistance from a church or religious organization.

This nonfault defense is not available in most cases if the eviction is a second or subsequent proceeding for criminal activity brought against the tenant. It may, however, succeed if the tenant can prove by clear and convincing evidence—a higher standard than the normal civil burden of proof—that no reasonable person could have foreseen the occurrence of the subsequent criminal activity or that the tenant did everything that could reasonably be expected under the circumstances to prevent the commission of the second instance of criminal activity.

Even if the landlord has proved grounds for eviction, a magistrate may choose not to evict the tenant if, considering the circumstances of the criminal activity and the condition of the tenant, the magistrate finds, by clear, cogent, and convincing evidence that immediate eviction or removal would be a serious injustice, the prevention of which overrides the need to protect

124. Stone v. Guion, 223 N.C. 831, 28 S.E.2d 510 (1944).
125. G.S. 42-63.

the rights, safety, and health of the other tenants. It is not a defense to an eviction to show that the criminal activity was an isolated incident or otherwise had not reoccurred or that the person who actually engaged in the criminal activity no longer resides in the tenant's individual unit. However, the magistrate can consider such evidence if it is offered in support of an affirmative defense; he or she may also consider it as grounds for a decision not to evict the tenant because it would create a serious injustice.[126]

Conditional eviction orders. When the landlord proves that the criminal activity was committed by someone other than the tenant, the magistrate may issue a *conditional eviction* order against a tenant but deny eviction of the tenant himself or herself.[127] Conditional eviction may also be used when the magistrate finds that a member of the tenant's household or the tenant's guest has engaged in criminal activity but was not named as a party in the action.[128] A conditional eviction order does not evict the tenant; rather, it forbids the tenant as an express condition of the tenancy to give permission to or invite to return to or re-enter any portion of the entire premises the person named in the conditional order as barred from the premises. The tenant must immediately notify law enforcement or the landlord if the person who is barred returns to the tenant's rental unit. The tenant must acknowledge in writing that he or she understands the terms of the conditional eviction and that failure to comply with the court's order will result in mandatory termination of the tenancy.[129]

A landlord who believes that a tenant has violated a conditional eviction order may enforce the order in one of two ways: First, the landlord may file a motion in the cause in the original eviction case, and the clerk must set a hearing on the motion within fifteen days of the motion's filing and provide notice of the hearing. The landlord is responsible for bringing the motion and having notice served on the defendant in any manner authorized by G.S. 1A-1, Rule 4 or Rule 5, but the defendant must be served at least five days before the time specified for the hearing.[130] If he or she has not been given sufficient notice, the magistrate should continue the case to allow time for proper notice, unless the defendant affirmatively waives notice requirement.

At the hearing, the magistrate must order the immediate eviction of the tenant if he or she finds that (1) the tenant has given permission to any person removed or barred from the premises to return to any portion of the entire premises, (2) the tenant has failed to notify appropriate law enforcement authorities or the landlord as soon as the tenant discovered that a previously barred person has returned to the tenant's individual rental unit, or (3) the tenant has otherwise knowingly violated an express term or condition of any order issued by the court under this statute. *Immediate eviction* under the statute does not mean that the writ to remove the defendant may be served as soon as the judgment is entered. It merely means that, like any other summary ejectment judgment, the tenant is ordered to give immediate possession of the

---

126. G.S. 42-67.

127. G.S. 42-64(a).

128. G.S. 42-63(c).

129. The magistrate would use the form "Judgment In Action For Summary Ejectment Criminal Activity," AOC-CVM-403, checking the block for conditional eviction.

130. G.S. 1A-1, Rule 6(d).

premises to the landlord. However, the judgment cannot be enforced until the time for appeal has run (ten days in small claims cases).[131]

The second way in which a landlord may enforce a conditional judgment is to file a new summary ejectment action. To file a new action, the landlord must have the new complaint and summons served on the defendant and must pay court costs. The ground for eviction in this action should be criminal activity based on the allegation that the tenant gave permission to a person to return to the property after that person was barred from the entire premises or that the tenant failed to notify a law enforcement officer or the landlord immediately upon learning that a person barred from the tenant's individual unit had returned to that unit. If the landlord proves the case by the greater weight of the evidence, the magistrate will enter a judgment for complete eviction of the tenant.[132]

Partial eviction. The criminal activity statute includes an unusual provision authorizing a magistrate to order removal from a tenant's premises of a person other than the tenant—without evicting the tenant—when the magistrate finds that the person has engaged in criminal activity on or in the immediate vicinity of the entire premises. For the magistrate to have jurisdiction to remove a person who is not the tenant, that person must be named as a defendant in the ejectment action. Any person removed by the magistrate also is barred from re-entering any portion of the entire premises. In addition to removing a person who is not the tenant, the magistrate may issue a conditional order of eviction against the tenant, if appropriate.[133]

Effect of criminal charge on eviction. A landlord may pursue an eviction for criminal activity even though no criminal charge has been brought against the tenant, a member of the tenant's household, or the tenant's guest. The statute allows eviction for conduct that would constitute criminal activity as defined in the statute; it does not require criminal charges or conviction. Moreover, if criminal charges have been brought, the eviction may occur before the criminal proceeding is concluded or even if the defendant was acquitted or the case was dismissed. On the other hand, if a criminal prosecution involving the criminal activity results in a final conviction or adjudication of delinquency, the conviction or adjudication is conclusive proof in the eviction proceeding that the criminal activity took place. These differences result because the standard of proof for eviction—by the preponderance of the evidence—is lower than the standard of proof for conviction of a crime—beyond a reasonable doubt.

Breach of Lease Condition

Before the criminal activity statute became law a landlord could evict a tenant for criminal activity only if the lease agreement had a specific provision prohibiting criminal activity that included an automatic forfeiture clause for breach of that condition. Landlords who have those

---

131. G.S. 1A-1, Rule 62(a). The form the magistrate should use in this situation is "Order For Eviction After Violation of Conditional Order of Eviction," AOC-CVM-405.

132. The magistrate should use the form "Judgment In Action For Summary Ejectment Criminal Activity," AOC-CVM-403.

133. The magistrate would use the form "Judgment In Action For Summary Ejectment Criminal Activity," AOC-CVM-403 to enter the partial eviction and, if conditional eviction is entered against the tenant, both judgments would be entered on the same form.

provisions in their leases can still use them as grounds for evicting their tenants. If the landlord is suing based on violation of such a lease provision, the magistrate should read the provision in the written lease to ensure the conduct it covers and that the evidence proves that the tenant violated that provision. For example, a landlord who has evidence that the tenant is engaging in criminal activity cannot evict him or her under a lease providing that "the tenant can be evicted if convicted of any criminal offense" if the tenant has not been convicted in a court of law; nor can the landlord evict the tenant under this provision if the tenant's son, a household member, has been convicted of a crime.

Because North Carolina's new eviction for criminal activity statute provides that it is not the only remedy for eviction based on criminal activity, landlords can continue to include lease provisions regarding criminal activity and provide for forfeiture if those provisions are violated. In that case the landlord could bring a summary ejectment action based on the tenant's breach of a lease condition prohibiting unlawful activities on the premises or possession of illegal drugs. However, the criminal activity statute allows actions based on express provisions in the lease only to the extent that they are not contrary to the new law.[134] Therefore, a lease provision that requires a landlord to wait until the second occurrence of criminal activity before evicting a tenant or a provision that does not allow a tenant to plead ignorance of the criminal activity might be unenforceable because it is contrary to the new law. The landlord may, however, choose to sue under the statutory provision even if the lease contains a condition covering criminal activity.

Since the law applies only to residential leases, a landlord may only evict a commercial tenant for criminal activity on the basis of breach of a condition in the lease.

Public housing agencies. Perhaps the most common situation in which landlords proceed under a lease provision rather than the statute is federally subsidized housing. Believing in 1988 that drug dealers were 'increasingly imposing a reign of terror on public and other federally assisted low-income housing tenants,"[135] the U.S. Congress passed the Anti-Drug Abuse Act. The act requires that leases utilized by public housing agencies and other federally funded programs provide that any criminal activity that threatens the health, safety, or right to peaceful enjoyment of the premises by other tenants or "any drug-related criminal activity on or off such premises, engaged in by a public housing tenant, any member of the tenant's household, or any guest or other person under the tenant's control, shall be cause for termination."[136] Generally, public housing agencies cannot evict a tenant who is not personally at fault for a breach of the lease.[137] Nonetheless, in *Department of Housing & Urban Development v. Rucker*,[138] the Supreme

---

134. G.S. 42-75.

135. 42 USC § 11901.

136. 42 U.S.C. § 1437d (l)(6) (2003). The lease must provide that the tenant is obligated "to assure that no tenant, member of the tenant's household or a guest engages in any criminal activity that threatens the health, safety or right to peaceful enjoyment of the premises by other residents; or any drug-related criminal activity on or off the premises; to assure that no other person under the tenant's control" engages such activity. 24 CFR § 966.4(f)(12).

137. Maxton Hous. Auth. v. McLean, 313 N.C. 277, 328 S.E.2d 290 (1985); Charlotte Hous. Auth. v. Patterson, 120 N.C. App. 552, 464 S.E.2d 68 (1995).

138. 535 U.S. 125 (2002). *Rucker* overturned the holding in *Charlotte Hous. Auth. v. Patterson*, 120 N.C. App. 552, 464 S.E.2d 68 (1995).

Court held that the federal statute does not require the public housing authority to prove that the tenant knew or should have known of the criminal activity committed by a household member, guest, or person under the control of the tenant before evicting the tenant. The Court said the statute was clear that "knowledge" on the part of the tenant is not required and held that the statute entrusts the decision to evict to the public housing authority. That authority is in the best position to take account of the degree to which the housing project suffers from rampant drug-related or violent crime, attest to the seriousness of the offending action, and judge the extent to which the tenant has taken all reasonable steps to prevent or mitigate the offending action.[139] If the public housing authority brings an action under the clause prohibiting criminal activity, the tenant cannot use as a defense the claim that he or she committed no personal fault. If the authority proves a violation of the criminal activity provision in the lease and shows that the lease includes an automatic forfeiture for breach of that condition, the only possible defense left for the tenant is that enforcing the forfeiture would be unconscionable.[140]

Ejectment of Tenants in Publicly Assisted Housing

Tenants of publicly assisted housing have certain additional rights under federal law that must be followed in a summary ejectment proceeding. Sometimes the law distinguishes between *public housing*—housing operated by a local public housing authority (PHA)—and *Section 8 housing*—housing operated by private landlords but rented to tenants who receive public assistance with respect to their rental payments. The term *publicly assisted housing* is used in this chapter to refer to both PHA and Section 8 housing.

"Good Cause" Requirement

Under federal law a tenant who lives in publicly assisted housing may not be evicted except for "good cause."[141] This means that a landlord (or a PHA) cannot evict a tenant from publicly assisted housing unless the landlord can prove (1) a serious or repeated violation of a material term of the rental agreement or other good cause,[142] (2) criminal activity that threatens the health, safety, or right to peaceful enjoyment of the premises by other tenants, or (3) any drug-related criminal activity.[143] *Good cause* has been held to mean that public landlords cannot evict for arbitrary, discriminatory, or otherwise manifestly improper reasons.[144]

The good cause requirement for PHAs and some Section 8 housing differs in one situation. In PHAs and older Section 8 housing programs, the good cause requirement applies to renewals of leases as well as to ejectment during the term of the lease. In the Section 8 Vouchers Program, however—except for enhanced vouchers in multifamily projects in which the owner has prepaid

---

139. *Rucker,* 535 U.S. at 134.

140. For more on the defense of unconscionability, *see* text discussion at footnote 60, p. 160.

141. Swann v. Gastonia Hous. Auth., 675 F.2d 1342 (4th Cir. 1982); Joy v. Daniels, 479 F.2d 1236, 1241 (4th Cir. 1973); Goler Metro. Apartments, Inc. v. Williams, 43 N.C. App. 648, 260 S.E.2d 146 (1979). The good cause requirement also applies to PHAs under state law. G.S. 157-29(c).

142. *See* G.S. 157-29(c); 24 C.F.R. § 966.4 (l) (2) (1995); Maxton Hous. Auth. v. McLean, 313 N.C. 277, 328 S.E.2d 290 (1985).

143. 42 U.S.C. § 1437d (l)(5),(6) (2003).

144. Bogan v. New London Hous. Auth., 366 F. Supp. 861, 868 (D. Conn. 1973).

the mortgage or opted out of project-based Section 8[145]—the good cause requirement applies only during the term of the lease.[146] Other voucher landlords, therefore, may terminate the lease without cause at the end of the lease term unless the lease agreement provides otherwise.

The failure of a tenant to make the payments due under the lease agreement (both rent and utilities) is a breach of the material terms of the contract if the payments were properly calculated according to the applicable HUD regulations. The tenant's failure to comply with any of the following obligations also constitutes violation of material terms of the contract. Public housing tenants, therefore,

(1) may not assign or sublease the lease.

(2) may not provide accommodations for boarders or lodgers.

(3) must use the premises solely as a private dwelling for the tenant and his or her household as identified in the lease and may not to use or permit the unit to be used for any other purpose;

(4) must abide by necessary and reasonable regulations promulgated by the PHA for the benefit and well-being of the housing project and tenants (which regulations must be posted in the project office and incorporated by reference in the lease);

(5) must comply with all obligations imposed on tenants by applicable housing and building codes that materially affect health and safety;

(6) must keep the tenant's premises in a clean and safe condition;

(7) must dispose of garbage and other waste in a sanitary and safe manner;

(8) must use all electrical, plumbing, sanitary, heating, ventilating, air-conditioning and other facilities, including elevators, in a reasonable manner;

(9) must refrain from and cause his or her guests and household to refrain from destroying, defacing, damaging, or removing any part of the premises;

(10) must pay reasonable charges for repair of damages (above normal wear and tear) to the premises caused by the tenant, the tenant's household, or guests;

(11) must conduct himself or herself—and cause guests and household members on the premises to conduct themselves—in a manner that will not disturb neighbors' peaceful enjoyment of their accommodations and will be conducive to maintaining the project in a safe, decent, and sanitary condition; and

(12) must ensure that no tenant, member of the tenant's household, guest, or other person under the tenant's control will engage in any criminal activity that threatens the health, safety, or right to peaceful enjoyment of the PHA's premises by other residents or employees, or engage in any drug-related criminal activity on or near such premises.[147]

With regard to eviction for tenant's failure to pay rent (brought either as an action for breach of a condition of the lease or an action for failure to pay rent), a 1985 decision by the North Carolina Supreme Court held that proof that a public housing tenant failed to pay rent is sufficient

145. National Law Housing Project, HUD Housing Programs: Tenants' Rights (3d ed. 2004) §14:2.1.4. (The National Housing Law Project).

146. 42 U.S.C. § 1437f(o)(7)(C) (2003).

147. 24 C.F.R. § 966.4(f).

to find good cause for eviction and that that showing shifts the burden to prove lack of fault to the tenant.[148] Thus the court equated good cause with the tenant's fault. Three months after the court's decision, the General Assembly amended G.S. 157-29 to provide that "[e]xcept in the case of failure to make payments due under a rental agreement, fault on the part of a tenant may be considered in determining whether good cause exists to terminate a rental agreement."[149] That statutory amendment eliminates fault on the part of the tenant as an issue when the breach is failure to make payments due and overrules the decision of the court insofar as it was based on the North Carolina Public Housing Authority Act. However, since good cause is a federal requirement, a court could, presumably, continue to hold that federal law requires a showing of fault or could, at least, allow a tenant to avoid eviction by showing that he or she had no ability to pay the rent.[150]

Examples of situations in which a tenant may be evicted from publicly assisted housing include (1) failure to provide Social Security Number and documentation,[151] (2) failure to sign consent forms allowing verification of employee income information,[152] (3) chronic delinquency in making rent payments,[153] and (4) vandalism and destruction of PHA property by a tenant's children.[154]

Notice Requirements

Federal law requires publicly assisted housing landlords to give notice of termination of the lease, but the provisions regarding grounds for termination, what the notice must include, and the number of days before termination that notice must be given vary according to the particular program. There is one set of regulations for public housing agencies and separate regulations for each of the several types of Section 8 housing programs. If at trial a question is raised about the landlord's compliance with the federal regulations governing the particular publicly assisted housing involved in the eviction, the magistrate may require the landlord to indicate the specific program under which the lease operates and bring a copy of the regulations governing that program to trial. The magistrate may also refer to Appendix I, at the end of this chapter, which sets out some of the requirements of the various programs.

---

148. Maxton Hous. Auth. v. McLean, 313 N.C. 277, 328 S.E.2d 290 (1985) (in which tenant whose rental and water and sewer payments were in arrears, avoided eviction by showing lack of fault because rent was based on her husband's income, and when he left she had no income until her AFDC was restored some months later).

149. 1985 N.C. Sess. Laws ch. 741.

150. *Cf.* Charlotte Hous. Auth. v. Patterson, 120 N.C. App. 552, 464 S.E.2d 68 (1995).

151. *E.g.,* 24 C.F.R. § 880.607(b)(3).

152. *Id.*

153. Scott v. Peekskill Hous. Auth., 313 N.Y.S. 220 (1970), *aff'd,* 268 N.E.2d 802 (N.Y. 1971).

154. Johnson v. Tamsberg, 430 F.2d 1125 (4th Cir. 1970).

General Provisions about Leases

When Rent Is Due

The rental agreement ordinarily specifies when the rent is payable. If the lease is silent on this point, however, the common law provides that it is payable at the end of the term or period, not in advance.[155] As a practical matter, however, the parties almost always agree, either expressly or by implication from their actions, that rent is payable at the beginning of the term. For example, if there is no specific agreement in an oral lease but the landlord requires the tenant to pay the first week's rent before moving in, the parties have agreed that the rent is due in advance by the first of the week.

Terms of a Written Lease

If a lease is in writing, its terms govern the relationship of the parties unless it includes a provision that is in violation of a state or federal statute. The parties should not be allowed to vary the lease's written terms by testifying to conversations, statements, or negotiations that took place before the lease was executed.[156] Either party may, however, introduce evidence of an oral agreement to change the terms of the lease made after it was executed. The magistrate must then decide whether there was a valid contract to modify the terms of the lease.

What Leases Must Be Written

Many leases litigated before the magistrate will be periodic leases (week-to-week or month-to-month) or leases for fixed terms of a short duration. Such leases need not be in writing; an oral agreement for a week-to-week or month-to-month tenancy is perfectly valid and enforceable, as is an oral lease for one or two years. But a lease for a fixed term that will expire more than three years from the date it is made must be in writing and signed by the party against whom the lease is being enforced.[157] The three-year period runs from the date the lease was signed, not from the time the lease term begins (which may be sometime later). Thus, to be enforceable in court, a three-year lease executed on March 1 to go into effect April 1 must be in writing and signed by the party against whom enforcement is sought. If a lease is unenforceable because it is not in writing, the landlord still may recover a reasonable rental for any period of occupancy.[158] When the magistrate finds the lease unenforceable, he or she should determine what the reasonable rental would be and award that amount as damages rather than the rate agreed to in the lease.

Registration of Leases and Selling Property Subject to Lease

Under G.S. 47-18 no lease of land for more than three years is valid against third-party lien creditors (one whose claim for payment of a debt is secured by a charge against the specific property involved) or against someone who purchases the property from the lessor unless the lease is registered in the county where the land lies. Unless such a lease is filed with the register of deeds, therefore, it is valid only between the parties; a person who buys the land from the

---

155. 49 AM. JUR. 2D, *Landlord & Tenant* § 579 (2006).
156. Merchants Oil Co. v. Mecklenburg County, 212 N.C. 642, 194 S.E. 114 (1937).
157. G.S. 22-2.
158. G.S. 42-4.

lessor is not bound by the lease, even if he or she knew about the lease. On the other hand, if the lease is for fewer than three years, a person who buys leased property is bound by the terms of the lease, even if it is unwritten or unrecorded, as long as the buyer has notice of the tenancy. Actual possession by the tenant is treated as notice.[159]

The existence of an outstanding lease on a particular piece of property does not prevent the landlord from selling his or her interest in the property. Such sales are not uncommon, particularly with commercial property subject to long-term leases. When this occurs, the buyer takes the property subject to the interest of the lessee as long as the buyer has notice of the lease.[160] Registration of a lease under G.S. 47-18 or possession by a tenant under a lease for a term of three or fewer years constitutes notice.

Subleases and Assignments

Unless the lease has a contrary provision, the tenant is free to transfer the leasehold, either by assignment or sublease.[161] A tenant who "sells" the entire leasehold is making an *assignment*, and the assignee then becomes the tenant of the original landlord. The original tenant (lessee-assignor) is still liable for the rent to the original landlord until he or she obtains a release. The landlord's acceptance of rent from the assignee does not constitute a release.[162] Although the landlord may be able to pursue an action against the original tenant, the assignee, or both for the rent, the assignee is the appropriate defendant in a summary ejectment action.[163]

If the original tenant wants to dispose of only part of the leasehold—as, for example, when the lease is for one year and the tenant wants to rent the premises for the summer months only—he or she may sublet. In this situation the lessee becomes a landlord to the sublessee for the summer months and can bring an ejectment action against the sublessee for violating the sublease. The original lessor–lessee relationship also continues in force until the end of the year, and the original lessee remains responsible for payment of the rent. If the rent is not paid, the landlord can evict the tenant, which would also remove the sublessee. If the lease prohibits subletting or requires the landlord's consent before subletting, the landlord may pursue an action against a tenant who sublets the premises based on breach of a condition in the lease.

Lease provisions prohibiting assignment or subletting are strictly construed, but a provision prohibiting subleasing does not bar the tenant from assigning the lease and vice versa.[164]

---

159. Perkins v. Langdon, 237 N.C. 159, 165, 74 S.E.2d 634, 640 (1953).

160. *Id. But see* Adams v. Woods, 169 N.C. App. 242, 609 S.E.2d 429 (2005) (ruling that no landlord–tenant relationship existed between new owner and original month-to-month tenant but seeming to rely on the district court's finding that the parties never entered into a lease agreement was binding because no objection was raised to it)

161. *See* HETRICK & MCLAUGHLIN, *supra* note 54, § 6-20.

162. Coulter v. Capitol Fin. Co., 266 N.C. 214, 220, 146 S.E.2d 97, 102 (1966); Fidelity Bank v. Bloomfield, 246 N.C. 492, 498, 98 S.E.2d 865, 869 (1957).

163. Atlantic & East Coast Ry. Co. v. Wheatly Oil Co., 163 N.C. App. 748, 594 S.E.2d 425 (2004).

164. Rogers v. Hall, 227 N.C. 363, 42 S.E.2d 347 (1947).

Entry to Leased Premises

Unless the lease reserves the right, a landlord has no right to enter the leased premises during the term of the lease and may be sued for trespass for any unauthorized entry.[165] He or she also could be prosecuted for the crime of misdemeanor breaking or entering, or trespass.[166]

Security Deposits

Residential Leases

State law regulates the handling of security deposits given for rental of residential dwelling units (other than the rental of single rooms).[167] The maximum security deposit depends on the type of lease agreement. If the tenancy is a week-to-week tenancy, the maximum allowable security deposit is an amount equal to two weeks' rent. In a month-to-month tenancy, the maximum allowable security deposit is an amount equal to one and one-half months' rent. If a tenancy is for longer than month-to-month, the maximum is an amount equal to two months' rent.

The landlord may use or retain the security deposit to cover the following expenses: nonpayment of rent, nonpayment of costs for water or sewer services that are provided directly by the landlord under the procedures adopted by the North Carolina Utilities Commission,[168] damage to the premises above normal wear and tear, nonfulfillment of the rental period, unpaid bills that become a lien against the rented property because of the tenant's occupancy, costs of re-renting after the tenant's breach, and court costs for bringing a summary ejectment action and for removing and storing tenant's property after eviction. The landlord may not apply the deposit to any other use. In addition to a security deposit, a landlord may charge a reasonable, nonrefundable fee for pets kept by the tenant.

The landlord must either (1) place the tenant's security deposit in a trust account with a licensed and insured bank or savings institution located in North Carolina or (2) furnish a bond covering the deposits issued by an insurance company licensed in the state. The landlord (or the landlord's agent) must notify the tenant within thirty days after the beginning of the lease of the name and address of the institution where the deposit is kept or the name of the insurance company providing the bond.

No later than thirty days after a tenancy ends, the landlord must itemize any damages charged against the tenant and deliver to the tenant a written statement indicating how much of the security deposit will be retained and for what reason. The landlord must refund any balance of the security deposit due to the tenant. If the landlord does not know the tenant's address, he or she must hold the balance of the deposit due to the tenant for at least six months. It is unclear whether this provision cuts off the right of the tenant to recover the security deposit after six months or merely authorizes the landlord to remove it from the trust account after that time. The latter is probably the better reading of the statute.

---

165. Rickman Mfg. Co. v. Gable, 246 N.C. 1, 16, 97 S.E.2d 672, 683 (1957); Barneycastle v. Walker, 92 N.C. 198 (1885).

166. *Cf.* State v. Cooke, 246 N.C. 518, 98 S.E.2d 885 (1957); State v. Piper, 89 N.C. 551 (1883).

167. G.S. 42-50 through -56.

168. G.S. 62-110(g).

A landlord who transfers ownership of the dwelling unit may relieve himself or herself of any liability with respect to the security deposits of tenants by withholding any amount due for damages and transferring the remaining amounts to his or her successor in interest or to the tenants. If the deposits are transferred to the landlord's successor, the original landlord must notify the tenants of the transfer by mail.

A tenant may file a civil action to require the landlord to account for and refund the balance of the security deposit. The tenant is entitled to damages resulting from noncompliance; and if the noncompliance was willful, the magistrate may award a reasonable attorney's fee to the attorney representing the tenant. The only special remedy given for violating the security deposit law is the award of attorneys' fee. However, a tenant may also be able to sue the landlord for an unfair and deceptive practice based on the violation of the security deposit law.[169]

Commercial Leases

Parties to commercial leases may contract for a security deposit in their leases. Such contractual agreements regarding the amount and application of the deposit control are enforced according to their terms.

Responsibility for Tenant's Property Left on Premises

Residential Premises

In 1995 the General Assembly streamlined the procedures residential landlords should use to dispose of personal property left by tenants on residential premises after eviction. With the one exception specified below, a landlord has no authority to move or dispose of a tenant's property until he or she has brought a summary ejectment action, won a judgment for possession, and had the sheriff execute a writ of possession to enforce the judgment.[170] A writ of possession may be executed by having the sheriff remove the tenant's personal property and store it for one month at the expense of the landlord; or the sheriff, upon request of the landlord, may padlock the premises and leave the personal property on the premises.[171] If the sheriff executes the writ by padlocking the premises, the landlord has several alternatives for dealing with the tenant's personal property remaining on the premises.

Premises other than mobile home spaces. ANY PROPERTY WITHOUT REGARD TO VALUE. The first alternative may be used for all personal property remaining on residential premises, no matter what its aggregate value. The landlord, after being placed in possession by the sheriff under a writ of possession, may immediately remove the property and store it for the tenant for ten days or may leave the tenant's property on the premises for ten days. If the tenant requests the property during that ten-day period, the landlord must return the property to the tenant during regular business hours or at another agreed-upon time. If the tenant has not removed the property within ten days after the sheriff places the landlord in lawful possession of the premises, the landlord may throw away, dispose of, or sell any items of personal property

---

169. *See* Borders v. Newton, 68 N.C. App. 768, 315 S.E.2d 731 (1984).

170. G.S. 42-25.9(g), (h).

171. G.S. 42-36.2.

remaining on the premises.[172] Because the value of the personal property is not at issue in this procedure, it is the one most commonly used by landlords.

A landlord who decides to sell the tenant's property must give written notice to the tenant of when and where the sale will occur. The notice also must state that any surplus proceeds will be disbursed to the tenant, upon request, within ten days after the sale or, if the tenant fails to make a timely request, will be delivered to the government of the county where the real property is located. The notice must be sent by first class mail to the tenant's last known address at least seven days before the date of the sale. The sale may be public or private, and there is no requirement to advertise a public sale. The tenant is entitled to return of the property, upon request, any time before the day of the sale, even if more than ten days have elapsed since the sheriff served the writ of possession. If the tenant's property is sold, the landlord may apply the proceeds of the sale to unpaid rent, other damages, storage fees, and sale costs. Any surplus must be disbursed to the tenant, upon request, within ten days of the sale. If the tenant fails to request the surplus proceeds within ten days of the sale, the landlord must give the surplus to the government of the county where the real property is located.

PROPERTY VALUED AT LESS THAN $100. An alternative procedure may be used if the total value of all the personal property left on the premises is less than $100. The statute considers the property abandoned five days after execution of a writ of possession, and at that time the landlord may throw away or dispose of the property.[173] If the tenant requests the property before expiration of the five-day period, the landlord must return the property to the tenant during regular business hours or at a time agreed upon. A landlord who uses this provision is open to a lawsuit charging that the property was worth $100 or more; whereas, if the landlord waits five more days before disposing of the property, the value of the property is not at issue.

PROPERTY VALUED AT $500 OR LESS. If a tenant abandons personal property with a total value of $500 or less or fails to remove such property at the time of execution of a writ of possession, the landlord may immediately remove the property and deliver it to a nonprofit organization that regularly provides clothing and household furnishings to people as long as that organization agrees to identify and separately store the tenant's property for thirty days.[174] If the tenant asks for its return during the thirty-day period, the organization must return the property to the tenant at no charge. A landlord who uses this alternative must post notice at the rented premises and at the place where the rent is received; he or she must also send, by first-class mail to the tenant's last known address, a notice stating the name and address of the organization to which the tenant's property was delivered.

This third method of disposing of the tenant's property may also be used without getting a summary ejectment judgment and a writ of possession when a tenant vacates the premises and abandons his or her property. The statute provides that abandonment occurs if

---

172. G.S. 42-25.9(g), -36.2(b).

173. G.S. 42-25.9(h). Most landlords use the procedure outlined in G.S. 42-25.9(g) rather than this provision because it eliminates any argument about the value of the property remaining on the premises.

174. G.S. 42-25.9(d) to -(f).

1. the premises have been voluntarily vacated after the paid rental period has expired,
2. the landlord has received no notice of a disability that caused the vacancy, and
3. the landlord has conspicuously posted a notice of suspected abandonment both inside and outside the premises for at least ten days and has received no response from the tenant.

This alternative is rarely used because most charitable organizations will not separately store the tenant's property for thirty days.

Mobile home spaces. MOBILE HOME WORTH $500 OR LESS. If the tenant rents a mobile home space (that is, brings a mobile home onto the landlord's lot) and the mobile home has a current value of $500 or less, the landlord may dispose of it and all other items of personal property as described above in "Any property without regard to value."

MOBILE HOME WORTH MORE THAN $500. If the mobile home has a current value of more than $500, the landlord must dispose of it and its contents and other personal property left on the premises as provided in G.S. 44A-2(e2). This statute gives the landlord a lien on the property left on the premises if the landlord has a lawful claim for damages against the tenant and the property is not claimed by the tenant within twenty-one days after a writ of possession is served.[175] However, title to the mobile home must be in the name of the tenant; if it is owned by someone else, the landlord cannot acquire a landlord's lien on it.

To enforce the lien, the landlord must get a judgment for possession, obtain a writ of possession, and have the sheriff serve it on the tenant. After the writ has been executed, the landlord may either immediately remove the mobile home and its contents and store it or leave it on the premises for the twenty-one days. During that period the landlord must release the mobile home and its contents to the tenant during regular business hours or at a time they mutually agree upon. Twenty-one days after the writ has been executed—whether the property remains on the premises or is stored elsewhere—the landlord has a lien on the property for the following amounts: rent due at the time the tenant vacated the premises, rent due for up to sixty days from the date tenant vacated the premises to the date of sale, cost of physical damage to the property beyond normal wear and tear, and reasonable expenses related to the sale. The landlord must dispose of the property by selling it at a public auction, as provided in G.S. 44A-4. The statute requires the landlord to post a notice of sale at the courthouse, give notice of the sale to the tenant, and, in certain instances, advertise it in a newspaper. Because the mobile home is a motor vehicle, the landlord may not sell the mobile home without notifying the North Carolina Division of Motor Vehicles and getting permission to do so.[176]

Commercial Leases

The landlord's possessory lien statute, G.S. 44A-2(e), also applies to commercial leases. That statute allows the landlord of a commercial lease who has a lawful claim for damages against the tenant to assert a lien in and sell a tenant's personal property if it is left on the premises at least twenty-one days after the tenant has vacated the premises. The landlord must comply with the specific advertising and sale requirements set out in G.S. 44A-4.

175. G.S. 44A-2(e2).
176. G.S. 44A-4(b)(1).

Tenant's Rights and Remedies

Residential Rental Agreements Act

Landlord–tenant law has been based historically on the premise that a lease is a property transaction conveying to a tenant an interest in land for a specified period of time. Treating a lease as an interest in real estate made sense in an agrarian society when a tenant leased land for farming. In modern times, however, a tenant who rents a residential dwelling is interested not in the land, but rather in living space, utilities, facilities, and services suitable for occupation. Recognizing this change, many courts began interpreting residential leases as contracts rather than transfers of property and have recognized in a contract to lease a dwelling unit an implied warranty by the landlord that the premises are habitable.

In North Carolina the General Assembly established a warranty of habitability in residential leases by statute when it enacted the Residential Rental Agreements Act (RRAA).[177] This act requires landlords to keep premises in a fit and habitable condition and requires tenants to keep premises clean, sanitary, and free from damage and to pay rent. The landlord's and tenant's obligations are mutually dependent. The law applies to all rental agreements for dwelling units, including rental of mobile homes but does not apply to transient occupancy in a hotel, motel, or similar lodging; to occupancy in a dwelling furnished without charge or rent; or to vacation rentals entered into under G. S. Chapter 42B.[178] It is not clear whether the rental of a mobile home space is "a rental agreement for a dwelling unit." Clearly, when the tenant brings a mobile home to a rented space, the landlord has no responsibility to keep the mobile fit and habitable or to comply with any of the other provisions regarding the mobile home itself; but it is unclear whether the landlord and tenant have the duty to comply with their obligations outside the mobile home. The RRAA does not apply to commercial leases and there is no implied warranty of habitability for commercial leases.[179]

Landlord's Duties

The act places six duties on the landlord:

1. To comply with the current applicable building and housing codes to the extent that the dwelling is covered by the codes.
2. To make all repairs and do whatever is necessary to put and keep the premises in a fit and habitable condition. Because the statute does not define *fit and habitable*, the magistrate will have to determine whether the premises meet that requirement on the basis of the facts of each case. The only North Carolina case to define lack of habitability indicated that it meant that "the premises were in material violation of the local housing code or were otherwise not fit and habitable."[180] That standard corresponds

---

177. G.S. 42-38 through -44. *See generally* Joan Brannon, *North Carolina's New Landlord–Tenant Law*, Administration of Justice Memorandum 07/77 (Chapel Hill: Institute of Government, Dec. 1977); Theodore Fillette, *North Carolina's Residential Rental Agreements Act: New Developments for Contract and Tort Liability in Landlord–Tenant Relations*, 56 N.C. L. Rev. 785 (1978).

178. G.S. 42-39. *See* Conley v. Emerald Isle Realty, Inc., 350 N.C. 293, 513 S.E.2d 556 (1999).

179. K & S Enter. v. Kennedy Office Supply, Inc., 135 N.C. App. 260, 266, 520 S.E.2d 122, 126 (1999).

180. Miller v. C.W. Myers Trading Post, Inc., 85 N.C. App. 362, 369–70, 355 S.E.2d 189, 194 (1987).

to a standard used by other states that habitability is measured by standards set out in the applicable housing codes—a building is habitable if it substantially complies with the applicable codes.[181] Minimal violations are not enough; the defect must affect habitability.[182] Another standard followed by one state is whether the defect renders the dwelling wholly or partially uninhabitable in the eyes of a reasonable person.[183] Courts from other states have indicated that several factors should be considered in determining whether a violation is substantial enough to render the premises unfit and uninhabitable: (a) whether the applicable building or housing codes or sanitary regulations have been violated, (b) whether the defect or deficiency affects a vital facility, (c) the potential or actual effect of the defect on safety and sanitation, (d) the length of time the defect has persisted, and (e) whether the tenant was responsible for the defective condition.[184]

3. To keep all common areas of the premises in safe condition.

4. To maintain in good, safe working order and promptly repair all electrical, plumbing, sanitary, heating, ventilating, air-conditioning, and other facilities and appliances actually supplied or required to be supplied. This means that a landlord who supplies an air-conditioner, a refrigerator, and a stove must keep them in safe and working order and repair them when they break even if the landlord is not required by the housing and building codes to provide those items.[185] Similarly, if codes require every bathroom in a house to have a toilet, the landlord must repair a broken toilet even if there are other working ones in the house.

5. To provide operable smoke detectors that are properly installed and to place new batteries in battery-operated detectors at the beginning of each tenancy.

6. If the landlord provides water or sewer services to a tenant as authorized by G.S. 42-42.1, to notify the tenant if the water being supplied exceeds the maximum contaminant level.

Notice Requirements

The RRAA provides that a tenant must give the landlord written notice of a malfunctioning smoke detector before the landlord's obligation to repair it applies. The tenant also must give the landlord written notice, except in emergencies, of needed repairs to electrical, plumbing, or other facilities or appliances. In an emergency the tenant may give oral notice of a needed repair. However, if repairs to electrical, plumbing, sanitary, heating, and ventilating facilities are needed to bring the dwelling into a fit and habitable condition, the written notice requirement of G.S. 42-42(4) does not apply.[186]

---

181. Javins v. First Nat'l Realty Corp., 428 F.2d 1071 (D.C. Cir.) (1970); Green v. Superior Court, 517 P.2d 1168, 1183 (Cal. 1974).

182. McKenna v. Begin, 362 N.E.2d 548 (Mass. 1977).

183. Berzito v. Gambino, 308 A.2d 17, 22 (N.J. 1973).

184. Mease v. Fox, 200 N.W.2d 791, 797 (Iowa 1972); *Berzito,* 308 A.2d at 22.

185. Mendenhall-Moore Realtors v. Sedoris, 89 N.C. App. 486, 366 S.E.2d 534 (1988).

186. Surratt v. Newton, 99 N.C. App. 396, 393 S.E.2d 554 (1990).

The statute is silent on whether the tenant must give the landlord notice before any of the other three obligations—providing a fit and habitable dwelling, complying with applicable building and housing codes, and keeping common areas clean—are breached. The court has indicated, however, that the tenant does have to give the landlord notice—either oral or written—and reasonable time and opportunity to correct the defect before attempting to hold the landlord liable for damages for any breach of the warranty of habitability or breach of failure to comply with the housing code.[187] Although no North Carolina case has yet determined the issue, it may be argued that notice need not be given if the conditions that caused the breach existed before the tenant began living on the premises; the law presumes that the landlord knows the condition of the premises when he or she delivers possession.[188]

Tenant's Remedies

If the landlord breaches any of the obligations under the law, the tenant has several remedies. G.S. 42-44(a) states that any right or obligation of the landlord–tenant law is enforceable by civil action, including recoupment, counterclaim, defense, set-off, and any other legal or equitable remedy. Some states allow the tenant to withhold rent when the landlord violates a condition, but North Carolina's law specifically provides that a tenant may not unilaterally withhold rent without a court order authorizing it.

Termination of the lease. One possible remedy for a tenant who believes the landlord has violated one of the six obligations is to declare the lease ended and move out. Although it has been recognized that a tenant can refuse to move into premises that are not fit and habitable and is not responsible for paying rent in that situation,[189] no case has yet held that a tenant can move out when the landlord breaches an obligation. The breach of a covenant or warranty by the landlord does not necessarily justify the tenant's abandonment of the premises without affording the landlord the opportunity to comply with the lease.[190] Not every breach justifies termination of the lease. Essentially, the breach must be material in a way that constitutes a breach of the covenant of quiet enjoyment.[191] Although it is possible to argue that the statutory provision making payment of rent dependent on the landlord's provision of fit premises allows the tenant to terminate the lease for any violation by the landlord, it is more likely that the court will allow termination only for a material violation. For example, the tenant could terminate the lease if the landlord fails to provide fit and habitable premises but not if the breach is failure to repair a broken dishwasher.

Rent abatement action. The tenant may also choose to continue to live on the premises, pay rent, and bring an action against the landlord seeking a rent abatement based on landlord's breach of his or her obligations under the RRAA. The tenant also could file a rent abatement action as a counterclaim to a summary ejectment action brought against him or her. In a rent abatement action, the tenant is entitled to recover from the landlord the difference between the

---

187. Cotton v. Stanley, 86 N.C. App. 534, 539, 358 S.E.2d 692, 695–96 (1987).

188. *Cf.* Abram v. Litman, 150 Ill. App. 3d 174 (1986); McKenna v. Begin, 325 N.E.2d 548, 550 (Mass. 1975); Boston Hous. Auth. v. Hemingway, 293 N.E.2d 831, 844 n.18 (Mass. 1973).

189. *Mendenhall-Moore Realtors,* 89 N.C. App. at 490, 366 S.E.2d at 537.

190. Brewington v. Loughran, 183 N.C. 558, 112 S.E. 257 (1922).

191. Dobbins v. Paul, 71 N.C. App. 113, 321 S.E.2d 537 (1984).

fair rental value of the premises as warranted (in other words, as if they were in full compliance with G.S. 42-42) and the fair rental value of the premises as they are (with the defects) plus any special and consequential damages the tenant proves.[192] For example, assume that the tenant rents a dwelling for $300 per month but that its fair rental value as warranted is $400 per month. Because the landlord fails to make certain required repairs, the fair rental value of the premises with the defects is $250 per month. Under the measure of damages adopted in North Carolina, the tenant is therefore entitled to sue to recover $150 per month for all the months that the landlord failed to comply with the statute after receiving notice of the deficiencies and having a reasonable opportunity to correct them. However, the amount recovered by the tenant cannot exceed the amount actually paid in rent.[193]

Fair rental value is the amount that would be agreed upon as fair rent by a landlord who wishes to rent but is not compelled to do so, and a tenant who wishes to rent but is not compelled to do so. The fact that the landlord is prohibited by a housing ordinance from renting a vacant structure because the unit is uninhabitable does not automatically reduce the unit's fair rental value to zero. The measure of damages is not the price at which the owner could lawfully rent the unit to a new tenant on the open market but the price at which the landlord could rent the premises if it were lawful to do so.[194] In determining the fair rental value of the dwelling, the magistrate may consider evidence of what the premises would rent for in the open market, the rent agreed upon by the parties in the lease, the magistrate's own experience with living conditions, and any other evidence presented.[195] Although expert testimony by a realtor or someone familiar with the property to show fair rental value may be used, it is not required. The tenant is entitled to give his or her opinion of the fair rental value of the dwelling in its unfit condition.[196] The absence of opinion evidence as to the fair rental value of an unfit dwelling does not mean that the magistrate should deny rent abatement. Testimony about the deteriorated condition of the premises is sufficient for the magistrate to determine fair rental value as is: "From their own experience with living conditions, the jury [magistrate] could determine the 'as is' fair rental value of plaintiffs' units by considering the testimony of both plaintiffs and Mr. Bartholomew [the housing inspector]."[197] A party is not required to put on direct evidence to show fair rental value. In the absence of other evidence, the contract rent may be taken as the fair rental value of the premises as warranted.[198]

192. Miller v. C.W. Myers Trading Post, Inc., 85 N.C. App. 362, 371, 355 S.E.2d 189, 194 (1987); Cotton v. Stanley, 86 N.C. App. 534, 537, 358 S.E.2d 692, 694 (1987).

193. Dean v. Hill, 171 N.C. App. 479, 486–87, 615 S.E.2d 699, 703 (2005); Von Pettis Realty, Inc. v. McKoy, 135 N.C. App. 206, 210, 519 S.E.2d 546, 549 (1999); Surratt v. Newton, 99 N.C. App. 396, 407, 393 S.E.2d 544, 560 (1990).

194. *Cotton*, 86 N.C. App. at 538, 358 S.E.2d at 695.

195. *Surratt*, 99 N.C. App. at 408, 393 S.E.2d at 561; *Cotton*, 86 N.C. App. at 539, 358 S.E.2d at 695.

196. *Miller*, 85 N.C. App. at 371, 355 S.E.2d at 194.

197. *Cotton*, 86 N.C. App. at 539, 358 S.E.2d at 695.

198. Martin v. Clegg, 163 N.C. 528, 530, 79 S.E. 1105, 1106 (1913); *Cotton*, 86 N.C. App. at 539; 358 S.E.2d at 695.

The statute of limitations in a rent abatement action is three years,[199] which means that the tenant can sue to recover for a breach that occurred up to three years before the suit was begun. If the tenant is still living on the premises and wants to continue to live there, the magistrate may also enter an order authorizing the tenant to pay future rent at the rate equal to the fair rental value of the premises as is until the landlord corrects the defects.

Example 9. Larry rents a three-bedroom house to Samantha for $350 a month. Samantha moves in and finds major code violations—a large leak in the roof, a rotten front porch, nonworking bathroom plumbing, and no running hot water. Samantha telephones Larry asking that he make the repairs, but six months later none of the repairs have been made. Samantha sues Larry for failure to provide premises in a fit and habitable condition. She testifies that the fair rental value of the house as warranted is $500 because that is the amount of rent paid for three-bedroom houses with two baths in comparable neighborhoods. She also testifies that the fair rental value of the house with the defects is $200 per month.

The magistrate could determine fair rental value from that testimony. The evidence of rental rates at similar houses indicates a fair rental value as warranted that is higher than the contract rate, and the magistrate can determine the fair rental value as is from the evidence of the condition of the premises—a dwelling with three bedrooms and one functioning bathroom, no hot water, a leaking roof, and rotten front porch. If the magistrate agreed with Samantha, he or she would award damages of $300 per month times the number of months after the repairs should have been made until judgment. The $300 figure is the difference between the fair rental value as warranted ($500) and the fair rental value as is ($200). The magistrate should also enter an order allowing Samantha to pay future rent at the rate of $200 per month until the landlord makes the repairs. If the magistrate's own understanding led him or her to believe that the fair rental value as is was $250 per month (or any other amount), he or she would enter judgment accordingly.

Similarly, if Samantha had testified about the deteriorated condition of the premises without giving any indication of the fair market value of the premises "as is," the magistrate would have determined the fair rental value based on the testimony regarding the condition of the premises.

Defense to summary ejectment action. The RRAA most likely will be raised before a magistrate as a defense to a summary ejectment action brought for the tenant's failure to pay rent. The landlord seeks possession and back rent, and the tenant defends on the grounds that the landlord violated RRAA.[200] Two questions are raised in this situation. May the tenant use the act to defeat the landlord's right to possession? May the tenant use the act to decrease or offset the amount of back rent that is owed? North Carolina's appellate courts have not yet heard a case that answers either of these questions.

G.S. 42-40(1) does, however, make it clear that the tenant may raise the landlord's breach as a defense against the amount of monetary damages to which the landlord is entitled. In Example 9, suppose that Samantha had stopped paying rent and Larry sued her for $2,100 ($350 per month for the six months she had not paid rent). If Samantha defended on the grounds of

199. *Miller*, 85 N.C. App. at 369, 355 S.E.2d at 193.

200. G.S. 42-40(1) specifically authorizes a tenant to raise the Residential Rental Agreements Act as a defense.

breach of warranty of habitability and the magistrate found the fair rental value "as is" as $250 per month, Larry would be entitled to money damages of only $1,500 (six months' rent at the fair rental value as is).[201]

But what is not clear from the statutes is whether Samantha can defeat Larry's right to possession. The difficulty is how to interpret two seemingly conflicting provisions in the RRAA. G.S. 42-41 provides that "the tenant's obligation to pay rent under the rental agreement . . . and the landlord's obligation to comply with G.S. 42-42(a) [duty to provide fit premises] are mutually dependent," while G.S. 42-44(c) provides that "the tenant may not unilaterally withhold rent prior to a judicial determination of a right to do so." Two commentators have indicated that the tenant should be able to avoid eviction if the reason the tenant withheld rent was a failure to provide fit and habitable premises.[202] A third commentator indicates that the courts have attempted to reconcile the two by recognizing the tenant's right to bring a rent abatement action.[203] As originally introduced, the bill proposing the RRAA included the provision regarding mutuality of tenant's and landlord's obligations but did not include the provision prohibiting unilaterally withholding rent. That provision was added by the House in its committee substitute.[204] Because the provision prohibiting a tenant from unilaterally withholding rent was added to the bill, a court might hold that the tenant's withholding of the rent entitles the landlord to a judgment for possession. On the other hand, because the statute specifically authorizes the tenant to raise the act as a defense or set-off to a summary ejectment action, it is also possible that a court would hold that in certain instances a tenant might be able to avoid eviction when he or she has withheld the rent.[205]

Until a court determines the issue, it would probably be appropriate for a magistrate to follow the approach taken by the leading case on the doctrine of breach of implied warranty.[206] This means that the magistrate first determines the amount of unpaid rent under the lease and then the amount of damages the landlord owes the tenant for breach of the implied warranty of habitability. After offsetting these two amounts, the magistrate should deny the ejectment if the landlord owes the tenant a balance or the balance is zero. If the tenant still owes the landlord rent after the offset is applied, the remedy imposed would depend on the basis of the ejectment action. If the action was brought for breach of a condition in the lease (the breach being not paying rent and the lease included an automatic forfeiture clause), the magistrate would award a judgment for possession to the landlord. However, if the action was brought for failure to pay rent (with no forfeiture clause in the lease), G.S. 42-33 allows the tenant to cure the breach any time up until judgment is rendered by tendering the amount of rent owed and court costs. In that situation the magistrate should give the tenant the opportunity to tender the amount of

201. Surratt v. Newton, 99 N.C. App. 396, 411, 393 S.E.2d 544, 562–63 (1990) (Greene, J., concurring).

202. HETRICK & McLAUGHLIN, *supra* note 54, § 6-4(b); Fillette, *supra* note 177, at 789.

203. JANICE L. MILLS, NORTH CAROLINA LANDLORD AND TENANT—BREACH AND REMEDIES § 2-6 (1991).

204. H 949, 1977 N.C. Sess. Laws ch. 770 (from original bill file, School of Government).

205. *Cf.* Cardwell v. Henry, 145 N.C. App. 194, 549 S.E.2d 587 (2001) (Trial court dismissed summary ejectment action on finding failure to provide fit and habitable premises and an unfair and deceptive practice in which damages exceeded back rent owed.).

206. Javins v. First Nat'l Realty Corp., 428 F.2d 1071, 1082–83 (D.C. Cir. 1970).

unpaid rent owed before entering judgment. If the tenant is able to pay that amount in cash, the action should be dismissed. If the tenant fails to tender the amount owed, then a judgment for possession in favor of the landlord is appropriate.

> **Example 10.** Billie files a summary ejectment action on June 20 against George for failure to pay rent. At the trial on July 15, Billie proves that they had a verbal month-to-month lease with rent of $400 due on the first of the month, that George failed to pay rent for June and July, and that on June 7, Billie telephoned George and demanded that he pay the rent. Billie asks for a judgment of possession and $600 (one and one-half months' rent). George offers evidence that he didn't pay the rent because Billie had not repaired the stove. George had written Billie on May 15 telling her that the stove did not work and asking her to repair it. Billie never responded, so George didn't think he had to pay rent. George testifies that the fair rental value of the dwelling without a stove is $300 per month. He asks the magistrate not to evict him.
>
> Billie's claim for $600 back rent is offset by George's claim of violation of the RRAA. George's damages would be the difference between the fair rental value of the premises as warranted and the fair rental value of the premises with the defect. In this case the only evidence of fair rental value as warranted is the contract rental value. If the magistrate finds that the landlord had a duty to make the repairs by May 31 and that the fair rental value of the premises as is was $300, the magistrate would award George $150 (the difference between $400 per month and $300 per month for the one and one-half months that George has not paid rent). Thus Billie would be entitled to a judgment for only $450 back rent.

With regard to entering a judgment for possession for Billie, the best procedure would be as follows: Before announcing judgment, the magistrate should indicate to George that he or she has determined that the fair rental value of the premises is $300 per month. Since George is entitled to tender the full amount of the rent due and owing, he can remain on the premises by tendering in cash at this moment the amount of $600 plus court costs, which is two full months' rent at the rate of $300. (George would have to tender all of July's rent, not just fifteen days.) If George pays that amount, the magistrate dismisses the action because of the tender. If George fails to do so, the magistrate would award a possession judgment and a money judgment for $450.

Repair and deduct. If the landlord is given notice of needed repairs and does not make them, the tenant may be able to make the repairs and deduct the reasonable expense of these repairs from the rent. The right to offset the cost of repairs against the rent is limited to reasonable costs, in light of the value of the leasehold.[207] The limitation is necessary because without it the tenant conceivably could spend a year's rent making major repairs to the premises.

North Carolina courts have held that when a landlord has agreed in the lease to make needed repairs and fails to do so after notice and a reasonable time period, the tenant may make them and recover the cost in an action against the landlord for that purpose or on a counterclaim in

---

207. Marini v. Ireland, 265 A.2d 526, 535 (N.J. 1970). *See* MILLS, *supra* note 203, § 2-7; Jonathan M. Purver, Annotation, *Tenant's Right, Where Landlord Fails to Make Repairs, to Have Them Made and Set Off Against Rent,* 40 A.L.R.3d 1369 (1991).

an action for back rent.[208] Although precedent exists for using the repair-and-deduct remedy in North Carolina, it is unclear whether the RRAA's prohibition of unilateral withholding of rent would prevent the tenant from deducting the cost of repairs from the rent. It would seem unreasonable to allow the tenant to make the repair but require him or her to recover the costs of repair by bringing an action instead of deducting them from the rent. Until a court rules otherwise, a magistrate can allow the tenant, as a defense to an eviction, to show that failure to pay rent was the result of the tenant's having deducted from rental payments the amount expended to make repairs that the landlord was required to make but did not make within a reasonable time after being notified of the need to do so. However, the tenant who the uses repair-and-deduct defense takes a risk that the landlord is not required to make the repairs or that the amount spent on repairs was unreasonable in light of the value of the lease.

Landlord's defenses. One issue that may be raised before the magistrate is whether the landlord must repair the premises if the damage is caused by the tenant. G.S. 42-43(a) provides that the tenant may not deliberately or negligently destroy or damage the dwelling or permit anyone else to do so and that the tenant is responsible for any damage to the dwelling, other than normal wear and tear, caused by himself or herself, family, or guests. If the tenant breaches these duties, that breach certainly does not impose on the landlord an obligation to repair. The landlord's obligation to repair is mutually dependent on the tenant's obligation not to deface or damage the property. The general contract principle that one cannot benefit from his or her own wrong also applies. Therefore, if the landlord proves that the tenant, the tenant's family, or guests deliberately or negligently caused the damage, the tenant is responsible for the repairs.

Another issue that may arise is whether the tenant can waive the landlord's obligation to repair and keep the premises habitable. The landlord might attempt to defend against an action for breach by arguing that the tenant knew about the breach and implied that it was acceptable by continuing to pay the rent; or the landlord might argue that the tenant had moved into the premises knowing of the defect. The landlord is not released from his or her obligations by the tenant's implicit or explicit acceptance of the landlord's failure to provide premises that comply with the act.[209] For example, the tenant's paying rent while knowing of a defect does not relieve the landlord from the obligation to correct that defect. The landlord and the tenant may enter a written contract under which the tenant agrees to do specified work on the premises, but that contract must be separate from the lease, must be entered into after the lease, must be written, and must be supported by consideration other than rental of the dwelling.[210]

Tenant's Obligations

The tenant also has certain obligations under the RRAA. He or she

1. must keep the premises clean and safe, dispose of ashes and garbage in a clean and safe manner, and keep the plumbing fixtures clean;

---

208. Leavitt v. Twin County Rental Co., 222 N.C. 81, 82, 21 S.E.2d 890, 891 (1942).
209. G.S. 42-42(b). *See* Mendenhall-Moore Realtors v. Sedoris, 89 N.C. App. 486, 490–91, 366 S.E.2d 534, 537 (1988); Miller v. C.W. Myers Trading Post, Inc., 85 N.C. App. 362, 370, 355 S.E.2d 189, 194 (1987).
210. G.S. 42-42(b).

2. must not deliberately or negligently destroy the premises, render inoperable the smoke detector provided by the landlord, or knowingly permit anyone else to do so;

3. must comply with housing and building code obligations placed on tenants;

4. is responsible for all damage inside the unit unless the damage was caused by the landlord or was due to ordinary wear and tear or natural forces; and

5. must notify the landlord in writing of the need for replacement of or repairs to a smoke detector.

The statute requires the landlord to notify the tenant in writing of any breach of those conditions except in emergencies, when verbal notice will suffice. The tenant then presumably has a reasonable opportunity to correct the breach before becoming liable for damages. If the tenant fails to correct the breach, the landlord can either sue the tenant for monetary damages for breach of the tenant's obligation or make the repairs and sue the tenant for the costs.[211]

May the landlord evict the tenant for breach of one of these statutory obligations? Since the statute does not specifically provide for eviction for breach, the landlord can evict only when the lease between the parties provides (1) that a condition of the lease is that the tenant not violate any of the obligations set out in G.S. 42-43(a), and (2) that breach of that condition will terminate the lease or authorize the landlord to re-enter the premises and evict the tenant.[212]

Unfair and Deceptive Practice Claim

In some landlord–tenant cases, the tenant may join a claim for unfair and deceptive practices with an action for breach of duties under the RRAA or with an action for violation of another law applying to landlords. G.S. 75-1.1 makes it unlawful for any person to engage in unfair or deceptive acts or practices in or affecting commerce. The rental of residential housing is considered commerce under the Unfair and Deceptive Practices Act.[213] A landlord need not rent units on a large scale to be covered by the act; anyone who rents a single unit operates in commerce.[214] Conduct is *unfair* or *deceptive* if it has the capacity or tendency to deceive the average consumer[215] or "when it offends established public policy as well as when the practice is immoral, unethical, oppressive, unscrupulous, or substantially injurious to consumers."[216] Examples of unfair and deceptive practices in or affecting commerce in residential leases include the following:

---

211. Technically, the tenant's damage to the property is called *waste*, and the measure of damages for waste is diminution in the value of the property or the difference in the value immediately before and immediately after the injury. However, reasonable costs for repair are considered in determining diminution of value. *See* Huberth v. Holly, 120 N.C. App. 348, 353, 462 S.E.2d 239, 243 (1995).

212. G.S. 42-41 provides that the landlord's duty to keep the premises in a fit and habitable condition and to make repairs and the tenant's duties to keep the premises clean, etc., are mutually dependent; however, there are no cases that discuss this provision, and it is unclear whether our courts would hold that a landlord need not provide fit and habitable premises if the tenant violates the duty to keep the tenant's premises clean.

213. Love v. Pressley, 34 N.C. App. 503, 239 S.E.2d 574 (1977).

214. Stoflo v. Kernodle, 118 N.C. App. 580, 455 S.E.2d 869 (1995).

215. Canady v. Mann, 107 N.C. App. 252, 260, 419 S.E.2d 597, 602 (1992).

216. Johnson v. Phoenix Mut. Life Ins. Co., 300 N.C. 247, 263, 266 S.E.2d 610, 621 (1980); Dean v. Hill, 171 N.C. App. 479, 485, 615 S.E.2d 699, 702 (2005).

1. trespassing by the landlord on the premises rented to the tenant and conversion of the tenant's personal property,[217]
2. evidence that the premises were uninhabitable and that landlord knew that the premises needed repair but failed to correct the defects,[218]
3. continued collection of rent after the housing inspector declared the premises unfit and uninhabitable (where a local housing code provided that no person shall receive rental payments after the owner was notified that the unit was uninhabitable and the time for vacating the premises has expired),[219] and
4. delivering notices to tenants warning them that a tenant who calls the housing inspector before making a repair request to the landlord will be evicted.[220]

If the tenant proves the claim of unfair and deceptive practices, the magistrate must treble (triple) the award of actual damages found.

Retaliatory Evictions

In 1979 the General Assembly gave residential tenants the statutory right to raise retaliatory eviction as a defense.[221] This law protects the tenant from reprisals for the following acts:

1. a good faith complaint or request for repairs to the landlord about conditions or defects in the premises that the landlord is required to repair;
2. a good faith complaint to a government agency about a landlord's alleged violation of any health or safety law, code, or ordinance regulating premises used for dwellings;
3. a government's issuance of a formal complaint to a landlord concerning premises rented by a tenant;
4. a good faith attempt to exercise, secure, or enforce any rights existing under a valid lease or rental agreement or under state or federal law; or
5. a good faith attempt to organize, join, or become involved with an organization promoting tenants' rights.

A tenant may raise as an affirmative defense to a summary ejectment action the claim that the landlord's action is substantially in response to the occurrence within the previous twelve months of one or more of the five protected activities listed above. Because the claim of retaliatory eviction is an affirmative defense, the tenant must raise it as a defense at the trial; and if the tenant files a written answer, it must be asserted in that answer. If the tenant raises retaliatory eviction as a defense, he or she has the burden of proving that the eviction was retaliatory. To avoid eviction, the tenant must prove three things: (1) that one or more of the protected activities occurred; for example, that the tenant gave the landlord notice of needed repairs, (2) that the activity took place no more than twelve months before the summary ejectment complaint

217. *Love,* 34 N.C. App. at 515, 239 S.E.2d at 582.
218. *E.g., Dean,* 171 N.C. App. at 485, 615 S.E.2d at 702–03; Allen v. Simmons, 99 N.C. App. 636, 643, 394 S.E.2d 478, 483 (1990).
219. Cardwell v. Henry, 145 N.C. App. 194, 197, 549 S.E.2d 587, 589 (2001).
220. Creekside Apartments v. Poteat, 116 N.C. App. 26, 37–38, 446 S.E.2d 826, 834 (1994).
221. G.S. 42-37.1 through -37.3.

was filed, and (3) that the summary ejectment action was substantially in response to the activity. The tenant is not required to prove that retaliation is the "sole" reason for eviction but only that the ejectment action is "substantially" in retaliation. The tenant might prove the third element by direct evidence; for example by testimony that the landlord told the tenant (or a third party) that he or she wanted to get rid of the tenant because the tenant undertook one or more of the five protected activities. The tenant might also prove the landlord's motive by indirect evidence, such as the proximity of the occurrence of a protected activity to the summary ejectment action or evidence that other tenants who did not engage in the protected activities were not evicted for similar breaches. For example, evidence that the landlord gave the tenant notice to terminate a month-to-month lease two days after the tenant complained to the city housing inspector about conditions might be accepted as evidence that the eviction was substantially in retaliation for the tenant's complaints.

The retaliatory eviction law provides that the landlord may prevail in the summary ejectment action if he or she proves that the tenant breached the covenant to pay rent or any other substantial covenant of the lease for which the tenant may be evicted and that the tenant's breach is the reason for eviction. For example, if a lease includes a covenant not to sublease and the landlord proves breach of that condition, he or she must also show that the tenant's subletting was the reason for the ejectment action. The tenant might still prevent eviction if he or she can prove that other tenants had subleased their premises and that the landlord had not evicted them; therefore that the reason for the eviction was not that the tenant had sublet the premises for one month but rather that the tenant had demanded that the landlord make needed repairs. A tenant whose breach is failure to pay the rent would find it very difficult to sustain a defense of retaliatory eviction because of the difficulty of showing that failure to pay rent was not the reason for the eviction.[222] A tenant might be able to show retaliation if he or she had been late paying the rent several times previously but the landlord had not then filed for eviction, whereas on this occasion—when the tenant paid the rent late after exercising his or her rights under the statute—the landlord had moved quickly to evict the tenant.

In a tenancy for a definite period of time in which the tenant has no option to renew but holds over after the term expires, the landlord may prevail even if the tenant proves a retaliatory motive. For example, the landlord can win a judgment for possession if the summary ejectment action is being brought for holding over after the end of the year in a one-year lease. This exception does not apply to holding over after a periodic tenancy, such as a week-to-week or month-to-month lease, or to holding over at the end of a tenancy for years with an option to renew. In periodic tenancies or tenancies for years with options to renew, the tenant can avoid eviction after the end of the term by proving that the eviction was retaliatory.

If the tenant raises retaliatory eviction as a defense and proves that the eviction is retaliatory, the landlord may still prevail. To do so the landlord must (1) prove that the violation of the RRAA complained of by the tenant was caused primarily by the willful or negligent conduct of the tenant, the tenant's family, or guests; (2) show that compliance with the building or housing codes requires demolition or major alteration or remodeling that cannot be accomplished

---

222. *See* Maxton Hous. Auth. v. McLean, 70 N.C. App. 550, 320 S.E.2d 322 (1984).

without completely displacing the tenant; or (3) prove that he or she gave the tenant good faith notice to quit the premises before any of the protected activities occurred. For example, the landlord decides to rent the premises to someone else and gives the tenant notice to quit the premises at the end of the month. Two days after receiving the notice to quit, the tenant, who had never said anything to the landlord about the defective condition of the premises, files a complaint about the conditions with the local housing inspector. The landlord will prevail in the summary ejectment action because good faith notice to quit was given before the tenant filed the complaint. Another way of analyzing these three statutory exemptions is that the tenant could not prove that an eviction in these situations was in retaliation for the exercise of protected rights.

The landlord also can win the summary ejectment action despite a retaliatory eviction defense if the landlord (1) seeks in good faith to recover possession of the premises at the end of the tenant's term to use as his or her own dwelling, (2) seeks in good faith to make major alterations that requires the tenant's displacement, or (3) seeks in good faith to demolish the dwelling or terminate its use as a rental dwelling unit for at least six months. This last provision allows the landlord to remove the premises from the housing market rather than make needed repairs. For example, if the tenant complains of a defect to the housing inspector, who finds that the premises are not habitable, the landlord may end the tenancy at the end of the month and demolish the premises rather than make the necessary repairs.

A tenant may not waive the right to raise a defense of retaliatory eviction, and any waiver he or she gives is void and cannot be enforced. If the magistrate finds that an ejectment action is retaliatory, the magistrate must deny the request for ejectment. In this situation the tenant is entitled to remain on the premises under the existing rental agreement but must, of course, continue to pay rent.

One issue unresolved by the retaliatory eviction statute is whether a tenant who reports unsafe conditions or engages in one of the other protected activities can prevent a landlord from retaliating by raising the rent to an artificially high level. Courts from other states have said that retaliatory acts such as diminution of services or disproportionate rent increases are prohibited to the same extent as a direct retaliatory eviction.[223] These courts reasoned that public policy prohibits increasing rent in retaliation for the tenant's exercise of the statutory right to obtain repair. North Carolina's retaliatory eviction law establishes as the state's public policy protection for tenants who seek to exercise their rights to decent, safe, and sanitary housing;[224] that same public policy should also prevent landlords from raising the rent artificially high to evict tenants who assert their protected rights. If tenants are not protected from retaliatory rent increases, landlords will be able to violate the state's public policy by doing indirectly what they are prohibited from doing directly.

Another unanswered issue is whether the tenant can raise a violation of the retaliatory eviction statute in an action for monetary damages for wrongful eviction. The retaliation statute speaks in terms of an affirmative defense to a summary ejectment action and does not indicate

---

223. Schweiger v. Superior Court of Alameda County, 476 P.2d 97 (Cal. 1970); E. & E. Newman, Inc. v. Hallock, 281 A.2d 544 (N.J. 1971).

224. G.S. 42-37.1(a).

that it gives the tenant a cause of action. The tenant can, however, bring an unfair and deceptive practice action based on a retaliatory eviction against the landlord.

Example 11. Henrietta rents a house from Bohanan Inc. for $400 per month in a month-to-month periodic tenancy. Upon moving into the house, she discovers that the roof is leaking, the toilet does not work, the bathroom floor is rotted, there are no screens on the windows, and every time she plugs in the iron, the circuit breaker is tripped. She complains to Bohanan's manager, but two months later nothing has been done to correct the problem. She calls the local housing inspector who, after inspecting the apartment, notifies Bohanan Inc. that the house is uninhabitable and that the company must replace the roof, the bathroom, and the electrical wiring to bring it into compliance with codes. On May 15 Bohanan gives Henrietta notice that the tenancy is terminating at the end of May because major alterations that require the tenant to move out will be made to the dwelling. Henrietta goes to see an attorney who indicates that Bohanan has the right to terminate the tenancy on that basis even though Henrietta might be able to show that the eviction was in response to her complaint to the housing inspector. Henrietta decides not to fight and moves out. Her new rent is $550 per month, and she spends $500 moving all of her property to the new house. On July 30, while visiting her former neighbor, Henrietta discovers that Bohanan has made no attempt to repair the house and has, in fact, rented it to someone else, who moved in on June 15. Clearly Henrietta should have some remedy against Bohanan Inc. for violating the retaliatory eviction act by not terminating the tenancy in good faith. The remedy would be an unfair and deceptive practice claim for treble the amount of actual damages suffered. Her actual damages would include $500—the moving expenses—and $150 per month for June and July at least—the difference between the monthly rent at her new residence and the $400 rate under the lease with Bohanan.

Tenant's Rights in Self-Help Eviction

In 1981 the court held that a landlord could use peaceful self-help methods in evicting tenants who are in default of rental payments.[225] Ten days later the General Assembly barred all self-help evictions, peaceful or not, for residential tenants,[226] while retaining the authority of commercial landlords to evict without a court order if they can do so peaceably. For residential tenants, however, the landlord must file a summary ejectment action and enforce a judgment by having the clerk issue a writ of possession, which requires the sheriff to remove the tenant from the premises and put the landlord in possession. The prohibition against self-help eviction includes "constructive," as well as actual, eviction, meaning that a landlord cannot turn off the utilities, remove outside doors, or take other actions to force a tenant to vacate.

The 1981 legislation also bars residential landlords from holding a tenant's personal property until tenant pays money owed to the landlord and from disposing of a tenant's property except

---

225. Spinks v. Taylor, 303 N.C. 256, 278 S.E.2d 501 (1981).

226. S.L. 1981 ch. 566, codified as G.S. 42-25.6 through -25.9. *See* Kathleen Pepi Southern, *Landlord–Tenant—Spinks v. Taylor and G.S. 42-46: Abolition of Self-Help Evictions in North Carolina,* 60 N.C. L. Rev. 885 (1982).

as specifically authorized by G.S. 42-25.9 or -36.2.[227] Nor may landlords authorize self-help evictions by provisions in their residential leases or obtain a security interest or other rights in the tenant's property in violation of the law. Any lease provision that is contrary to the statute is void and against public policy.[228]

If a landlord uses self-help eviction or attempts to interfere improperly with a residential tenant's possession of his or her personal property, the tenant may sue to recover possession of the rental premises or the personal property taken and may sue for any actual damages. The statute provides that these remedies are supplementary to all existing common law and statutory rights and remedies. Therefore, a tenant can also bring a separate unfair and deceptive practice claim based on a self-help eviction. If the tenant prevails, the magistrate will be required to treble the damages.[229]

> **Example 12.** Murph and Betsy rent a mobile home from Fast Eddie. They had a one-year lease and paid the monthly rent of $300 regularly for ten months. Murph lost his job and was not able to pay the rent for June. Fast Eddie asked Murph to leave if he couldn't pay the rent by the tenth of the month. Murph found another job on June 15, and he and Betsy went out to celebrate that evening. When they came home, Fast Eddie had taken all their belongings from the mobile home and changed the lock on the door.
>
> Murph and Betsy were forced to spend two nights in a motel at a cost of $50 per night. They found another comparable mobile home to rent, but it cost $400 per month. They asked Fast Eddie to return all of their belongings, but Fast Eddie said he wouldn't return them until Murph and Betsy paid him the rent for June and July. The fair market value of the personal property was $1,000.
>
> Murph and Betsy sued Fast Eddie in small claims court. They are entitled to their actual damages for wrongful eviction—$300 ($100 for renting the motel room and $200 for the higher rent they had to pay for the remaining two months on the lease). With regard to their personal belongings, Murph and Betsy have two choices: they can sue to recover the property from Fast Eddie and sue for monetary damages for loss of the use of the property while it was wrongfully withheld; or they can let Fast Eddie keep the property and sue for conversion, seeking $1,000—the value of the property at the time it was wrongfully taken.
>
> Murph and Betsy could also sue Fast Eddie for unfair and deceptive practices. If they proved that claim, the magistrate would treble any actual damages awarded; in other words, the magistrate would award them $3,900.

Victims of Domestic Violence, Sexual Assault, or Stalking

In 2005 the General Assembly enacted three statutes dealing with the rights of tenants or household members who are victims of domestic violence, sexual assault, or stalking (referred to under the statute as *protected tenants*).

---

227. See section above, "Responsibility for Tenant's Property Left on Premises," p. 190.
228. G.S. 42-25.8.
229. Stanley v. Moore, 339 N.C. 717, 454 S.E.2d 225 (1995).

Changing Locks

One statute provides procedures for changing the locks of residential premises rented by pro-tected tenants.[230] The cost of changing the locks is borne by the tenant.

If the perpetrator of the domestic abuse, sexual assault, or stalking is not a tenant of the same dwelling as the protected tenant, the latter may request the landlord to change the locks and provide written or oral notice of his or her status as a protected tenant. The tenant need not show any documentation of the domestic violence, assault, or stalking. The landlord must change the locks within forty-eight hours or give the tenant permission to change them. If the landlord fails to act within the required time, the tenant may change the locks without the landlord's permission but must give a key to the new locks to the landlord within forty-eight hours of changing the locks. The statute does not specify what happens if the tenant fails to give a key to the landlord. Presumably, a landlord could make that requirement a condition of a lease with a right-of-re-entry clause and evict the tenant for failure to provide the key. The landlord could also hire a locksmith to make a key and require the tenant to reimburse the landlord for the cost.

If the perpetrator is a tenant in the same dwelling unit as the protected tenant, the protected tenant may request the landlord to change the locks to keep the perpetrator out. In this situa-tion, the tenant must provide the landlord with a copy of a court order ordering the perpetrator to stay away from the dwelling unit. Although the statute does not specify what constitutes a court order, it probably includes a regular or ex parte[231] domestic violence protective order and a judgment suspending sentence in a criminal case in which the court orders the defendant to stay away from the dwelling unit. It is questionable whether it also includes a pretrial release order that requires the defendant to stay away from the dwelling unit. It could be argued that an "order" means one that could be enforced by contempt of court, in which case a pretrial release order would not qualify. On the other hand, since the underlying reason for policy is protection of the victim of domestic violence, sexual assault, or stalking, the need for protection may be highest soon after a criminal offense against the victim has occurred. The landlord must change the locks or give the tenant permission to change the locks within seventy-two hours after receiving the request. If he or she fails to act, the tenant may change the locks without per-mission but must give a key to the landlord within forty-eight hours after changing the locks. The landlord has no duty to allow the perpetrator access to the dwelling unit unless the court order allows the perpetrator to return to the dwelling to retrieve personal belongings; nor does the landlord have a duty to provide keys to the perpetrator. The statute specifically provides that the landlord is not liable for civil damages for loss of use of the dwelling or for loss of use or damage to the perpetrator's personal property brought by a perpetrator excluded from the dwelling. Nonetheless, a perpetrator excluded from the dwelling remains liable under the lease, along with any other tenant, for payment of rent or damage to the dwelling unit.

---

230. G.S. 42-42.3.

231. The fact that another section in the same session law allows victims to terminate residential leases that specifically exclude ex parte orders is some indication that this statute is intended to cover ex parte orders.

Early Termination of the Lease

A protected tenant may terminate his or her rental agreement by providing the landlord with a written notice of termination effective on a date that is at least thirty days after the landlord receives the notice.[232] The tenant must include with the notice of termination a copy of a valid regular (not ex parte) order of protection issued under G.S. Chapter 50B or 50C, "a criminal order that restrains a person from contact with a protected tenant," or a valid Address Confidentiality Program card issued to the protected tenant.[233] Unlike the statute about changing locks, this provision specifically excludes ex parte orders. It does not define what is meant by "criminal order that restrains a person from contact with a protected tenant." However, the fact that it does not cover ex parte domestic violence or no-contact orders under G.S. Chapters 50B and 50C would indicate that "criminal order" means an order that is part of a suspended sentence after conviction and not a pretrial release order.

If the protected tenant is a victim of domestic violence or sexual assault, the tenant must attach a copy of a safety plan to the notice to terminate. This plan must be provided by a domestic violence or sexual assault program, must be dated during the term of the tenancy to be terminated, and must recommend relocation of the protected tenant. The tenant is liable for the rent due under the rental agreement prorated to the effective date of the termination but is not liable for any rent thereafter or for fees for early termination. If tenants other than the protected tenant reside in the dwelling unit, the tenancy continues for those tenants. A perpetrator who has been excluded from the dwelling unit under a court order remains liable under the lease, along with any other tenant of the dwelling unit, for rent or damages to the dwelling unit.

The provisions of this statute may not be waived by the landlord and tenant.

Retaliation or Discrimination against Domestic Violence Victims

Another statute prohibits a landlord from terminating a tenancy, failing to renew a lease, refusing to enter into a rental agreement, or otherwise retaliating in the rental of a dwelling based substantially on the status of the tenant, applicant, or a household member as a victim of domestic violence, sexual assault, or stalking. It also prohibits discrimination against a tenant or applicant who has lawfully terminated a lease because of domestic violence, sexual assault, or stalking.[234] The law provides that the landlord may be provided evidence of the domestic violence, sexual assault, or stalking in the form of copies of law enforcement, court, or federal agency records or files; documentation from a domestic violence or sexual assault program; or documentation from a religious, medical, or other professional. Presumably, if the tenant provides the landlord with any of these documents, the latter cannot base a defense on ignorance of the covered status of the tenant, applicant, or household member. The tenant may raise this statute as an affirmative defense in a summary ejectment action or may bring an action to recover actual damages for breach of the statute.

---

232. G.S. 42-45.1.
233. *See* G.S. Chapter 15C.
234. G.S. 42-42.2.

Termination of Lease by Military Tenant

G.S. 42-45 sets out a procedure for early termination of a residential lease by members of the armed forces who are required to move because of a permanent change of station orders, premature discharge from the military, or deployment for at least ninety days. The member who wishes to terminate a lease must give written notice of termination to the landlord and must attach to the notice a copy of the official military orders or a written verification signed by his or her commanding officer. If the termination is because of deployment, it is effective thirty days after the next rental payment is due or forty-five days after the landlord receives the notice of termination, whichever is shorter.[235] If the termination is for a permanent change of orders or a premature discharge, the termination date must be at least thirty days after notice is received by the landlord.

The statute includes a liquidated damages provision: If the tenant has completed less than six months of the tenancy as of the date of termination and the landlord will suffer actual damages due to loss of the tenancy, the landlord may assess the tenant for liquidated damages equal to one month's rent. If the tenant has completed at least six months but less than nine months of the tenancy as of the effective date of the termination, the landlord may impose damages equal to one-half month's rent.

This statute cannot be waived or modified by agreement of the landlord and tenant.

The federal Servicemembers Civil Relief Act also includes a provision authorizing a member of the armed services to terminate a residential lease under certain circumstances.[236] The termination provision applies when a tenant enters military service or when he or she receives military orders for a permanent change of station or deployment for a period of not less than ninety days.[237] The service member must give notice to the landlord by delivering a written notice of termination, along with a copy of the official military orders, to the landlord or the landlord's agent by hand delivery, private business carrier, or first class mail with return receipt requested. If the rent is paid monthly, the termination is effective thirty days after the first date on which the next rental payment is due after the date on which the notice is delivered. In any other lease, the termination is effective on the last day of the month following the month in which the notice is delivered.

---

235. The statute assumes that there is a lease for a definite period of time of at least one year. If the tenant has a month-to-month or week-to-week periodic tenancy, the tenant need not use this statute because a tenant can end those tenancies by giving notice at least seven days before the end of the month or two days before the end of the week and may leave at the end of that term without any penalty. If the tenant is leasing a mobile home space, he or she may—rather than giving sixty days notice to terminate under the general law—use this statute to terminate the periodic tenancy earlier than allowed under the general law.

236. The act applies to any member of the armed services (Army, Navy, Marines, Air Force, Coast Guard), commissioned corps of the National Oceanic and Atmospheric Administration, and commissioned corps of the Public Health Service. 10 U.S.C. § 101(a)(5).

237. 50 App. U.S.C. 535.

Tenant in Foreclosed Property

In 2007 the General Assembly authorized tenants in residential property of fewer than fifteen units to terminate their rental agreement when the property is being foreclosed under a power of sale. The tenant's written notice to the landlord must be effective on a stated date no fewer than ten days later; the tenant is liable only for rent prorated to the effective date of termination.[238] The authority to terminate the lease applies only after the tenant has received a notice of sale under the foreclosure statute, not when a foreclosure hearing has been scheduled or the clerk has entered an order authorizing foreclosure.

Fair Housing Act

The federal Fair Housing Act[239] makes it unlawful to refuse to rent a dwelling unit to a person or to discriminate against a person in the terms, conditions, or privileges of rental because of race, color, religion, sex, familial status, or national origin. Discrimination on the basis of *familial status* means discrimination against tenants with children.

The act also makes it unlawful to discriminate against a tenant because of the tenant's disability. Discrimination on the basis of handicap includes refusal to permit reasonable modifications of the premises at the expense of the tenant or to make reasonable accommodations in rules, policies, or services when such accommodations may be necessary to afford a person equal opportunity to use and enjoy a dwelling.[240] For example, a landlord with a no pets policy would have to accommodate a blind tenant by allowing the tenant's seeing-eye dog to live in the apartment. The federal law does not require that a dwelling be made available to an individual whose tenancy would constitute a direct threat to the health or safety of other individuals or whose tenancy would result in substantial physical damage to the property of others.[241]

Although claims based on violations of the Fair Housing Act generally will be filed in federal court, a federal district court in New Hampshire has indicated that a tenant might raise as a defense to a summary ejectment that he or she was being evicted for conduct that was a result of his handicap.[242] In that case a landlord of federally assisted housing attempted to evict the tenant for threatening and harassing conduct toward other residents. The landlord claimed that he did not have to consider making reasonable accommodation because of the federal law's exception for tenants who constitute a direct threat to other residents. The court held that the exception applies only after the landlord has attempted reasonable accommodations; therefore, before the landlord may lawfully evict a tenant he or she must prove that no reasonable accommodations will eliminate or acceptably minimize the risk a tenant poses to other residents.

---

238. G.S. 42-45.2.

239. 42 U.S.C. §§ 3601 through -3619 (2003). North Carolina also has a Fair Housing Act (G.S. Chapter 41A), but it requires a person to file a claim with the Human Relations Commission before that person is authorized to proceed to a court action and requires any court action to be brought in superior court.

240. 42 U.S.C. § 3604(f)(3)(B) (2003).

241. 42 U.S.C. § 3604(f)(9).

242. *See* Roe v. Sugar River Mills Assoc., 820 F. Supp. 636 (D.N.H. 1993).

Appendix I

Publicly Assisted Housing Notice Requirements

Program/Code of Federal Regulation Citation	Grounds for Eviction	Requirements of Notice	When Notice Must be Given
Public Housing (PHA) 24 C.F.R. § 966.4(k), (l)	1. Serious or repeated violation of material terms of lease. 2. Being over income limit. 3. Other good cause including criminal activity and other factors listed.	1. Written notice. 2. Specify grounds for termination. 3. Tell tenant has right to reply and examine documents relevant to termination. 4. State whether tenant entitled to grievance procedure required before eviction. 5. State whether eviction is for criminal activity or drug-related criminal activity.	Failure to pay rent or utilities—14 days. When health or safety of other tenants or PHA staff threatened or criminal or drug-related activity, reasonable notice but not longer than 30 days. In all other cases, 30 days notice.
§8 Housing—Voucher Program 24 C.F.R. § 982.310(e)	1. Serious or repeated violation of terms of lease. 2. Violation of federal, state, or local law that imposes obligations on tenant regarding occupancy or use of premises. 3. Other good cause (specified in regulation). 4. PHA's failure to pay housing assistance payment is not grounds for eviction of tenant.	1. Written notice. 2. Specify grounds for termination. 3. Must give PHA copy of eviction notice.	At or before beginning ejectment (may be given in summary ejectment complaint)
§8 Housing—New Construction & Substantial Rehabilitation Programs 24 C.F.R. § 880.607 24 C.F.R. § 881.601	1. Material noncompliance (defined in regulation). 2. Material failure to carry out obligations under state landlord–tenant law. 3. Criminal activity. 4. Other good cause (only if landlord has given tenant prior notice that the grounds constitute a basis for termination).	1. Written notice. 2. State grounds & giving date on which lease terminated. 3. Indicate tenant's opportunity to respond. 4. Landlord may not rely on any ground not set forth in notice.	When eviction based on other good cause, notice is effective at end of term in accordance with the lease but no earlier than 30 days after notice is received. If based on material noncompliance or failure to carry out terms, notice required under NC law.
§8 Housing—Moderate Rehabilitation Programs 24 C.F.R. § 882.511	1. Serious or repeated violation of terms of lease. 2. Violation of applicable federal, state, or local law. 3. Other good cause.	1. Written notice. 2. Give date lease terminated. 3. State reasons for termination. 4. Advise tenant that if summary ejectment action filed, tenant may present defense at that proceeding.	For failure to pay rent—not less than 5 days after receipt of notice. For serious or repeated violation of lease or violation of federal, state, or local law—in accordance with NC law. Other good cause—at least 30 days after notice. Notice must be served by first class mail return receipt requested or by delivering copy to dwelling unit.

Chapter VII

Motor Vehicle Mechanic and Storage Liens

Section 7A-211.1 of the North Carolina General Statutes (hereinafter G.S.) authorizes the chief district judge in each judicial district to assign to magistrates actions for enforcement of motor vehicle mechanic and storage liens under G.S. 44A-2(d) and motor vehicle liens arising under G.S. 20-77(d). The law does not authorize magistrates to hear actions to enforce motor vehicle liens under G.S. 44A-2(e2) (landlord's lien in tenant's mobile home worth more than $500), G.S. 42-25.9(g) (landlord's lien in mobile home worth $500 or less), or G.S. 20-28.3 (vehicles seized from drunk drivers). The judge may assign motor vehicle lien cases to magistrates by specific order or according to a general rule. The procedure in small claims actions to enforce motor vehicle liens differs from other small claims cases in three respects.

1. Actions to enforce motor vehicle liens must be brought in the county where the claim arose rather than the county where the defendant resides.
2. The defendant may be served by publication and other methods of service not authorized for other small claim actions.
3. The remedy sought is not money, possession of personal property, or summary ejectment. Rather, the plaintiff seeks a judgment declaring the lien in the motor vehicle valid and enforceable. The judgment will allow the plaintiff to sell the motor vehicle and apply the proceeds to the amount owed for repairing, storing, or towing the vehicle.

Who Is Entitled to a Lien

G.S. 44A-2(d) and G.S. 20-77(d) specify the particular persons who are entitled to a lien in motor vehicles.

- Any person who repairs, services, tows, or stores motor vehicles in the ordinary course of business pursuant to an express or implied contract with owners or legal possessors has a lien on a motor vehicle for reasonable charges for repairs, service, towing, or storage.[1]

---

1. N.C. GEN. STAT. § 44A-2(d) (hereinafter G.S.).

- An operator of a place of business that garages, repairs, parks, or stores vehicles for the public has a lien on a vehicle remains unclaimed for ten days.[2]
- A landowner has a lien on a motor vehicle left abandoned on his or her property for more than thirty days.[3]

Such a lien has priority over all perfected and unperfected security interests, which means that it takes precedence over a person holding a security interest in the property that was perfected before the motor vehicle lien attached. The lien is against the motor vehicle only, not the contents or any property that is not part of the motor vehicle.

Establishing the Lien

When the Lien Arises

A lien under G.S. 44A-2(d) arises when a person acquires possession of the motor vehicle for the purpose of storing, towing, or repairing it. This lien is called a *possessory lien* because it is established when the person who repairs, tows, or stores the motor vehicle (hereafter called the *lienor*) acquires possession of the vehicle. The lienor does not file a written lien with the Division of Motor Vehicles (hereafter DMV) or with the clerk of court. Although the lien arises when the vehicle is stored, towed, or repaired, the lienor may not begin to enforce the lien until the debt for storing, repairing, or towing the vehicle is at least thirty days past due. However, if the debt is for towing and storing expenses only, enforcement may begin ten days after the debt becomes due.

The lien under G.S. 20-77(d) arises when a vehicle has been unclaimed for at least ten days at a place for garaging, parking, or repairing vehicles for the public and the lienor has notified DMV of the unclaimed vehicle. The lien also arises under this statute when a vehicle has been abandoned on a landowner's property for at least thirty days and the landowner has notified DMV of the unclaimed vehicle.

When the Lien Terminates

The lien terminates when the lienor voluntarily relinquishes possession of the motor vehicle or when the owner, legal possessor, or secured party pays the amount secured by the lien plus reasonable storage and other expenses incurred by the lienor. Thus, a lienor who allows the owner to take his or her motor vehicle before paying fully for the services has given up the lien in the vehicle and can only proceed to sue the owner for money owed. Even if the lienor regains possession of the motor vehicle at a later time, the lienor cannot assert a lien against the vehicle for the prior service.

The lien is not terminated if possession is involuntarily relinquished. Involuntary relinquishment includes only those situations in which the owner or another party takes possession of the motor vehicle without the lienor's permission or without judicial process.[4] Surrendering

---

2. G.S. 20-77(d).

3. G.S. 20-77(d).

4. G.S. 44A-6.1. Although this statutory definition of involuntary relinquishment applies to a lawsuit by a lienor to regain possession of property wrongfully taken by the owner, it also should apply to an action to enforce

the vehicle in obedience to a court order is not a forfeiture of the lienor's rights.[5] For example, a lienor who was storing vehicles seized by the sheriff under a writ of attachment is not considered to have voluntarily relinquished the vehicle when he turned it over to the sheriff for sale; the amount owed to the lienor remains collectable from the proceeds of the sale.[6] It is also an involuntary relinquishment if a vehicle's owner takes the vehicle without paying by tricking the lienor's employee.[7] In two cases the court held that property was not voluntarily relinquished when the lienor returned it to the owner upon receipt of a check that was subsequently returned for insufficient funds.[8] In a third case the court found that the motor vehicle was not voluntarily relinquished when the owner of the vehicle stopped payment on the check.[9] At the time these cases were decided, *voluntary relinquishment* was not defined in the statute. It is possible that a court today might still determine that the current definition of involuntary relinquishment—loss of the motor vehicle when an owner or other party takes possession of it without the lienor's permission or without judicial process—excludes the situation in which the lienor accepts a check that is returned for insufficient funds or on which a stop payment order is issued. The court in *Maxton Auto Co. v. Rudd*,[10] in which the vehicle owner stopped payment on the check given to the repairman, based its finding on an estoppel theory, not on voluntary relinquishment; it found that a party cannot hold to an advantage acquired in the course of a business deal when that party has renounced the deal and refused to abide by its terms. The estoppel theory applies regardless of the definition of voluntary relinquishment. The lienor's remedy for the situation in which a motor vehicle is taken by the owner without the lienor's permission is discussed below under "Lienor's Action to Recover Vehicle and Establish Lien."

Example 1. Bob takes his Chevrolet to Abe's Auto Repair Shop to have the muffler replaced and some other work done on the car. When Bob goes to pick up the car, he says he doesn't have $300, the cost of repair, but can pay Abe $150 and pay him the remaining $150 the following month. Abe says Bob can't have the car back until he pays the full $300 and that he charges $3 per day storage charges for cars that remain on the premises for more than ten days after the work is completed. Abe has a possessory lien in the Chevrolet and may hold it until the debt is paid.

But what if Abe said fine and let Bob take the car? At that point Abe would have voluntarily relinquished the lien. Assume, further, that Bob pays $250 and stops paying. Then he takes the car back to Abe to have a flat tire repaired. When Bob comes to pick up the car, he pays for repairing the flat, but Abe says he will hold the car for the $50 owed for the previous repair. In this situation

---

the lien since the identical issue of voluntary and involuntary relinquishment applies in that action.

5. Case v. Miller, 68 N.C. App. 729, 723, 315 S.E.2d 737, 739 (1984).

6. *Id.*

7. N.C. Farm Bureau Mut. Ins. Co. v. Weaver, 134 N.C. App. 359, 517 S.E.2d 381 (1999).

8. Adder v. Holman & Moody, Inc., 288 N.C. 484, 219 S.E.2d 190 (1975) (holding that lien was not extinguished when check returned for insufficient funds); Reich v. Triplett, 199 N.C. 678, 155 S.E. 573 (1930) (Owner fraudulently obtained possession by stating that check was good.).

9. Maxton Auto Co. v. Rudd, 176 N.C. 497, 97 S.E. 477 (1918).

10. *Id.* The court said that when the vehicle owner stopped payment, he had a duty to return the vehicle to the lienor and put him in position to enforce the mechanic's lien for the amount due. The owner was estopped from resisting enforcement of the lien by reason of possession thus acquired. *Maxton*, 176 N.C. at 499; 97 S.E. at 478.

Abe does not have the right to hold the car because the lien for the $300 service was extinguished when the car was voluntarily relinquished. The lien cannot be reactivated when Bob brings the car back to Abe for more repairs. Abe's only remedy is to release the vehicle to Bob and sue him for the $50 he is owed. If Abe does not give him the vehicle, Bob would be entitled to recover possession of the vehicle if he brought an action against Abe.

Procedure to Enforce Lien before Court Proceeding

A lienor must file an unclaimed vehicle report with the DMV within five days after the date the lien may be enforced;[11] the lienor must then notify the division that he or she asserts a lien in the motor vehicle and intends to sell it.[12] Upon receipt of notice from the lienor, DMV sends a certified letter, return receipt requested, to the registered owner of the motor vehicle, the person with whom the lienor dealt if not the registered owner, and all secured parties known to DMV. The notice informs them that the lienor intends to sell the vehicle for a lien and specifies the amount of the lien and the services performed. It advises recipients that they have ten days from receipt of the letter in which to notify DMV that they wish to request a judicial hearing to determine the validity of the lien. The lienor may, instead of notifying DMV and having DMV send the notices, send the notices directly to the owner or secured party.

If one of the recipients requests a hearing, DMV will notify the lienor that he or she must get a court declaration that the lien is valid before DMV will authorize the sale. If none of the recipients of the DMV notice request a court hearing, the division will authorize the lienor to sell the vehicle without any court involvement. The purchaser of the vehicle will be issued a title upon filing a title application and presenting the DMV form letter authorizing the lienor to sell the vehicle, which letter the seller will give to the purchaser upon completion of the sale.[13]

But what if DMV's certified letter is never delivered to the owner of the vehicle or a secured party known to DMV? Because the state's integral role in the sale of a motor vehicle constitutes state action, due process requires that a judicial hearing be held to determine the validity of the lien before DMV can authorize a sale.[14] Therefore, if the owner or a secured party cannot be notified by DMV, DMV will require the lienor to bring a judicial proceeding before authorizing the sale of the motor vehicle.

11. G.S. 44A-4 and 20-77(c). The form "Report of Unclaimed Vehicle," ENF-260, is available from the local Division of Motor Vehicles (DMV) License and Theft Office. The consequences of failure to file the report on time are discussed below in the discussion of Examples 5 and 6.

12. G.S. 44A-4. The form, "Notice of Intent to Sell a Vehicle to Satisfy Storage and/or Mechanic's Lien," ENF-262, is available from the local DMV License and Theft Office.

13. The DMV form is ENF-265. The form letter authorizing the sale includes a "Record of Sale and Notice of Purchase" in which the lienor fills in with the name of the person buying the vehicle and the price and date of the sale. The purchaser acquires title to the motor vehicle by submitting a completed application for title, accompanied by the completed form ENF-265 to the local license plate agency.

14. Caesar v. Kiser, 387 F. Supp. 645 (M.D.N.C. 1975). See also Mitchell v. W.T. Grant Co., 416 U.S. 600, 94 S. Ct. 1895, 40 L. Ed. 2d 406 (1974), Fuentes v. Shevin, 407 U.S. 67, 92 S. Ct. 1983, 32 L. Ed. 2d 349 (1972); Sniadach v. Family Fin. Corp., 395 U.S. 337, 89 S. Ct. 1820, 23 L. Ed.2d 349 (1969).

Small Claims Case or Special Proceeding?

There are two separate court proceedings used to enforce a motor vehicle lien: a civil action in small claims, district, or superior court (depending on the amount in controversy) and a special proceeding before the clerk of superior court. Only a civil action was available until 1985, when the General Assembly authorized a special proceeding before the clerk[15] as a simplified and less-expensive court proceeding in two limited situations.

- The DMV was able to mail letters to the registered owner of the vehicle and secured parties but the certified letter to one of them was returned as undeliverable.
- The name of the owner cannot be determined, and the vehicle has a fair market value of less than $800. The fair market value is determined by the schedule of values that G.S. 105-187.3 requires the commissioner of motor vehicles to provide.[16]

A lienor may always choose to bring a civil action before a magistrate or judge. However, in the two situations when a special proceeding can be filed, most lienors will choose that option because it is quicker, easier, and less expensive. In all other situations, when a judicial proceeding is required the lienor must file a civil action.[17]

Trial before Magistrate

Small claim actions to enforce motor vehicle liens are commonly brought in two situations.

- The owner of the motor vehicle (or secured party) requests a hearing because he or she is unhappy with charges for the repair.
- A motor vehicle is abandoned on the side of the highway and is towed at the request of a law enforcement officer, but DMV cannot determine the name or the address of the owner.

In the former case, the vehicle owner is likely to appear at the trial and contest the existence or amount of the lien. In the latter, the vehicle owner is not likely to appear, and the lienor's evidence proving the lien will not be contradicted.

15. 1985 N.C. Sess. Laws ch. 655 authorized a special proceeding when a certified letter is not deliverable. 1995 N.C. Sess. Laws ch. 635 authorized use of a special proceeding when the name of the owner cannot be determined and the value of the motor vehicle is less than $800.

16. This schedule sets out the use tax to be paid when applying for a certificate of title for a motor vehicle and is based on the wholesale value of the motor vehicle. The schedule is kept by local license plate agencies.

17. Appendix 1 at the end of this chapter provides examples of various letters that DMV sends to lienors and indicates the kind of judicial proceeding that may be filed in each situation.

Amount in Controversy and Venue

The amount in controversy is the amount of the lien, not the fair market value of the motor vehicle.[18] Therefore, the lienor may file the action as a small claim if the amount of the lien is $5,000 or less.[19]

Unlike other small claims actions, the proper county in which to file an action to enforce a motor vehicle lien is the county where the claim arose; in other words, the county where the motor vehicle was repaired, stored, towed, garaged, or abandoned[20] rather than the county where the defendant resides. This exception to the general rule for small claims actions is necessary because in so many of these cases the owner of the motor vehicle is unknown or his or her residence cannot be determined.

Nature of Action and Parties

An action to enforce a motor vehicle lien is what is called an *in rem* action—an action against the motor vehicle itself that does not assert any personal liability against the vehicle's owner. The lienor is not suing the motor vehicle owner for money, but is asking for a judgment to establish the amount of the lien and to allow the sale of the motor vehicle to satisfy that lien. If the sale does not bring the full amount of the lien, the lienor cannot have a writ of execution issued against the owner to satisfy the difference because no money judgment is entered.

All persons who have an interest in the motor vehicle must be named as defendants.[21] In motor vehicle lien cases, that includes any known secured parties as well as the owner of the motor vehicle.[22] Secured parties must be made defendants because the garage owner's lien is superior to all other liens, which means that sale of the motor vehicle extinguishes a secured party's lien, even if the secured party's lien was established before the garage owner's. If the motor vehicle is licensed in North Carolina, a secured party must notify DMV of a lien in order to have it effective against third-party purchasers. Therefore, if a security agreement on a motor vehicle titled in North Carolina is not listed with DMV, it would not be a "known" security interest. Although DMV is required to give notice to the person who contracted with the lienor if that person is not the owner, that person would not be a necessary party to the small claims action because he or she has no interest in the motor vehicle.

What if some, but not all, of the owners and secured parties receive the certified notice from DMV and waive their right to a hearing? A judicial hearing will be required if any of the persons who are required to receive notice (owner and secured parties) do not receive it. But the

---

18. G.S. 7A-243(3) provides that where no monetary relief is sought, but relief sought would establish, enforce or avoid an obligation, right, or title, it is the value of the obligation, right, or title that is in controversy.

19. The form "Complaint to Enforce Possessory Lien on a Motor Vehicle," AOC-CVM-203, is available for this purpose.

20. G.S. 7A-211.1.

21. See G.S. 1-75.8 and -75.9. Necessary parties are "all persons who have or claim material interests in the subject matter of a controversy, which interests will be directly affected by an adjudication of the controversy." Equitable Life Assurance Soc'y v. Basnight, 234 N.C. 347, 352, 67 S.E.2d 390, 394–95 (1951).

22. *Cf.* G.S. 44A-4(d) (authorizing secured parties to object to a private sale by lienor) and G.S. 105-364 (requiring lienholders to be made parties to a civil action by a city or county to foreclose on a property for unpaid property taxes).

question is must they all be made parties? In other words, does the fact that a person waives a right to a hearing under G.S. 44A-4 (by not requesting it) after being notified mean that that person should not be made a defendant to a lawsuit brought by the lienor to enforce the lien? Since G.S. 44A-4 deals only with the issue of whether a court hearing is required and not who are parties to the court proceeding and because G.S. 1-75.8 requires all persons with an interest in the motor vehicle to be parties to the action, the safest practice is to name all interested persons as defendants. The consequence of not naming a necessary party is that the unnamed person is not bound by the court order, even though the order remains valid as regards to all named parties. Therefore, whether all necessary parties are named is an issue for the lienor, not the magistrate. The magistrate can go forward with the case and enter judgment for the parties named and served.

Service of Process

Before trying an action to enforce a motor vehicle lien the magistrate must determine that the defendants were properly served and that, therefore, the court has jurisdiction to hear the case. The defendant(s) may be served by any of the normal small claims methods of service—by service in person, by leaving a copy of the summons and complaint at the defendant's residence with a person of suitable age and discretion who also resides in the dwelling, or by mailing a copy to the defendant by certified mail, return receipt requested. In addition, in motor vehicle lien cases only, the plaintiff may serve the defendant by using a designated delivery service such as Federal Express[23] or by mailing the service by signature confirmation.[24] If after due diligence the plaintiff is unable to serve the defendant by any of these methods, he or she may serve the defendant by publication.[25] Due diligence requires the plaintiff to use all resources reasonably available to attempt to locate the defendant[26] but not to undertake other, probably futile means of service when the plaintiff has no indication of the defendant's whereabouts.[27] Service by publication is the only possible method of service when a law enforcement officer requests the lienor to tow an abandoned motor vehicle with no license plate, and neither the lienor nor DMV can discover the name of the owner or, if the name is known, an address for that owner.

23. The designated private delivery services are: Airborne Express: Overnight Air Express Service, Next Afternoon Service, and Second Day Service; DHL Worldwide Express: DHL "Same Day" Service and DHL USA Overnight; Federal Express: FedEx Priority Overnight, FedEx Standard Overnight, and FedEx 2Day; United Parcel Service: UPS Next Day Air, UPS Next Day Air Saver, UPS 2nd Day Air, and UPS 2nd Day Air A.M. See 26 U.S.C. § 7502(f)(2); Notice 99-41.

24. G.S. 7A-211.1 and G.S. 1A-1, Rule 4(j)(1). G.S. 1-75.10 specifies how plaintiff proves service by designated delivery service or signature confirmation.

25. G.S. 7A-211.1.

26. Fountain v. Patrick, 44 N.C. App. 584, 587, 261 S.E.2d 514, 516 (1980). See G. Gray Wilson, N.C. Civil Procedure § 4-22 (3d ed. 2007).

27. Wilson, *supra* note 26.

Procedure for Service by Publication

To serve by publication, the plaintiff must publish a notice of service of process once a week for three successive weeks in a newspaper that is qualified for legal advertising[28] and is circulated in the relevant county. In most cases, the notice must be published in the county where the action is pending (that is, where the claim arose); but if the lienor has reliable information concerning a party's location, he or she must publish the notice in the county where the owner may be residing. The notice must identify the court in which the action has been commenced and the title of the action, state that a pleading has been filed seeking to enforce a lien in the motor vehicle, and direct the defendant to make a defense within forty days after the first date of publication.[29] Because the defendant has forty days from the first publication to respond, a plaintiff who serves by publication, either after a failed attempt to serve by one of the normal methods of service or for the initial service, should inform the clerk when asking for a summons or alias and pluries summons so that the clerk will set the trial date of the case more than forty days after issuance of the summons.

If the motor vehicle owner's name cannot be discovered, the publication notice and the lawsuit may be filed against the unknown owner of the specifically described motor vehicle. For example, the defendant in the lawsuit would be listed as "the unknown owner of a 1995 blue Toyota Camry, VIN # 333355554444."

Proving Service by Publication

A plaintiff who has served the defendant by publication proves service by filing (1) an affidavit from the newspaper publisher or printer showing the publication notice and indicating the date of the first and last publication and (2) an affidavit by the plaintiff indicating the circumstances that warranted use of service by publication and all information obtained, if any, regarding the location of the party served.[30] The magistrate must determine not only that the plaintiff's advertisement was proper but also that the plaintiff exercised due diligence before resorting to publication.

Action Brought by Business That Repairs, Stores, Tows Vehicles

A plaintiff in an action is brought under G.S. 44A-2(d) must prove the following six things by the greater weight of the evidence:

---

28. G.S. 1A-1, Rule 4(j1). To be qualified for legal advertising, the newspaper must have a general circulation with actual paid subscribers and be admitted to U.S. mails in the periodicals class in the county where such publication is required to be published; the newspaper must have been regularly and continuously issued in the county at least one day in each calendar week. G.S. 1-597 through -599 provide guidance if there is no qualifying newspaper in the county. *General circulation* refers to a publication to which the general public would resort for the general news of the community and not to the number of subscribers or geographic distribution in the county. The criterion is whether the newspaper contains news of a general character and interest to the community. Great S. Media, Inc. v. McDowell County, 304 N.C. 427, 284 S.E.2d 457 (1981).

29. The notice published in the newspaper must be substantially in the form specified in G.S. 1A-1, Rule 4(j1).

30. G.S. 1-75.10(2) and G.S. 1A-1, Rule 4(j2)(3).

1. The plaintiff in the ordinary course of his or her business repairs, services, tows, or stores motor vehicles.
2. The plaintiff entered into an express or implied contract with an owner or legal possessor of the motor vehicle for repairs, services, towing, or storage.
3. The lien attaches to the motor vehicle.
4. The plaintiff is owed unpaid charges of $_____.
5. The charges are reasonable charges for the repairs, services, towing, or storage.
6. The plaintiff gave notice to DMV that a lien was asserted and that he or she intended to sell the motor vehicle.

Ordinary Course of Business

To be entitled to a lien under G.S. 44A-2(d), the lienor must be in the business of towing, storing, or repairing motor vehicles and the actual towing, storing, or repair must be done in the course of that business. For example, a physician who fixes cars for his friends on the weekends as a hobby is not a person who in the ordinary course of business tows, stores, or repairs motor vehicles. Similarly, a person who owns an automobile repair shop may not be acting in the ordinary course of that business when he uses his private car to tow a neighbor out of a ditch.

Owner or Legal Possessor

The lienor must have contracted with an owner or legal possessor. An *owner* is a person who has legal title to the motor vehicle, a *lessee* of the person who has legal title, a debtor entrusted with possession of the vehicle by a secured party, a secured party entitled to possession (a secured party would be entitled to possession if the debtor had defaulted[31]), or any person entrusted with possession of the vehicle by that person's employer or principal who is an owner.[32] For example, a person who leases rather than buys a car is considered an owner of the leased car, and an employee driving the employer's truck to deliver goods would be an owner under the statute.

A *legal possessor* is a person entrusted with possession of the vehicle by its owner or a person in possession of the vehicle and entitled to possession by operation of law.[33] A family member or friend of the owner driving the car with the owner's permission is a person entrusted with possession. A law enforcement officer is a legal possessor when the officer contracts with a garage owner to tow a motor vehicle that has been parked or left standing on the right-of-way of a highway or has been parked or left standing in violation of the law and is interfering with the regular flow of traffic or otherwise constitutes a hazard.[34] A sheriff who seizes a motor vehicle under an order of attachment[35] or as evidence of a crime[36] is a legal possessor when the sheriff contracts for the towing and storage of the vehicle.

---

31. See G.S. 25-9-609.
32. G.S. 44A-1(3).
33. G.S. 44A-1(1).
34. G.S. 20-161.
35. Case v. Miller, 68 N.C. App. 729, 315 S.E.2d 737 (1984).
36. State v. Davy, 100 N.C. App. 551, 561, 397 S.E.2d 634, 639–40 (1990).

Example 2. Officer James sees a car pulled off the road onto shoulder of I-95. The officer tags the car,[37] and several days later when the car is still there he calls Johnson Tow Co. and asks them to remove and store the car. Johnson Tow Co. has a lien in the car for towing and storing it because it contracted with a legal possessor, Officer James.

Express or Implied Contract

The contract may be either express, which means the parties agreed to the specific terms of the contract, or implied, which means that the contract exists by virtue of the parties' conduct rather than in any explicit set of words.[38] Although the terms of an implied contract may not be expressed in words—or at least not fully in words—the legal effect is the same as that of an express contract in that it too is considered a "real" contract based on a genuine agreement between the parties.[39]

Example 3. Jean takes her car to Easy Auto Repair and asks the manager to align the front end; the shop manager agrees to do the work for $145. This is an express contract.

Example 4. Jean takes her car to Easy Auto Repair and asks them to fix her car. Easy Auto determines that her car needs new brake pads and charges her $150. This is an implied contract; the terms are not fixed, but Jean's actions in taking the car and in asking that it be fixed and Easy Auto's actions in repairing the car create an implied contract.

The Lien Attached

The lien attaches to the motor vehicle if the lienor has retained possession of the vehicle and not voluntarily relinquished it. The lienor may begin to enforce the lien if the charges remain unsatisfied for thirty days, or if the charges are for towing and storing only, if the lien remains unsatisfied for ten days.[40]

Amount of the Lien and Storage Costs

The lien is not for the amount charged by the lienor but rather for the reasonable charges for the services performed. Thus, the lienor must prove the reasonable value of the services performed. "Reasonable value" might be equivalent to "fair market value"[41] or a determination of what the services are reasonably worth based upon the time and labor expended and the skill, knowledge, and experience involved.[42] Generally, to show reasonable charges the lienor will have to show

---

37. G.S. 20-161 provides that when a vehicle is parked or left standing upon the right of way of a public highway for forty-eight hours or more, a law enforcement officer is a legal possessor of the motor vehicle for purposes of removing and storing the vehicle.

38. Ellis Jones, Inc. v. Western Waterproofing Co., 66 N.C. App. 641, 646, 312 S.E.2d 215, 218 (1984).

39. *Jones,* 66 N.C. App. at 645, 312 S.E.2d at 217.

40. G.S. 44A-3.

41. Cline v. Cline, 258 N.C. 295, 128 S.E.2d 401 (1962).

42. Turner v. Marsh Furniture Co., 217 N.C. 695, 697, 9 S.E.2d 379, 380 (1940).

that the lienor's charges are similar to charges made by other persons in the business of repairing, towing, or storing motor vehicles.

The lienor is not entitled to recover unlimited storage costs. There are two limitations on storage costs. First, a person who tows, repairs, or stores motor vehicles must file a report with DMV if the vehicle remains unclaimed for ten days. If the unclaimed vehicle report is not filed within fifteen days after the vehicle becomes unclaimed, the lienor may not collect storage costs for the period of time between the date the lienor was required to file the unclaimed vehicle report and when the lienor actually did send the report to DMV by certified mail.[43] Before the magistrate may award any storage costs, the lienor must prove when he or she sent the unclaimed vehicle report to DMV; and if the report was sent more than fifteen days after the vehicle became unclaimed, the lienor must prove that he or she sent the report by certified mail.

Example 5. On March 15, at the request of a police officer, Dave's Auto tows a Ford that has been left on the right-of-way of a street. Sixty days later, when Dave's Auto gets ready to sell the Ford, Dave, the owner, sends an unclaimed vehicle report and a notice of intent to sell the Ford to DMV by certified mail. He files a small claims action to enforce the motor vehicle lien 100 days after the car was towed, and the trial is held twenty days later. At the trial, Dave proves that he is entitled to a lien for towing and storing, shows the magistrate a certified mail certificate, and proves that $75 is a reasonable charge for towing and $5 per day is a reasonable charge for storage. Dave seeks $75 for towing and $600 for storage. However, Dave is entitled to a lien of only $450—$75 for towing and $375 for storage costs because he is not entitled to storage costs for the forty-five days between the time he was required to notify DMV and the time he actually notified DMV (between the fifteenth day and sixtieth day after vehicle was towed). If Dave had sent the unclaimed vehicle report within fifteen days after the car was towed, he would be entitled to storage costs of $600 dollars (for 120 days).

Second, failure of the lienor to bring an action on the debt within 180 days after the commencement of storage constitutes a waiver of the right to collect storage charges that accrue (become due) after such period.[44] Thus a lienor who has towed or repaired a vehicle is not entitled to storage for more than 180 days unless the lawsuit to enforce the lien is filed within 180 days after storage began. However, if the property is placed in storage under an express contract of storage, the lien continues and the lienor may bring an action to enforce the lien within 120 days following default on the obligation to pay storage costs.[45]

Example 6. On November 15 Big Joe's Towing and Repair Shop tows a Toyota from the side of a highway at the request of a law enforcement officer. Big Joe's puts the car in its storage lot, notifies DMV of the unclaimed vehicle, and promptly forgets about it. Eight months later, Big Joe's realizes the Toyota is still sitting in the lot and notifies DMV of its intent to sell the vehicle for its lien. DMV cannot determine the name of the owner of the vehicle and informs Big Joe's that

---

43. G.S. 20-77(d). If the lienor files the unclaimed vehicle report with DMV within fifteen days of the towing, the report need not be filed by certified mail. The form is "Report of Unclaimed Vehicle," ENF-260, and is available from the local DMV License and Theft Office.

44. G.S. 44A-4(a).

45. *See* Case v. Miller, 68 N.C. App. 729, 733, 315 S.E.2d 737, 740 (1984).

it must bring a court proceeding. Big Joe's files a small claim action on August 15, 270 days after the vehicle was towed and placed in storage. Big Joe's is entitled to a lien for reasonable charges for towing the Toyota and for 180 days of storage. If Big Joe's had filed the lawsuit 179 days after storage began but the trial was not held until the 200th day, Big Joe's Towing and Storage would be entitled to a lien for all of the storage costs until sold because the 180-day period stops running when the lawsuit to enforce the lien is filed.

If Big Joe's had not sent the notice of unclaimed vehicle until eight months after the car was towed, it would only be entitled to fifteen days of storage costs. One statute would say that Big Joe's is not entitled to storage fees between the time it should have filed the report (fifteen days after towing) and the time it filed the report (eight months after towing), and the other statute provides that failure to bring the lawsuit within 180 days waives the right to collect storage costs after that period.

Example 7. Tamara is being transferred to Japan for a six-month tour of duty. She arranges with Big Joe's Towing and Storage to store her vehicle for six months while she is gone. Big Joe's agrees to store the vehicle for $150 per month and requires Tamara to pay for the first three months before the storage begins and indicates that the monthly storage fee thereafter will be due by the fifth of the month. Tamara pays Big Joe's $450 and delivers the vehicle on March 1. She does not pay the storage fee due June 5. Big Joe's files a lawsuit to enforce the lien on September 30, 215 days after the storage began but 113 days after the default on the payment (the default occurred on June 5). Because there was an express contract for storage, the 180-day period from commencement of the storage does not apply. Rather, Big Joe's had up to 120 days after the default on the storage contract to file the lawsuit. In this case Big Joe's would be entitled to a lien for reasonable storage costs from June 1 until the vehicle is sold.

Requirement to Notify DMV of Lien and Intent to Sell

Although G.S. 44A-4(b) requires the lienor to give notice to DMV of the lien and the lienor's intent to sell the motor vehicle, it is not clear whether the lienor must prove that he or she has met that requirement to be entitled to a judgment. The purpose of the statute is to allow DMV to notify those persons with an interest in the motor vehicle of the lien and their right to require a judicial hearing. If the lienor does not notify DMV but rather initiates a small claim action to enforce the lien, the owner and secured parties will be given notice of the lawsuit and the opportunity to contest the lien, so the purpose of the G.S. 44A-4 provision will have been served.[46]

Action Brought by Business That Stores or Garages Vehicles

For the most part the provision in G.S. 20-77(d), which allows businesses that store, repair, garage or park motor vehicles for the public to assert a lien, is subsumed by G.S. 44A-2(d). A business that stores or repairs motor vehicles will rely on G.S. 44A-2 to enforce its lien. However, if the business garages or parks motor vehicles, it may use G.S. 20-77(d) as the basis for

---

46. The practical question is whether DMV will transfer title to the vehicle when it receives a copy of the magistrate's judgment.

asserting a lien. Under G.S. 20-77(d) the plaintiff must prove the following five things to be entitled to judgment.

1. The plaintiff operates a place of business for garaging, repairing, parking, or storing vehicles for the public.[47]
2. The motor vehicle has remained unclaimed for at least ten days.
3. The plaintiff filed an unclaimed vehicle report with DMV.[48]
4. The charges have not been paid.
5. The charges are reasonable.

A typical place of business for garaging would be a city or privately owned parking deck.

Action Brought by Landowner

A landowner who files an action because a motor vehicle has been abandoned on his or her property must prove four things to be entitled to judgment.

1. The plaintiff is the landowner on whose property a motor vehicle is located. If the motor vehicle, including a mobile home, was left on the property by a tenant, the landowner must file a landlord's lien with DMV under G.S. 42-25.9(g) or G.S. 44A-2(e2) and not a motor vehicle lien under G.S. 20-77.[49]
2. The motor vehicle has been abandoned on the property for more than thirty days.
3. The plaintiff filed an unclaimed vehicle report with DMV.
4. The amount of damages the landowner is seeking to recover.

G.S. 20-77(d) specifies that the landowner is entitled to sell the vehicle under the provisions of G.S. Chapter 44A. Since the landowner is not a person who is in the business of storing, repairing, or towing vehicles, it is not clear that the plaintiff can ask for monetary damages. However, G.S. 44A-5 provides that the proceeds from the sale shall be applied first to the expenses of sale and specifically states that such expenses include reasonable storage expenses beginning after the landowner gives notice of the sale. Therefore, a plaintiff always is entitled to recover the expenses of sale, including reasonable charges for storage from the date he or she gives notice of the sale to the date of the sale itself. The landowner must, however, offer evidence that the storage costs are reasonable.

---

47. Although G.S. 20-77(d) applies to all vehicles that are left unclaimed in businesses for storing, repairing, garaging, or parking for the public, the magistrate only has jurisdiction to hear cases involving "motor vehicles." Motor vehicles are defined as self-propelled vehicles and vehicles designed to run upon the highway, which are pulled by a self-propelled vehicle. It does not include mopeds or bicycles. G.S. 20-4.01(23).

48. The form that must be filed with DMV is ENF-260, "Report of Unclaimed Motor Vehicles," and is available from DMV's local License and Theft Office.

49. The landlord can seek authority to sell the motor vehicle (including mobile homes) under the landlord's lien by filing with DMV the form "Notice of Sale of Motor Vehicle—20-Day Advance Notice with DMV," ENF-261. The landlord should check Block E and state that the lien is for a landlord's lien under G.S. 44A-2(e) or G.S. 42-25.9(g). In the case of a mobile home left by an ejected tenant, the landlord must also attach a certified copy of the magistrate's summary ejectment judgment granting possession of the premises to the landlord and a copy of the return of the sheriff indicating that a writ of possession was served.

Judgment

In an action to enforce a motor vehicle lien, the magistrate does not award a specific sum of money to the plaintiff who proves his or her case. Rather, the magistrate enters a judgment either (1) authorizing the plaintiff to enforce a lien in the motor vehicle for an amount determined by the magistrate and for the daily rate of storage to be charged from the date of judgment until the vehicle is sold or (2) finding that the plaintiff has failed to prove the case by the greater weight of the evidence and ordering that the case be dismissed with prejudice. In an action by a landowner on whose property the motor vehicle was abandoned, in which there are no damages other than expenses and storage costs from the date notice of sale was given, the magistrate may authorize the plaintiff to enforce the lien, specify the daily amount of storage costs to be awarded, and specify the date from which the storage costs are awarded until the date of the sale.[50]

Lienor's Duties after Judgment

DMV Permission to Sell Vehicle

If the magistrate renders a judgment in favor of the lienor, the lienor must send a copy of the judgment to DMV along with a notice of sale.[51] DMV will send a letter[52] authorizing the lienor to proceed with a private or public sale as provided in G.S. 44A-4(c) through (f). The lienor may purchase the vehicle at a public sale but not at a private sale.[53] The owner, the person with whom the lienor dealt, a secured party, or any other person who claims an interest in the vehicle may object to a private sale any time before the date the sale is set and may require the lienor to hold a public sale.[54]

Redeeming the Vehicle

Although the statute does not include a provision for redeeming the property, the owner can terminate the lien at any time before the sale by paying the lienor the amount of money secured by the lien plus reasonable storage charges and other expenses incurred by the lienor. In fact, any person who has an interest in the vehicle, including a secured party, can terminate the lien by paying the charges owed. An owner who wishes to contest the amount of the lien may redeem the vehicle by filing an action to recover possession of the vehicle and paying into the office of the clerk of superior court the amount of the lien asserted. (See below, "Action by Owner to Recover Vehicle.")

---

50. The magistrate should use the form "Judgment in Action on Possessory Lien on Motor Vehicle," AOC-CVM-402 to enter judgment in a motor vehicle lien case.

51. DMV Form ENF-263, "Notice of Sale of Motor Vehicle, is available from the local DMV License and Theft Office.

52. Form ENF-265 is the form used. It tells the lienor that he or she can sell the vehicle and includes a place for the lienor to write the name and address of the purchaser.

53. G.S. 44A-4(c) & (e)(3).

54. G.S. 44A-4(d).

Sale Procedure

Public or Private Sale

The lienor may choose to sell the motor vehicle by public or private sale. A public sale is a public auction held at a time and place advertised. Any other sale is a private sale. If the lienor chooses to hold a private sale, that sale must be conducted in a manner that is commercially reasonable. For example, selling motor vehicles by private sale through wholesalers or placing them on the lienor's own lot for sale to the first buyer at a set and reasonable price may be commercially reasonable. The lienor himself or herself may not purchase the motor vehicle at a private sale; if the lienor does so, the sale is voidable.[55]

If the lienor chooses to hold a public auction, the sale must be held in the county where the claim arose on a day other than Sunday between the hours of 10:00 a.m. and 4:00 p.m. The lienor may purchase the vehicle at a public sale.

Notice to DMV and Parties

Whether the sale is public or private, the lienor may not sell the motor vehicle until he or she has given DMV advance notice of the sale—at least twenty days before the date of the public sale or the date the vehicle will be offered for private sale.[56]

The lienor also must mail a notice of the sale to the titleholder, if his or her identity is known; the person with whom the lienor dealt, if this person is different from the titleholder; and each secured party who is known or whose identity can be reasonably ascertained. The notice must include

a. the name and address of the lienor,
b. the name of the person who has legal title to the vehicle if it can be reasonably ascertained,
c. the name of the person with whom the lienor dealt,
d. a description of the motor vehicle,
e. the amount due to lienor for which the lien is claimed,
f. the place of sale, and
g. the date on or after which the lienor will offer the vehicle for private sale or the date and hour of the proposed public sale.

The statute provides that the lienor does not have to give notice to the titleholder and secured parties if the first notice he or she gave to DMV when beginning the process of enforcing the lien contained all the necessary information.[57] Nonetheless, because the earlier notice sent to

---

55. G.S. 44A-4(c).

56. DMV form "Notice of Sale of Motor Vehicle," ENF-263, is the proper form to use. It is available from the local DMV License and Theft Office.

57. G.S. 44A-4(e)(1)a1 provides that "notices provided pursuant to subsection (b) hereof shall be sufficient for these purposes if such notices contain the information required by subsection (f) thereof." Subsection (b) refers to G.S. 44A-4(b) and the form "Notice of Intent to Sell a Vehicle to Satisfy a Lien." In *AT&T Family Fed. Credit Union v. Beaty Wrecker Serv., Inc.*, 108 N.C. App. 611, 614, 425 S.E.2d 427, 428 (1993), the court apparently misread the statute as referring to sub-subdivision G.S. 44A-4(e)(1)b. instead of subsection G.S. 44A-4(b).

DMV[58] does *not* include all of the required information for a sale notice, the lienor must send a separate notice of sale. If a public sale is being held, the notice of sale must be sent to the owner and secured parties at least twenty days before the sale date; and if a private sale is contemplated, the notice must be sent at least thirty days before the date the motor vehicle will be offered for sale. The lienor may draft a notice or send a copy of the completed DMV Form ENF-263 sent to DMV, which includes the necessary information.

Posting and Publication for Public Sale

If a public sale is to be held, the lienor must post a copy of the notice of sale at the courthouse door in the county where the sale is to be held at least twenty days before the sale. In addition, the lienor must publish the notice of sale once a week for two consecutive weeks in a newspaper of general circulation[59] in the county where the sale is to be held. The last notice in the newspaper must be published not less than five days before the sale. However, if the motor vehicle has a market value of less than $3,500 as determined by the schedule of values adopted by the commissioner of motor vehicles under G.S. 105-187.3,[60] the lienor is not required to publish the notice in a newspaper.

Allocation of the Proceeds of Sale

The lienor must allocate the proceeds of the sale as follows:

- First, the lienor must pay the reasonable expenses incurred in connection with the sale, which may include any storage expenses incurred after notice of sale was sent.
- Second, the lienor pays the obligation secured by the lien.
- Third, the lienor must pay the surplus to the person(s) entitled to it, who may be secondary lienholders or, if none, the titleholder.

If the person entitled to the surplus cannot be found, the lienor must the pay the surplus to the clerk of superior court of the county where the sale took place; the clerk will hold it for the person entitled to it.[61]

Owner's Remedies for Lienor's Failure to Comply

A lienor who fails to comply substantially with the procedures for enforcing the lien by sale is liable to the titleholder or to any other person injured by noncompliance for $100, a reasonable attorney's fee, and any actual damages to which the party is entitled.[62] The actual damages titleholder or secured party suffered as a result of lienor's failure to comply with the sale procedures is the difference between the fair market value of the motor vehicle at the time of sale and the

---

58. ENF-262, "Notice of Intent to Sell a Vehicle to Satisfy a Storage and/or Mechanic's Lien."

59. *See supra* note 28.

60. *See supra* note 16.

61. G.S. 44A-5.

62. G.S. 44A-4(g). *See* AT&T Family Fed. Credit Union v. Beaty Wrecker Serv., Inc., 108 N.C. App. 611, 615, 425 S.E.2d 427, 429 (1993).

amount for which the motor vehicle actually sold.[63] If the lienor purchased the vehicle at a private sale, the sale is voidable and the titleholder or secured party can bring an action in district or superior court—but not in small claims court—to set aside the sale.

Action by Owner to Recover Vehicle

If an owner of a motor vehicle contests the lienor's right to a lien or contests the amount of the lien, the owner may, instead of waiting to defend an action to enforce the lien brought by the lienor, file a complaint seeking to recover the motor vehicle and establish the amount of the lien.[64] For the owner, the advantage of filing this action is that he she can sue immediately when the lienor refuses to return the vehicle and need not wait until the lienor files an action to establish the lien. A trial will be scheduled within thirty days after the owner's action is filed, and the magistrate will determine whether there is a lien against the vehicle and, if so, the amount of the lien.

Moreover, if the owner wishes to obtain immediate possession of the motor vehicle without waiting until trial, he or she may deposit with the clerk of court, in cash, the full amount of the lienor's claim. After the cash is deposited, the clerk will order the lienor to relinquish the vehicle to the owner immediately.[65] The full amount the lienor is claiming will be held pending the magistrate's determination of how much should be paid to the lienor. The lienor is therefore protected and need not sell the vehicle to satisfy the lien. Conversely, the owner gets the vehicle, and if the magistrate determines that the lienor was not entitled to a lien or is entitled to a smaller lien than the lienor is asserting, the owner will receive back from the clerk the difference between the lienor's claim and the magistrate's determination. If the lienor refuses to relinquish the vehicle when ordered to do so, the clerk may proceed to issue a show cause order for a contempt hearing before a district court judge.[66]

An owner of a motor vehicle who files an action to recover possession of the vehicle and determine the amount of the lien is required in the complaint to indicate the amount of the lien claimed by the lienor and the amount that is undisputed. If the owner also posts a cash bond to obtain immediate possession of the vehicle, the clerk may, at the request of the lienor, disburse to the lienor that portion of the cash bond that the plaintiff/owner states is not in dispute.

Amount in Controversy

The amount in controversy in an action by the owner to recover the motor vehicle and establish the amount of the lien is the disputed amount of the lien,[67] not the value of the motor vehicle or the total amount of the lien claimed. If the amount in dispute is $5,000 or less, the plaintiff may file the action as a small claim.

---

63. Drummond v. Cordell, 73 N.C. App. 438, 441, 326 S.E.2d 292, 293 (1985).

64. G.S. 44A-4(a). The form "Complaint to Recover Personal Property Held for Lien and to Contest Amount of Money," AOC-CVM-900M, is available for this action.

65. The form is "Order for Release of Motor Vehicle Held for Lien," AOC-CVM-901M.

66. A district court judge must hold the criminal contempt hearing for indirect criminal contempt or civil contempt. G.S. 5A-15, G.S. 5A-23(b).

67. G.S. 7A-243(3).

Magistrate's Judgment

In an action to recover possession of the motor vehicle and establish the amount of the lien, if any, the plaintiff/owner has the burden of proving that he or she is entitled to relief. In other words, the plaintiff must prove by the greater weight of the evidence either (1) that the lienor is not entitled to a lien and the plaintiff is therefore entitled to possession of the vehicle or (2) the actual amount of the lien to which the lienor is entitled and that upon payment the plaintiff is entitled to recover the vehicle.[68]

No Cash Deposit by Owner

If the plaintiff brings a motion to recover the vehicle and establish the amount of the lien but does not deposit a cash bond with the clerk, the magistrate has three options for judgment.

1. If the plaintiff/owner proves that the defendant/lienor is not entitled to a lien in the vehicle, the plaintiff is entitled to recover possession of the vehicle and the defendant is not entitled to a lien in the property. The defendant is entitled to a lien if he or she repairs, services, tows, or stores motor vehicles in the ordinary course of business and provided service to the vehicle pursuant to an express or implied contract with the owner or legal possessor.[69]

2. If the plaintiff/owner fails to prove that there is not a lien on the property, the defendant/lienor is entitled to a judgment for possession of the vehicle and can assert a claim of lien for the amount determined by the magistrate. After judgment, the defendant can get permission from DMV to sell the vehicle and to proceed with the sale unless the vehicle's owner pays the amount of the lien set by the magistrate.

3. If the plaintiff/owner fails to appear to prosecute the action, the magistrate must dismiss the lawsuit. The lienor/defendant remains in possession of the vehicle and follows the general procedure to assert the lien and sell the vehicle.

Plaintiff Deposits Cash Bond

If the plaintiff has deposited a cash bond with the clerk before trial, the magistrate can issue one of three possible judgments.

1. If the plaintiff proves that the lienor is not entitled to a lien, the magistrate must find that the plaintiff is entitled to recover possession of the motor vehicle and the defendant is not entitled to a lien on the property. The magistrate must also direct the clerk of court to return any of the cash bond remaining to the plaintiff.

2. If the plaintiff fails to prove that the lienor is not entitled to a lien on the vehicle, the magistrate must determine the amount of the lien—in other words the reasonable charges for the service performed. The magistrate must find that the plaintiff is entitled to possession of the motor vehicle and the defendant is entitled to a lien in that amount.

---

68. The magistrate enters judgment using "Judgment to Recover Personal Property Held for a Lien and to Award Amount of Money Owed," AOC-CVM-902M.

69. *See* above, "Action Brought by Business That Repairs, Stores, Tows Vehicles."

Remember that, in this case, the plaintiff is entitled to possession because the cash bond held by the clerk is used to pay the lien. The magistrate must, therefore, direct the clerk to disburse to the defendant from the cash bond any portion of the amount of the lien awarded that has not already been disbursed to the defendant and to return any remaining amount of the cash bond to the plaintiff.

3. If the plaintiff fails to appear at trial, the magistrate must dismiss the action and direct the clerk to disburse any amount of the cash bond remaining to the defendant. In this situation, the plaintiff will have possession of the vehicle but the lienor will receive from the clerk the amount of money to which he or she is entitled.

Example 8. Susan Owner takes her car, which has a fair market value of $25,000, to Quick Auto Repair Shop and asks that the mechanic install a new engine in the car. Quick Auto Repair Shop installs an engine. When Susan comes to pick up the car, Quick Auto Repair Shop says the bill is $3,500. Susan is astonished because she believes the engine should not have cost more than $2,500. Susan says she will pay $2,500 now and the rest later. Quick Auto Repair says that it won't release the vehicle until the full $3,500 is paid. Further, Susan notices a large sign that says there will be a $5 per day storage charge for cars left over ten days after the repairs are finished. Susan needs her car and does not want to wait for Quick Auto Repair to enforce its lien. On the other hand, she doesn't want to pay Quick Auto Repair the extra $1,000 she doesn't believe she owes. Susan may file an action to recover possession of her motor vehicle and to establish the amount of the lien on the vehicle, The action may be filed in small claims court because the disputed amount of the lien ($1,000) is within the small claims jurisdiction. But if Susan merely files the lawsuit, Quick Auto Repair will keep possession of the vehicle and can charge daily storage fees until trial. At the trial, the magistrate will determine if Quick Auto Repair Shop is entitled to a lien and, if so, the amount of the lien. If Quick Auto Repair is entitled to a lien, it may enforce its lien by selling the vehicle unless Susan pays Quick Auto Repair the amount of lien set by the magistrate.

Example 9. But what if Susan wants immediate possession of her car and does not want to incur $5 per day storage costs? When she files her lawsuit, she may deposit $3,500 in cash with the clerk of superior court. The clerk will order Quick Auto Repair Shop to relinquish the vehicle to Susan because the clerk is now holding $3,500 in cash that will be paid to Quick Auto Repair Shop if at the trial the magistrate rules that Quick Auto Repair is entitled to the full $3,500. Assume that at the trial the magistrate determines that Quick Auto Repair Shop is entitled to a lien of $3,000. The magistrate's judgment must award possession of the vehicle to Susan and direct the clerk to disburse $3,000 of the cash bond (or any amount up to $3,000 that has not already been distributed) to Quick Auto Repair Shop and $500 to Susan.

Example 10. Susan agreed that she owed $2,500 but didn't want to pay the $3,500 that Quick Auto Repair Shop claimed as the lien. She indicated that $2,500 of the asserted lien was not in dispute. After releasing the car, Quick Auto Repair Shop could make application to the clerk for payment and the clerk could pay them the $2,500 that was not in dispute. At trial the clerk would hold the remaining $1,000 for disbursement according to the magistrate's judgment. Upon receiving the magistrate's judgment that the lien was $3,000, the clerk would send another $500 to Quick Auto Repair and the remaining $500 to Susan.

What if the lienor comes to the trial and indicates he or she is owed more than the amount alleged by the owner in the complaint? The lienor has three days after being served with the complaint to file a contrary statement with the clerk of court saying that the amount alleged by the owner is not correct and stating the correct amount. If the lienor files a statement, the clerk will not force the lienor to relinquish the vehicle unless the owner pays the additional amount into the clerk's office. However, if the lienor does not file a statement with the clerk within the proper time, the amount alleged in the complaint is the maximum amount of the lien and the lienor may not claim more at the trial.

What if the lienor is entitled to a lien but has ignored the order to relinquish the property and is still in possession at trial? The magistrate would indicate that the plaintiff is entitled to possession of the vehicle and the defendant is entitled to the amount determined as the lien. However, the magistrate must modify the judgment form to order the clerk not to disburse the money until the lienor turns the car over to the plaintiff.

Lienor's Action to Recover Vehicle and Establish Lien

What if the owner has taken the vehicle without the lienor's permission? In other words, the lienor has not voluntarily relinquished the vehicle but had it taken from him or her? In that situation the lienor may institute an action to regain possession of the motor vehicle.[70] In the lawsuit to regain possession, the lienor also asks the court to determine the amount of the lien so that after judgment the lienor can enforce the lien without having to bring a second lawsuit.[71]

The lienor may file the action as a small claim if the amount of the asserted lien is $5,000 or less.[72]

Because the lienor is seeking to enforce the lien as well as get possession of the vehicle, all persons with an interest in the motor vehicle should be made defendants, which means secured parties as well as the owner.

What is the appropriate county in which to file the lawsuit—the county where the claim arose or where one of the defendant resides? Although this action combines a request to recover possession of the motor vehicle with a determination of the amount of the lien, it is at its core an action to enforce a motor vehicle lien. Therefore, it should be filed in the county where the lien arose (where the motor vehicle was repaired, towed, or stored).

A defendant who is served with a complaint to recover the vehicle and establish a lien and wishes to keep the vehicle and extinguish the potential for an order to return the vehicle, may post a cash bond with the clerk in the lien amount the plaintiff alleges in the complaint.[73]

---

70. G.S. 44A-6.1.

71. The form is "Complaint to Recover Motor Vehicle to Enforce Possessory Lien and to Establish Amount of Lien," AOC-CVM-903M.

72. G.S. 7A-243(3).

73. The form is "Bond To Keep Possession of Motor Vehicle Taken From Lienor," AOC-CVM-904M.

The plaintiff must prove, by the greater weight of the evidence, the following six things:

1. that the plaintiff is a person who in the ordinary course of business repairs, services, tows, or stores motor vehicles;
2. that the plaintiff entered into an express or implied contract with an owner or legal possessor for repairs, services, towing, or storage;
3. that the lien attached to the motor vehicle;
4. that the motor vehicle was not voluntarily relinquished;
5. the charges have not been paid; and
6. the charges are reasonable charges for the repairs, services, towing, or storage provided.

If the defendant or a secured party has not filed with the clerk of court a statement alleging a different amount of the lien within three working days after service of the summons, the amount alleged in the complaint is deemed to be the amount of the lien. In other words, at trial the defendant cannot contest the amount of the lien, only whether there is a lien. When no contrary statement is filed, the statute seems to indicate that the amount alleged by the plaintiff is assumed to be the reasonable charge and that the magistrate would not make a separate determination of the reasonable charge.

If the defendant has not put up a cash bond and the plaintiff proves that he or she is entitled to a lien in the vehicle, the magistrate must grant possession of the vehicle to the plaintiff and determine the amount of plaintiff's lien.[74] If the plaintiff fails to prove that he or she is entitled to a lien, the magistrate must dismiss the action.

If the defendant has posted a cash bond and the plaintiff proves he or she is entitled to a lien, the magistrate determines the amount of the lien and directs the clerk (a) to disburse that amount to the plaintiff from the cash bond and (b) to return any remaining amount to the defendant. The plaintiff is not entitled to recover possession of the vehicle since the defendant has deposited the amount owed with the clerk. If the plaintiff fails to prove that he or she is entitled to a lien, the magistrate dismisses the action and directs the clerk to return the cash bond to the defendant.

Example 11. Babe Sampson goes away for the weekend. When she returns, she notices that her car is not in the driveway. Her 24-year-old son, who had been forbidden to drive her car, calls her and said he drove the car while she was gone. Something was wrong with the front end so he dropped it off at Main Street Ford dealership to be fixed. Babe immediately goes to the Ford dealership and demands her car. The manager says she owes $250 for the repair work and he will not release the vehicle until she pays for it. She says, "You don't have a lien in the car because you did not contract with an owner or legal possessor of the vehicle." He responds, "Tough! The car stays here until you pay $250." Babe waits until Sunday morning and then goes to the Ford dealership and takes the car. (She, of course, had an extra set of keys.) Main Street Ford dealership files an action to recover the vehicle claiming a lien of $250, plus storage costs at $5 per day for the week the car was on its lot. Babe does not file anything in response to the complaint and summons but does appear at

---

74. At the trial the magistrate should enter judgment on the form "Judgment to Recover Possession of Motor Vehicle to Enforce Possessory Lien and to Establish Amount of Lien." AOC-CVM-905M.

trial. She argues that Main Street Ford was not entitled to hold the vehicle because it did not have an express or implied contract with an owner or legal possessor. If the magistrate believes Babe's evidence, he or she will find that the son was not a legal possessor since he was not entrusted with the car by its owner; in fact, he was specifically told he could not drive the car. In that case, the plaintiff, Main Street Ford, would fail to prove that it was entitled to a lien in the vehicle and the action would be dismissed. Main Street Ford would not be entitled to possession of the vehicle and would have to sue the son, who entered into the contract, for the $250 repair bill, plus storage.

Example 12. But what if the magistrate determined that the son had permission to drive the car? Babe does not file a statement in response to the lawsuit but at trial argues that the reasonable charge for the repair is $100. In that situation, Main Street Ford would be entitled to a judgment for possession and the magistrate would find that it has a lien for $250. The amount alleged in the complaint is deemed to be the amount of the lien because Babe did not file a statement alleging a different amount.

The Motor Vehicle Repair Act

The North Carolina Motor Vehicle Repair Act[75] (MVRA) requires motor vehicle repair shops to give customers written estimates of work that will exceed $350 and to notify the customer before performing the work if it determines that actual charges will exceed the written estimate by more than 10 percent. The act also requires a shop to provide an invoice to customers and sets out a number of prohibited practices, including charging for repairs that have not been made and making fraudulent promises. MVRA further provides that a customer injured by a violation of the act may file an action for damages and attorneys' fees or may bring an action for injunctive relief. Because MVRA does not provide that the repair shop loses the right to a lien under G.S. 44A, for most violations the act has no impact on the motor vehicle lien law. However, it does specify that it is a violation for a repair shop to refuse to return a motor vehicle to the customer because the customer refuses to pay for repair charges that exceed the written estimate by more than 10 percent if the customer has paid the shop the amount of the estimate, plus 10 percent. In that one instance only, the customer could raise the act (1) as a defense to an action to enforce a motor vehicle lien or (2) as the basis of an action to recover possession of a vehicle held for a lien.

75. G.S. 20-354 through -354.9.

Appendix 1

Division of Motor Vehicle Letters to Lienor

1. "The Division has given notice of your intent to sell the vehicle . . . to the registered owner, garageman(s), and person authorizing the storage. We have not received a request for a judicial hearing from any of these persons. Therefore, North Carolina General Statutes 20-114(c) requires that you furnish twenty days advance notice of the sale to the Division." *Lienor can sell without any court proceeding. Sends ENF-262 to DMV; receives ENF-265 from DMV; and conducts sale under G.S. 44A-4 provisions.*

2. "As a result of your notice of intent to sell the vehicle described above, we have been unable to secure delivery of certified mail to . . . . Therefore, if you wish to sell the vehicle to satisfy your lien, you may have a judicial hearing before a court of competent jurisdiction. . . . You may also contact the clerk of court in your county and file a petition with the clerk for authorization to sell the vehicle to satisfy your lien." *Lienor can bring special proceeding before the clerk or a civil action (small claims if amount of lien is $5,000 or less).*

3. "As a result of your notice of intent to sell the vehicle. . . . we have received a request from . . . for a judicial hearing to determine the validity of your storage and/or mechanic's lien. If you wish to sell the vehicle, you should initiate the necessary action in a court of competent jurisdiction." *Lienor must file a civil action (small claims if amount of lien is $5,000 or less).*

4. "Thank you for the ENF-262. . . . We have checked our registration files and do not find this vehicle registered in North Carolina (or in the State of _____). Therefore, we cannot notify the legal owner as required by G.S. 44A-4. . . . If you wish to sell this vehicle to satisfy your lien, it will be necessary for you to have a judicial hearing before a court of competent jurisdiction to determine the validity of your lien." *Lienor must file a civil action if the value of the motor vehicle is at least $800 (small claims if amount of lien is $5,000 or less) and may file a special proceeding or civil action if the value of the motor vehicle is less than $800.*

5. "[W]e have received information which indicates that the vehicle . . . ; however, the title has not been submitted to the Division of Motor Vehicles for transfer of ownership. If you wish to satisfy your lien, it will be necessary for you to have a judicial hearing before a court of competent jurisdiction to determine the validity of your lien." *Lienor must file a civil action (small claims if amount of lien is $5,000 or less).*

6. "We have reviewed your file and find you did not furnish the name and address of the person authorizing storage and/or repairs. Therefore, we cannot notify that person as required by General Statute 44A-4. If you wish to sell this vehicle to satisfy your lien, it will be necessary for you to have a judicial hearing before a court of competent jurisdiction." *Lienor may file a special proceeding or civil action if value of vehicle is less than $800. The lienor must file a civil action if value is $800 or more.*

Appendix 2

Time Line for Awarding Storage Fees

A	B	C	D
Date lien arises= 10 days after towing if only charges are for towing and storage or 30 days after repairing or servicing a vehicle	10 days after lien arises= lienor required to file unclaimed vehicle report with DMV	15 days after lien arises= date by which unclaimed vehicle report finally due or lienor not entitled to storage until files report	180 days after lien arises= lienor loses right to collect storage fees from this date forward unless already filed small claim action

Lienor must file unclaimed vehicle report by C. Failure to file by that date means lienor is not entitled to storage costs from C until the date lienor files an unclaimed vehicle report with DMV by certified mail.

Lienor who has not filed a lawsuit by D is not entitled to any storage fees after D.

Chapter VIII

Evidence

Evidence is anything that tends to establish or to disprove a disputed fact. The law of evidence is a set of rules that regulates (1) what evidence a party can use in support of his or her claim or to refute the other party's claim and (2) how much evidence is necessary to prevail on the claim. While the concept of evidence is something anyone can understand, the law of evidence is quite complicated. Most of the North Carolina rules of evidence are set out in Chapters 8 and 8C of the North Carolina General Statutes (hereinafter G.S.).

How much evidence law magistrates should know and apply in small claims court is by no means obvious. G.S. 7A-222 provides that the "rules of evidence applicable in the trial of civil actions generally are observed" in small claim actions; but this language does not clarify what the word *generally*" describes—*applicable* or *are observed*. If generally modifies *applicable*, then magistrates must always follow the rules that apply in most civil cases; on the other hand, if generally modifies *are observed*, magistrates need not always apply the rules of evidence in small claims court. Several good arguments support the latter reading.

First, the purpose of small claims court is to provide a readily accessible, low-cost way to resolve civil disputes. Part of what makes this goal possible is the simplified version of legal process that small claims court uses. A plaintiff may file a complaint simply by filling in the blanks on the form supplied by the clerk's office; the defendant is not required to answer the complaint and cannot have the plaintiff's complaint dismissed for failure to state a sufficient legal claim. Small claims actions are not only easier to initiate than other court actions, they are also easier to conduct in terms of the trial itself. As a matter of course, parties appear without attorneys. Because of this emphasis on simplified process, it makes little sense to expect lay persons, either parties or magistrates, to strictly observe a body of law as highly technical as the rules of evidence.

Second, many judicial districts are using court-ordered arbitration of civil cases with an amount in controversy of $15,000 or less. Arbitrators must be lawyers, yet the rules of evidence are not binding in these hearings. It therefore does not make sense that magistrates, who generally are not lawyers, should have to apply the rules of evidence strictly while attorney–arbitrators need not do so.

Third, the fact that parties dissatisfied with a magistrate's ruling have the right to a trial de novo before a district court judge or jury[1] minimizes the prospect that a magistrate's consideration of inadmissible evidence will affect a party's substantial rights or create a serious injustice.

But even if magistrates are not always required to apply the rules of evidence in small claims court, there are good reasons for them to have some familiarity with this body of law. First, if magistrates were not required to use any evidence law, then that portion of G.S. 7A-222 providing that the "rules of evidence applicable in the trial of civil actions generally are observed" in small claims court would be meaningless.

Second, attorneys will appear occasionally in small claims court and make objections to the admissibility of evidence based on the law of evidence. Magistrates should have some sense of how to deal with such objections.

Finally, some rules of evidence are based on public policy concerns that touch on issues or rights that are important outside of the trial context: for example, the right to confidentiality in communications between attorneys and clients, doctors and patients, and husbands and wives. If a magistrate ignores these rules and admits evidence that should be excluded on the basis of confidentiality, he or she may violate a party's rights. For instance, if a magistrate forces an unwilling spouse, over the other spouse's objection, to testify about their communications, the disclosure of that information violates both spouses' right to privacy. Even if the magistrate later ignores this testimony in rendering a judgment, the privacy violation is not corrected. Of course, if the party does not object to introduction of this kind of evidence, this concern does not arise.

The answer, then, to the question posed at the beginning of this chapter—"How much evidence law should magistrates know and apply in small claims court?"—is still not entirely clear. The most satisfactory answer seems to be that magistrates should know enough evidence law to deal with an attorney's or a party's objections about admissibility. The amount of evidence law magistrates need to know for this purpose is not overwhelming. Because most evidence *is* admissible, the magistrate should not exclude evidence to which no one objects.

If an attorney is present and makes objections to the admission of certain evidence, a magistrate may pursue one of two courses. One course is to note the objection but refrain from making an immediate ruling on it or to ask the attorney to hold objections until all the evidence is presented and then indicate to the magistrate what evidence he or she should not consider. When the attorney makes an objection, the magistrate may indicate that he or she will receive all the evidence for what it is worth and at the close of the proceeding will base his or her judgment on the competent evidence. It is entirely within the magistrate's power to admit evidence that may be inadmissible because, as an expert on North Carolina evidence puts it, "there is a distinction between admission of incompetent evidence and reliance upon it in making findings . . . . [T]he judge with knowledge of the law is able to eliminate from the testimony he hears that which is immaterial and incompetent, and consider that only which properly tends to prove

---

1. N.C. Gen. Stat. § 7A-228(a) (hereinafter G.S.).

the facts to be found."[2] The magistrate can point out to the attorney that he or she is in small claims court, where the rules of evidence are not strictly followed. The magistrate can also tell the attorney that he or she will take the objection to the evidence into account in rendering judgment and that if, after judgment is rendered, the attorney believes the judgment is based on inadmissible evidence, he or she may, of course, appeal for a trial de novo in district court.

The second course open to the magistrate is to rule on the objection immediately. In making a ruling the magistrate should keep in mind two factors. First, the magistrate can and should require the attorney to explain the objection in detail by asking "Please give me the basis for your objection." If necessary, the magistrate also may ask the attorney to point out (and provide a copy of) the specific rule of evidence on which the objection is based. Second, because the rules of evidence are difficult; oftentimes attorneys themselves do not have as comprehensive an understanding of them as they should. Magistrates, therefore, should not be cowed into excluding evidence just because an attorney objects to it.

General Principles of Evidence

Kinds of Evidence

Anything perceptible by the senses can be evidence if it makes the existence of a fact material to a party's case more or less likely. Distinctions between kinds of evidence are made not because one kind is necessarily more important, reliable, or persuasive than another, but mainly because different rules apply to them.

Documentary and Testimonial Evidence

The two most important kinds of evidence for magistrates are documentary and testimonial evidence. *Documentary evidence* is tangible evidence in the form of a written document (such as a lease or a bill of sale), a photograph, or a recording. *Testimonial evidence* is given by a witness who is sworn and then placed on the stand to verbally relate facts that he or she knows from personal experience or observation; the witness may testify by answering specific questions, by telling his or her story in narrative form, or by both forms of testimony. In small claims court, most of the testimony is narrative. Rules governing these kinds of evidence are discussed below.

Judicial Notice

One other kind of evidence with which a magistrate should be familiar is judicially noticed evidence. Judicially noticed evidence is evidence about which there can be no reasonable dispute, such as "I-95 is an interstate highway." Taking judicial notice of evidence means the court declares it to exist without requiring the production of further evidence to establish it. It would be a waste of the court's time and the taxpayers' money to require proof of facts that are well known to everyone or that are readily verifiable, and magistrates should take judicial notice of such matters. A magistrate can judicially notice evidence either at a party's request, or on his or

---

2. Henry Brandis and Kenneth Broun, North Carolina Evidence (6th ed. 2004) § 5 (*citing* Cameron v. Cameron, 232 N.C. 686, 61 S.E.2d 913 (1950)).

her own initiative. Once judicial notice is taken of a matter, it is proven and no longer subject to dispute.[3]

No precise rules cover this area of the law of evidence, and a magistrate should take a common sense approach to it. Case law shows that the following facts are among those that have been considered proper subjects of judicial notice: that a municipality is located in a certain county, that the Neuse River in Pamlico County is large and navigable, that gasoline alone or in a mixture with kerosene is inflammable and highly explosive, the distance between two stations on a railroad, and the population of a region as shown by the last census reports.[4]

Direct and Circumstantial Evidence

A final evidentiary distinction may be useful to magistrates: that between direct and circumstantial evidence. *Direct evidence* is any evidence that, if believed, proves or disproves a material fact in a case. For example, on the issue of whether a traffic light was red when the defendant drove through it, testimony from a witness who was in the car behind defendant's that the witness saw that the light was red is direct evidence. *Circumstantial evidence* is evidence that, even if believed, will not conclusively establish the fact at issue; it is evidence of one fact that, if established, will *tend* to show that another fact—the one at issue—existed. On the issue of the defendant's speed as he or she drove through the light, testimony that shortly before the collision and four blocks from the light the defendant passed the witness traveling at a speed of approximately 25 mph is circumstantial evidence. A good example of the distinction between direct and circumstantial evidence can be illustrated by our national anthem, "The Star-Spangled Banner." Francis Scott Key wrote:

> Oh, say can you see by the dawn's early light,
> What so proudly we hailed at the twilight's last gleaming?
> Whose broad stripes and bright stars, through the perilous fight,
> O'er the ramparts we watched were so gallantly streaming?
> And the rockets' red glare, the bombs bursting in air,
> Gave proof through the night that our flag was still there.

Seeing the flag through the rockets' red glare and bombs bursting in air was direct evidence that the flag was still there; and the fact that the American flag was still there was circumstantial evidence that the fort had not fallen to the British.

The most important thing to remember about the distinction between direct and circumstantial evidence is that either or both may be used to prove a point, and a case established by circumstantial evidence is no less valid than one proven by direct evidence. A form of circumstantial evidence that magistrates may encounter frequently is evidence of a habit, custom, or usual practice of doing something introduced to show that the same thing was done in a routine

---

3. G.S. 8C-1, Rule 201.

4. State v. Painter, 261 N.C. 332; 333, 134 S.E.2d 638, 639 (1964); Miller v. Coppage, 261 N.C. 430; 435, 135 S.E.2d 1, 5 (1964); Stegall v. Catawba Oil Co., 260 N.C. 459, 462, 133 S.E.2d 138, 141 (1963); Johnson v. R.R., 140 N.C. 581, 587, 53 S.E. 362, 367 (1906); Mallard v. Eastern Carolina Reg'l Hous. Auth., 221 N.C. 334, 338, 20 S.E.2d 281, 285 (1942).

way on the occasion in question. Often this involves evidence of business practices such as giving receipts for certain payments but not for others, a usual method of accounting or bookkeeping, or a bank's custom of mailing notices of insufficient funds. Such evidence is admissible if it meets the tests of relevance and competence discussed later in this chapter. This kind of evidence should not be confused with circumstantial evidence of bad character used to show a propensity for the kind of behavior of which the defendant stands accused—for example, testimony from defendant's mother that the defendant has been stealing money from her purse since the age of ten and is therefore likely to have committed the bank robbery in question. This kind of circumstantial evidence is not admissible.

Presentation of Evidence

In the ordinary small claims case, the plaintiff first presents his or her witnesses and other evidence; then the defendant presents evidence in an effort to either weaken or disprove the plaintiff's case or to establish a defense. In most contested small claims cases, the presentation of evidence is likely to stop at this point. The plaintiff may, however, challenge the defendant's evidence by introducing rebuttal witnesses who will explain, modify, or contradict the testimony of the defendant's witnesses.

Formal examination of witnesses proceeds as follows: the party calling the witness first conducts what is known as the direct examination; then the opposing party may cross-examine the witness. The party who called the witness then may want to conduct a redirect examination, and his or her adversary may wish to conduct a recross-examination on any new information introduced on the redirect. The questioning of witnesses generally does not proceed beyond these four stages.

In small claims court, in fact, questioning of witnesses may take on a less-formal structure, with witnesses and parties engaging in more immediate back-and-forth conversation with the magistrate. The magistrate may address questions to a witness at any time[5] and should do so whenever the testimony needs clarifying or explaining.

Weight of the Evidence

The party requesting relief in a small claim action has the burden of proof. The plaintiff most often has this burden because he or she filed the complaint that initiated the action. However, the defendant may also present a claim for relief against the plaintiff (a counterclaim) and thus also bear the burden of proof on that claim. An easy way to remember who has the burden of proof is to ask "who would care if this claim was dismissed?"

The burden of proof is a two-pronged standard. First, the party requesting relief in a small claims action has the burden of presenting enough evidence in support of each legal element of his or her claim to prevent the magistrate from dismissing it: this duty is called the *burden of production* or the burden of going forward. If a party has satisfied the burden of producing enough evidence to avoid dismissal, he or she is said to have established a *prima facie* case.

---

5. G.S. 8C-1, Rule 614(b).

A *prima facie* case means the party has produced evidence sufficient to justify but not compel a favorable verdict.[6] In a negligence action, for example, the plaintiff's prima facie case consists of proving duty, breach of duty, causation, and damages. If the plaintiff does not present enough evidence on any one of these elements to persuade the magistrate that, if uncontradicted, this evidence is sufficient to support a judgment for the plaintiff, the magistrate must dismiss the case before hearing evidence from the defendant. G.S. 7A-222 explicitly states this proposition: "At the conclusion of plaintiff's evidence, the magistrate may render a judgment of dismissal if plaintiff has failed to establish a prima facie case."

If, on the other hand, the magistrate thinks that the evidence presented by the plaintiff, standing alone and uncontradicted, would support a judgment in the plaintiff's favor, then the magistrate must not render a judgment of dismissal. At this point the defendant can either produce evidence to support a defense or choose not to offer evidence and risk judgment for the plaintiff.

If the magistrate determines that a party with the burden of proof has presented sufficient evidence on each and every legal element of a claim to avoid dismissal, then the second part of the burden of proof—the burden of persuasion—becomes primary. The term *burden of persuasion* is essentially a fancy way of saying that a party must convince the magistrate that, based on all the evidence presented by both sides, his or her version of the facts is supported by the greater weight of the believable evidence (preponderance) and therefore that that party is entitled to prevail. The plaintiff has the burden of persuasion for every contested issue in his or her claim. A plaintiff who fails to persuade the magistrate will lose the case. On the other hand, if the defendant has presented an affirmative defense (for example, in a suit on an overdue account, argues that the statute of limitations has run) or a counterclaim, then the defendant has the burden of persuading the magistrate that his or her version of every contested issue in the defense or counterclaim is correct.

To satisfy the burden of persuasion, the party seeking relief must prove the case only by a *preponderance* of the evidence—sometimes called the greater weight of the evidence. A party's evidence preponderates when (1) it is more convincing than the other party's, and (2) it leads the magistrate to conclude that the facts as the party alleges them are more likely than not.

Determining whether the comparative weight and credibility of a party's evidence entitles that party to judgment is not an exact science. Weight and credibility are not functions of the number of witnesses or the volume of testimony presented on either side; the magistrate should not grant judgment to a party merely because he or she presented the most witnesses or the greatest amount of evidence. It is simply a question of whether the party with the burden of proof, on the basis of all of the evidence presented, has satisfied the magistrate by a preponderance (the greater weight) of the believable evidence.

Example 1. Barnes sues his neighbor, Whitaker, for $150 and testifies that he lent Whitaker $150 six months earlier, and Whitaker has never paid him. Whitaker testifies that he borrowed the money from Barnes but that before paying Barnes back, Barnes asked him to pick up his newspapers and mail and walk his dog while Barnes went on a two-week vacation. Whitaker testified that

---

6. BRANDIS AND BROUN, *supra* note 2, § 32.

Barnes told him if he would take care of these items while Barnes was away, "they would be even about the money lent." Barnes says he never said that. The magistrate finds both witnesses credible and is unable to determine which one is truthful. In that case Barnes, the plaintiff, has failed to meet the burden of persuasion, and therefore the magistrate should find that Barnes has failed to prove the case by the greater weight of the evidence and should dismiss the action.

The inexact process of weighing evidence may be complicated by the fact that formal presentation of evidence often is not observed in small claims court. The party bearing the burden of proof on an issue may not present all of his or evidence in a discrete chunk. The other party may intersperse his or her own evidence in the presentation, thus obscuring the need to assess whether the first party has met the burden of proof. Nonetheless, making this determination is the magistrate's first order of business.

Example 2. In a summary ejectment case the landlord testifies that he and the tenant entered into an oral month-to-month lease under which the tenant agreed to pay a rent of $300 on the first of every month. On February 1 the tenant did not pay rent, so on February 8 the landlord filed this action. The tenant testifies that she paid her rent in cash on February 3 but was not given a receipt. The landlord testifies that he always gives receipts for cash payments and the tenant agrees that in the past he did give receipts, but insists that this time he did not. Even if the magistrate finds the landlord's version of the facts more compelling than the tenant's, the landlord is not entitled to a judgment in his favor because he failed to meet the burden of proof. The landlord in a summary ejectment action must show (1) a landlord–tenant relationship, (2) when the rent was due, and how much it was, (3) that the tenant failed to pay the rent, and (4) that the landlord made a demand for the rent and waited ten days after that demand before bringing the action. The landlord failed to present evidence of element (4) and, therefore, the magistrate should dismiss his claim.

Admissibility of Evidence and Rules of Exclusion

An important concept in the law of evidence is *relevance*. Any evidence that makes the existence of an important fact in a party's case more or less likely than it would be without that evidence is relevant.[7] The connection between the evidence presented and the point to be proved must be reasonable and observable, not remote or conjectural. The line between what is relevant and what is irrelevant is difficult to draw and may change in given circumstances. For example, the North Carolina Supreme Court has held that evidence that the defendants were seen racing their automobiles twenty minutes before an accident occurred is irrelevant (on grounds of remoteness),[8] while evidence of the speed of the plaintiff's automobile one-quarter of a mile before an accident is relevant.[9]

All relevant evidence should be admitted unless a party makes a valid objection to it under the rules of evidence. The rules of evidence provide two specific exclusionary rules that parties frequently raise—the original writing rule and the ban on hearsay, which are discussed below.

---

7. G.S. 8C-1, Rule 401.

8. Corum v. Comer, 256 N.C. 252, 123 S.E.2d 473 (1962).

9. Honeycutt v. Strube, 261 N.C. 59, 134 S.E.2d 110 (1964).

Other rules, called testimonial privileges, deal with the circumstances in which witnesses who have special relationships to one party in a case can be barred from testifying. (These rules are discussed below in the section "Competency of Witnesses.") It bears repeating, though, that magistrates should admit all evidence unless a party specifically raises one of these objections.

The Original Writing or Best Evidence Rule

The original writing (sometimes called best evidence) rule deals with documentary evidence and states that if the contents of a document are in dispute, the original document must be introduced into evidence;[10] in other words, the document itself is the best evidence of its contents.[11] Under the original document rule, an exact copy of a document—such as a copy produced by photocopier, carbon paper, or photography—is usually considered the same as the original document. A handwritten copy of the contents of a typed document, on the other hand, would not qualify as a duplicate. The method of duplicating must ensure exact replication of the original and not allow human error. The only circumstance in which an original rather than a duplicate must be produced is when the authenticity of the original is being questioned.[12]

The best evidence rule most commonly applies when a document whose contents are in dispute is a legal document. For example, in a suit for summary ejectment in which the length of the tenant's term as specified in a written lease agreement is in dispute, the lease sets the legally binding terms of the agreement and must be produced. If the original document is lost and no exact copies are available, the party may prove the contents of the document by other evidence and must satisfactorily explain the failure to produce it.

The original writing rule does not come into play when the disputed facts exist independently of any document. A good example of a fact that exists independently of any document is a person's birth. Although most persons have birth certificates, it is impossible to argue that someone was never born if he or she cannot produce one. Compare this situation to one in which the question is whether a person is divorced. Because a person can only obtain a divorce by judicial order, it is quite possible to argue successfully that that person is still married if he or she cannot produce the decree.

Another example of a fact that exists independently of any documentation (and an important one for magistrates) is payment for goods received. Without producing bills, receipts, or canceled checks, a party may testify orally to expenses he or she incurred as a result of damage allegedly inflicted by the opposing party. If the party paid someone, that person received money regardless of whether the party can produce a receipt.

This last example raises an important point for a magistrate to remember. Much of the evidence a party presents to prove his or her point will be oral testimony, not documentary or other physical evidence. If oral testimony is credible—that is, if the magistrate believes it—he or she should give it as much weight and as much consideration as documentary or other physical evidence. Under the law, no kind of evidence counts more than another.

---

10. G.S. 8C-1, Rule 1002.
11. Wooten v. Grand United Order of Odd Fellows, 176 N.C. 52, 62, 96 S.E. 654, 659 (1918).
12. G.S. 8C-1, Rule 1003.

Authentication

Whenever a document is produced, the party offering it must prove that it is genuine, that is, must authenticate it.[13] The easiest, and perhaps most common, way to do this is to have both parties agree to the document's authenticity. If the document is a signed writing and the party against whom it is being introduced will not admit its authenticity, the party seeking to introduce it may have a witness testify that he or she is familiar with the handwriting or signature and that it belongs to the plaintiff or the defendant, as the case may be; or the witness may testify that he or she saw the paper being written or signed. A witness need not be a handwriting expert to give an opinion as to the genuineness of a particular specimen of handwriting or a signature so long as the witness is familiar with the handwriting of the person to whom the specimen or signature is imputed.[14] The magistrate, as the fact finder, may personally compare the handwritings and determine that a given person signed a particular document.

If the document in question is an unsigned writing or a writing produced entirely by mechanical means (such as a bill), the party seeking to introduce it may authenticate it with testimony from someone familiar with its production. Statements of account (discussed in more detail below) may be authenticated with an affidavit from a person qualified to testify in court about the account; oral testimony is not necessary to authenticate a statement of account unless one party disputes the accuracy of the statement.

A type of evidence closely akin to both documents and physical objects is the class that includes photographs, maps, and diagrams. These articles may be introduced in evidence to illustrate the testimony of a witness, thereby making the testimony more intelligible to the magistrate. For example, a tenant testifying as to the unfit condition of the premises as a violation of the Residential Rental Agreements Act might show photographs to illustrate the testimony. A photograph need not have been taken by the witness so long as he or she can identify it and attest to its accuracy. A photograph should not necessarily be excluded because it is not an exact reproduction or because it was not made at the time of the event to which the accompanying testimony relates. The magistrate may, however, exclude it if he or she thinks it is inaccurate or misleading because of changes that have occurred over time. A photograph may also be admissible as substantive evidence, that is, as evidence of what the photograph itself shows; for example, a picture showing the defendant pointing a gun at the plaintiff and the plaintiff gasping in fear may be evidence of assault without any accompanying testimony from a witness.[15] A photograph is also admissible to illustrate the testimony of a witness; for example, where an accident scene has been reconstructed, a witness may use a photo of that reconstruction to explain how the accident occurred.

13. G.S. 8C-1, Rule 901.
14. G.S. 8C-1, Rule 901(b)(2).
15. G.S. 8-97.

Hearsay

Hearsay is a statement, other than one made by a witness while testifying in court, that is offered to prove the truth or falsity of the matter contained in the statement. Generally, hearsay evidence is inadmissible.[16] The hearsay rule expresses a preference for live, in-court testimony subject to cross-examination. The main reason for excluding hearsay is that the person who made the out-of-court statement was not under oath at that time or subject to cross-examination. As there is no assurance that he or she was telling the truth or knew what he or she was talking about, the evidence is not reliable enough. Hearsay evidence can come in the form of oral testimony or documentary evidence.

Not all evidence about what someone said outside of court is hearsay. To be hearsay, testimony about an out-of-court statement must be introduced by a party seeking to use the statement to prove the truth of what it says. For example, in an automobile crash case in which the defendant allegedly ran a red light, the plaintiff's testimony that a man standing on the corner said "Geez, that guy drove straight through a red light into your car" is hearsay;[17] the plaintiff wants to use the statement to prove a part of his or her case. In-court testimony from the man himself that at the time of the accident he made the above statement would also be hearsay. It would not be hearsay, however, for the man to simply state that the light was red at the time of the accident.

When a statement is not introduced to prove the truth of what it asserts, but for some other purpose, it is not hearsay. Another example might help to clarify this point. In a battery case, Smith, the defendant, is trying to prove that he punched Jones, the plaintiff, in self-defense. Smith testifies that a friend of Jones told him an hour before the battery that "Jones is carrying around a baseball bat and he's coming to get you." If Smith is trying to prove that Jones was carrying a baseball bat and intended to beat him up, the statement made by Jones's friend is hearsay and inadmissible. If, on the other hand, Smith is only trying to prove that, because of the conversation with Jones's friend, he had a reasonable belief that he was in danger of great bodily harm—whether or not the statement was actually true—then the statement is not hearsay and should be admitted.

The above are examples of *testimony* that is and is not hearsay. Hearsay may also come in the form of documentary evidence. A very simple example of documentary hearsay is an affidavit introduced to prove the truth of its contents. An affidavit is an out-of-court statement reduced to writing and sworn to before a person authorized to administer an oath (e.g., a notary public). Another example of documentary hearsay might be a letter from the National Dry Cleaners' Association introduced by the defendant; in it, the association states that the plaintiff's sweater shrank because the fabric was defective, not because the defendant was negligent in cleaning the sweater.

Magistrates should keep in mind that hearsay, like other evidence subject to exclusion under the rules of evidence, should be admitted unless a party objects to it. In addition, the rules of evidence themselves create many exceptions to the rule excluding hearsay. These exceptions are

16. G.S. 8C-1, Rule 802.

17. It is possible that this statement would be admissible under an exception to the hearsay rule for excited utterances that is discussed below.

too numerous and complicated to make remembering them practical; the important thing to remember about these exceptions is that they admit hearsay evidence that is considered fairly reliable. Some of these exceptions require that the person who made the statement be unavailable to testify; others do not require unavailability. When an objection is raised to hearsay testimony, the party seeking to introduce it must indicate to the magistrate the specific basis on which it should be admissible.

The following subsections explain the most important of these exceptions. When appropriate, they provide an example of the sort of evidence that would be admitted under that exception.

Declarations against Interest

When a person has made a statement that is against his or her own interest—generally a financial interest—and is unavailable to testify, a witness who heard the statement may testify to it. Unavailable to testify does not mean that the witness had another appointment the day of the trial; it means that the witness is dead, out of the country, or that after due diligence a party cannot secure the live testimony of the witness. The rationale underlying this exception is that no one would make a statement that harms his or her interest if it were not true.

> *Example 3.* Jacobson brings an action against Young for recovery of possession of a cow. A witness for Jacobson testifies that one year ago, when Young and Brown were operating the farm jointly and Brown was still alive, Brown told him that Jacobson's cow had strayed over onto their farm and that he and Young were going to keep it and fatten it. Since Brown is now dead and the statement, when made, was against his ownership interest, the statement will be admitted under this exception to the hearsay rule.

Admissions

Any out-of-court statement a party to the action (either plaintiff or defendant) has made, if relevant to the issues and not subject to some specific exclusionary rule, is admissible. Such an admission will usually, though not always, be against the interest of the party making it. The reason for this exception to the hearsay rule is that a party to an action cannot object that he or she was not under oath or had no opportunity to cross-examine himself or herself when the statement was made; in effect, the party will not be allowed to call himself or herself a liar.

> *Example 4.* In a suit by Samson against Green to obtain payment for repairs he did on Green's house, the parties dispute whether or not they agreed that Samson would be paid for the work he did. Samson may introduce testimony from Green's neighbor, Gray, that Green said he owed Samson a bundle for all the work he did on the house. Because Green is a party to the action, this statement is an admission and may be allowed in evidence.

Spontaneous (or Excited) Utterances

If a person makes a statement during the excitement of an occurrence, or so soon thereafter that he or she would have had no time to think of a lie, that statement may be given in testimony by a witness who heard it.

> *Example 5.* Harry brings an action against Dewey for property damage resulting from a car crash in which Dewey's rate of speed is an issue. Minerva, a witness, may testify that she heard a passenger in Dewey's car say immediately after the accident, "I told you you were going too fast!" But if Minerva plans to testify that the statement by Dewey's passenger was made some four hours after the accident, it could no longer be classified as a spontaneous or excited utterance and would be inadmissible under the hearsay exclusion rule.

Regular Business Entries

When the record of a business transaction, or business entry, is made in the regular course of business at or near the time of the transaction and is authenticated by a witness who is familiar with the system under which it was made, it is admissible.

> *Example 6.* Smith brings an action on an account against Jones. At trial Jones says he paid the bill. Smith says Jones paid with a check that was returned for insufficient funds. If for some reason Smith cannot produce Jones's returned check, he may use properly authenticated bank records as evidence to establish whether Jones had a balance in his account on the date the check was delivered to Smith sufficient to cover the check in question.

Verified Statement of Account

G.S. 8-45 states: "In any action instituted in any court of this State upon an account for goods sold and delivered, for rents, for services rendered, or labor performed, or upon any oral contract for money loaned, a verified itemized statement of such account shall be received in evidence, and shall be deemed prima facie evidence of its correctness." This statute can be very useful in speeding up the collection of accounts when there is no real dispute and is relied upon by some creditors in small claim actions.

An account is sufficiently itemized under the statute if it sets forth a description of each item with price and catalogue number, if applicable. To be properly verified, the account must be accompanied by an affidavit (in this case, allowable hearsay) from a person who (1) would be a competent witness if called at the trial, (2) has personal knowledge of the account or is familiar with the books and records of the business,[18] and (3) who swears that the account is correct and just and that it presently constitutes a debt owing from the defendant to the plaintiff. The affidavit must be from someone who has first-hand familiarity with the accounts; so an affidavit, for instance, from a party's attorney that the statement of account is correct generally would not satisfy the requirement.

---

18. Johnson Serv. Co. v. Richard J. Curry & Co., 29 N.C. App. 166, 167–68, 223 S.E.2d 565, 567 (1976).

Usually the verified, itemized statement is attached to the complaint itself when it is filed, but it may be brought to trial and introduced at that time. The party seeking payment then offers the statement into evidence at trial. If undisputed, this statement of account can constitute the entirety of the plaintiff's evidence. If, however, the defendant disputes the accuracy of the statement—for example, by saying that he or she made payments that are not reflected in the account or that he or she never bought some of the items listed—the plaintiff will have to produce more evidence. Such evidence might include (1) a witness to testify about how the statement is produced, who produced it, and why it is unlikely to be in error; (2) a witness who can testify that he or she had seen the defendant purchase the items in question; or (3) a receipt signed by the defendant for the items in question.

Example 7. Jones Service Station brings an action on an unpaid account against Smith for three tires. If the service station bookkeeper verifies the account and the brand, size, and cost of each tire are itemized in it, the account should be admitted in evidence. If the defendant does not dispute the account's accuracy, no further evidence is needed. The bookkeeper need not be present in court; the plaintiff or the plaintiff's attorney need only submit the verified itemized statement.

Competency of Witnesses

As a general rule, any person who has the mental capacity to understand the nature of an oath and to relate his or her experience or observations in an understandable manner is permitted to testify.[19] This means that a child or a person who is mentally retarded can be a competent witness as long as he or she understands the oath and is able to relate his or her testimony to the magistrate in an intelligible manner. There is no age below which a child, as a matter of law, is incompetent to testify.[20]

Even though all persons are presumed competent to testify, not all persons can be compelled to testify. Rules that prohibit forcing certain people to testify are called *testimonial privileges* and are based on the state's desire to encourage and protect confidential relations between certain persons. The following list discusses these privileged communications.

1. Neither husband nor wife may be compelled in a civil lawsuit to testify about confidential communications between them, though each may voluntarily consent to testify. Spouses may be compelled to testify, however, about other evidence.[21]
2. An attorney cannot, without his or her client's consent, testify about confidential communications received from the client. Three requirements must be met before the client can successfully claim the attorney–client privilege: (a) the relation of attorney and client must have existed when the communication was made; (b) the communication must have been made in confidence—that is, not in the presence of third parties or with the intent that it be divulged; and (c) the communication must relate to the matter for which the attorney was being consulted. The client alone may waive the privilege.

19. G.S. 8C-1, Rule 601.
20. State v. Jenkins, 83 N.C. App. 616, 621, 351 S.E.2d 299, 302 (1986).
21. G.S. 8-56.

3. A member of the clergy cannot testify to confidential communications made to him or her in his or her professional capacity under such circumstances that disclosure would violate a sacred or moral trust.[22] In open court, the communicant may waive the privilege.

4. A doctor cannot, over the objection of his or her patient, testify to confidential communications the patient made to him or her. However, a magistrate who believes that the testimony is necessary for the proper administration of justice may compel disclosure. This privilege extends to hospital records prepared by doctors or at their direction as well as to oral statements made by the patient to his or her doctor. The communications or information must have been necessary for the doctor to the treat or prescribe for the patient properly.[23] The doctor–patient privilege does not apply in cases of child abuse.[24] The same rules apply to psychologists, nurses, licensed marital and family therapists, private social workers, licensed counselors, and optometrists.[25]

5. A certified school counselor cannot testify concerning information acquired as part of his or her service unless the student waives the privilege in open court. However, the magistrate may compel disclosure if he or she believes the information is necessary for the proper administration of justice.[26]

Another testimonial privilege is the Fifth Amendment constitutional privilege against self-incrimination: no person may be compelled to give incriminating evidence against himself or herself.[27] An ordinary witness in a civil case can be compelled to take the witness stand but cannot be compelled to answer a question when the answer would incriminate him or her. A statement is incriminating if it tends to show that the witness has committed some criminal act or been engaged in some activity for which he or she could be criminally prosecuted. Mere damage to the witness's reputation or liability to civil suit because of the answer is not enough to permit the witness to claim the privilege. The privilege should not be granted automatically whenever the witness claims it. The magistrate must determine from the circumstances that the question probably calls for an incriminating answer (in other words, an answer that would require the witness to admit to a criminal act). The magistrate must be careful not to abuse the privilege during this inquiry. To claim the privilege successfully, the witness need not show that his or her answer would be a direct admission of guilt; he or she need only show that it would be a link in a chain of evidence that might lead to conviction. If the defendant in a civil case pleads the Fifth Amendment right against self-incrimination, the magistrate may use that invocation of the right to infer that the defendant's truthful testimony would have been unfavorable to him or

---

22. G.S. 8-53.2.
23. G.S. 8-53.
24. G.S. 8-53.1.
25. G.S. 8-53.3, G.S. 8-53.13, G.S. 8-53.5, G.S. 8-53.7, G.S. 8-53.8, G.S. 8-53.9.
26. G.S. 8-53.4.
27. U.S. CONST. amend. IV (as made applicable to the states through the Fourteenth Amendment); N.C. CONST. art. I, § 23. See Malloy v. Hogan, 378 S. U. 1, 84 S. Ct. 1489, 12 L.Ed.2d 653 (1964).

her.[28] On the other hand, the privilege to refuse to answer a proper question on the basis of self-incrimination is intended to be a shield and not a sword. Therefore, the plaintiff cannot claim the Fifth Amendment right against self-incrimination and refuse to answer questions that are material and essential to the defendant's defense and continue on with the claim; he or she must decide whether to testify or to claim the Fifth Amendment right against self-incrimination and dismiss the claim.[29]

A witness in an ordinary civil case cannot claim a blanket privilege for his or her entire testimony and thereby refuse to testify at all. The witness must claim the privilege for each specific question as it is asked if he or she thinks the answer would incriminate him or her. The witness may, of course, waive the privilege by voluntarily testifying about transactions upon which a criminal prosecution could be based; once he or she relates part of the details of an incriminating transaction, he or she cannot claim the privilege with respect to the rest of that transaction.

> *Example 8.* A landlord brings a summary ejectment action against a tenant on the basis of criminal activity. At the trial, landlord puts on evidence that the tenant sold controlled substances from his apartment. The tenant has been charged with sale of controlled substances but not yet tried. When asked about whether he was involved in the sale of controlled substances, the tenant asserts his Fifth Amendment right against self-incrimination and asks that the lawsuit be postponed until the criminal matter has been disposed of. The magistrate may rule on the case and may infer guilt from the defendant's assertion of the privilege against self-incrimination.

Conclusion

Magistrates need to have some familiarity with the rules discussed above. They need not, however, commit them to memory or understand every nuance of them. As discussed above, the rules are unlikely to come into play unless an attorney is present; and in such cases, magistrates do not have to rule on the attorney's objections unless they want to. It is sufficient in small claims court to try not to base a judgment on inadmissible evidence.

The most important evidentiary concepts magistrates must remember are that (1) all relevant evidence is admissible unless a rule specifically excludes it; and (2) no relevant evidence should be excluded unless a party or his or her attorney raises an objection based on such a rule.

---

28. *In re* Estate of Trogdon, 330 N.C. 143, 151–52, 409 S.E.2d 897, 902 (1991); Fedoronko v. Am. Defender Life Insur. Co, 69 N.C. App. 655, 658, 318 S.E.2d 244, 246 (1984).

29. Sugg v. Field, 139 N.C. App. 160, 164, 532 S.E.2d 843, 845–46 (2000); McKillop v. Onslow County, 139 N.C. App. 53, 62–64, 532 S.E.2d 594, 600–01 (2000).

Chapter IX

The Marriage Ceremony

Probably the most common civil duty the magistrate is requested to perform is the marriage ceremony. To accomplish this function properly, it is useful for the magistrate to have a general knowledge of the legal prerequisites for a man and woman to become husband and wife, and the magistrate must have specific knowledge of the statutory requirements of his or her role as the solemnizing official in this ceremony.

General Requirements

The requirements for a valid marriage are set out in Chapter 51 of the North Carolina General Statutes (hereinafter G.S.).[1] A marriage license, issued by the register of deeds of any county in the state, is a requisite for the marriage of a consenting male and female. Unmarried persons eighteen years of age or older may apply for a license; persons between the ages of sixteen and eighteen may do so with the consent of a parent, guardian, or person having legal custody of the applicant. A person between the ages of fourteen and sixteen may marry only if a district court judge, after determining that he or she meets the statutory requirements, enters an order authorizing that person to marry.[2] Residence in North Carolina is not required to obtain a license.

Bigamous marriages are void. A marriage between persons nearer of kin than first cousins is voidable,[3] as is the marriage of a person who is underage, has certain physical defects such as impotency, or lacks the will or understanding to contract for marriage at the time of the ceremony. Under certain circumstances, marriages entered into under false representations of

---

1. For a detailed description of the marriage laws, *see* Janet Mason, *North Carolina Marriage Laws and Procedures,* 4th ed. (Chapel Hill, N.C.: UNC School of Government, 2002).

2. An unmarried female who is more than 14 years of age, but less than 16 years of age, and is pregnant or has given birth to a child or a male who is more than 14 years of age but less than 16 years of age who is the putative father of a child, either born or unborn, may marry if the district court judge finds that the person is capable of assuming the responsibilities of marriage and that the marriage will serve the best interests of the underage party. N.C. GEN. STAT. § 51-2.1 (hereinafter G.S.).

3. First cousins may marry in North Carolina, but double first cousins (fathers and mothers of both are brother and sister) may not marry.

pregnancy are also voidable. Interracial marriages are lawful.[4] Persons of the same gender may not wed in North Carolina; nor does the state recognize marriages between two men or two women entered into in another state.

Marriage by consent of the couple alone (common law marriage) is not recognized in North Carolina.

The duty to determine whether a couple meets the requirements to marry falls to the register of deeds, not the magistrate.

G.S. 51-1 and G.S. 7A-292 set out the magistrate's basic authority to perform the marriage ceremony. In North Carolina, only magistrates and ministers are authorized to perform marriages. Performing marriages is a duty of the office of magistrates like any other duty, such as issuing warrants or trying small claims cases. A magistrate may decline to perform the ceremony only if he or she has legitimate doubts about the validity of the license or the lawfulness of the proposed marriage.

Marriage License

Before marrying a couple, the magistrate must be given a marriage license signed by the register of deeds or a deputy or assistant register of deeds of any county in North Carolina; the license must have been issued within sixty days before the magistrate performs the ceremony. A magistrate who performs a ceremony more than sixty days after the license was issued or without a license is guilty of a misdemeanor and subject to a penalty of $200. Notwithstanding the penalty to the magistrate, the marriage itself is valid.[5] Also, the requirement that the license be in the magistrate's possession is strictly enforced. In one court case a justice of the peace who married a couple knowing that the license was in the mail and addressed to him was held by the North Carolina Supreme Court to be liable for the $200 penalty.[6]

The magistrate receives two copies of the marriage license. A certificate the magistrate must complete after performing the marriage ceremony is included as a part of the license. The magistrate must fill in the necessary information on both copies, sign both copies, obtain the signatures of at least two witnesses (with their places of residence) on both copies, and return them both to the office of the register of deeds who issued the license. The reason both copies must contain original signatures is that the magistrate is creating two originals—one will be kept by the register of deeds office and one by the state registrar in the Department of Health and Human Services.[7] The copies must be returned to the register's office within ten days after the ceremony is performed. Failure to complete the certificate and return the license to the register within ten days after the ceremony constitutes a misdemeanor and subjects the magistrate to a penalty of $200.

---

4. In 1967 the United States Supreme Court declared miscegenation statutes unconstitutional (Loving v. Virginia, 388 U.S. 1, 87 S. Ct. 1817, 18 L. Ed. 2d 1010 (1967)), and North Carolina repealed its statute in 1973 (G.S. 14-81 repealed by 1973 N.C. Sess. Laws ch. 108).

5. Magget v. Roberts, 112 N.C. 71, 16 S.E. 919 (1893); State v. Parker, 106 N.C. 711, 11 S.E. 517 (1890).

6. Wooley v. Bruton, 184 N.C. 438, 114 S.E. 628 (1922).

7. G.S. 130A-110.

Pre-Ceremony Checks

Before performing the ceremony, the magistrate should check the license and certificate to determine that

1. It bears the correct names of the prospective bride and groom. If it does not, only the issuing register deeds can correct it and the ceremony should not be performed until this correction has been made.
2. It was issued within sixty days immediately preceding the date of the ceremony. If more than sixty days have elapsed since it was issued, the license is void and the magistrate should refuse to conduct the ceremony.
3. The license was filled out and signed by the register of deeds or an assistant or deputy register of deeds of any county in North Carolina.
4. The fee for conducting the ceremony has been collected.

Location of the Ceremony

A magistrate may marry a couple anywhere within the magistrate's county; however, the magistrate is not required to go outside his or her office to perform a wedding. Nor is a magistrate required to perform a marriage at times other than those when the magistrate is on duty. Whether he or she performs marriages outside the office or only in the office during normal office hours is within the magistrate's discretion.

Sometimes a magistrate is asked to perform a marriage outside the magistrate's county of appointment, usually for a relative or close friend. Because G.S. 51-1 specifies that a magistrate is a proper official to marry persons in North Carolina and does not limit his or her authority to one county, a magistrate may perform a marriage ceremony anywhere in the state.

Marriage Ceremony

No particular marriage ceremony is prescribed by law; therefore any ritual that satisfies the moral convictions of the parties concerned is sufficient if the following requirements are fulfilled: (1) the man and woman must consent to take each other as husband and wife; (2) this consent must be "freely, seriously and plainly, expressed by each in the presence of the other . . . in the presence of . . . a magistrate"; and (3) the magistrate must declare that such persons are husband and wife.[8] G.S. 51-6 requires that at least two witnesses must be present. The witnesses must be persons capable of testifying that they were present at the marriage and able to sign their names. Sometimes the couple will bring minor children from a previous marriage to be witnesses, and the fact that the children are minors does not automatically prohibit them from being witnesses. Under general North Carolina law, minors are not disqualified from testifying as witnesses in court cases;[9] therefore since the marriage statute does not require witnesses to be adults, minors can be witnesses in that situation as long as they are capable of understanding what they are witnessing.

8. G.S. 51-1.
9. G.S. 8C-1, Rule 601; State v. Jenkins, 83 N.C. App. 616, 351 S.E.2d 299 (1986).

Marriages by proxy (in other words, someone standing in for the groom or the bride) and marriage ceremonies conducted over the telephone are not authorized in North Carolina. G.S. 51-1 clearly requires the parties being married to recite their vows in the presence of each other and in the presence of a magistrate or minister.

A legally sufficient ceremony would be: "Do you (name man) take (name woman) to be your lawful wedded wife? [Pause for response.] Do you (name woman) take (name man) to be your lawful wedded husband? [Pause for response.] I now pronounce you husband and wife." However, most magistrates prefer to conduct a ceremony with more ritual.

A new magistrate would do well to consult an experienced magistrate for advice concerning the conduct of the marriage ceremony. For convenient reference, examples of ceremonies that may be used are set out as an appendix at the end of this chapter. The magistrate may not to refuse to perform a marriage because the applicants do not meet certain religious tests. For couples who want a strictly civil ceremony, sample ceremony No. 1 has been included. Many couples select a magistrate to perform the marriage ceremony specifically because they do not want a religious ceremony. Therefore, magistrates should be prepared to conduct a nonreligious ceremony if the couple asks for it. In fact, some magistrates always use a civil ceremony. Some couples may prefer a more traditional ceremony with religious references; sample ceremony No. 2 or No. 3 in the appendix can then be used if it suits the couple. A sample civil ceremony in English and Spanish is also included as Ceremony No. 4.

Customarily, the man and woman stand facing the magistrate, the man to the woman's right, with the witnesses standing slightly behind and to the side of the couple. The ceremony should be conducted with dignity and seriousness.

Reasons for Refusing to Conduct Ceremony

In certain circumstances the magistrate may refuse to marry a couple who appears before him or her during regular office hours with a valid marriage license and the cash to pay the fee. The most common reason is that the couple must freely, seriously, and plainly consent to marry each other. If the magistrate believes they are not able to do that either because of coercion or because one or both of the parties is too drunk to "freely and seriously" consent, the magistrate may refuse to conduct the ceremony. Another issue that may arise is whether one party cannot speak or understand English. The question for the magistrate is whether the person either understands enough English to be able to consent to the marriage or brings an interpreter. As mentioned above, a sample marriage ceremony in both English and Spanish is included in the appendix; this may be helpful when the magistrate can speak Spanish or when the person who may not fully understand English can read Spanish.

Certificate

When the ceremony is over, the magistrate must fill out and sign, and have both witnesses sign, both copies of the certificate that appears on the license. If this is not done, or if the license and certificate (both copies) are not returned to the register of deeds who issued them within ten days after the ceremony, the magistrate is subject to a penalty of $200. Some magistrates have the witnesses sign before the ceremony because in the excitement of the event, they may leave as soon as the ceremony is over. However, since the witnesses are signing that they witnessed the marriage ceremony, the better practice is for the magistrate to have the witnesses sign the certificate after the ceremony. In no event should the magistrate sign the certificate before conducting the ceremony. Both copies of the license and certificate must be returned to the register of deeds, not given to the couple. In some counties, the register of deeds prepares an unofficial "certificate" of marriage that the magistrate may sign and give to the couple at the end of the ceremony.

Fees

Magistrates are required by G.S. 7A-309 to charge a fee of $20 for performing the marriage ceremony. Generally, this fee should be collected before the ceremony is performed. The magistrate must give the couple a receipt for the $20 and must remit the fee to the clerk of superior court in the magistrate's county. Even if the magistrate performs a marriage outside his or her county of appointment, the fee should be returned to the clerk of the magistrate's home county, and the magistrate should note on the receipt the county where the ceremony was performed. The magistrate is not authorized to collect any additional fees or to accept any voluntary gift or gratuity for performing the ceremony.

> ***Example 1.*** Magistrate Jones is a magistrate in Camden County. Her best friend, Tamika, is getting married and wants Magistrate Jones to officiate at the wedding on the beach in Dare County. Tamika and her fiancé work in Pasquotank County so they get their marriage license there on June 1. Magistrate Jones conducts the marriage ceremony in Dare County on June 30. Magistrate Jones and the two witnesses must sign both copies of the marriage license, and Magistrate Jones must send both copies to the Register of Deeds Office of Pasquotank County. Magistrate Jones collects $20 and sends it to her clerk in Camden County, writing on the receipt "For a marriage performed in Dare County."

Appendix 1

Sample Marriage Ceremonies

No. 1 (Civil)

We are assembled here at this time to join (name man) and (name woman) in marriage according to the laws of the State of North Carolina. It is our firm belief that those who enter this relationship do cherish a mutual esteem and love; and do promise to bear with each other's infirmities and weaknesses; to comfort each other in sickness, trouble and sorrow; in honesty and industry to provide for each other and for their household, and to be mindful always that marriage is designed for the happiness and welfare of mankind and therefore to be entered into advisedly and discreetly and in good faith.

(*Then the magistrate shall say to the man:*)

_____, will you have this woman to be your wife, and will you love her, comfort her, honor and keep her in sickness and in health; and, forsaking all others, keep only unto her as long as you both shall live? (*Then the man shall answer, "I will." Then the magistrate shall say to the woman:*)

_____, will you have this man to be your husband, and will you love him, comfort him, honor and keep him in sickness and in health; and forsaking all others, keep only unto him as long as you both shall live? (*The woman shall answer "I will." Then the magistrate shall cause the man with his right hand to take the woman by her right hand, and to say after him as follows:*)

"I, _____, take you _____ to be my wife; to have and to hold from this day forward, for better, for worse, for richer, for poorer, in sickness and in health, to love and to cherish, and thereto I pledge you my faith." (*The woman shall likewise say after the magistrate:*)

"I, _____, take you _____ to be my husband; to have and to hold from this day forward, for better, for worse, for richer, for poorer, in sickness and in health, to love and to cherish, and thereto I pledge you my faith.'

(*If the parties desire a ring ceremony, the man shall then hand a ring to the magistrate, who shall return it to him and direct him to place it on the third finger of the woman's left hand, and shall direct the man to repeat after him the following words to the woman:*)

This ring I give you, in token and pledge of my constant faith and abiding love. (*For a double-ring ceremony the magistrate shall do similarly as above.*)

(*Then the magistrate shall say to all present:*)

By the authority committed to me as a magistrate of the State of North Carolina I declare that _____ and _____ are now husband and wife according to the laws of the State.

No. 2 (Religious)

My friends, you stand now in the presence of God and the faces of these witnesses, to be united, under the law of this state, in the bonds of holy matrimony; and since marriage is ordained of God and is an institution for the preservation of the race and the happiness of all mankind, it is recognized as such everywhere and approved of all men as an honorable estate. Our nation and its prosperity are founded upon the homes of the people and for this reason our government has set up laws for its protection and preservation.

For inasmuch as you declared your love for each other and have determined between yourselves to enter into this holy and honorable estate, and I require you now to give truthful answers to the questions ordained by the laws of the State of North Carolina. Do you (*man's first name*), take this woman to be your lawful wedded wife to have and to hold, to love, honor and cherish, and to keep yourself only unto her as long as ye both shall live? (*The man shall answer, "I do."*)

Do you (*woman's first name*), take this man to be your lawful wedded husband, to have and to hold, to love honor and cherish, and to keep yourself only unto him so long as ye both shall live? (*The woman shall answer "I do."*)

You will now join hands, (*man's name*), repeat after me: "I, (*name of man*) take thee (*woman's name*) to be my lawful wedded wife and I promise before God and these witnesses to be thy loving and faithful husband, in riches and in poverty, in sickness and in health, and, forsaking all others to keep me only unto thee, so long as we both shall live."

(Woman's name), repeat after me: "I, (*woman's name*) take thee (*man's name*), to be my lawful wedded husband and I promise before God and these witnesses to be thy loving and faithful wife, in riches and in poverty, in sickness and in health, and, forsaking all others to keep me only unto thee, so long as we both shall live."

(*The magistrate shall then ask for the ring, returning it to the man, who shall then place it on the third finger of the woman's left hand. Then the magistrate shall say:*)

For inasmuch as you (*man's name*) and you (*woman's name*) have made these vows and plighted your troth before God and these witnesses, by the authority vested in me by the laws of the State of North Carolina, I now pronounce you husband and wife. What, therefore, God hath joined together, let no man put asunder. Amen.

No. 3 (Religious)

We are gathered here in the sight of God, and in the presence of these witnesses, to join together this man and this woman in holy matrimony; which is an honorable estate, instituted of God in the time of man's innocence. Into this holy estate these two persons present come now to be joined.

I require and charge you both, that if either of you know any impediment why you may not be lawfully joined together in matrimony, you do now confess it.

(*Then the magistrate shall say to the man:*)

_____, wilt thou have this woman to be thy wedded wife, to live together after God's ordinance in the holy estate of matrimony; wilt thou love her, comfort her, honor and keep her, in sickness and in health; and forsaking all others, keep thee only unto her, so long as ye both shall live? (*Then the man shall answer "I will." Then the magistrate shall say to the woman:*)

_____, wilt thou have this man to be thy wedded husband, to live together after God's ordinance in the holy estate of matrimony; wilt thou love, honor, and keep him in sickness and in health; forsaking all others, keep thee only unto him, so long as ye both shall live?" (*Then the woman shall answer, "I will." If the parties desire a ring ceremony, the man shall then hand a ring to the magistrate, who shall return it to him, and direct him to place it on the third finger of the woman's left hand, and shall direct the man to repeat after him the following words to the woman:*)

With this ring, I thee wed, and with my worldly goods I thee endow.

(*The magistrate and those present may then repeat the Lord's Prayer, as follows:*)

Our Father, Who Art in heaven, Hallowed be Thy Name. Thy kingdom come, Thy will be done, on earth as it is in heaven. Give us this day our daily bread. And forgive us our trespasses, as we forgive those who trespass against us. And lead us not into temptation, but deliver us from evil. For thine is the kingdom, and the power, and the glory forever. Amen.

(*Then the magistrate shall join right hands of the man and woman, and say:*)

Forasmuch as (*name of woman*) and (*name of man*) have consented together in holy wedlock, and have given and pledged their troth, each to the other, and have declared the same by joining hands; and by virtue of the power vested in me as a magistrate of _____ County, North Carolina, I do pronounce you husband and wife.

No. 4 (Civil Spanish)

We are gathered here at this time to join _____ (man's name) and _____ (woman's name) in marriage according to the laws of the Great State of North Carolina.

Estamos aquí congregados para unir en matrimonio a _____ y _____ de acuerdo con las leyes del gran estado de Carolina del Norte.

Being mindful always that marriage is designed for the happiness and welfare of mankind and therefore, to be entered into advisedly and discreetly and in good faith, come _____ (man's name) and _____ (woman's name) to be wedded together in this honorable estate.

Consciente de que el matrimonio es para la felicidad y el bienestar de la humanidad, se deberá iniciar con conocimiento de causa, con discreción y en buena fe. Se presentan ahora _____ y _____ para casarse e iniciar la vida conyugal.

I now require and charge you both, that if either of you know of any reason why you may not lawfully be joined together in matrimony you do now confess it.

Ahora, les exijo y ordeno a los dos que si saben de alguna razón por la cual no se pueden unir legalmente en matrimonio, la confiesen ahora.

(the Magistrate shall say to the man)

_____ (man's name), will you have this woman to be your wife, and will you love her, comfort her, honor and keep her in sickness and health and forsaking all others, keep only unto her as long as you both shall live?

_____ ¿ quieres recibir a esta mujer como esposa, amándola y respetándola en lo favorable y en lo adverso, con salud o enfermedad, y prometes serle fiel todos los días de tu vida?

(the Magistrate shall say to the woman)

_____ woman's name), will you have this man to be your husband, and will you love him, comfort him, honor and keep him in sickness and health and forsaking all others, keep only unto him as long as you both shall live?

_____ ¿ quieres recibir a este hombre como esposo, amándolo y respetándolo en lo favorable y en lo adverso, con salud o enfermedad, y prometes serle fiel todos los días de tu vida?

You will join hands.

Dense la mano.

(If they have rings—man places ring on woman's finger)

_____ (man's name), repeat after me:

_____ repite lo que digo:

(continued)

I, _____ (man's name), take you (woman's name), to be my lawful wedded wife and I promise to be your loving and faithful husband.

Yo, _____, te recibo, _____ a ser mi legítima esposa y prometo ser tu esposo para amarte fielmente durante nuestra vida.

(If they have rings—woman places ring on man's finger)

_____ (woman's name), repeat after me:

_____ *repite lo que digo:*

I _____ (woman's name), take you (man's name), to be my lawful wedded husband and I promise to be your loving and faithful wife.

Yo, _____, te recibo, _____, a ser mi legítimo esposo y prometo ser tu esposa para amarte fielmente durante nuestra vida.

By the authority committed to me as a Magistrate of the Great State of North Carolina I declare that (man's name) and (woman's name) are now husband and wife according to the laws of this state.

Por la autoridad que se me ha conferido como juez magistrado del gran estado de Carolina del Norte, yo declaro que _____ y _____ ahora son nuevos esposos de acuerdo con las leyes de este estado.

Chapter X

Miscellaneous Duties and Powers of a Magistrate

In addition to the power to try civil and criminal cases, magistrates are authorized under Section 7A-292 of the North Carolina General Statutes (hereinafter G.S.) to perform various other functions. Some of these functions are quasi-judicial, civil, or simply ministerial. One of these functions, the civil ceremony of marriage, is the subject of separate treatment in Chapter IX.

Assignment of a Year's Allowance

Article 4[1] of G.S. Ch. 30 provides for assignment of a year's allowance in the amount of $10,000 to a decedent's surviving spouse and an allowance of $2,000 to certain of the decedent's children. The allowances come from the decedent's money or other personal property but not from any real property in the estate.

The purpose of these allowances is to provide support for the spouse and children in the year following the decedent's death. The spouse and children take their allowances free from any lien or judgment against the decedent's estate, which means that the allowances take precedence over a general creditor's claim against the estate for money owed. The spouse and children do not, however, take better title to an item of personal property than the decedent had: if, for example, the spouse receives as part of the allowance a car on which a lien exists, the lien remains.[2]

Because either the clerk of court or a magistrate may assign the year's allowance, magistrates in some counties no longer perform this function.[3]

---

1. N.C. GEN. STAT. §§ 30-15 through -26 (hereinafter G.S.).

2. Williams v. Jones, 95 N.C. 504, 507 (1886).

3. In 1997 the law was changed to allow the clerk as well as the magistrate to assign year allowances. S.L. 1997-310.

Persons Entitled to an Allowance

A surviving spouse of a decedent is entitled to the allowance unless he or she has forfeited the right in a legally binding contract,[4] such as a separation agreement,[5] or by forfeiting his or her rights under G.S. 31A-1. Under the latter statute, a spouse forfeits his or her rights by abandoning a spouse,[6] committing adultery that has not been condoned,[7] or knowingly contracting a bigamous marriage. It makes no difference whether the surviving spouse is a husband or a wife[8] or whether the decedent died intestate or left a will. If the decedent did leave a will, the allowance is charged against the share of the estate left to the surviving spouse. If the surviving spouse claims an elective share,[9] however, he or she is entitled to the year's allowance in addition to the statutory share.[10]

Since the purpose of the statute is to protect the state's residents by providing them with money to live on while an estate is being settled,[11] the surviving spouse must be a resident of North Carolina to receive the allowance. If the surviving spouse resided in another state when his or her spouse died and the decedent owned personal property in North Carolina, the surviving spouse is not entitled to have a year's allowance assigned in North Carolina.[12] Even if the couple had resided in another state and after the death the surviving spouse moves to and becomes a resident of North Carolina, he or she is not entitled to assignment of a year's allowance in North Carolina.[13] If the decedent was a resident of another state but owned personal property in North Carolina and the surviving spouse was a resident of North Carolina at the time of the spouse's death, the surviving spouse may be assigned a year's allowance in North Carolina.[14]

Each of the decedent's children under the age of eighteen is entitled to the allowance.[15] "Child" includes a natural child of the decedent, an adopted child, a child with whom the widow is pregnant at the time of her husband's death, or any other child residing with the deceased and to whom the deceased or surviving parent stood in loco parentis.[16] An illegitimate

---

4. *In re* Estate of Cline, 103 N.C. App. 83, 404 S.E.2d 178 (1991) (antenuptial agreement).

5. Lane v. Scarborough, 19 N.C. App. 32, 198 S.E.2d 45, *rev'd on other grounds,* 284 N.C. 407, 200 S.E.2d 622 (1973).

6. Locust v. Pitt County Mem'l Hosp., Inc., 358 N.C. 113, 121, 591 S.E.2d 543, 548 (2004).

7. *In re* Estate of Trogdon, 330 N.C. 143, 146–47, 409 S.E.2d 897, 899 (1991).

8. G.S. 30-15. Formerly, only the wife was entitled to the allowance.

9. G.S. 30-3.1 through -3.6. A surviving spouse who is left less than a certain percentage of his or her spouse's estate may claim a certain statutory share of the estate—called an elective share.

10. First Union Nat'l Bank v. Melvin, 259 N.C. 255, 130 S.E.2d 387 (1963). However, any year's allowance awarded is included in the property passing to the spouse to determine whether the spouse qualifies for an elective share. G.S. 30-3.3.

11. "[It is] a humane provision to keep her and her children from suffering and from being a county charge." Jones v. Layne, 144 N.C. 600, 602, 57 S.E. 372, 373 (1907).

12. Simpson v. Cureton, 97 N.C. 112 (1887).

13. Medley v. Dunlap, 90 N.C. 527 (1884); 40 N.C. Op. Att'y Gen. 35 (1969).

14. Jones v. Layne, 144 N.C. 600, 604, 57 S.E. 372, 373 (1907).

15. G.S. 30-17.

16. *In loco parentis* means in the place of the parent and applies to a person who has assumed the status and obligations of a parent without a formal adoption. *In re* A.P., 165 N.C. App. 841, 845, 600 S.E.2d 9, 12 (2004).

child of a deceased father is not entitled to an allowance unless the father has recognized his paternity of the child by deed, will, or other writing. In addition, the law provides that a child younger than twenty-two years of age who is a full-time college student or a child younger than twenty-one years of age who has been declared mentally incompetent or who is totally disabled is entitled to the allowance. The child's allowance is paid to the surviving parent if the child resides with a parent. If the child does not reside with a parent, it is paid to the child's guardian if one has been appointed or to the clerk of superior court if there is no guardian.[17]

It is unclear to whom the allowance should be paid in the two situations in which the decedent's adult children are entitled to the allowance: that is, when they are full-time students who are at least eighteen but under twenty-two years of age or are under twenty-one but are totally disabled or have been declared mentally incompetent. If the adult student has a parent who is providing support, it probably will not be an issue; if he or she has been declared mentally incompetent, the child will have a guardian to whom the allowance will be paid. However, if the adult son or daughter has no living parent and has not been adjudicated incompetent, he or she will not have a guardian, and in many cases it probably does not make sense to pay the allowance to the clerk rather than directly to the adult child.

Whether the residency requirement applies to the decedent's children is also unclear: no state court has ruled specifically on the question, and the statute does not address it. The statute itself provides that allowance shall be paid to "any child under the age of 18 years" and specifies that the allowance be paid to the surviving spouse if he or she is the parent of the child in question, or to a surviving parent who is other than the decedent's surviving spouse. Thus the statute clearly contemplates a situation in which the decedent has children from a former relationship—children whose right to the allowance does not depend on being members of the surviving spouse's family. Nonetheless, as case law long ago established the principle that the allowance's purpose is to support residents of the state and prevent them from becoming county charges,[18] it is likely that the court would apply the same residency requirements to the decedent's children as to the surviving spouse.

Who Must File Claim

The decedent's personal representative[19] must file the claim for the surviving spouse, upon written application by the surviving spouse.[20] If there is no personal representative, if the surviving spouse is the personal representative, or if the personal representative has refused to apply for the

---

17. G.S. 30-17.

18. *E.g.,* Jones v. Layne, 144 N.C. 600, 602, 57 S.E. 372, 373 (1907) ("provision to keep [wife] and children from . . . being a county charge").

19. The *personal representative* is the executor under the decedent's will or, if there is no will, the administrator appointed by the clerk to administer the estate. In rare instances a collector under G.S. 28A-11-1 may be appointed by the clerk to handle the estate when there is a delay in appointing a personal representative. In such cases the collector may file for a year's allowance for the surviving spouse. This collector is not a *collector by affidavit* under G.S. 28A-25-1; if a collector by affidavit has been appointed, the surviving spouse must file for the year's allowance herself or himself because there is no personal representative.

20. G.S. 30-16.

allowance within ten days after being requested to do so by the surviving spouse, the surviving spouse may make application for his or her allowance.

The personal representative must also file the claim for the children; or, if there is no personal representative or if the personal representative fails to act within ten days after a written request by the child's guardian or next friend, the guardian or next friend may make application to the clerk for the allowance.[21] If the child has a living parent who is also the surviving spouse, that person files on the child's behalf. *Next friend* is an outdated term no longer provided for in North Carolina law; it has been essentially replaced by the term *guardian ad litem*. If the child has a living parent who is not the surviving spouse or does not have a living parent, a guardian ad litem under G.S. 1A-1, Rule 17 can be appointed to seek the year's allowance.[22] It is more likely, however, that if the child has no living parent, the court will appoint a guardian for the child under G.S. Ch. 35A to handle all of the child's affairs; the guardian may then apply for the allowance.

Filing for the Allowance

Assignment of the allowance is not automatic, and the right to it may be waived by failure to make a timely application.[23] An application must be made within one year of the decedent's death.[24] The statutes governing the assignment expressly limit only the application filing to the year after the decedent's death, thus raising the question of whether the assignment of the allowance may be made after the passage of the year—for instance, if the personal representative files the application on the three hundred and sixty-fourth day after the decedent's death. Since the statutes do allow a full year within which to file the application, it makes no sense to say that an application filed on the three hundred and sixty-fourth day or the three hundred and sixty-fifth day will not be acted on. The reasonable answer would seem to be that actual assignment of the allowance can be made outside the one-year-limitation-period. However, since the statute of limitations for filing a special proceeding for the superior court to assign a year's allowance is one year from the date of decedent's death,[25] it is not clear whether a magistrate can assign an allowance after the year is over. In *Cook v. Sexton*,[26] the surviving spouse requested the personal representative to assign the allowance within the first year after the decedent's death, but the personal representative denied that request on the basis that the spouse had forfeited her right to the allowance. Five years after the decedent's death, the spouse filed a special proceeding in superior court to assign the allowance,[27] and the court held that the proceeding had to be filed

21. G.S. 30-17.

22. One could argue that a living parent who is not the surviving spouse can seek the allowance on behalf of the child as the natural guardian. *Cf.* G.S. 35A-1220. However, the safer practice is to appoint the parent as the guardian ad litem for the purpose of seeking the allowance.

23. Wachovia Bank & Trust Co. v. U.S., 234 F. Supp. 897, 899 (M.D.N.C. 1964).

24. G.S. 30-16. *See* Cook v. Sexton, 79 N.C. 305 (1878).

25. G.S. 1-54(5) (statute of limitations for filing a special proceeding for assignment of an allowance under G.S. 30-27).

26. 79 N.C. 305 (1878).

27. The current statute is G.S. 30-27; now, as well as when *Cook* was decided, it allows the surviving spouse or child to file a special proceeding in superior court for a year's allowance with or without having asked the personal representative to have the allowance assigned.

within one year of the decedent's death. Even though application was made to the personal representative within a year of the decedent's death, the court indicated that if the personal representative did not assign the allowance, the spouse's remedy was to file a superior court special proceeding and to do so within the year. Thus, if the spouse or child asks the personal representative to have the year's allowance assigned and the personal representative refuses to do so, the spouse must file the special proceeding within a year.

However, that case does not tell the magistrate whether he or she should assign the year's allowance after the year is over if the personal representative failed to make the application to the clerk within a year of the decedent's death. The most logical reading of the statute is that the magistrate should assign the allowance in that situation.

Where to File for Allowance

The personal representative (or other authorized persons) must make application for the allowance to the clerk of superior court of the county where the deceased resided.[28] If the decedent's personal property is located outside the county where the decedent resided at the time of his or her death, the personal representative (or other authorized persons) may apply for the allowance in the county where the property is located.[29] This provision also applies to the situation in which the deceased was not a resident of North Carolina but had personal property in North Carolina and the surviving spouse resided in North Carolina at the time of the death.

The clerk of court may either assign the allowance himself or herself or send it to a magistrate for assignment.[30]

Procedure for Assigning Year's Allowance

Upon receiving from the clerk the application to assign the year's allowance,[31] the magistrate must (1) determine if the persons named in the application are entitled to an allowance, (2) ascertain the money and personal property in the decedent's estate, (3) establish the value of the property, and (4) assign property to the persons entitled to allowances. Before proceeding, the magistrate must also collect the $8 fee for allotting the allowance[32] and remit the fee to the clerk.

In determining whether the persons named in the application are entitled to the allowance, the magistrate must determine that (1) the application was filed with the clerk within a year after the decedent's death, (2) the applicant is the spouse or qualifying child of the decedent, and (3) if the issue is raised, the spouse is not disqualified by statute or contract from taking the year's allowance.

---

28. G.S. 30-20.

29. G.S. 30-17.

30. G.S. 30-20. Although G.S. 30-16 seems to indicate that the application may be made directly to the magistrate, G.S. 30-20 specifies that the clerk shall assign the inquiry to the magistrate of the appropriate county.

31. The form an applicant for the year's allowance should file is "Application and Assignment Year's Allowance," AOC-E-100.

32. G.S. 7A-309(2).

In most instances, the personal representative or surviving spouse will list the items of personal property or money belonging to the deceased that he or she wishes to have assigned. It will then be the duty of the magistrate to value the items and assign only so much of the property as the petitioner is entitled to. If the personal representative does not list the personal property to be assigned, the magistrate can ask the clerk for the ninety-day inventory filed in the estate, which lists the decedent's property.[33] If the inventory has not yet been filed, the magistrate can use the preliminary inventory found in the application for letters testamentary[34] or letters of administration[35] filed with the clerk. The most common types of property sought by applicants are bank accounts and motor vehicles, but any personal property in the decedent's estate is subject to assignment. Personal property may be owned jointly, usually as tenants-in-common; in that case only the decedent's share in the property becomes part of his or her estate and subject to the year's allowance. Bank accounts and stocks can be held jointly as tenants-in-common or held jointly with a right of survivorship. If an account is held jointly with the right of survivorship, the asset does not become part of the decedent's estate but at death passes entirely to the joint owner and cannot be assigned as a year's allowance.[36] The contract setting up the bank account or stock account will indicate whether it is held jointly with right of survivorship.

Other nonprobate assets that are not subject to assignment are insurance proceeds, 401(k) accounts, and pensions that have designated beneficiaries—unless the estate is the beneficiary.[37] As mentioned above, real property cannot be assigned. Moreover, even if real property in the estate is sold to provide assets to pay debts, the proceeds of the real property cannot be used to pay the year's allowance, because any part of those proceeds not needed to pay debts of the estate is treated as real estate assets.[38] Finally, if the decedent and surviving spouse owned a mobile home jointly and the mobile home is classified as personal property, it is held as tenancy-by-entirety and passes automatically to the surviving other spouse.[39]

> **Example 1.** Wife dies and leaves husband and three adult children. She had (1) a 2002 Ford Explorer, titled in her and her husband's name and valued at $10,500, (2) a joint bank account containing $5,600, owned jointly with her husband with right of survivorship, (3) a 401(k) account of $150,000, with her husband listed as the beneficiary, (4) an antique cabinet left to her by her mother valued at $3,500, and (5) various household belongings valued at $2,500. The magistrate could assign the allowance from the following property: (1) one half of the value of the Ford Explorer, $5,250 (because the husband already owns half of the car); the cabinet valued at $3,500;

---

33. The ninety-day inventory form is "Inventory for Decedent's Estate," AOC-E-505.

34. "Application for Probate and Letters Testamentary/Of Administration CTA," AOC-E-201. This form is used when the decedent had a will.

35. "Application for Letters Of Administration," AOC-E-202. This form is used when there is no will.

36. *See In re* Estate of Brown, 40 N.C. App. 61, 251 S.E.2d 905 (1979) (Right of survivorship bank accounts pass as rights under a contract and are not "property of the deceased spouse.").

37. *Id.*

38. Denton v. Tyson, 118 N.C. 542, 544, 24 S.E. 116 (1896).

39. G.S. 41-2.5. If the mobile home is permanently attached to the land and intended to be permanently attached, it becomes part of the real property. *See* Little v. Nat'l Serv. Indus., Inc., 79 N.C. App. 688, 340 S.E.2d 510 (1986).

and the household belongings at $2,500. The joint bank account with right of survivorship and the 401(k) account are not assets of the decedent's estate and pass by contract to the husband. If the bank account was one without a right of survivorship, one-half of the account could be assigned to the husband (because he already owns one-half).

After determining the personal property in the deceased spouse's estate, the magistrate must value the property. He or she can look at the value placed on the property in the inventory but should not rely solely on that value, which is set by the personal representative. In valuing motor vehicles, the "blue book" (available from a car dealer or public library) or some other information regarding fair market value[40] may be used. No standard guide is available to assist in valuing household belongings, but listings of similar property for sale in classified advertisements can be helpful guides. The magistrate will have to determine the fair market value of the items using whatever information he or she finds useful and reasonable, including trade periodicals. Once the fair market value is determined, the magistrate must determine if there are any liens or security agreements against the property to be distributed. Although no cases indicate whether the assigned value is the fair market value or the *equity value*—that is, the fair market value minus any liens and security interests against the property—the fairer valuation is the equity value since the spouse and children take their allowances subject to those specific liens.

> **Example 2.** Deceased spouse owned a 2006 V6 LE Toyota Camry with 35,700 miles on it. It has a fair market value of $16,400, but the decedent still owes Bank of America, which has a lien on the car, $6,800 for lending the money to purchase the car. The magistrate should value the car at $9,600 because that is the true value of the car to the spouse or child to whom it is assigned since that person will have to pay off the lien on the car to keep it.

Finally, the magistrate should assign property to the surviving spouse and children. The assigned allowances may not exceed $10,000 for the surviving spouse and $2,000 for each child.

The magistrate must make and sign three lists showing the money or other property assigned to each person. (If the money being assigned is in a bank account, some clerks of court require that a fourth copy be made for the bank.) The magistrate assigns the property on the bottom half of the form "Application and Assignment Year's Allowance," AOC-E-100, which he or she received from the clerk. The magistrate must return one list of each person's allowance within twenty days after the assignment to the clerk of superior court in the county where administration was granted or the will was probated. Another copy goes to the surviving spouse to whom the allowance is given. If one allowance is for a child, the copy goes to the surviving parent, guardian, or guardian ad litem of the child. If the "child" is over eighteen years of age without a surviving parent, guardian, or guardian ad litem, the copy may go to the child. The third copy is given to the decedent's personal representative.

If the personal property is insufficient to pay the full amount of allowance, the magistrate should indicate the amount of the deficiency on the award. The clerk will enter a deficiency

---

40. The personal representative may offer evidence of advertised sale prices for similar motor vehicles. Online sites such as www.edmunds.com also provide estimates of fair market values for motor vehicles.

judgment against the estate.[41] If other assets come into the estate, the personal representative may not come back to the magistrate for a supplemental award of an allowance. Rather, the personal representative must apply sufficient personal property to satisfy the deficiency judgment and notify the clerk of the assignment.

If there is insufficient property to fully satisfy all allowances, the issue for the magistrate is how to allocate whatever property is available. For several years the ratio of the surviving spouse's allowance to the allowance of any individual child has been 5:1;[42] as this ratio presumably reflects the judgment of the legislature about the appropriate division of assets, the magistrate should use it as a guideline in dividing the personal property available for allowances. Since the statute does not favor the surviving spouse over the children, allocations should be made to the surviving spouse and children in the same ratio as full allocations would be. The magistrate should not, when allocating allowances from insufficient personal property, make distinctions among children of the surviving spouse, children from a former relationship, or adopted children. When all the qualifying children live with the surviving parent, it may not make any practical difference in the way the allowance is allocated as all the allowances will be paid to the parent.

Any appeal from the magistrate's findings is brought in superior court.

Special Proceeding to Award Year's Allowance

If the decedent's personal estate exceeds $10,000, the surviving spouse and children may file a special proceeding for an allowance in superior court, regardless of whether the regular allowances have been awarded by the magistrate or clerk.[43] The surviving spouse and children also may bring a special proceeding in superior court if the personal representative denies the year's allowance.[44] If the clerk finds that the material allegations in the complaint are true, he or she enters judgment that the petitioner is entitled to the relief sought. The statute directs the clerk to issue an order to the sheriff to summon a magistrate and two persons qualified to act as jurors, who will act as commissioners to determine the allowance. However, in some counties the clerk selects the two persons to serve with the magistrate and directs the three to act as commissioners in determining the allowance. The magistrate administers the following oath to the persons acting with him or her as commissioners:

---

41. The form is "Deficiency Judgment," AOC-E-101.

42. Since 1981, this has been the ratio; from 1981 to 1995 the surviving spouse was entitled to $5,000 and the children $1,000 each.

43. G.S. 30-29.

44. *See* Cook v. Sexton, 79 N.C. 305 (1878), in which the court held that bringing the superior court action within one year of the death is the only way to stop the statute of limitations from running on the right to an allowance when the personal representative either refused or neglected to assign the allowance. At the time of *Cook*, the year's allowance statutes were substantially the same as today's statutes. 1868–69 N.C. Sess. Laws ch. 93 (Bat. Rev. ch. 117).

You and each of you swear (or affirm) that you will lay off and allot to the petitioner a year's provisions for herself [himself] and family, according to law, and with your best skill and ability; so help you, God.[45]

The three commissioners must ascertain what money and personal property are in the decedent's estate and assign allowances for support of the surviving spouse and children for one year from the decedent's death. The commissioners must assign an amount sufficient for the recipient's support "according to the estate and condition of the decedent"[46] without regard to the previously stated $10,000 and $2,000 limitations. The purpose of the special proceeding is "to provide the surviving spouse of a solvent decedent with a level of support commensurate with the support which he or she would have had from the deceased spouse during the first year after the spouse's death had the death not occurred, . . . [in other words] an amount sufficient to maintain for a period that standard of living to which he or she had become accustomed."[47]

The allowance is fixed with due consideration for other persons entitled to allowances, but the total value of all allowances may not exceed one-half the decedent's net income for one year, based on the decedent's average annual income for the three years preceding his or her death. *Net income* means after-tax income, defined as take home pay after federal and state income taxes are deducted, not adjusted gross income.[48] The average annual income is derived by adding the net income for the three years preceding the decedent's death and dividing the total by three.

The commissioners need not allocate the maximum amount allowed but must allot a value sufficient to maintain the spouse and children in the manner to which they are accustomed.[49]

Example 3. Sarah died on February 1, 2008, leaving her husband, Joe, and one child, Susan, who is fifteen years old. Sarah's gross income was $85,400 in 2005; $86,000 in 2006; and $90,000 in 2007. After taking out for federal and state income taxes, she took home $59,780 in 2005; $60,200 in 2006, and $61,200 in 2007. Her total net income for the three years preceding her death is therefore $181,180 and her average annual income for that three-year period is $60,393.33. Therefore the maximum year's allowance that the commissioners could assign to Joe and Susan is $30,196.66. If the maximum allowance is $225,000 but the couple lived very frugally, the commissioners might award a lesser amount because Joe was accustomed to living on much less than $225,000 a year.

The magistrate must return a report of these allowances assigned to the clerk of superior court. There is no form for the report, but the magistrate can either draft a form similar to the order part of the $10,000 year's allowance form or ask the petitioner's attorney to draft the report.

---

45. G.S. 11-11. If a commissioner chooses to affirm, magistrate should omit "so help you, God."
46. G.S. 30-31.
47. Pritchard v. First-Citizens Bank & Trust Co., 38 N.C. App. 489, 491, 248 S.E.2d 467, 469 (1978).
48. *Id.* at 493, 248 S.E.2d at 470.
49. *Id.*

The personal representative or any creditor or beneficiary of the decedent may file exceptions to the report; the clerk will rule on the exceptions and confirm the report. The property assigned is then transferred to the surviving spouse.

Administration of Oaths

G.S. 7A-292 and G.S. 11-7.1 authorize magistrates to administer oaths. Various oaths and the procedure for administering them are contained in G.S. Ch. 11. Additional oaths are found in other chapters dealing with specific offices or functions. Oaths for the more common offices and functions are set out in G.S. 11-11, which also contains a general oath for offices that do not have a specific oath. In addition to the oath for the specific office being assumed, an officer of the government must take two oaths swearing to support the U.S and North Carolina constitutions and laws.[50]

The oath for a witness in civil cases is as follows:

> You swear (or affirm) that the evidence you shall give to the court in this cause now on trial, wherein (*name plaintiff*) is plaintiff and (*name defendant*) defendant, shall be the truth, the whole truth, and nothing but the truth; so help you, God.[51]

The oath for a witness in criminal actions is as follows:

> You swear (or affirm) that the evidence you shall give to the court in this action between the state and (*name defendant*) shall be the truth, the whole truth, and nothing but the truth; so help you, God.[52]

The person taking the oath may either swear on the "Holy Scriptures" or may affirm. Courts have held that non-Christians may take an oath on their holy book or according to the form of their religion.[53] To swear on the Bible or another holy book, the person normally places his or her left hand on the book and lifts the right hand. A person who has conscientious scruples

---

50. N.C. Const. art. VI § 7; G.S. 11-7.

51. G.S. 11-11.

52. *Id.*

53. In *Shaw v. Moore*, 49 N.C. 25 (1856), the North Carolina Supreme Court pointed out that at common law Jews could swear upon the Old Testament or Tanach and other non-Christians can swear "according to the form which they hold to be most sacred and obligatory on their consciences." The court then determined that the sole object of the statute requiring swearing on the Holy Scriptures (which means the Christian bible) was "to prescribe forms, adapted to the religious belief of the general mass of the citizens, for the sake of convenience and uniformity," and that if the legislature's intent in adopting the statute had been to alter the common law so as to exclude persons of other religions, the statute would be void because it would violate the provision found in the North Carolina Constitution that "all persons have a natural and inalienable right to worship Almighty God according to the dictates of their own consciences." N.C. Const. art. I, § 13. Therefore, the court held that the common law still applies in North Carolina. A recent superior court case reaffirmed the law set out in *Shaw* in a case challenging a Guilford County judge's ruling prohibiting a Muslim from swearing on the Quran. American Civil Liberties Union of North Carolina v. North Carolina, Wake County Superior Court 05 CVS 9872, May 24, 2006.

against taking an oath may be affirmed.[54] To affirm, the witness does not place his or her hand on a holy book but raises his or her right hand and the magistrate gives the same oath except the word *affirm* replaces the word *swear* and the phrase "so help you, God" is omitted.

The magistrate must charge a fee of $2, to be remitted to the clerk, for performing an oath when it is not incident to a criminal or civil action.[55] Generally a magistrate administers oaths to witnesses appearing before him or her in civil or criminal proceedings in which no separate fee is assessed. However, if the magistrate is asked to swear in a new sheriff or county commissioner, he or she should collect the fee and remit it to the clerk.

Issuance of Subpoenas

The magistrate may issue subpoenas and capiases that are valid throughout the county.[56] Subpoenas are issued to compel the appearance of witnesses before the magistrate to give testimony in a civil or criminal action. The magistrate will not often need to exercise this power—and then primarily in contested small claim actions. Subpoenas may also be issued to compel the production of documents in an action before the magistrate.

The provision for issuing capiases has been modified by G.S. Ch. 15A. Although G.S. 7A-292 still uses the word *capias* in granting authority to the magistrate, G.S. Ch. 15A-304, the Criminal Pretrial Procedure Code, uses the term "order for arrest" instead. Moreover, G.S. 15A-305 and G.S. 7A-273(3) authorize magistrates to issue orders for arrest that are valid throughout the state, not just the county.

Affidavits for the Verifications of Pleadings

The magistrate may take the affidavit of a person for verification of a *pleading.*[57] The purpose of verification is to bind the signer under oath to his or her statement of the facts.[58] Verification is not required for most pleadings, but several statutes specifically require verification of pleadings for (among others) (1) a complaint in an action for divorce,[59] (2) a petition for adjudication of incompetence,[60] (3) a motion for the appointment of an interim guardian,[61] and (4) a petition for adoption.[62] Even if verification is not required, it can be used for any pleading or motion. For example, a verified complaint can be used as the affidavit required for an order of attachment[63]

---

54. G.S. 11-4.
55. G.S. 7A-309(5).
56. G.S. 7A-292(4). Although the statute does not limit magistrates to issuing subpoenas to appear in proceedings before the magistrate himself or herself, it is unlikely that a magistrate would ever be asked to issue a subpoena for a person to appear in any other civil or criminal proceeding.
57. G.S. 7A-292(5). A pleading includes a complaint, answer, or reply to a counterclaim in a civil lawsuit.
58. G. Gray Wilson, North Carolina Civil Procedure §11-5 (3d ed. 2007).
59. G.S. 50-8.
60. G.S. 35A-1105.
61. G.S. 35A-1114.
62. G.S. 48-2-304.
63. G.S. 1-440.11(b).

or for a default judgment for a sum certain.[64] It would be rare for a person filing a pleading to come to the magistrate to take the verification. However if someone did ask the magistrate to take the affidavit to verify the pleading, the affidavit could be executed by the pleading party or by one of the parties—if there are several parties united in interest and pleading together.[65]

There is no prescribed form for the verification, but it must state that the pleading is true to the knowledge of the affiant except that, as to matters stated to be on information and belief, he or she believes them to be true. The magistrate must take the oath or affirmation of the person verifying the pleading, sign and date the oath, fill in the county and state in which the pleading is verified, and have the affiant pay the $2 fee,[66] which he or she will remit to the clerk. The common form for verification is as follows:

> A.B., being duly sworn, deposes and says: That he is the plaintiff in the foregoing action; that he has read the foregoing complaint and knows the contents thereof; that the same are true of his own knowledge, except as to those matters alleged on information and belief, and as to those matters he believes them to be true.

_____

s/ A.B.
Sworn/Affirmed and Subscribed to Before Me
Date   (Signature of Magistrate)
_____ County, North Carolina   Magistrate

Habeas Corpus ad Testificandum

The magistrate has the power, upon application by a party to an action pending before the magistrate, to issue a writ of habeas corpus ad testificandum.[67] The writ is used to compel the appearance of any person confined in a jail in the county of the magistrate's jurisdiction for the purpose of having the prisoner become a witness before the magistrate.[68] A writ for the appearance of a prisoner confined outside the magistrate's county must be issued by a superior or district court judge. The application for the writ must be verified by the applicant and must state the title and nature of the proceeding for which the testimony of the prisoner is desired and declare that the testimony is believed to be material and necessary to the proceeding. The most common request for a magistrate to issue a writ of habeas corpus ad testificandum comes from an incarcerated party who wishes to testify at a small claims trial.

A party who seeks to have a writ issued must pay the person with custody of the prisoner the fees and expenses involved in bringing the prisoner to the trial and must sign a bond, with sufficient sureties, that he or she will pay the charges for carrying the prisoner back to the place

---

64. G.S. 1A-1, Rule 55(b)(1).
65. If the action is for adoption it must be verified by each of the petitioners. G.S. 48-2-304.
66. G.S. 7A-309(5).
67. G.S. 7A-292(6), G.S. 17-41.
68. The form application and writ is "Application and Writ of Habeas Corpus Ad Testificandum," AOC-G-112.

of custody. The jail or prison has no duty to carry out the writ until the expenses are paid and the bond is signed.

Acknowledgments

Magistrates are authorized to acknowledge the execution of any instrument pertaining to real property and all instruments of any kind that are required to or allowed to be filed with the register of deeds; included are deeds, deeds of trust, powers of attorney, and assignments.[69] Usually magistrates send persons seeking to have instruments acknowledged to a notary public rather than doing the acknowledgement themselves. However, on rare occasions a magistrate acknowledges an instrument, assessing a fee of $2 and remitting the fee to the clerk.[70]

Forms for the acknowledgment are contained in Article 3 of G.S. Ch. 47. An instrument executed by an individual should read substantially as follows:[71]

I (*name of magistrate*) magistrate, do hereby certify that (*name(s) of the individual(s) whose acknowledgement is being taken*) personally appeared before me this day and acknowledged that he or she signed the foregoing [or attached] instrument.

Date: (*date of acknowledgement*)   (*Signature of Magistrate*)

_____ County, North Carolina   Magistrate

69. G.S. 7A-292(8).
70. G.S. 7A-309(4).
71. G.S. 47-38.